Intelligence Analysis: A Target-Centric Approach

Intelligence Analysis: A Target-Centric Approach

Third Edition

Robert M. Clark

CQ PRESS
A Division of SAGE
Washington, D.C.

CQ Press
2300 N Street, NW, Suite 800
Washington, DC 20037

Phone: 202-729-1900; toll-free, 1-866-4CQ-PRESS (1-866-427-7737)

Web: www.cqpress.com

Cover design: Silverander Communications
Composition: C&M Digitals (P) Ltd.

☺ The paper used in this publication exceeds the requirements of the American National Standard for Information Sciences—Permanence of Paper for Printed Library Materials. ANSI: Z39.48-1992.

Printed and bound in the United States of America

13 12 11 10   3 4 5

Library of Congress Cataloging-in-Publication Data

Clark, Robert M.
   Intelligence analysis : a target centric approach / Robert M. Clark. — 3rd ed.
      p. cm.
   Includes index.
   ISBN 978-1-60426-543-9 (pbk. : alk. paper)
   1. Intelligence service—Methodology. I. Title.

JF1525.I6C548 2010
327.12—dc22   2009026772

Contents

Part 3   Predictive Analysis

Tables, Figures, and Boxes

Part 3 Predictive Analysis

Preface

Two events in the early 2000s focused the world's attention on apparent failures of the U.S. intelligence community—the terrorist attack on U.S. soil of September 11, 2001, and the U.S.-led invasion of Iraq, more commonly called the Iraq war, on March 20, 2003. Each event caused enough consternation within the United States to spawn bipartisan commissions of inquiry, resulting in the 9/11 Commission report (published in September 2004) and the Iraqi Weapons of Mass Destruction (WMD) Commission report (published in March 2005). These two documents have provided perhaps the most detailed assessments of intelligence failures ever written at the unclassified level. The reports have led directly to dramatic changes in the structure and function of the U.S. intelligence community.

Most books on intelligence, whether critical or descriptive, focus on structure and function. But if an intelligence community is interested in real improvement, it must begin by rethinking *process*: the form and structure of a new community will naturally follow. A major contribution of both the 9/11 and the Iraqi WMD Commissions was their focus on a failed process. Thus, the first objective of this book is to redefine the intelligence process—specifically the analytic process—to help make all parts of what is commonly referred to as the "intelligence cycle" run smoothly and effectively.

The intelligence process should accomplish three basic tasks. First, it should make it easy for customers of intelligence to ask questions. Second, it should use the existing base of intelligence information to provide immediate responses to the customer. Third, it should manage the expeditious creation of new information to answer remaining questions. To do these things intelligence analysts must be collaborative and predictive—collaborative to engage *all* participants while making it easy for customers to ask questions and get answers; predictive because intelligence customers above all else want to know what will happen next.

What I call a target-centric intelligence process helps analysts and customers accomplish these three tasks by bringing together all participants in the production of sound intelligence. Although intelligence communities are organized hierarchically, the target-centric process outlines a collaborative approach for intelligence collectors, analysts, and consumers to operate cohesively against increasingly complex enemies. We cannot simply provide more intelligence to customers; they already have more information than they can process, and information overload encourages intelligence failures. The intelligence community must provide intelligence that is relevant to customer needs—known as actionable intelligence. Collaboration enables such intelligence. The convergence of computers and multimedia communications allows intelligence producers and customers to interact more closely as they move from traditional hierarchies to networks—a process that already had begun to emerge before the restructuring of the U.S. intelligence community that followed the enactment of the Intelligence Reform and Terrorism Prevention Act of 2004.

The second goal of this book is to clarify and refine the analysis process by drawing on existing prediction methodologies. These include the analytic tools used in organizational planning and problem solving, science and engineering, law, and economics. In many cases, these are tools and techniques that have endured despite dramatic changes in information technology over the past fifty years. All can be useful in making intelligence predictions, even in seemingly unrelated fields. In fact, a number of unifying concepts can be drawn from these disciplines and applied when creating scenarios of the future, assessing forces, and monitoring indicators. The book highlights these concepts in short information boxes called "Analysis Principles" and treats them as fundamental principles of intelligence analysis. These boxes should make the book a valuable reference even as the world continues to change.

This book is written primarily for the practicing intelligence analyst, though it will be of interest to all intelligence professionals, students, and customers of intelligence. Intelligence professionals can spend their entire careers on specialized topics, such as behavioral analysis, and many publications are devoted to topics covered only briefly here. This book, rather, is intended as a general guide, with references to lead the reader to in-depth studies and reports on specific techniques. But it also aims to go beyond that role in defining a better intelligence analysis process, putting specific analysis techniques in context, and showing how they interrelate within the process. The book offers insights amplifying why intelligence consumers and analysts alike need to become more proactive in the changing world of intelligence and to extract more useful intelligence than has been possible before.

Many examples of intelligence failures are discussed in the book, possibly leading a reader to get the impression that we experience more failures than successes. Quite the opposite is true. Every major intelligence service probably has more analytical successes than failures. But the failures are more visible, and this book concentrates on failures for two reasons. First, sharing our intelligence successes openly ensures that there will be fewer of them in the future. Second, we learn more from our failures than from our successes.

This third edition has been prepared primarily in response to suggestions made by readers. The wide use of the previous edition in academia and by government agencies and contractors has resulted in a number of excellent recommendations, and I have attempted to incorporate those ideas throughout this new edition. As a result, all of the chapters have undergone changes. In particular, chapter 6, "Sources of Intelligence Information," has been completely rewritten to present a more logical explanation of intelligence collection, and chapter 15, "The Analyst and the Customer," has been substantially expanded to discuss the challenge of getting intelligence understood and accepted by our customers.

All statements of fact, opinion, or analysis expressed are those of the author and do not reflect the official positions or views of the CIA or any other U.S. government agency. Nothing in the contents should be construed as asserting or implying U.S. government authentication of information or agency endorsement of the author's views. This material has been reviewed by the CIA to prevent the disclosure of classified information.

Acknowledgments

Many people throughout the U.S. and British intelligence communities, academia, and the business intelligence world have provided wisdom that I have incorporated into this edition. I cannot name them all, but I appreciate their help. I am especially grateful to reviewers within and outside the U.S. intelligence community who have contributed their time to improving the text. In addition to several anonymous reviewers, I wish to thank Professors Matthew Degn and Jason Thomas for their reviews. I also want to thank Elise Frasier, Emily Bakely, Ann Davies, and Christina Mueller at CQ Press for shaping the finished product.

Robert M. Clark
Reston, Virginia

Introduction

The greatest derangement of the mind is to believe in something because one wishes it to be so.

Louis Pasteur

We learn more from our failures than from our successes. As noted in the preface to this book, there is much to be learned from the two major U.S. intelligence failures of this century—the attacks of September 11, 2001, and the miscall on Iraqi weapons of mass destruction. So this book begins with an overview of why we fail.

Why We Fail

As a reminder that intelligence failures are not uniquely a U.S. problem, it is worth recalling some failures of other intelligence services in the last century:

- *Operation Barbarossa, 1941.* Josef Stalin acted as his own intelligence analyst, and he proved to be a very poor one. He was unprepared for a war with Nazi Germany, so he ignored the mounting body of incoming intelligence indicating that the Germans were preparing a surprise attack. German deserters who told the Russians about the impending attack were considered provocateurs and shot on Stalin's orders. When the attack, named Operation Barbarossa, came on June 22, 1941, Stalin's generals were surprised, their forward divisions trapped and destroyed.[1]

- *Singapore, 1942.* In one of the greatest military defeats that Britain ever suffered, 130,000 well-equipped British, Australian, and Indian troops surrendered to 35,000 weary and ill-equipped Japanese soldiers. On the way to the debacle, British intelligence failed in a series of poor analyses of their Japanese opponent, such as underestimating the capabilities of the Japanese Zero fighter and concluding that the Japanese would not use tanks in the jungle. The Japanese tanks proved highly effective in driving the British out of Malaya and back to Singapore.[2]

- *Yom Kippur, 1973.* Israel is regarded as having one of the world's best intelligence services. But in 1973 the intelligence leadership was closely tied to the Israeli cabinet and often served both as policy advocate and information assessor. Furthermore, Israel's past military successes had led to a certain amount of hubris and belief in inherent Israeli superiority. Israel's leaders considered their overwhelming military advantage a deterrent to attack. They assumed that Egypt needed to rebuild its air force and forge an alliance with Syria before attacking. In this atmosphere, Israeli intelligence was vulnerable to what became a successful Egyptian deception operation. The Israeli intelligence officer who correctly predicted the impending attack had his report suppressed by his superior, the chief intelligence officer of the Israeli Southern Command. The Israeli Defense Force was caught by surprise when, *without* a rebuilt air force and having kept their agreement with Syria secret, the Egyptians launched an attack on Yom Kippur, the most important of the Jewish holidays, on October 6, 1973. The attack was ultimately repulsed, but only at a high cost in Israeli casualties.[3]

- *Falkland Islands, 1982.* Argentina wanted Great Britain to hand over the Falkland Islands, which Britain had occupied and colonized in 1837. Britain's tactic was to conduct prolonged diplomatic negotiations without giving up the islands. There was abundant evidence of Argentine intent to invade, including a report of an Argentine naval task force headed for the Falklands with a marine amphibious force. But the British Foreign and Commonwealth Office did not want to face the possibility of an Argentine attack because it would be costly to deter or repulse. Britain's Latin America Current Intelligence Group (dominated at the time by the Foreign and Commonwealth Office) accordingly concluded, on March 30, 1982, that an invasion was not imminent. On April 2 Argentine marines landed and occupied the Falklands, provoking the British to assemble a naval task force and retake the islands.[4]

The common theme of these and many other intelligence failures discussed in this book is *not* the failure to collect intelligence. In each of these cases, the intelligence had been collected. Three themes are common in intelligence failures.

Failure to Share Information

From Pearl Harbor to 9/11 and the miscall on Iraq's possession of weapons of mass destruction (WMD), the inability or unwillingness of collectors and analysts to share intelligence has been a recurring cause of failure.

Intelligence is a team sport. Effective teams require cohesion, formal and informal communication, cooperation, shared mental models, and similar knowledge structures—all of which contribute to sharing of information.

Without such a common process, any team—especially the interdisciplinary teams that are necessary to deal with complex problems of today—will quickly fall apart.[5]

Nevertheless, the Iraqi WMD Commission (the Commission on the Intelligence Capabilities of the United States Regarding Weapons of Mass Destruction, which issued its formal report to President George W. Bush in March 2005) found that analysts failed to work as a team.[6] They did not effectively share information. And the root causes for the failure to share remain, in the U.S. intelligence community as well as in almost all intelligence services worldwide.

Sharing requires openness. But any organization that requires secrecy to perform its duties will struggle with and often reject openness.[7] Most governmental intelligence organizations, including the U.S. intelligence community, place more emphasis on secrecy than on effectiveness.[8] The penalty for producing poor intelligence is modest. The penalty for improperly handling classified information can be career ending.[9] There are legitimate reasons not to share; the U.S. intelligence community has lost many collection assets because details about them were too widely shared. So it comes down to a balancing act between protecting assets and acting effectively in the world. Commercial organizations are more effective at intelligence sharing because they tend to place more emphasis on effectiveness than on secrecy; they also have less risk of losing critical sources from compromises.

Experts on any subject have an information advantage, and they tend to use that advantage to serve their own agendas.[10] Collectors and analysts are no different. At lower levels in the organization, hoarding information may have job security benefits. At senior levels, unique knowledge may help protect the organizational budget. So the natural tendency is to share the minimum necessary to avoid criticism and to protect the really valuable material. Any bureaucracy has a wealth of tools for hoarding information, and this book discusses the most common of them.

Finally, both collectors of intelligence and analysts find it easy to be insular. They are disinclined to draw on resources outside their own organizations.[11] Communication takes time and effort. It has long-term payoffs in access to intelligence from other sources, but few short-term benefits.

In summary, collectors, analysts, and intelligence organizations have a number of incentives to conceal information and see few benefits in sharing it. The problem is likely to persist until the incentives to share outweigh the benefits of concealment.

Failure to Analyze Collected Material Objectively

In each of the cases cited at the beginning of this introduction, intelligence analysts or national leaders were locked into a *mindset*—the consistent thread in analytical failures. Falling into the trap that Louis Pasteur warned about in the observation that I quoted above, they believed because, consciously or unconsciously, they wished it to be so. Mindset can manifest itself in the form of many biases and preconceptions, a short list of which would include the following:

- *Ethnocentric bias* involves projecting one's own cultural beliefs and expectations on others. It leads to the creation of a "mirror-image" model, which looks at others as one looks at oneself, and to the assumption that others will act "rationally" as rationality is defined in one's own culture. The Yom Kippur attack was not predicted because, from Israel's point of view, it was irrational for Egypt to attack without extensive preparation.
- *Wishful thinking* involves excessive optimism or avoiding unpleasant choices in analysis. The British Foreign Office did not predict an Argentine invasion of the Falklands because, in spite of intelligence evidence that an invasion was imminent, they did not want to deal with it. Josef Stalin made an identical mistake for the same reason prior to Operation Barbarossa.
- *Parochial interests* cause organizational loyalties or personal agendas to affect the analysis process.
- *Status quo biases* cause analysts to assume that events will proceed along a straight line. The safest weather prediction, after all, is that tomorrow's weather will be like today's. An extreme case is the story of the British intelligence officer who, on retiring in 1950 after forty-seven years' service, reminisced: "Year after year the worriers and fretters would come to me with awful predictions of the outbreak of war. I denied it each time. I was only wrong twice."[12] The status quo bias causes analysts to fail to catch a change in the pattern.
- *Premature closure* results when analysts make early judgments about the solution to a problem and then defend the initial judgments tenaciously. This can lead the analyst to select (usually without conscious awareness) subsequent evidence that supports the favored solution and to reject (or dismiss as unimportant) evidence that conflicts with it.

All of these mindsets can lead to poor assumptions and bad intelligence if not challenged. And as the Iraqi WMD Commission report notes, analysts often allow unchallenged assumptions to drive their analysis.[13]

Failure of the Customer to Act on Intelligence

In some cases, as in Operation Barbarossa and the Falkland Islands affair, the intelligence customer failed to understand or make use of the available intelligence.

A senior State Department official once remarked, half in jest, "There are no policy failures; there are only policy successes and intelligence failures."[14] The remark rankles intelligence officers, but it should be read as a call to action. Intelligence analysts should accept partial responsibility when their customer fails to make use of the intelligence provided, and also accept the challenges to engage the customer during the analysis process and to ensure that the resulting intelligence is taken into account when the customer must act.

In this book I devote considerable discussion to the vital importance of analysts being able objectively to assess and understand their customers and their customers' business or field. The first part of the book describes a collaborative, "target-centric" approach to intelligence analysis that demands a close working relationship among all stakeholders, including the customer, as the means to gain the clearest conception of needs and the most effective results or products. The last chapter of the book discusses ways to ensure that the customer takes the best available intelligence into account when making decisions.

Intelligence analysts have often been reluctant to closely engage one class of customer—the policymakers. In its early years the CIA attempted to remain aloof from its policymaking intelligence customers to avoid losing objectivity in the national intelligence estimates process.[15] The disadvantages of that separation became apparent, as analysis was not addressing the customer's current interests, and intelligence was becoming less useful to policymaking. During the 1970s CIA senior analysts began to expand contacts with policymakers. As both the Falklands and Yom Kippur examples illustrate, such closeness has its risks. But in many cases analysts have been able to work closely with policymakers and to make intelligence analyses relevant without losing objectivity.

What the Book Is About

This book is for intelligence analysts, and it develops a process for successful analysis—including avoiding those three themes of failure.

Studies have found that no baseline, standard analytic method exists in the U.S. intelligence community. Any large intelligence community is made up of a variety of disciplines, each with its own analytic methodology.[16] Furthermore, intelligence analysts routinely generate ad hoc methods to solve specific analytic problems. This individualistic approach to analysis has resulted in a great variety of analytic methods, more than 160 of which have been identified as available to U.S. intelligence analysts.[17]

There are good reasons for this proliferation of methods. Methodologies are developed to handle very specific problems, and they are often unique to a discipline, such as economic or scientific and technical (S&T) analysis (which probably has the largest collection of problem-solving methodologies). As an example of how methodologies proliferate, after the Soviet Union collapsed, economists who had spent their entire professional lives analyzing a command economy were suddenly confronted with free market prices and privatization. No model existed anywhere for such an economic transition, and analysts had to devise from scratch methods to, for example, gauge the size of Russia's private sector. [18]

But all intelligence analysis methods derive from a fundamental process. This book is about that process. It develops the idea of creating a model of the intelligence target and extracting useful information from that model. These two steps—the first called "synthesis" and the second called "analysis"—make up what is known as intelligence analysis. All analysts naturally do this. The key to avoiding failures is to share the model with collectors of information and customers of intelligence. While there are no universal methods that work for all problems, a basic process does in fact exist.

There also are standard, widely used techniques. An analyst must have a repertoire of them to apply in solving intelligence problems. They might include pattern analysis, trend prediction, literature assessment, and statistical analysis. A number of these techniques are presented throughout the book in the form of analysis principles. These analysis techniques together form a problem-solving process that can help to avoid the intelligence blunders discussed earlier.

Sherman Kent noted that an analyst has three wishes: "To know everything. To be believed. And to exercise a positive influence on policy." [19] This book will not result in an analyst's being able to know everything—that is why we will continue to have estimates. But chapters 1–14 should help án analyst to learn the tradecraft of analysis, and chapter 15 is intended to help an analyst toward the second and third wishes.

Summary

Intelligence failures have three common themes that have a long history:

- Failure of collectors and analysts to share information. Good intelligence requires teamwork and sharing, but most of the incentives in large intelligence organizations promote concealment rather than sharing of information.

- Analysts' failure to analyze the material collected objectively. The consistent thread in these failures is a mindset, primarily biases and preconceptions that hamper objectivity.

- Failure of customers to act on intelligence. This lack of response is not solely the customer's fault. Analysts have an obligation to ensure that customers not only receive the intelligence but fully understand it.

This book is about an intelligence process that can reduce such failures. A large intelligence community develops many analytic methods to deal with the variety of issues that it confronts. But the methods all work within a fundamental process: creating a model of the intelligence target (synthesis) and extracting useful information from that model (analysis). Success comes from sharing the target model with collectors and customers.

Notes

1. John Hughes-Wilson, *Military Intelligence Blunders* (New York: Carroll and Graf, 1999), 38.
2. Ibid., 102.
3. Ibid., 218.
4. Ibid., 260.
5. Rob Johnson, *Analytic Culture in the U.S. Intelligence Community* (Washington, D.C.: Center for the Study of Intelligence, Central Intelligence Agency, 2005), 70.
6. *Report of the Commission on the Intelligence Capabilities of the United States Regarding Weapons of Mass Destruction,* March 31, 2005, Overview.
7. Johnson, *Analytic Culture,* xvi.
8. Ibid., 11.
9. There exists some justification for the harsh penalty placed on improper use of classified information; it can compromise and end a billion-dollar collection program or get people killed.
10. Steven D. Leavitt and Stephen J. Dubner, *Freakonomics* (New York: HarperCollins, 2005), 13.
11. Johnson, *Analytic Culture,* 29.
12. Amory Lovins and L. Hunter Lovins, "The Fragility of Domestic Energy," *Atlantic Monthly,* November 1983, 118.
13. *Report of the Commission.*
14. William Prillaman and Michael Dempsey, "Mything the Point: What's Wrong with the Conventional Wisdom About the C.I.A.," *Intelligence and National Security* 19, no. 1 (March 2004): 1–28.
15. Harold P. Ford, *Estimative Intelligence* (Lanham, Md.: University Press of America, 1993), 107.
16. Johnson, *Analytic Culture,* xvii.
17. Ibid., 72.
18. Center for the Study of Intelligence, Central Intelligence Agency, "Watching the Bear: Essays on CIA's Analysis of the Soviet Union," Conference, Princeton University, March 2001, www.cia.gov/cis/books/watchingthebear/article08.html, 8.
19. Ibid., 12.

1

The Intelligence Process

Future conflicts will be fought more by networks than by hierarchies, and whoever masters the network form will gain major advantages.

John Arquilla and David Ronfeldt, RAND Corp.

George Lucas's original *Star Wars* movie describes the final stages of a human intelligence operation. The heroine, Princess Leia, obtains the plans for the evil Galactic Empire's ultimate battle machine, the Death Star, from the robot R2-D2, which is functioning as a mobile dead drop.[1] Leia gives the plans to the rebel forces, whose scientific intelligence analyst briefs the rebel command on the plans, pinpoints the weak spot on the Death Star, and presents a brilliant analysis of the enemy defenses. Rebel fighter jockeys deliver proton torpedoes to the weak spot and destroy the Death Star. End of movie.

This *Star Wars* vignette accurately summarizes the intelligence process as it is popularly viewed. The people who collect intelligence information and execute the operations get the glory, the press, and the money. The intelligence analyst, working behind the scenes, gets the interesting problems to solve to make it all work.

Although the popular focus is on collection, most of the major failures in intelligence are due to inadequate or nonexistent analysis, and most of the rest are due to failure to act on the analysis, as noted in the introduction. The information is usually there, at least in hindsight. So, unfortunately, is a large volume of irrelevant material that has to be examined and discarded. All intelligence organizations today are saturated with incoming information. Furthermore, in large intelligence communities critical information about an intelligence matter may not be effectively shared because the intelligence activity is organized around the flawed concept of an "intelligence cycle." Before we explore this flawed concept we should define the term *intelligence*.

The Nature of Intelligence: Reducing Uncertainty in Conflict

Intelligence is about reducing uncertainty in conflict. Because conflict can consist of any competitive or opposing action resulting from the divergence of two or more parties' ideas or interests, conflict is not necessarily physical combat. If competition or negotiation exists, then two or more groups are in conflict. There can be many different levels of conflict, ranging from friendly competition to armed combat. Context determines whether another party is an opponent or an ally. As a rule, friends and allies do not conduct intelligence operations on one another. However parties can be allies in one conflict, opponents in another.[2] For example, France and the United States are usually military allies, but they are opponents in commercial affairs.

Reducing uncertainty requires that intelligence obtain information that the opponent in a conflict prefers to conceal. This definition does not exclude the use of openly available sources, such as newspapers or the Internet, because competent analysis of such open sources frequently reveals information that an opponent wishes to hide. Indeed, intelligence in general can be thought of as the complex process of understanding meaning in available information. A typical goal of intelligence is to establish facts and then to develop precise, reliable, and valid inferences (hypotheses, estimations, conclusions, or predictions) for use in strategic decision making or operational planning.

How, then, is intelligence any different from the market research that many companies conduct or from traditional research as it is carried out in laboratories, think tanks, and academia? After all, those types of research are also intended to reduce uncertainty. The answer is that most of the methods of intelligence and nonintelligence research are identical, with one important distinction: In intelligence, when accurate information is not available through traditional (and less expensive) means, then a wide range of specialized techniques and methods unique to the intelligence field are called into play. Academics are unlikely to have intercepted telephone communications at their disposal as a means for collection and analysis. Nor must academics deal routinely with concealment, denial, or deception.

Because intelligence is about conflict, it supports *operations* such as military planning and combat, diplomatic negotiations, trade negotiations and commerce policy, and law enforcement. The primary customer of intelligence is the person who will act on the information—the executive, the decision maker, the combat commander, or the law enforcement officer. Writers therefore describe intelligence as being *actionable* information. Not all actionable information is intelligence, however. A weather report is actionable, but it is not intelligence.

What distinguishes intelligence from plain news is support for operations. The operations customer does (or should do) something about intelligence, whereas TV viewers normally do not do anything about the news—though they may do something about the weather report. The same information can be both intelligence and news, of course: Food riots in Somalia can be both if the customer takes action on the information.

Finally, intelligence is always concerned with a *target*—the focus of the problem about which the customers want answers. In the *Star Wars* example the target was the Death Star. The rebel intelligence effort supported operations by locating its weak point.

Logic dictates that the intelligence process should revolve around how best to approach the target. That is exactly what the remainder of this book is concerned with: the steps to solving an intelligence problem, using a target-centric approach. This process is different from that depicted in most introductory texts and courses, but it is the new direction that intelligence is taking in practice. A brief review of the traditional intelligence cycle will illustrate why.

The Traditional Intelligence Cycle

Intelligence has traditionally been described as following a series of steps called the *intelligence cycle*. Figure 1-1 illustrates the cycle in elementary form.

The cycle typically begins with a *requirements*, or *needs* step, which amounts to a definition of the intelligence problem. Usually it takes the form of a rather general question from an intelligence customer, such as, How stable is the government of Ethiopia?

Then comes *planning*, or *direction*—determining how the other components of the cycle will address the problem. Collectors have to be tasked to gather missing bits of information. Analysts have to be assigned to do research and write a report on Ethiopian government stability.

The cycle then proceeds to *collection*, or gathering information. Ethiopian newspapers have to be acquired. Communications intelligence (COMINT) has to be focused on Ethiopian government communications. Human intelligence (HUMINT) operatives have to ask questions of sources with knowledge of Ethiopian internal affairs.

From there, the information has to be *processed*. Foreign language material must be translated. Encrypted signals must be decrypted. Film or digital signals

Figure 1-1   Traditional Intelligence Cycle

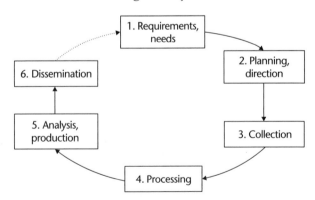

Note: The dotted line represents the transition from one cycle to the next, during which the customer reviews the analysis product and formulates new requirements and needs.

must be translated into visible imagery. Responses from HUMINT sources must be validated and organized into a report format.

The newly collected and processed material must be brought together with relevant historical material to create intelligence in an *analysis* phase. An analyst must create outcome scenarios based on the current Ethiopian situation, generate profiles of Ethiopian leaders, and assess their likely responses to possible events. The analysis phase also typically includes a peer and supervisory review of the finished product, except in fast-moving, combat intelligence situations, in which simple fusion (discussed in chapter 4) is done.

The finished intelligence must be *disseminated* to the customer in a written report (usually sent electronically) or a briefing. Then comes a transition to new requirements or needs, and a new cycle begins.

Over the years, the intelligence cycle has become almost a theological concept: No one questions its validity. Yet when pressed, many intelligence officers admit that the intelligence process "really doesn't work like that." In other words, effective intelligence efforts are not cycles. Here are some reasons why.

The cycle defines an *antisocial* series of steps that constrains the flow of information. It separates collectors from processors from analysts and too often results in "throwing information over the wall" to become the next person's responsibility. Everyone neatly avoids responsibility for the quality of the final product. Because such a compartmentalized process results in formalized and relatively inflexible requirements at each stage, it is more predictable and therefore more vulnerable to an opponent's countermeasures. In intelligence, as in most forms of conflict, if you can predict what your opponents will do, you can defeat them.

The cycle-defined view, when it considers the customer at all, tends to treat the customer in the abstract as a monolithic entity. The feedback loop inherent in a true cycle is absent; a gap exists between dissemination and needs. Customers, being outside the loop, cannot make their changing needs known. Why does this gap exist?

In government, intelligence officers and policymakers often are almost totally ignorant of one another's business.[3] In the military the gap may be less severe—the importance of intelligence has been ingrained in military culture over a long time. But as in the civilian side of government, an organizational demarcation usually exists. Most commanders and their staffs have not had intelligence assignments, and intelligence officers usually have not had operations assignments. They tend to speak different jargons, and their definitions of what is important in an operation differ. Military intelligence officers often know more about an opponent's capability than they do about their own unit's capability, and the commander often has the inverse problem.

In large intelligence organizations, such as those of the U.S. government, the collection element (see Figure 1-1) typically is well organized, well funded, and automated to handle high volumes of traffic. In contrast, the step wherein one moves from disseminated intelligence to new requirements is almost completely unfunded and requires extensive feedback from intelligence consumers. The system depends on the customers voicing their needs. Military organizations have a formal system for that to occur. Policymakers do not. The policymaker's input is largely informal, dependent on feedback to the analyst, and often passes through several intermediaries. And for the newest class of customers of U.S. intelligence—law enforcement—the feedback is rudimentary. No entity has the clear responsibility to close the loop. Analysts and their managers, who normally have the closest ties to intelligence customers, usually determine customer needs. But it is often a hit-or-miss proposition because it depends on the inclination of analysts who are dealing with other pressing problems.

The traditional conception of the intelligence cycle also prevails because it fits a conventional paradigm for problem solving. It flows logically from the precept that the best way to work on an intelligence problem is to follow a sequential, orderly, and linear process, working from the question (the problem) to the answer (the solution). One begins by understanding the question; the next step is to gather and analyze data. Analysis techniques are then applied to answer the question. This pattern of thinking is taught in the simplest problem-solving texts, and we use it almost instinctively. In fact, conventional wisdom says that the more complex the problem, the more important it is to follow this orderly flow. The flaw of this linear problem-solving approach is that it obscures the real, underlying cognitive process: The mind does not work linearly; it jumps around to different parts of the problem in the process of reaching a solution. In practice, intelligence officers might jump from analysis back to collection, then to requirements, to collection again, then back to analysis, in what seems a very untidy process, and which in no way resembles a cycle.

Despite its irrelevance to the real world of intelligence, the concept of an intelligence cycle persists. Some of the foremost experts in U.S. and British intelligence, such as Mike McConnell, former U.S. director of national intelligence, and noted British author Michael Herman, have questioned its relevance. Both McConnell[4] and Herman[5] noted that the so-called cycle is actually a series of feedback loops. But old habits tend to fade very slowly, and so the intelligence cycle continues to be taught in introductory intelligence courses.

U.S. intelligence analysis guru Sherman Kent noted that the problems with the intelligence cycle—the compartmentation of participants, the gap between dissemination and needs, and the attempt to make linear a nonlinear process—are worse in large organizations and in situations far removed from the heat of conflict.[6] As Keith Hall, former director of the National Reconnaissance Office, observed, "During crisis the seams go away and all the various players pull together to create end-to-end solutions . . . but we don't do that well in a noncrisis situation."[7]

In summary, the traditional cycle may adequately describe the structure and function of an intelligence community, but it does not describe the intelligence process. In the evolving world of information technology, the traditional cycle may be even less relevant. Informal networks (communities of interest) increasingly are forming to address the problems that Kent identified and enable a nonlinear intelligence process using secure Web technology.

The cycle is still with us, however, because it embodies a convenient way to organize and manage intelligence communities like those in large governments and large military organizations. And it is in some respects a defensive measure; it makes it difficult to pinpoint responsibility for intelligence failures.

Fifty years ago, the automobile production "cycle" looked a lot like the traditional intelligence cycle. Marketing staff would come up with requirements for new cars. Designers would create a design and feed it to production. Production would retool the factory and produce the cars in a long assembly line. The cars came out at the end and went to a sales force that sold the cars to customers. And then marketing started on a new requirements set, beginning the cycle anew. No one had responsibility for the final result. Today automobile production is a team effort—with marketing, sales, design, and production staff sitting in the same room with consumer representatives, working together on a common target: the new automobile. This complex, interactive, collaborative, and social process results in faster production of higher quality, more market-oriented products. Although producing intelligence is a more complex undertaking than automobile manufacturing, the interactive approach works for both. This book defines an alternative approach, one that is gaining currency in intelligence communities, for a world where intelligence problems are becoming increasingly complex.

Intelligence as a Target-Centric Process

An alternative to the traditional intelligence cycle is to make all stakeholders (including customers) part of the intelligence process. Stakeholders in the intelligence community include collectors, processors, analysts, and the people who plan for and build systems to support them. U.S. customers on a given issue could include, for example, the president, the National Security Council staff, military command headquarters, diplomats, the Department of Homeland Security, local law enforcement, and the commanders of U.S. naval vessels. To include them in the intelligence process, the cycle must be redefined, not for convenience of implementation in a traditional organizational hierarchy but so that the process can take full advantage of evolving information technology and handle complex problems.

Figure 1-2 defines this *target-centric*, or objective-oriented, view of the intelligence process. Here the goal is to construct a shared picture of the target, from which all participants can extract the elements they need to do their jobs and to which all can contribute from their resources or knowledge, so as to create a more accurate target picture. It is not a linear process, nor is it a cycle (though it contains many feedback loops, or cycles); it is a *network process*, a social process, with all participants focused on the objective. It has been

Figure 1-2   Target-Centered View of the Intelligence Process

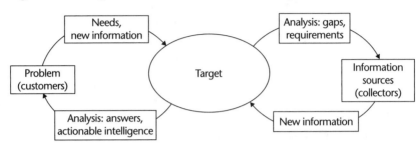

accurately described within the U.S. intelligence community as a "network-centric collaboration process."[8]

In the process depicted in Figure 1-2, customers who have operational problems look at the current state of knowledge about the target (the current target picture) and identify the information they need. Intelligence analysts, working with collectors who share the same target picture, translate the needs into "knowledge gaps" or "information requirements" for the collectors to address. As collectors obtain the needed information, it is incorporated into the shared target picture. From this picture, analysts extract actionable intelligence, which they provide to the customers, who may in turn add their own insights to the shared target picture. They may also add new information needs.

Let us bring some meaning to the process shown in Figure 1-2: The date is December 2, 1993. Colombian police lieutenant Hugo Martinez watches the signal display on his computer screen and listens to his headphones as his police surveillance van moves through the streets of Medellin, Colombia. Electronic intelligence has traced the cell telephone calls of drug kingpin Pablo Escobar to this neighborhood. Martinez is trying to find the exact house where a desperate Escobar is talking to his son about getting the family out of Colombia.

The signal on the computer screen and in the headphones strengthens and peaks. The van stops next to a house, and Martinez looks up to see a fat man standing at a window, holding a cell phone. The man turns away, and the cell phone conversation abruptly ends. Martinez reports to his commander: "I've got him located. He's in this house." The commander snaps out orders for all units to converge and surround the building. Five police officers force their way in the front door and exchange gunshots with the occupants. Ten minutes later, the gunfire stops. On the building rooftop, Pablo Escobar lies dead.[9]

This example, a true story, was the end of an intense cooperative effort between U.S. and Colombian intelligence officers that had endured for more than a year. In this case, the intelligence effort had several customers—an operations team comprising the Colombian police, the U.S. Army support team in Colombia, and the Colombian and U.S. governments, each with different intelligence needs. The information sources included COMINT focused on Escobar's cell phones and those of his associates, HUMINT from Escobar's associates, and financial information from other sources. The operations team focused on finding Escobar; the intelligence analysts who supported them had a more extensive target that included Escobar's family, his business associates, his bankers, and his agents in the Colombian government. Escobar would not have been caught if the intelligence search had focused solely on him and had ignored his network.

In the Escobar case, as in other, less time-critical operations, intelligence analysis is implicit and pervasive. But it is not all done by analysts. The customers and the providers of information also participate and will do so whether the analyst welcomes it or not. Both customers and providers possess valuable insights about the target, and both want their insights included in the final analytical product. However, someone must make the process work: create and maintain the picture of the target, elicit customer needs and change them into requirements for new information, accept new information and incorporate it into the target picture, and then extract actionable intelligence and ensure that it gets to the customer. All of these are functions that analysts have always performed. In the target-centric process, analysts still perform these functions, but collectors and customers can see into the process and have more opportunity to contribute to it. The analyst's job becomes more like that of a process manager and a conduit of information to the other participants.

The team-generated picture of the target is intended to facilitate and encourage interaction among collectors, analysts, and customers, who may be geographically remote from one another, via an electronic web. Because the team view is more interactive, or social, than the intelligence cycle view, it is a better way to handle complex problems. Because all participants share knowledge of the target, they are better able to identify gaps in knowledge and understand the important issues surrounding the target. The team-generated view brings the full resources of the team to bear on the target. During U.S. operations in Afghanistan in 2002, intelligence officers used screens similar to Internet chat rooms to share data in an interactive process that in no way resembled the traditional intelligence cycle,[10] and they continued that successful pattern during Operation Iraqi Freedom. But the method that has worked at the tactical level remains a work in progress at the national intelligence level. As the WMD Commission report says, "Information sharing still depends too much on physical co-location and personal relationships as opposed to integrated, community-wide information networks."[11]

The process shown in Figure 1-2 is resilient. Because the participants collaborate, there is no single point of failure; another member of the network could step in to act as facilitator; and the whole team accepts responsibility for the product.

The process is also able to satisfy a wide range of customers from a single knowledge base. There are usually many customers for intelligence about a given problem, and each customer has different needs. For example, military, foreign relations, financial, and foreign trade organizations all may need information about a specific country. Because there is a common target, their needs will overlap, but each organization also will have unique needs.

The target-centric approach has more promise for complex problems and issues than the traditional cycle view. Though depicted as a cycle, the traditional process is in practice linear and sequential, whereas the target-centric approach is collaborative by design. Its nonlinear analytic process allows for participation by all stakeholders, so real insights into a problem can come from any knowledgeable source. Involving customers increases the likelihood that the resulting intelligence will be used. It also reminds the customers of (or introduces them to) the value of an analytical approach to complex problems. It has been asserted that in the United States, government has detached itself from the analytical process and relied too much on the intelligence community to do its analytical thinking.[12] Increasing policymakers' exposure to the analytical process could help reverse that trend.

The collaborative team concept also has the potential to address two important pressures that intelligence analysts face today:

- *The information glut.* Analysts are overloaded with incoming material from collectors. The team approach expands the team of analysts to include knowledgeable people from the collector, processor, and customer groups, each of whom can take a chunk of the information glut and filter out the irrelevant material. Business organizations have been doing this for years, and they now rely heavily on Web-based means. Unfortunately, large intelligence communities, such as that in the U.S. government, have not succeeded in applying this remedy to the information glut. The barriers among collectors, processors, analysts, and customers still hold firm, and compartmentalization constrains collaboration.

- *The customer demand for more detail.* All intelligence customers are demanding increasingly greater detail about intelligence targets. This should not be surprising given that targets are more complex and the range of the customer's options to deal with opponents has become richer. If the operations target is a building (such as an embassy or a command and control center), for example, target intelligence may need to include the floor plan; the number of levels; whether it has a basement; the type of construction; roof characteristics; what type of heating, ventilation, and air conditioning it uses; when the building is empty; and so forth. Such details become critical when the objective is to place a smart bomb on the building or to take out the building's electric power.

For collaboration to work—for the extended team to share the data overload and provide the needed target detail—intelligence organizations have to provide incentives to share that outweigh the disincentives discussed in the introduction. Team members have to have a wealth of mutual trust and understanding; both require team building and extended social interaction. Some companies have been highly successful at collaboration; the U.S. government still is working at it, and most government intelligence services worldwide haven't even started.

It is important to note also what the collaborative process is not. As Mark Lowenthal has stated, it is not a substitute for competitive analysis—the process by which different analysts present alternative views of the target.[13] Collaboration, properly handled, is intended to augment competitive analysis by ensuring that the competing views share as much information about the target as possible.

The Target

In Norfolk, Virginia, a young intelligence officer controls a Predator Unmanned Aeronautical Vehicle on patrol over Afghanistan. The Predator's video display shows a vehicle racing along a mountain road. Moving the Predator closer for a better view, the officer identifies the vehicle as a BMP, a type of armored personnel carrier. He calls in an AC-130 Spectre gunship on patrol nearby. As the Spectre appears on the scene, the BMP lurches to a stop. The rear doors open, and the BMP disgorges Taliban soldiers running for cover. The Spectre's guns open up. In the Predator's video, the soldiers crumple one by one as the stream of gunship fire finds them.

The intelligence officer was able to order the attack by the AC-130 Spectre gunship because he had a mental picture of potential Taliban targets, and the BMP fit the picture in its location and characteristics. The BMP in Afghanistan was a specific operations target; the intelligence view of the target was much larger. It included details of the road network in Afghanistan that could support the BMP and maps delineating areas of Taliban control. A good mental model is essential when intelligence provides such close support to operations. The intelligence officer is under intense pressure to distinguish quickly between a troop carrier and a bus full of villagers, and the consequences of an error are severe.

The Target as a Complex System

As the BMP example suggests, the typical intelligence target is a system, not a single vehicle or building. Intelligence analysis therefore starts by thinking about the target as a system. A system comprises structure, function, and process, and the analyst has to deal with each of the three in systems thinking.[14] The *structure* of a system is defined by its components and the relationships among them. *Function* involves the effects or results that the system produces, that is, the system outputs. *Process* refers to the sequence of events or activities that produce results.

The Escobar drug cartel is (or was) an example of a system. Figure 1-3 is a macro-level picture of a cocaine cartel's structure, showing the major

Figure 1-3   Example Target: Cocaine Network

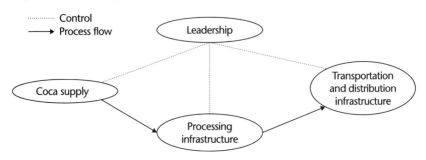

components and the relationships among them. Each of the components has a structure of its own, comprising subcomponents and their relationships. The coca supply component, for example, has subcomponents such as the farmers, land, seed, and farm equipment. A cocaine cartel also has several major functions, such as survival in the face of state opposition, making a profit, and providing cocaine to its customers. Each component also has additional functions that it performs. The transportation and distribution infrastructure has the functions of getting cocaine from the processor to the customer, selling the drugs, and obtaining payment for them. As this example illustrates, most intelligence targets are systems that have subordinate systems, also called *subsystems*. The Escobar leadership comprised a subsystem whose structure included components such as security and finance; it had a function (managing the cocaine network) and a process for carrying it out.

As a counterexample, a geographical region is not a system. A geographical region is much too abstract a concept to be treated as a system. It does not have structure, function, or process, though it contains many systems that have all three. Consequently, a geographical region could not be considered an intelligence target. The government of a region *is* a system—it has structure, function, and process.

All intelligence targets are systems. Furthermore, most are *complex systems* because

- They are dynamic and evolving.
- They are nonlinear, in that they are not adequately described by a simple structure such as a tree diagram or the linear structure that I used in Figure 1-1 to illustrate the traditional intelligence cycle.

A cocaine supply network is a complex system. It is constantly evolving, and its intricate web of relationships does not yield easily to a hierarchical breakout. It can, however, usually be described as a network. Most complex systems of intelligence interest are, in fact, networks.

The Complex Target as a Network

Although intelligence has always targeted opposing systems, it has often tended to see them as individual, rather than connected, entities. Such a narrow focus downplays the connections among organizations and individuals—connections that can be the real strength or weakness of an opposing system taken as a whole. That is the reason why we focus on networks.

Networks, by definition, comprise *nodes* with *links* between them. Several types of networks have been defined, and they vary in the nature of their nodes and links. In communications networks, the nodes are points, usually geographically separated, between which the communications are transmitted. A communications satellite and its ground terminals are communications nodes. The links are the communications means—for example, fiber optics, satellite communications, and wireless (cellular) telephones. In social networks, the nodes are people. The links show the relationships between people and usually the nature of those relationships. A social network exists, for example, at a cocktail party or in an investment club.

In this book, unless otherwise specified, *network* means a *generalized network,* in which the nodes can be almost any kind of entity—people, places, things, concepts. A cocaine supply system is a generalized network. The links define relationships among the nodes. Sometimes the links quantify the relationship. Whereas communications networks and social networks are useful concepts in intelligence, the more powerful generalized network is the preferred concept for intelligence analysis and is widely used.

In intelligence, the opposing generalized network typically is some combination of governments; individuals; nongovernmental organizations (NGOs), such as environmental, human rights, and religious groups; commercial firms; or illicit organizations—all tied together by some purpose, as suggested by the diagram in Figure 1-4. In conflicts, the goal of intelligence is to develop an understanding of the opposing network, so as to make the analyst's own network as effective as possible and render the opponent's network ineffective.

Analysts responsible for assessing the capabilities of an air defense network, a competing commercial firm or alliance, or a narcotics production and distribution network must take a network view. As an example, intelligence organizations

Figure 1-4   Netwar Competition: Network versus Network

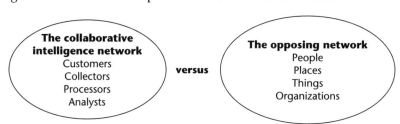

concerned with the balance of power in the Middle East sometimes look at Syria, Saudi Arabia, Iran, and Iraq separately. Yet no assessment of the future of the Middle East should ignore the continuing tensions among them—the constraining effects of past hostilities on any country's likely future actions and the opportunities that they provide for opponents. These individual countries are part of a larger target network bound by ties of mutual mistrust and suspicion.

It is also important to look at both sides as networks. It may be easier, especially in a bureaucracy, to see the opponent's side as a network than to see that one's own intelligence assets form a network and fully exploit its strengths. The collaborative, collector-analyst-customer, target-centric approach creates an effective network to deal with the opposing network. Figure 1-5 shows the example of a cocaine supply target network and some components of the opposing (that is, U.S. and Colombian) intelligence customer network. As the figure indicates, it makes sense that U.S. law enforcement would target the transportation and distribution infrastructure, because much of that infrastructure is located within U.S. borders. U.S. law enforcement would not normally be able to target the cartel leadership in Colombia. Colombian law enforcement, on the other hand, could target both the cartel leadership and its transportation and distribution infrastructure, but it would probably find the leadership a more profitable target. The customer network shown in the figure is far from complete, of course; it might include political leadership in the United States and Colombia, for example, or regional and European government entities concerned about the cocaine trade.

Figure 1-5   **Netwar Example against a Cocaine Network**

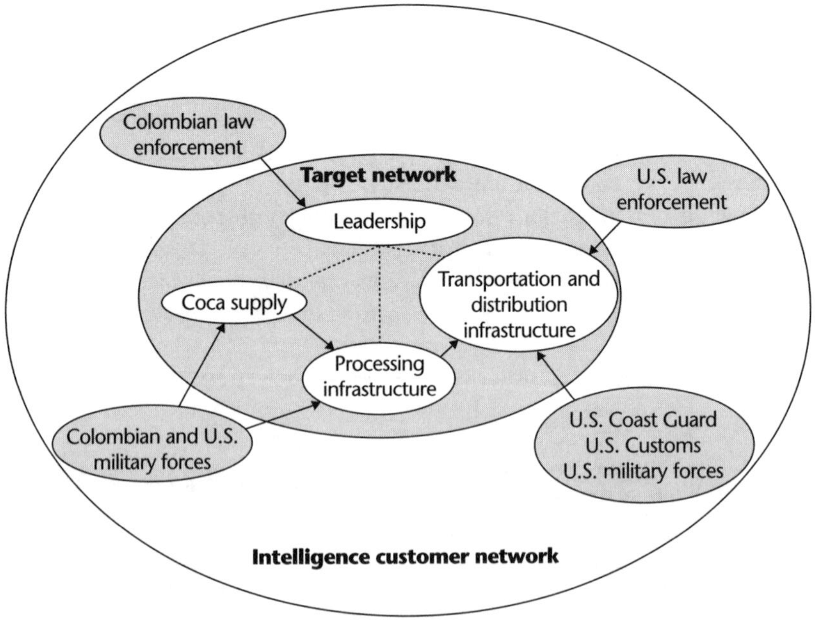

Note: Dotted lines represent the control that leadership exerts; solid lines entering the target network indicate targeting by the intelligence customer network.

John Arquilla and David Ronfeldt of RAND Corporation described the network target in their discussion of the impact of new communications and information technologies on military structures, doctrines, and strategies. They coined the term *netwar* and defined it as a form of information-related conflict, in which opponents form networks. Specifically, Arquilla and Ronfeldt use the term to describe the "societal struggles" that make use of new technologies.[15] The technologies they discuss are available and usable anywhere, as demonstrated by the Zapatista netwar: In January 1994, a guerrilla-like insurgency in Chiapas, Mexico, by the Zapatista National Liberation Army, and the Mexican government's repressive response, caused a collection of activists associated with human-rights, indigenous-rights, and other types of nongovernmental organizations elsewhere to link electronically with similar groups in Mexico to press for nonviolent change. What began as a violent insurgency in an isolated region mutated into a nonviolent but disruptive social netwar that engaged the attention of activists around the world and had both nationwide and foreign repercussions for Mexico. The Zapatista insurgents skillfully used a global media campaign to create a supporting network of NGOs and embarrass the Mexican government in a form of asymmetric attack (a form of conflict that exploits dissimilarities in capability between two opponents).[16]

Netwar is not the same as information warfare, though the two may overlap in some problems. Information warfare, also called *information operations,* encompasses the use of information systems, including computers, communications networks, and databases, for competitive advantage against an opponent. Thus information warfare can be one of the "levers" that are pulled in netwar; computer networks may be a part of the target. But one can engage in netwar without attacking the opponent's information systems.

Within the U.S. Department of Defense, netwar is currently referred to as *network-centric warfare.*[17] Defense planners have identified three themes:

- a shift in focus from the single-node target to the network target
- a shift from viewing actors as independent to viewing them as part of a continuously adapting system
- the importance of making strategic choices to adapt—or merely to survive—in the changing system

Network-centric warfare is not a new concept in the business world.[18] Companies such as Royal Dutch Shell were creating networks of this kind, including allied outsiders, more than a decade ago. Participants in that network found it a powerful mechanism for bringing a wide range of expertise to bear on problems.[19] The World Wide Web has speeded the formation of such networks, and the network-centric approach has been adopted widely in the commercial world. Companies such as Cisco Systems and Wal-Mart have made the collaborative network a key part of their business strategy. In Wal-Mart's network-centric retailing approach, the company shares sales information with suppliers in near-real time so that they can better control production and distribution, as well as manage their own supply chains for Wal-Mart products.[20] Another example is the network-centric securities trading system Autobahn, created by Deutsche Morgan Grenfell.[21] Autobahn replaces the traditional, trader-centered (hierarchical) system of securities trading with a network system in which participants have equal access to securities pricing information. The advantage that the network-centric approach gives companies such as Wal-Mart and Deutsche Morgan Grenfell forces their competitors to adopt similar approaches or lose out in competition.

Business intelligence might be ahead of government intelligence in applying the netwar strategy. Even military organizations, with their traditions of hierarchical structure, are considering the advantages of the network structure.[22] In cases when national intelligence efforts must deal with commercial entities, as they do in economic matters, weapons proliferation, and money-laundering cases, intelligence analysts increasingly must understand network-centric conflict. Furthermore, NGOs are becoming more involved in military, economic, political, and social issues worldwide, and NGO involvement usually makes any conflict network-centric, as it did with the Zapatistas in Mexico.

Summary

Intelligence is about reducing uncertainty in conflict. It supports operations, and it is always concerned with a target. Traditionally, intelligence has been described as a cycle: from requirements to planning or direction, collection, processing, analysis and production, dissemination, then back to requirements. That traditional view has several shortcomings. It separates the customer from the process and intelligence professionals from one another. A gap exists in practice between dissemination and requirements. The traditional cycle is useful for describing structure and function and serves as a convenient rationale for organizing and managing a large intelligence community. But it does not describe how the process works or should work.

Intelligence as a process is becoming a nonlinear and target-centric network, that is, a collaborative team of analysts, collectors, and consumers collectively focused on the intelligence target. The rapid advances in information technology are aiding this transition.

All significant intelligence targets of this target-centric network are complex systems in that they are nonlinear, dynamic, and evolving. As such, they can almost always be represented structurally as dynamic networks—opposing networks that constantly change with time. Conflict with such networks has been called *netwar* or *network-centric conflict*. In dealing with opposing networks, the intelligence network must be highly collaborative. Historically, however, large intelligence organizations, such as those in the United States, provide disincentives to collaboration. If those disincentives can be removed, U.S. intelligence will increasingly resemble the most advanced business intelligence organizations in being both target-centric and network-centric.

Having defined the target, the first question to address is, What do we need to learn about the target that our customers do not already know? This is the intelligence problem, and for complex targets, the associated intelligence problems are also complex. The next chapter discusses how to define the intelligence problem.

Notes

1. A *dead drop* is a temporary concealment place for material that is in transit between two clandestine intelligence operatives who cannot risk a face-to-face meeting. A tin can next to a park bench or the interior of a personable robot are classic examples of dead drops.
2. Walter D. Barndt Jr., *User-Directed Competitive Intelligence* (Westport, Conn.: Quorum Books, 1994), 21–22.
3. David Kennedy and Leslie Brunetta, "Lebanon and the Intelligence Community," case study C15-88-859.0, Kennedy School of Government Case Program, Harvard University.
4. William J. Lahneman, *The Future of Intelligence Analysis,* University of Maryland, Center for International and Security Studies at Maryland, final report, vol. I, March 10, 2006, E-8.
5. Michael Herman, *Intelligence Power in Peace and War* (Cambridge: Cambridge University Press, 1996), 100.
6. Quoted in Sherman Kent, "Producers and Consumers of Intelligence," in *Strategic Intelligence: Theory and Application,* 2nd ed., ed. Douglas H. Dearth and R. Thomas Goodden (Washington, D.C.: U.S. Army War College and Defense Intelligence Agency, 1995), 129.
7. Stew Magnuson, "Satellite Data Distribution Lagged, Improved in Afghanistan," *Space News,* September 2, 2002.
8. V. Joseph Broadwater, "I Would Make the T-PED Pain Go Away," memorandum for the record (U.S. National Reconnaissance Office, Washington, D.C., August 3, 2000), photocopy.
9. Mark Bowden, "A 15-Month Manhunt Ends in a Hail of Bullets," *Philadelphia Inquirer,* December 17, 2000.
10. Magnuson, "Satellite Data Distribution."
11. *Report of the Commission on the Intelligence Capabilities of the United States Regarding Weapons of Mass Destruction,* March 31, 2005, www.wmd.gov/report/wmd_report.pdf, 14.
12. Robert D. Steele, "The New Craft of Intelligence," advance review draft intended for general circulation, July 6, 2001, available from the author at bear@oss.net.
13. Mark M. Lowenthal, "Intelligence Analysis," address to the Intelligence Community Officers' Course, at CIA University, July 19, 2002.
14. Jamshid Gharajedaghi, *Systems Thinking: Managing Chaos and Complexity* (Boston: Butterworth-Heinemann, 1999), 110.
15. John Arquilla and David Ronfeldt, "Cyberwar Is Coming," in *Athena's Camp: Preparing for Conflict in the Information Age,* ed. John Arquilla and David Ronfeldt (Washington, D.C.: RAND Corporation, 1997).
16. David Ronfeldt and Armando Martinez, "A Comment on the Zapatista 'Netwar,'" in *Athena's Camp,* 369.
17. Arthur K. Cebrowski and John J. Garstka, "Network-Centric Warfare: Its Origin and Future," *Proceedings of the Naval Institute* 124, no. 1 (January 1998): 28–35.
18. Liam Fahey, *Competitors* (New York: John Wiley and Sons, 1999), 206.
19. Peter Schwartz, *The Art of the Long View* (New York: Doubleday, 1991), 90.
20. James F. Moore, *The Death of Competition: Leadership and Strategy in the Age of Business Ecosystems* (New York: HarperBusiness, 1996).
21. Cebrowski and Garstka, "Network-Centric Warfare."
22. Qiao Liang and Wang Xiangsui, *Unrestricted Warfare* (Beijing: PLA Literature and Arts, 1999), 57.

2

Defining the Intelligence Problem

Indeed, they disbelieve what they cannot grasp.

The Koran

The preceding chapter focused on the intelligence target—in most cases, a complex network. For such targets, there are typically several people who are interested in receiving intelligence, and those customers typically have different interests or different intelligence problems to which they want answers. For example, the U.S. Department of Energy might be interested in Iraqi oil well activity to estimate current production; a military field commander might be interested in the same oil well activity to prevent the wellheads from being destroyed. All intelligence analysis efforts therefore start with some form of problem definition.

The initial guidance that customers give analysts about a problem, however, is almost always incomplete, and it may even be unintentionally misleading. Therefore, the first and most important step an analyst can take is to understand the problem in detail. He or she must determine why the intelligence analysis is being requested and what decisions the results will support. The success of analysis depends on an accurate problem definition. As one senior policy customer commented concerning intelligence failures, "Sometimes, what they [the intelligence officers] think is important is not, and what they think is not important, is." [1]

The poorly defined problem is so common that it has a name: the *framing effect.* It has been described as "the tendency to accept problems as they are presented, even when a logically equivalent reformulation would lead to diverse lines of inquiry not prompted by the original formulation." [2] We encounter it in many disciplines where the problem must be properly defined before it can be effectively solved. The classic example of the framing effect was a 1982 study in which U.S. doctors were presented with two different formulations for the outcome of an operation. One set of doctors was informed that the operation had a 93 percent survival rate; the other set was told that the operation had a 7 percent mortality rate. Rationally, there should have been no difference in the doctors' decisions, since both statistics have the same meaning. But the doctors showed a definite preference not to operate when they were quoted a mortality rate instead of a survival rate.[3] Intelligence analysts often run afoul of the framing effect; one of the best-known examples is the National Intelligence Council's estimate on the Iraqi weapons of mass destruction program that is discussed in the appendix.

For these reasons, veteran analysts go about the analysis process quite differently than do novices. At the beginning of a task, novices tend to attempt to solve the perceived customer problem immediately. Veteran analysts spend more time thinking about it to avoid the framing effect. They use their knowledge of previous cases as context for creating mental models to solve the problem. Veterans also are better able to recognize occasions when they lack information necessary to solve a problem,[4] in part because they spend enough time at the beginning, in the problem definition phase. In cases such as the complex problems that are discussed in this chapter, problem definition should be about half of an analyst's work.

Problem definition is the first step in a process that is known as *structured argumentation*. We will get into the details of structured argumentation in the following chapters. For now, the important thing to understand is that structured argumentation always starts by breaking down a problem into parts so that each part can be examined systematically.[5] In this chapter, that first step is called *strategies-to-task*.

Statement of the Problem

Defining a problem begins with answering five questions:

- *When is the result needed?* Determine when the product must be delivered. (Usually, the customer wants the report yesterday.) In the traditional intelligence process, many reports are delivered late—long after the decisions that generated the need have been made—in part because the customer is isolated from the intelligence process. Also, tight deadlines are increasingly a problem in all areas of intelligence; the customer values having immediate, precise, and detailed intelligence. The target-centric approach can dramatically cut the time required to get actionable intelligence to the customer because the customer is part of the process.

- *Who is the customer?* Identify the intelligence customers and try to understand their needs. The traditional process typically involves several intermediaries, and the needs inevitably become distorted as they move through the communications channels. Also, even if the intelligence effort is undertaken for a single customer, the results often go to many other recipients. It helps to keep in mind the second-order customers and their needs as well.

- *What is the purpose?* Intelligence efforts usually have one main purpose. The purpose should be clear to all participants when the effort begins and also should be clear to the customer in the result. For instance, the main purpose might be to provide intelligence to support trade negotiations between the United States and the European Union. A number of more specific intelligence purposes support that main purpose—such as identifying likely negotiating tactics and pinpointing issues that might split the opposing negotiators. Again, customer involvement helps to make the purpose clear to the analyst.

- *What form of output, or product, does the customer want?* Written reports (increasingly in electronic form) are standard in the intelligence business because they endure and can be distributed widely. When the result goes to a single customer, or when it is extremely sensitive, a verbal briefing may be the form of output. Briefings have the advantage of customer interaction and feedback, along with certainty that the intended recipient gets the message. Studies have shown that customers never read most written intelligence.[6] Subordinates may read and interpret the report, but the message tends to be distorted as a result. So briefings or (ideally) constant customer interaction with the intelligence team during the target-centric process helps to get the message through.

- *What are the real questions?* Obtain as much background knowledge as possible about the problem that lies behind the questions the customer asks, and understand how the answers will affect organizational decisions. The purpose of this step is to narrow the problem definition. A vaguely worded request for information is usually misleading, and the result will almost never be what the requester wanted.

Be particularly wary of a request that has passed through several nodes in the organization. The layers of an organization, especially those of an intelligence bureaucracy, will sometimes "load" a request, as it passes through, with additional guidance that may have no relevance to the original customer's interests. A question that travels through several such layers often has become cumbersome by the time it reaches the analyst. A question about Israel's current balance of payments, for example, could wind up on the analyst's desk as instructions to prepare a complete assessment of the Israeli economy. In such situations, the analyst must go back to the originator of the request and close the loop. The problem of the communications channel is so pervasive in intelligence that it is covered in detail in chapter 7.

The request should be specific and stripped of unwanted excess. This entails focused (and perhaps repeated) interaction with the customer responsible for the original request—the executive, the policymaker, or the operations officer. Ask the customer if the request is correctly framed. The time spent focusing the request saves time later during collection and analysis. It also makes clear what questions the customer does *not* want answered. When the United States was already involved in Lebanon, in 1983, U.S. policymakers did not want to hear from U.S. intelligence that there was no reasonable way to force Syrian president Hafez Assad to withdraw from Lebanon.[7] The result of the disconnect between intelligence and the customer was a foreign policy debacle for the United States: On October 23, 1983, terrorists blew up the Marine Corps barracks at Beirut International Airport with a truck bomb that killed 241 marines. The United States subsequently withdrew from Lebanon. But policymakers can sometimes choose not to be informed by intelligence on selected issues. Chapter 15 deals with how to respond when the customer is antipathetic to intelligence.

After answering these five questions, the analyst will have some form of problem statement. On large (multiweek) intelligence projects, this problem statement will itself be a formal product. The problem definition product helps explain the real questions and related issues. Once it is done, the analyst will be able to focus more easily on answering the questions that the customer wants answered.

The Problem Definition Product

When the final intelligence product is to be a written report, the problem definition product is usually in précis (summary, abstract, or terms of reference) form. The précis should include the problem definition or question, notional results or conclusions, and assumptions. For large projects, many intelligence organizations require the creation of a concept paper or outline that provides the stakeholders with agreed terms of reference in précis form.

If the intelligence product is to be a briefing, a set of graphics will become the final briefing slides. If possible, the slides should be turned into a "notional briefing" (that is, a briefing with assumptions, notional results, and conclusions) and shown to the customer; this approach will improve the chances that the final report will address the issues in the customer's mind.

Either exercise will help all participants (customers, collectors, and analysts) understand their assignments or roles in the process. Think of it as a going-in position; no one is tied to the précis or notional presentation should the analysis later uncover alternative approaches—as it often does.

Whether the précis approach or the notional briefing is used, the problem definition should conclude with a strategies-to-task view of the problem.

Detailed Problem Definition: Strategies-to-Task

The basic technique for defining a problem in detail has had many names. Nobel laureate Enrico Fermi championed the technique of taking a seemingly intractable problem and breaking it into a series of manageable subproblems. The classic problem that Fermi posed for his students was, How many piano tuners are there in Chicago? The answer could be reached by using the sort of indirect approach that is common in the intelligence business: estimating how many families were in the city, how many families in the city per piano, and how many pianos a tuner can tune a year.[8] Glenn Kent of RAND Corporation uses the name *strategies-to-task* for a similar breakout of U.S. Defense Department problems.[9]

Whatever the name, the process is simple: Deconstruct the highest level abstraction of the problem into its lower level constituent functions until you arrive at the lowest level of tasks that are to be performed or subproblems that are to be dealt with. In intelligence, the deconstruction typically details issues to be addressed or questions to be answered. Start from the problem definition statement and provide more specific details about the problem. The process defines intelligence needs from the top level to the specific task level via *taxonomy*—a classification system in which objects are arranged into natural or related groups based on some factor common to each object in the group. At the top level, the taxonomy reflects the policymaker's or decision maker's view and the priorities of that customer. At the task level, the taxonomy reflects the view of the collection and analysis team. These subtasks are sometimes called *key intelligence questions* (KIQs) or *essential elements of information* (EEIs).

The strategies-to-task approach has an instinctive appeal. We naturally tend to form hierarchical social arrangements and to think about problems hierarchically. The strategies-to-task breakdown follows the classic method for problem solving. It results in a requirements, or needs, hierarchy that is widely used in intelligence organizations. A few examples from different national policy problem sets will help to illustrate the technique.

Figure 2-1 shows part of a strategies-to-task breakdown for political intelligence on a given country or region of the world. For simplicity, only one part of the breakdown is shown down to the lowest level.

Figure 2-1 illustrates the importance of taking the breakdown to the lowest appropriate level. The top-level question, "What is the political situation in Region X?" is difficult to answer without first answering the more specific questions lower down in the hierarchy, such as, What progress is being made toward reform of electoral systems?

Another advantage of the linear problem breakdown is that it can be used to evaluate how well intelligence has performed against specific problems or how future collection systems might perform. Again referring to Figure 2-1, it is difficult to evaluate how well an intelligence organization is answering the question, What is the political situation in Region X? It is much easier to evaluate the organization's performance in researching the transparency, honesty, and legitimacy of elections, because those are very specific issues.

Obviously several different problems can be associated with a given intelligence target, or several different targets can be associated with a given problem. If the problem were an overall assessment of a country's economy, rather than its political situation, then the problem breakdown might look very much like that shown in Figure 2-2. Because of space limits, the figure shows only four of thirteen question sets. At the bottom level, issues such as terms of trade

Figure 2-1 Political Situation Strategies-to-Task Problem Breakdown

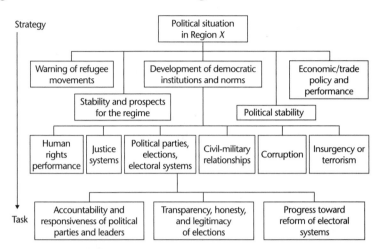

and corporate bankruptcies can be addressed with relative ease, compared with high-level questions such as, What is country X's financial stability?

These two strategies-to-task breakdowns are examples of the sorts of problems that intelligence analysts typically encounter with respect to a target, and both are oriented to broad information needs (here, political and

Figure 2-2 Country *X* Economic Problem Breakdown

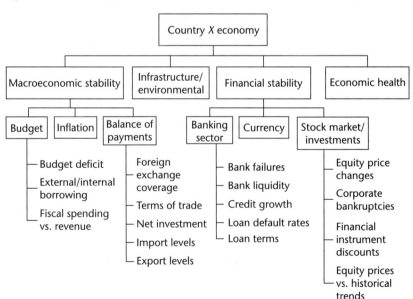

economic). But a strategies-to-task breakdown can be much more specific and more oriented to the customer's options for attacking the problem. Figure 2-3 illustrates an example—intelligence support to the design of economic sanctions against a country, such as might have been used to design sanctions against Iraq during the 1990s. An intelligence analyst might have difficulty directly answering this question from a policymaker: Tell me what I need to know to develop economic sanctions against country X. So the analyst would create a strategies-to-task breakdown of the problem, answer more specific questions such as, "What impact will sanctions have on the economy?" and integrate the answers to provide an answer to the top-level question.

No matter how narrow the top-level intelligence task, it still can likely be broken out into an array of specific questions. If the job is to assess the capabilities of an opponent's main battle tank, then an analyst would consider the tank's speed, range, armor, and firepower. Maintenance requirements, quality of crew training, logistics, and command and control supporting the tank should also be examined. Without these less-obvious components, the tank is simply an expensive piece of metal and a threat to no one.

Strategies-to-Task and Complex Problems

We have learned that the most important step in the intelligence process is to understand the problem accurately and in detail. Equally true, however, is that intelligence problems today are increasingly complex—often described as nonlinear, or "wicked." They are dynamic and evolving, and thus their solutions are, too. This makes them difficult to deal with—and almost impossible within the traditional intelligence cycle framework. A typical example of a complex problem is that of a drug cartel—the cartel itself is dynamic and evolving, and so are the questions being posed by intelligence consumers who have an interest in it.

Figure 2-3   Economic Sanctions Problem Breakdown

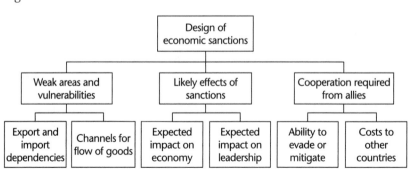

A typical real-world customer's problem today presents an intelligence officer with the following challenges:[10]

- *The problem represents an evolving set of interlocking issues and constraints.* There is no definitive statement of the problem. The intelligence officer may not understand the problem until he or she has finished the analysis, if then. Only by working through the problem to answers can one understand its ramifications. Often, even when the project is complete, an analyst learns from the customer that he or she didn't fully appreciate the issues involved. The narcotics example has an evolving set of interlocking issues and constraints. Take the constraints on possible solutions: Selectively introducing poison into the narcotics supply to frighten consumers and kill demand might reduce drug use, but it is not an acceptable option for the United States.

- *There are many stakeholders—people who care about or have something at stake in how the issue is resolved.* (This makes the problem-solving process a fundamentally social one, in contrast to the antisocial, traditional intelligence cycle.) The stakeholders in the contraband narcotics problem are on both sides: Among those trying to eliminate contraband narcotics are the Drug Enforcement Agency, other law enforcement agencies, U.S. Customs, the military, U.S. banks, and governments in drug-producing countries. Stakeholders on the opposing side include the cartel, its supporters in the foreign government, the financial institutions that it uses for funds laundering, farmers, processors, intermediaries, street forces, and drug users. And the stakeholders have different perspectives on the problem. Consider the Pablo Escobar example in chapter 1. From the U.S. point of view, the problem was to stem the flow of narcotics into the United States. From the Colombian government point of view, the problem was stopping the assassinations and bombings that Escobar ordered.

- *The constraints on the solution, such as limited resources and political ramifications, change over time.* The target is constantly changing, as the Escobar example illustrates, and the customers (stakeholders) change their minds, fail to communicate, or otherwise change the rules of the game. Colombians didn't want highly visible "gringos" involved in the hunt for Escobar, though they relaxed that constraint as they gained confidence in the U.S. operatives.[11] The U.S. government didn't want to be associated with killings of Escobar's relatives, business associates, and lawyers. The result is that the problem definition is dynamic; it cannot be created once and left unchanged.

- *Because there is no final problem definition, there is no definitive solution.* The intelligence process usually ends when time runs out, and the customer must act on the most current available information. Killing Escobar did not solve the narcotics problems of the United States or Colombia. Instead the rival Cali cartel became the dominant narcotics supplier in Colombia—an example of an unintended consequence. Many Colombian officials still live in fear of assassination.

Harvard professor David S. Landes summarized these challenges nicely when he wrote, "The determinants of complex processes are invariably plural and interrelated." [12] Because complex or wicked problems are evolving sets of interlocking issues and constraints, and because the introduction of new constraints cannot be prevented, the strategies-to-task breakdown of a complex problem must be dynamic; it will change with time and circumstances. As intelligence customers learn more about their targets, their needs and interests will shift.

Furthermore, the complex problem breakdown should be created as a network rather than as a hierarchy because of the interrelationships among the elements. In Figure 2-1 the political stability block is related to all three of the lowest blocks under "Political parties, elections, and electoral systems," though they appear in different parts of the hierarchy; political stability being enhanced, for example, when elections are transparent, honest, and legitimate. In Figure 2-3 "Ability to evade or mitigate" sanctions is clearly related to "Expected impact on the economy," or "Expected impact on leadership," though they also are in different parts of the hierarchy. Iraq's ability to evade or mitigate sanctions during the 1990s was sufficient to minimize the impact on its leadership but insufficient to keep the Iraqi economy healthy. If lines connected all of the relationships that properly exist within these figures, they would show very elaborate networks. The resulting dynamic network becomes quite intricate and difficult to manage at our present stage of information technology development.

The linear problem breakdown or strategies-to-task approach may be less than ideal for real-world, complex problems, but it works well enough if it is constantly reviewed and revised during the analysis process. It allows analysts to define the problem in sufficient detail and with sufficient accuracy that the rest of the process remains relevant. There may be redundancy in a linear hierarchy, but the human mind can usually recognize and deal with the redundancy. To keep the problem breakdown manageable, analysts should continue to use the strategies-to-task hierarchy, recognizing the need for frequent revisions, until information technology comes up with a better way. To illustrate, let us take an example of a very complex problem that has all of the challenges listed above, that of counterintelligence.

Example: Defining the Counterintelligence Problem

It is easy to begin with a wrong definition of the intelligence problem. If that happens, and if the problem definition is not revised, as discussed above, then the best analysis in the world will not avert a bad outcome. The counterintelligence problem has been poorly addressed in many countries for many years because the effort to do so began from a wrong problem definition that was never reconsidered.

Counterintelligence (CI) in government usually is thought of as containing two subordinate problems: security (protecting sources and methods) and catching spies (counterespionage). CI posters, literature, and briefings inevitably focus on the spies caught—probably because their primary purpose is to discourage treason. In doing so they are also catering to the popular media perception of counterintelligence.

If the problem is defined that way—counterespionage and security—the response in both policy and operations is defensive: Personnel background security investigations are conducted. Annual financial statements are required of all employees. Profiling is used to detect unusual patterns of computer use that might indicate computer espionage. Cipher-protected doors, badges, and personal identification numbers and passwords are used to ensure that only authorized persons have access to sensitive intelligence. The focus of communications security is on denial, typically by encryption. Leaks of intelligence are investigated to identify their source.

But whereas the focus on counterespionage and security is basically defensive, the first rule of strategic conflict is that *the offense always wins*. So, for intelligence purposes, you are starting out on the wrong path if the problem breakdown starts with managing security and catching spies. The Iraq WMD Commission recognized that flawed approach when it observed that U.S. counterintelligence has been criticized as focusing almost exclusively on counter-HUMINT, that is, on catching spies.[13]

A better approach to problem definition starts with consideration of the real target of counterintelligence: the foreign intelligence service. Good counterintelligence requires good analysis of the hostile intelligence services. As we will see in several examples later in the book, if you can model an opponent's intelligence system, you can defeat it. So we start with the target as the core of the problem and begin a strategies-to-task breakdown. Figure 2-4 illustrates the result: a simple first-level problem breakdown.

Figure 2-4   Counterintelligence Problem Breakdown

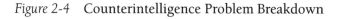

If the counterintelligence problem is defined in this fashion, then counter-intelligence activity will be forward-leaning and will focus on managing foreign intelligence perceptions through a combination of covert action, denial, and deception. The best way to win the strategic CI conflict is to take the offense (model the target, anticipate the opponent's actions, and defeat him). Instead of denying information to the foreign service, for example, you feed it false information that eventually degrades the opponent's confidence in his intelligence services.

To do this one needs a model of the foreign intelligence system that can be subjected to target-centric analysis, one that includes its communications channels and nodes, its requirements and targets, and its preferred sources of intelligence. How one uses such a model is discussed in the next chapter.

Summary

Before beginning intelligence analysis, the analyst must understand the customer's problem. That usually involves close interaction with the customer until the important issues are identified. The problem then has to be deconstructed in a strategies-to-task process so that collection, synthesis, and analysis can be effective.

All significant intelligence problems, however, are complex and nonlinear. The complex problem is a dynamic set of interlocking issues and constraints, with many stakeholders and no definitive solution. The linear strategies-to-task process is not an optimal way to approach such problems, but it can work if it is frequently reviewed and updated during the analysis process.

Problem definition is the first step in a process known as *structured argumentation.* As analysts work through that process, they collect and evaluate relevant information, fitting it into a target model (which may or may not look like the problem breakdown); that part of the process is discussed in chapters 5 to 7. The analyst identifies information gaps in the target model and plans strategies to fill them (the subject of chapter 8). The analysis of the target model then provides answers to the questions posed in the problem definition process. The next chapter discusses the concept of a model and how it is analyzed.

Notes

1. Stew Magnuson, "Satellite Data Distribution Lagged, Improved in Afghanistan," *Space News,* September 2, 2002, 6.
2. Matthew Herber, "The Intelligence Analyst as Epistemologist," *International Journal of Intelligence and Counterintelligence* 19, no. 4 (December 2006): 666–684.
3. Barbara J. McNeill, Stephen G. Paulker, and Amos Tversky, "On the Framing of Medical Decisions," in *Decision Making: Descriptive, Normative, and Prescriptive Interactions,* ed. David E. Bell, Howard Raiffa, and Amos Tversky (Cambridge: Cambridge University Press, 1988), 562–568.
4. Rob Johnson, *Analytic Culture in the U.S. Intelligence Community* (Washington, D.C.: Center for the Study of Intelligence, Central Intelligence Agency, 2005), 64.
5. Jill Jermano, "Introduction to Structured Argumentation," Project Genoa Technical Report (Washington, D.C.: DARPA, Department of Defense, May 2002).

6. Jack Davis, "Intelligence Changes in Analytic Tradecraft in CIA's Directorate of Intelligence," CIAPES ICATCIADI-9504 (Washington, D.C.: Central Intelligence Agency, April 1995), 2.

7. David Kennedy and Leslie Brunetta, "Lebanon and the Intelligence Community," case study C15-88-859.0 (Cambridge: Kennedy School of Government, Harvard University, 1988), 15.

8. Hans Christian von Baeyer, *The Fermi Solution* (Portland: Random House, 1993).

9. Glenn Kent and William Simon, *New Challenges for Defense Planning: Rethinking How Much Is Enough* (Santa Monica: RAND Corp., 1994).

10. E. Jeffrey Conklin, "Wicked Problems and Social Complexity," CogNexus Institute, March 24, 2003, www.cognexus.org/wpf/wickedproblems.pdf.

11. Mark Bowden, "Martinez Pushes Ahead with the Hunt," *Philadelphia Inquirer,* December 3, 2000.

12. David S. Landes, *The Wealth and Poverty of Nations* (New York: W. W. Norton and Company, 1998), 577.

13. *Report of the Commission on the Intelligence Capabilities of the United States Regarding Weapons of Mass Destruction,* March 31, 2005, www.wmd.gov/report/wmd_report.pdf, chap. 11.

3

An Analysis Approach to the Target

If we are to think seriously about the world, and act effectively in it, some sort of simplified map of reality . . . is necessary.
Samuel P. Huntington, *The Clash of Civilizations and the Remaking of World Order*

The target-centric approach and the problem definition process described in the preceding chapter naturally lead to the creation of a model of the target, if a model does not already exist. Models are so extensively used in intelligence that analysts seldom give them much thought, even as they use them. For example:

- Imagery analysts can recognize a nuclear fuel reprocessing facility because they have a mental model of typical facility details, such as the use of heavy reinforced concrete to shield against intense gamma radiation.
- In signals intelligence (SIGINT), a communications or radar signal has standard parameters—it can be recognized because it fits an existing model in its radio frequency, its modulation parameters, and its modes of operation.
- Clandestine or covert radio communications signals can be recognized because they fit a specific model: They are designed to avoid intercept by, for example, using very short (burst) transmissions or jumping rapidly from one radio frequency to another.
- Economic analysts recognize a deteriorating economy because they have a checklist (a simple form of model) of indicators, such as a budget deficit, an unfavorable balance of payments, and inflation. The strategies-to-task problem breakdown shown in Figure 2-2 provides such a checklist.

The model paradigm is a powerful tool in many disciplines. As political scientist Samuel P. Huntington noted in the quote that begins this chapter, "If we are to think seriously about the world, and act effectively in it, some sort of simplified map of reality, some theory, concept, model, paradigm, is necessary."[1] In this book the map, theory, concept, or paradigm is merged into a single entity called a model.

Modeling is usually thought of as being quantitative and using computers. However, all models start in the human mind. Modeling does not require a computer, and many useful models exist only on paper. Models are used widely in fields such as operations research and systems analysis. With modeling, one can analyze, design, and operate complex systems. One can use simulation models to evaluate real-world processes that are too complex to analyze with spreadsheets or flowcharts (which are themselves models, of course) to test hypotheses at a fraction of the cost of undertaking the actual activities. Models are an efficient communication tool for showing how the target functions and stimulating creative thinking about how to deal with an opponent.

Models are essential when dealing with complex targets. Without a device to capture the full range of thinking and creativity that occurs in the target-centric approach to intelligence, an analyst would have to keep in mind far too many details. Furthermore, in the target-centric approach, the customer of intelligence is part of the collaborative process. Presented with a model as an organizing construct for thinking about the target, customers can contribute pieces to the model from their own knowledge—pieces that the analyst might be unaware of. The primary supplier of information (the collector) can do likewise.

Because the model concept is fundamental to everything that follows, it is important to define it.

Analysis Principle 3-1 •————————————————————

The Essence of Intelligence

All intelligence involves creating a *model* of the target and extracting knowledge therefrom. (So does all problem solving.)

The Concept of a Model

A model is a replica, or representation, of an idea, an object, or an actual system. It often describes how a system behaves. Instead of interacting with the real system, an analyst can create a model that corresponds to the actual one in certain ways. For example, the results of a political poll are a model of how a population feels about a topic; today's weather map is a model of how the weather is expected to behave.

Figure 3-1   Model Hierarchy

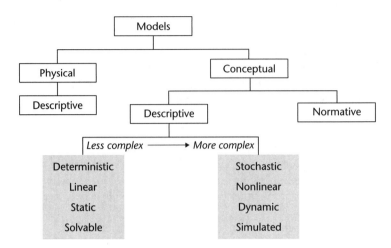

Figure 3-1 shows a hierarchy of models and forms the basis for the discussion that follows. As the figure indicates, models can be classified as physical or conceptual (abstract).

A *physical model* is a tangible representation of something. A map, a globe, a calendar, and a clock are all physical models. The first two represent the earth or parts of it, and the latter two represent time. Physical models are always descriptive.

Conceptual models—inventions of the mind—are essential to the analytical process. They allow the analyst to describe things or situations in abstract terms both for estimating current situations and for predicting future ones. A conceptual model is not a tangible item, although the item it represents may be tangible. Mathematical models are conceptual. A conceptual model may be either descriptive or normative. A normative model may contain some descriptive segments, but its purpose is to describe a best, or preferable, course of action. A decision-support model—that is, a model used to choose among competing alternatives—is normative.

In intelligence analysis, the models of most interest are conceptual and descriptive rather than normative. Some common traits of these conceptual models are the following:

- *Descriptive models can be deterministic or stochastic.* In a deterministic model the relationships are known and specified explicitly. A model that has any uncertainty incorporated into it is a stochastic model (meaning that probabilities are involved), even though it may have deterministic properties.[2] Consider the anecdote in chapter 1 about drug kingpin Pablo Escobar. A model of the home in which Escobar was located and the surrounding buildings would have been deterministic—the details were known and specified exactly. A model of the people expected to be in the house at the time of the attack would have been stochastic, because the presence or absence of Escobar and his family could not be known in advance; it could only be estimated as a probability.

- *Descriptive models can be linear or nonlinear.* Linear models use only linear equations (for example, $x = Ay + B$) to describe relationships. It is not necessary that the situation itself be linear, only that it be capable of description by linear equations. The number of automobiles produced in an assembly line, for example, is a linear function of time. In contrast, nonlinear models use any type of mathematical function. Because nonlinear models are more difficult to work with and are not always capable of being analyzed, the usual practice is to make some compromises so that a linear model can be used. It is important to be able to justify doing so because most real-world intelligence targets are complex, or nonlinear. A combat simulation model is nonlinear because the interactions among the elements are complex and do not change in ways that can be described by linear equations. Attrition rates in combat, for example, vary nonlinearly with time and the status of remaining military forces. A model of an economy is inherently nonlinear; but the econometric models used to describe an economy are simplified to a set of linear equations to facilitate a solution.

- *Descriptive models can be static or dynamic.* A static model assumes that a specific time period is being analyzed and that the state of nature is fixed for that time period. Static models ignore time-based variances. For example, one cannot use them to determine the impact of an event's timing in relation to other events. Returning to the example of a combat model, a snapshot of the combat showing where opposing forces are located and their direction of movement at that instant is static. Static models do not take into account the synergy of the components of a system, in which the actions of separate elements can have a different effect on the system than the sum of their individual effects would indicate. Spreadsheets and most relationship models are static.

A dynamic model, on the other hand, considers several time periods and does not ignore the impact of an action in time period 1 on time period 2. A combat simulation model is dynamic; the loss of a combat unit in time period 1 affects all succeeding time periods. Dynamic modeling (also known as *simulation*) is a software representation of the time-based behavior of a system. Whereas a static model involves a single computation of an equation, a dynamic model is iterative—it constantly recomputes its equations as time changes. It can predict the outcomes of possible courses of action and can account for the effects of variances or randomness. One cannot control the occurrence of random events. One can, however, use dynamic modeling to predict the likelihood and the consequences of their occurring. Process models usually are dynamic because they envision flows of material, the passage of time, and feedback. Structural and functional models are usually static, though they can be dynamic.

- *Descriptive models can be solvable or simulated.* A solvable model is one in which there is an analytical way of finding the answer. The performance model of a radar, a missile, or a warhead is a solvable problem. But other problems require such a complicated set of equations to describe them that there is no way to solve them. Worse still, complex problems typically cannot be described in a finite set of equations. In complex cases—such as the performance of an economy or a person—one can turn to simulation. Rather than seeking the optimal solution, simulation requires the user to propose a set of possible solutions. The proposals are then introduced into the model, which typically is coded on a computer and verified for feasibility. From the courses of action proposed, the user can then select the one with the best result.

Simulation involves designing a model of a system and performing experiments on it. The purpose of these "what if" experiments is to determine how the real system performs and to predict the effect of changes to the system as time progresses. For example, an analyst can use simulation to answer questions such as these: What is the expected balance of trade worldwide next year? What are the likely areas of deployment for mobile surface-to-air missiles (SAMs) in country X? What is the expected yield of the nuclear warheads on country Y's new medium-range ballistic missiles?

Using Target Models for Analysis

Often, particularly in military combat or law enforcement operations, the creation and analysis of a target model occur as a quick and intuitive process. Let us begin with a simple example, one that is relevant to military combat operations.

Consider the BMP personnel carrier racing along an Afghan mountain road that was described in chapter 1. The problem definition in that example was very simple: Locate Taliban forces in the region. This time, however, the intelligence officer has an additional problem: He must determine when the BMP will reach a nearby village, where a Doctors Without Borders team is currently providing medical assistance.

The officer has a mental model of the BMP's performance; he knows its maximum speed on typical mountain roads. He has the Predator's information giving the present position of the BMP. And he has a map—a geographical model—that allows him to determine the distance between the BMP's present position and the village. Combining these models and performing a simple computation (analysis), he produces a predictive scenario (a combination of several models into a more comprehensive target model), concluding that the BMP will arrive in the village in twenty-five minutes, and the Doctors Without Borders team will be toast unless the Spectre gunship arrives first.

When the intelligence customer is a national leader or policymaker or a business executive, the analysis process is typically more deliberate than in this example. Consider the intelligence problems defined in the breakdowns in Figures 2-1 and 2-2 in the preceding chapter. The problem breakdown in each case, when populated with specific intelligence, is also a type of target model that can serve many purposes. It can be used as a basis for requesting intelligence collection on the specific topics shown in the boxes at the bottom level of the diagrams—a subject explored in detail in chapter 8. It can be a framework in which to incorporate incoming intelligence—a subject discussed in chapter 7, "Evaluating and Collating Data."

To illustrate, let us use the problem breakdown of a country's economy shown in Figure 2-2 and focus on one part of the overall economy: the country's financial stability, specifically the stability of the banking sector. There are five components that contribute to an assessment of the banking sector: bank failures, bank liquidity, credit growth, loan default rates, and loan terms. Most of these components can be described effectively by a simple type of model that is discussed in chapter 5: a temporal graphic. Using the available raw intelligence information, one can draw curves showing

- bank failures over the last few years (a flat curve)
- bank liquidity over the same time period (steadily decreasing)
- credit growth (rising sharply)
- loan default rates (stable until last year, then started increasing)

One can also prepare a comparative graphic that shows how loan terms compare with those offered in other countries (terms are much more favorable to lenders in the target country).

Combining all of these models into an overall picture of the banking sector, one might observe that although bank failures have been stable so far, the future does not look good. All of the other components of the model are showing unfavorable trends. On the basis of past experience, one can analyze the models to create a predictive model—another scenario—which indicates that bank failures will rise dramatically in the near future and that the banking sector of the economy is headed for serious trouble.

This example illustrates how the problem breakdown is closely related to the target model and how it can also be used to structure or organize the target model. Part 2 of this book explores the target model in more detail and illustrates the types of models that are used in analysis. Part 3 is devoted to analysis methodologies that use models—especially predictive methodologies.

As another example of how a good target model can be analyzed and used in policymaking and policy execution, let us revisit the counterintelligence analysis problem.

Counterintelligence Analysis

In chapter 2 we examined a simple counterintelligence (CI) problem breakdown model that has as its target a foreign intelligence service. We begin from the block in Figure 2-4 labeled *General Strategy* of the organization, which has three subcategories—targets, operations, and linkages (to other intelligence services). Let us look at these subcategories more closely.

Targets

Most intelligence services have preferred strategic targets that closely align with their national interests. As examples, consider four countries with sizable intelligence services having different targets—Russia, China, France, and Germany.

- Countries such as France and Germany are concerned with combating terrorism and promoting their economies through exports. So they focus on terrorism and economic intelligence.[3]

- China is particularly concerned with regional military threats, causing Chinese intelligence to target Taiwan. China also has a national interest in acquiring technology to develop both military and commercial strength.

- Russia's priorities center on internal security (particularly against terrorist threats) and on political, economic, and military events in neighboring countries, especially in the former Soviet republics. The Russian intelligence services divide these targets, with the SVU (successor to the KGB) going after political and economic targets and the GRU going after military targets.

Operations

Intelligence services prefer specific sources of intelligence, shaped in part by what has worked for them in the past, by their strategic targets, and by the size of their pocketbooks. The poorer intelligence services rely heavily on open sources (including the Web) and HUMINT, because both are relatively inexpensive. COMINT also can be cheap, unless it is collected by satellites. The wealthier services also make use of satellite-collected imagery intelligence (IMINT) and COMINT, as well as other types of technical collection (all of which are discussed in chapter 6).

- France and Germany make use of technical collection, including COMINT and computer intrusion techniques.[4] They are well equipped to do COMINT because two of the premier COMINT hardware developers are located in France (Thales) and Germany (Rohde & Schwartz).

- China relies heavily on HUMINT, working through commercial organizations, particularly trading firms, and academics far more than most other major intelligence powers do.[5]

In addition to being acquainted with opponents' collection habits, CI also needs to understand a foreign intelligence service's analytical capabilities. Many services have analytical biases, are ethnocentric, or handle anomalies poorly. It is important to understand their intelligence communications channels and how well they share intelligence within the government. In many countries the senior policymaker or military commander is the analyst. That provides a prime opportunity for "perception management," especially if a narcissistic leader like Hitler, Stalin, or Saddam Hussein is in charge and doing his own analysis. Leaders and policymakers find it difficult to be objective; they are men of action, and they always have an agenda. They have lots of biases and are prone to wishful thinking.

Linkages

Almost all intelligence services have liaison relationships with foreign intelligence or security services. It is important to model these relationships because they can dramatically extend the capabilities of an intelligence service.

- During the cold war, the USSR had extensive liaison relationships with the intelligence services of its East European satellites. The Soviet intelligence services, however, were always the dominant ones in the relationships. Since the breakup of the Soviet Union, Russia has been slowly developing new liaison relationships with some of the former Soviet republics.

- France and Germany share intelligence both directly and through NATO (the North Atlantic Treaty Organization) and have intelligence liaison arrangements with selected other countries.

- In the area of law enforcement, many countries share intelligence via Interpol, the international organization created to facilitate cross-border police cooperation.

Target Model Combinations

Often the problem breakdown provides a target model, or at least a starting point. Sometimes it does not. Sometimes the target model is built without detailed knowledge of the problem to be solved. Almost all target models are actually combinations of many models.

Let us illustrate with an example of organizing available intelligence concerning a biological weapons (BW) threat. The problem is to assess the ability of country *X* to produce, deploy, and use BW as a terror or combat weapon. One might start by synthesizing a generic model, or model template, based on nothing more than general knowledge of what it takes to build and use biological weaponry. Such a generic process model would probably look like Figure 3-2.[6]

But the generic model is only a starting point. From here the model has to be expanded and made specific to the target, the program in country *X,* in an iterative process that involves creation of more detailed models called *submodels* or *collateral models.*

Submodels

Like a Russian Matrushka doll, an overall target model can contain a number of more detailed component models. Participants in the target-centric process then can reach into the model set to pull out the information they need. The collectors of information can drill down into more detail to refine collection targeting and to fill specific gaps. The intelligence customer can drill down to answer questions, gain confidence in the analyst's picture of the target, and understand the limits of the analyst's work. The target model is a powerful collaborative tool.

One type of component model is a submodel, a more detailed breakout of the top-level model. Figure 3-3 illustrates a submodel of one part of the process shown in Figure 3-2.[7] In this scenario, as part of the development of the BW agent and a delivery system, a test area has to be established, and the agent must be tested on animals.

Figure 3-2   Generic Biological Weapons (BW) System Process Model

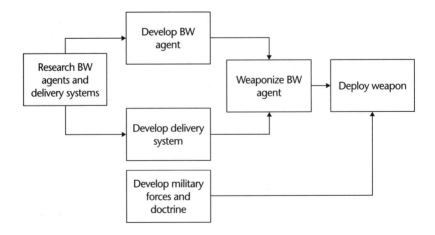

Figure 3-3   Biological Weapons (BW) System Test Process Submodel

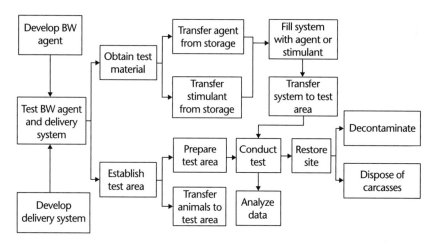

Collateral Models

In contrast to the submodel, a collateral model may show particular aspects of the overall target model, but it is not simply a detailed breakout of a top-level model. A collateral model typically presents a different way of thinking about the target for a specific intelligence purpose. For example, suppose that the customer needs to know how the BW organization is managed, where the operations are located, and when the country will deploy biological weapons.

Figure 3-4 is a collateral model intended to answer the first question: How is the organization managed? The figure is a model of the BW development organization, and like most organizational models, it is structural.

Figure 3-5 illustrates a spatial or geographical collateral model of the BW target, answering the second question, of where the BW operations are located. This type of model is useful in intelligence collection planning, as discussed in chapter 8.

Figure 3-4   Biological Weapons (BW) Development Organization Model

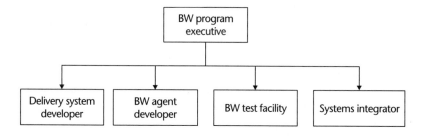

Figure 3-5   Collateral Model of Biological Weapons (BW) Facilities

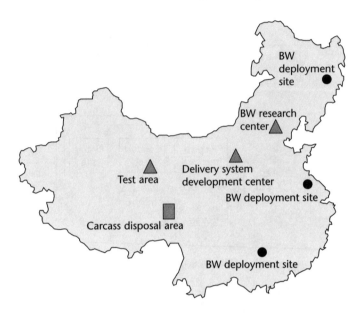

Another type of collateral model of the BW target is shown in Figure 3-6, a chronological model of BW development designed to answer the question of when the country will deploy biological weapons. This model also is of value to an intelligence collector for timing collection efforts.

The collateral models in Figures 3-4, 3-5, and 3-6 are examples of the three general types—structural, functional, and process—used in systems analysis. Figure 3-4 and Figure 3-5 are structural models. Figure 3-6 is both a process model and a functional model. In analyzing complex intelligence targets, all three types are likely to be used.

These models, taken together, allow an analyst to answer a wide range of customer questions. A model like Figure 3-5 can help determine the likely use and targets of the deployed BW system. The model shown in Figure 3-6 can help determine what stage the program is in and can help the intelligence customer with timing political, economic, or military action to halt the program or roll it back.

In practice, these models would be used together in an iterative analysis process. As an example of how the iterative approach works, begin with the generic model in Figure 3-3. From this starting point, the analyst might create the test process submodel shown in Figure 3-4. Prompted by the recognition that a BW testing program must have a test site, the analyst would ask collectors to search for test areas having associated animal pens and certain patterns of biological sensor deployment nearby. The analyst also would

Figure 3-6 Chronological Model of Biological Weapons (BW) Development

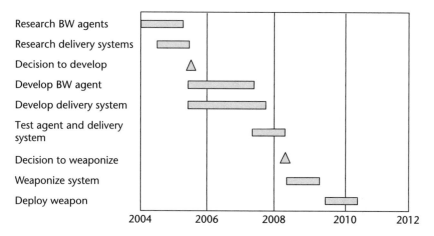

request that the collectors search for a carcass disposal area. Assuming the collectors are successful, the analyst can create a collateral model—a map display like that shown in Figure 3-5. Based on observation of activity at the test site and disposal area, the analyst can refine the chronological model shown in Figure 3-6.

The hunt for Pablo Escobar was another example of an iterative process. The Colombian and U.S. intelligence teams created models of Escobar's cell phone communication patterns, his network of associates, and his financial structure. From analysis of these, collectors could be aimed at specific targets—a process discussed in detail in chapter 8. As new intelligence was gathered on Escobar's cartel members, cell phone numbers, bank accounts, and pattern of operations, all of the models could be updated almost daily in a continuing, iterative process.

Summary

All intelligence involves extracting knowledge from a model of the target. Models in intelligence are normally conceptual and descriptive. The easiest ones to work with are deterministic, linear, static, solvable, or some combination of these models. Unfortunately, in the intelligence business the target models tend to be stochastic, nonlinear, dynamic, and simulated.

From an existing knowledge base, a model of the target is developed. Next, the model is analyzed to extract information for customers or for additional collection. The model of complex targets will normally be a collection of associated models that can serve the purposes of intelligence customers and collectors. Collateral models and submodels are examples. In an ongoing intelligence process, the analyst will continually incorporate new intelligence into the model for the purpose of refining it.

Notes

1. Samuel P. Huntington, *The Clash of Civilizations and the Remaking of World Order* (New York: Simon and Schuster, 1996), 29.
2. A stochastic process is one in which the events of the process are determined by chance. Such processes are therefore analyzed using probability theory.
3. "Telecommunications, Satellites Said to Be Targeted for Espionage by France," *Common Carrier Week,* May 17, 1993.
4. Samuel D. Porteous, "Economic Espionage: Issues Arising from Increased Government Involvement with the Private Sector," *Intelligence and National Security* 9, no. 4 (October 1994): 735–752; Wayne Madsen, "Intelligence Agency Threats to Computer Security," *International Journal of Intelligence and Counterintelligence* 6, no. 4 (Winter 1993): 413–488.
5. Nicholas Eftimiades, *Chinese Intelligence Operations* (Annapolis: Naval Institute Press, 1994), 22.
6. Michael G. Archuleta, Michael S. Bland, Tsu-Pin Duann, and Alan B. Tucker, "Proliferation Profile Assessment of Emerging Biological Weapons Threats," research paper, Directorate of Research, Air Command and Staff College, Maxwell AFB, Ala., April 1996.
7. Ibid.

4

The Analytic Spectrum

CAPTAIN MATTHEW GARTH (Charlton Heston):
Joe, you're guessing!
INTELLIGENCE OFFICER JOSEPH ROCHEFORT
(Hal Holbrooke): Sir, we like to call it analysis.
Midway, the movie, 1976

Analysis entails drawing conclusions from the target model. The type of intelligence that must be extracted from the model changes depending on the customer and on the time available to act on it. No intelligence categorization scheme works perfectly. The categorizations that I describe in this chapter have their own shortcomings and overlaps, but they encourage more effective collection and analysis than do disciplinary categorizations such as "political," "economic," and "military." They are equally applicable to government and to business intelligence.

The Conflict Spectrum

As we learned in chapter 1, intelligence is about conflict. Military organizations commonly define three levels of conflict: strategic, operational, and tactical.[1] Policymakers, law enforcement officers, and businesses experience similar levels of conflict. Types of intelligence are often defined to mirror these three levels, though the lines between them are often blurred.

Against any opponent in a conflict, three successive levels of action can be taken: *prevention, deterrence,* or *defeat.* Figure 4-1 shows a spectrum that includes these levels of action. Preventive operations tend to be strategic and to focus on planning. Actions intended to deter or defeat are mostly tactical; they center on executing the plans and managing the developing crisis.

- *Prevention.* Intelligence customers first try to prevent a disadvantageous situation from developing. Examples include preventing the opponent from acquiring or developing a capability, a strategy, or a new weapons system; preventing an unfavorable decision from being made; or preventing the opposing negotiations team from taking a certain position. Prevention can also include making an existing

Figure 4-1   Conflict Spectrum

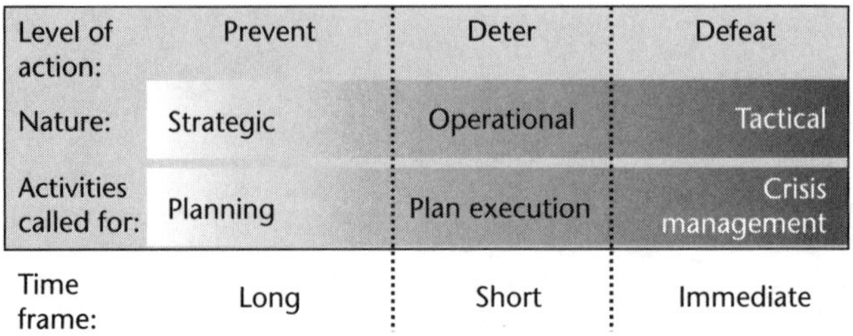

Level of action:	Prevent	Deter	Defeat
Nature:	Strategic	Operational	Tactical
Activities called for:	Planning	Plan execution	Crisis management
Time frame:	Long	Short	Immediate

situation more advantageous, for example, by encouraging an opponent to reverse an unfavorable decision that has been made; rolling back an opponent's existing capability; or inducing the opponent to abandon a favorable position or pull out of a contested area.

- *Deterrence.* Deterrence is used when it is too late for prevention. Examples include deterring an attack, deterring the use of a capability or weapons system; deterring the opponent from escalating or aggravating a crisis; or creating uncertainty that induces the opponent to be cautious. Prevention keeps a situation from becoming unfavorable; deterrence focuses on an opponent's potential actions as a way to resolve an already unfavorable situation.

- *Defeat.* When all else fails, the goal is to resolve the conflict on favorable terms. Examples include defeating the opponent in armed combat, destroying the opponent's weapons of mass destruction, or taking market share away from the opponent in commerce.

Until September 11, 2001, when terrorists attacked the World Trade Center and the Pentagon, the U.S. Department of Defense's Central Command (CENTCOM) was primarily focused on prevention and deterrence vis-á-vis the Taliban and al Qaeda in Afghanistan. After September 11, CENTCOM moved quickly into operational planning and then into tactics for defeating them.

We have said that intelligence supports operations across the spectrum of conflict. Intelligence, like operations, can be broadly defined at the top level as being *strategic, operational,* or *tactical.*

Strategic Intelligence

Strategic intelligence deals with long-range issues. For national customers generally, it is used to create national strategy and policy, monitor the international situation, and support such diverse actions as trade policymaking or national industrial policymaking. Strategic intelligence is also produced for the senior military leadership. It is used to prepare military plans, determine what weapon systems to build, and define force structures.[2] For corporations, it typically supports strategic planning.

Here an analyst must spend much time building a target model from scratch or updating an existing model. There are lots of options. One can consider many possible target models (scenarios), and the situation can evolve in many different ways. Intelligence takes a long-term, analytical view.

Strategic intelligence involves creating much the same target models whether in business or government. Both business and government look at the political structure and alliances of opponents; both create biographical or leadership profiles; both assess the opponent's technology.

Strategic intelligence is tougher than tactical intelligence. The analyst has to command more sophisticated analytic techniques. The models will be similar or identical to those used for tactical intelligence, but usually they are more complex because of the longer predictive time frame of strategic intelligence. Another problem is that the intelligence analyst is seldom able to put aside short-term, tactical support to customers while developing a clientele having the long-term view.[3] The analyst needs a champion in the customer suite to support him or her in strategic intelligence because tactical intelligence, dealing with immediate issues, usually consumes all available resources.

Operational Intelligence

Operational intelligence focuses on the capabilities and intentions of adversaries and potential adversaries. It is defined as the intelligence required for the planning and execution of specific operations. In the military it is primarily used by combatant and subordinate joint force commanders and their component commanders. It keeps them abreast of events within their areas of responsibility and ascertains when, where, and in what strength an opponent will stage and conduct campaigns and major operations.[4] Operational intelligence therefore has to be predictive also.

Operational intelligence in diplomatic efforts could support, for example, planning the negotiation of an arms reduction treaty. In law enforcement, it might support planning the takedown of an organized crime syndicate. In business intelligence, it might support a campaign to gain market share in a specific product line.

Tactical Intelligence

Tactical intelligence operates at the front line of any conflict. In the military it is used by field commanders for planning and conducting battles and engagements. Tactical intelligence locates and identifies the opponent's forces and weaponry, enhancing a tactical commander's ability to gain a combat advantage with maneuver, weaponry on target, and obstacles. It allows tactical units to achieve positional advantage over their adversaries.[5]

Tactical intelligence to support military operations became much more important during the 1990s because of weapons technology trends. The trend to employing highly precise weaponry and operations placed a premium on highly accurate data. Intelligence systems that can establish the location of enemy units to within a few meters became more important than before. The rapidly expanding field of geospatial analysis supports such surgical operations with mapping, charting, and geodesy data, which can be used for the guidance of "smart" weapons.[6]

Much of law enforcement intelligence also tends to be tactical in orientation. Both the Colombian police lieutenant and the Predator operator in chapter 1 were using tactical intelligence while engaged against individual opponents. But tactical intelligence is used every day in situations well removed from military actions and law enforcement, as the following example illustrates.

A satellite photo of the Earth spins slowly on a large plasma screen, with markers indicating the sources of online threats. At rows of computer workstations, analysts monitor firewalls and other online defenses. The displays, the layout, and the security guards all evoke the image of a war room—which it is, but for a new type of war.

This is Symantec's war room. Here, a different type of intelligence analyst deals with junk e-mailers who are trying to stay one step ahead of filters and blacklists that block spam; of the hackers that constantly work to bypass bank firewalls; and of the viruses that can flow into thousands of computers worldwide in a few seconds.

Symantec maintains the war room to defend banks and Fortune 500 firms against cyber threats. This room was the front line of the battle against SQL Slammer as it surged through the Internet, knocking out police and fire dispatch centers and halting freight trains; against MSBlaster, as it clogged corporate networks and forced web sites offline; and against the graffiti viruses with such innocuous names as Melissa and ILoveYou.[7]

The analysts in Symantec's war room succeed in their tactical combat because they have *shared models* of viruses, worms, and Trojans instantly available. They model the operational patterns of East European organized crime groups that use viruses such as SoBig to track a user's keystrokes and lift passwords and credit card numbers. They have models of the computers that are used to spread viruses. The great plasma screen itself displays a massive model of the Internet battlefront, where the beginning of new threats can be seen. Using these models and creating new ones on the fly, these tactical intelligence analysts can analyze and defeat a new virus in minutes.

The Temporal Analysis Spectrum

Figure 4-2 shows how intelligence analysis proceeds on a particular problem or issue over time. As the customer focuses on strategic issues and planning, intelligence concentrates on creating the target model via in-depth research, and the focus is on an opponent's capabilities and plans or intentions. The intelligence customer's focus is strategic, and so is the intelligence effort. Alternative target scenarios are created. Referring again to the illustration

Figure 4-2   Temporal Synthesis/Analysis Spectrum

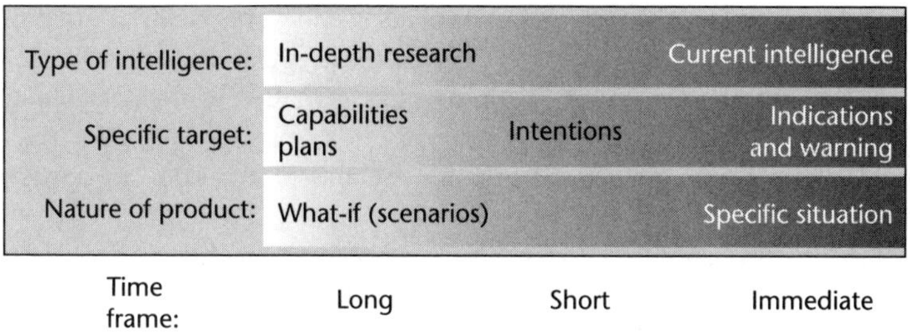

Type of intelligence:	In-depth research		Current intelligence
Specific target:	Capabilities plans	Intentions	Indications and warning
Nature of product:	What-if (scenarios)		Specific situation

Time frame:	Long	Short	Immediate

in Figure 4-2, on the right side the problem is tactical. The scenario or situation is known. The intelligence focus is not on building target models but on updating and exploiting them to determine current intentions and to provide indications and warning. In such a situation, intelligence is about current developments, and it reacts quickly to new information. The intelligence customers must make and execute decisions, and intelligence must help them.

As an example, consider operations in a diplomatic or a business negotiation context. In either type of negotiation, one plans strategy first, then develops tactics, and then modifies the tactics in response to the opponent's moves. On the left side of Figure 4-2, the process illustrated is one of data gathering and evaluation, followed by cool, reasoned, analytical research. On the right side it is a fast-paced, frenetic, news-gathering atmosphere, in which all of the carefully laid plans tend to go out the window if the process is poorly managed. The tempo of intelligence varies accordingly, from the normal maintenance of the target model and assembling of information as it comes in, to the surge of activity in the late operational phase. This increased tempo is well suited to support "swarm" operations against a target network, as discussed in the netwar strategy developed by John Arquilla and David Ronfeldt of RAND Corporation (see chapter 1).[8]

Long-Term Research versus Current Intelligence

Much of this book describes how to handle long-term research, often comprising major analytic efforts that take anywhere from days to weeks. Current intelligence goes through a similar process, but uses existing models, takes little time, and is cut to the essential message.

Current intelligence deals with matters that require immediate action. Supporting trade negotiations, providing relief to flood or famine victims, enforcing laws, and stopping narcotics or clandestine arms shipments are examples. At the tactical level the intelligence process is very fast. The model must already exist; ideally, it was created in the research phase in the normal course of things. Incoming intelligence is simply added to refine the model, and an analysis of changes is extracted and reported quickly.

On the right side of Figure 4-2, the customer wants details. Intelligence has to be fast and highly reactive. A military commander doesn't care, for example, what the tank can do; he already knows that. What he needs to know is where it is and where it is going. At the tactical level in diplomacy, the diplomat worries less about negotiating strategy and more about an opponent's likely reaction to the diplomat's initiatives.

One can also contrast current intelligence with intelligence research, or in-depth analysis. Current intelligence covers fast-breaking events and looks much like newspaper or television news reporting. Intelligence research much more resembles the world of a university or a research laboratory. It looks to the long term, or it looks at a specific issue in depth.

Both types of intelligence have their proponents in intelligence organizations and among policymakers. It is not useful to think of them in either-or terms when allocating time and resources because both are needed. Current intelligence allows analysts to be in close touch with policymakers and facilitates better understanding between the two. Intelligence research provides the background that allows an analyst to make credible judgments in current reporting.

Which area in Figure 4-2 to stress depends on the customers and where they are in operations. Almost all national leaders want current intelligence that is specific.[9] But as former CIA deputy director for intelligence Bruce Clarke once observed, "Intelligence research is putting money in the bank; current intelligence is making a withdrawal." The problem with abandoning in-depth research is that without it the intelligence models eventually become irrelevant to the problem. Without a clear picture of long-term trends, analysts cannot make short-term predictions. The intelligence outfit becomes bankrupt. It not only cannot provide strategic intelligence; it cannot even produce decent tactical intelligence.

Fusion Centers

A special category of current intelligence is the "fast synthesis" of data to support ongoing tactical operations and to allow additional collection to be done intelligently in a short period of time. This short-fuse synthesis—often called *fusion*—differs from normal synthesis and analysis only in the emphasis: Time is of the essence. Fusion is aimed at using all available data sources to develop a more complete picture of a complex event, usually with a short deadline. The target model exists, and the analyst's job is to fit in any new data. Analysts work only with the incoming data plus anything that is immediately accessible to them in a database or in memory. Fusion is commonly used by intelligence analysts when time is the critical element—such as in support of military operations, crisis management, law enforcement, and similar direct operations.

The need for this type of information domestically has led to the creation of *fusion centers* to support homeland security in the United States. These fusion centers integrate incoming streams of information from the private sector and from federal, state, local, and tribal governments. The original objective of the centers was to assess the risks to people, economic infrastructure, and communities from both natural disasters and terrorist attacks and to enable actions by first responders. Over time, the focus of many centers has evolved to support state and local law enforcement by providing criminal intelligence and even to address all types of hazards.

There is no one model for how a fusion center should be constructed. Ideally, it might function like the Symantec war room. In contrast to the Symantec model, though, state fusion centers must deal with more diverse sources and types of data and with a wider breadth of threats. State fusion centers have been criticized for doing very little true fusion—defined as analysis of disparate data sources, identification of intelligence gaps, and proactive collection of intelligence against those gaps which could contribute to prevention. They have also raised concern because of their potential for violations of privacy and civil liberties.[10]

Capabilities, Plans, and Intentions

The strategic intelligence target tends to divide into two major areas: capabilities and plans. This view of strategic intelligence is closely tied to the strategic planning process as it is done in government and industry. Such strategic planning proceeds from analysis of what is known as the *SWOT:* strengths, weaknesses, opportunities, and threats.

Strengths and weaknesses define *capabilities* and are determined by looking internally, inside the opposing organization. Opportunities and threats shape *plans* and are determined by looking externally—that is, perceiving the situation as the opponent perceives it. The job of strategic intelligence, in this view, is to assess the opposing organization's capabilities (strengths and weaknesses) and its consequent plans (shaped by the opportunities and threats it perceives).

The "specific targets" of intelligence depicted in Figure 4-2 can be tactical, strategic, or both. *Indications and warning* tend to be more tactical; *capabilities, plans,* and *intentions* tend to be more strategic. The division is based on the timeliness and quality of intelligence required.

In operational intelligence, an opponent's use of his capabilities to execute plans—specifically, his intentions—becomes important. Intent to launch a military attack, intent to impose an embargo, and intent to break off negotiations are all operational or even tactical. In Figure 4-2, intelligence about "intentions" is depicted as being somewhere between in-depth research and current intelligence. Plans and intentions tend to be lumped together in traditional intelligence definitions, but they are in fact two different targets, distinguished by their time scale: Plans are longer term, intentions are more immediate.

Indications and Warning

The category *indications and warning* (commonly referred to as I&W) for governments comprises detecting and reporting time-sensitive information on foreign developments that threaten the country's military, political, or economic interests. Providing indications and warning on threats to national security is traditionally an intelligence organization's highest priority. The failure of U.S. intelligence to provide indications and warning of the Japanese attack on Pearl Harbor was the primary reason that a U.S. intelligence community was formed in 1947. The failure of that community to provide I&W of the 9/11 terrorist attacks directly led to the most significant reorganization of U.S. intelligence since 1947.

The purpose of indications and warning is to avoid surprise that would damage the organization's or country's interests. Tactical indications and warning can include warning of enemy actions or intentions, imminent hostilities, insurgency, or terrorist attacks. Indirect and direct threats are the targets of indications and warning, including warnings of coups or civil disorder, third-party wars, and refugee surges, even if the events may not immediately and directly affect the country making the assessment.

Although I&W is shown on the right side of Figure 4-2, as if it were tactical or current intelligence, it can also be strategic. Strategic indications and warning involve identifying and forecasting emerging threats. Warnings about instability, new defense technologies, or breakthroughs that could significantly alter the relative advantages of opposing military forces are examples.

For forty years, from 1950 to 1990, U.S. national indications and warning was dominated by concern about a Soviet strategic attack. A secondary focus was persistent world hot spots: the likelihood of Arab-Israeli, India-Pakistan, or Korean conflict. National I&W for many Middle Eastern countries was dominated by the Arab-Israeli situation. Since 2001, indications and warning has become much more complex—many countries are focusing on the threat of terrorist attack, particularly an attack using weapons of mass destruction. Finally, since the fall of 2008, many governments have focused their indications and warning intelligence efforts on a worldwide economic crisis. The category of indications and warning also is closely related to (and overlaps with) two other categories of intelligence: (1) capabilities, plans, and intentions; and (2) crisis management and operations support.

The traditional approach to indications and warning has been to develop indicators, or norms, for military force deployments and activity. If a U.S. indications and warning organization had existed in December 1941, it would have had the following indicators, among others, about Japanese plans and intentions that year:[11]

- In January a HUMINT report from Peru's minister in Tokyo stated that in the event of trouble between the United States and Japan, the Japanese intended to begin with a surprise attack on Pearl Harbor.
- Intercepts of Japanese Foreign Ministry traffic on November 19 contained the message, "East wind rain," which some U.S. intelligence officers interpreted as indicating a decision for war in the near future.

- On November 22 Foreign Minister Togo Shigenori notified Ambassador Nomura Kichisaburo in Washington, D.C., that negotiations had to be settled by November 29, stating "after that things are going automatically to happen."

- In late November the Japanese began padding their radio traffic with garbled or redundant messages—a classic tactic to defeat COMINT operations.

- At the beginning of December the Japanese navy changed its ship call signs, deviating from its normal pattern of changing call signs every six months.

- On December 2 the Japanese Foreign Ministry ordered its embassies and consulates in London, Manila, Batavia, Singapore, Hong Kong, and Washington, D.C., to destroy most codes, ciphers, and classified documents.

- In early December the locations of Japan's aircraft carriers and submarines were "lost" by U.S. naval intelligence.

- Scattered reports came in of recent Japanese naval air practice torpedo runs against ships anchored in a southern Japanese harbor.

In hindsight, these bits of intelligence together clearly indicate an impending Japanese attack on Pearl Harbor. In practice, these bits would have formed a partial picture within a mass of conflicting and contradictory evidence, as Roberta Wohlstetter pointed out so well in her book *Pearl Harbor: Warning and Decision*.[12] At best, a cautiously worded warning could have been issued as to the likelihood and nature of an attack within days. In 1941, however, no national indications and warning organization existed.

Since World War II most countries of any size have created organizations to warn of impending military action and against other types of surprises. Despite some missteps based on poor analysis (e.g., the Yom Kippur and Falkland Islands surprises discussed in the introduction), I&W has done reasonably well in warning against conventional military attacks. Charlie Allen, CIA national intelligence officer for warning, issued a warning estimating a 60 percent chance of an Iraqi attack against Kuwait on July 25, 1990, more than a week before the Gulf War began.[13]

I&W successes, however, have tended to be in predicting the breakout of conventional armed conflict. The indicators of an impending Iraqi attack on Kuwait in 1990 were well established and were sufficient to allow a warning to be given. Warning norms for terrorism, instability, low-intensity conflict, and technological breakthroughs are much more difficult to deal with, and the indicators are more easily concealed.

Furthermore, the problem of pulling a coherent picture out of the mass of available information has not become easier since 1941. Lists of the evidence of an impending terrorist attack on the United States using airplanes have been compiled since the 9/11 attacks on the Pentagon and World Trade Center. Like the Pearl Harbor evidence, they can be judged fairly only when placed with all of the conflicting, contradictory, and often false raw intelligence that the U.S. intelligence community received before the attacks.

For commercial organizations, the highest indications and warning priority is on significant threats to the organization's survival—impending alliances among competitors or a competitor's impending product breakthrough, for example. But I&W has a broader role in business intelligence. Competitors often send out deliberate signals of their intentions. The business intelligence analyst must be attuned to those indicators and ensure that the customer is aware of the signals.[14] Analysis of the meaning of deliberate signals is a special skill that all analysts should possess, because governments send out deliberate signals, too.

Indications and warning intelligence always has had a trade-off problem: Analysts don't want to miss the indicators and fail to give a warning. That problem is complicated by the opponent's increasing use of denial and deception. On the other hand, if the analyst sets the warning threshold too low, false alarms result, and the analyst becomes vulnerable to the "cry wolf" problem—customers become desensitized, and in a genuine crisis the alarm is ignored.[15] The opposite desensitization problem happens to the analyst when a situation gradually worsens over time, or when warning indications persist for some time without the event happening. This desensitization pattern occurs frequently enough that British author Michael Herman has given it a name—"alert fatigue."[16] The trick is to have a set of indicators that are both necessary and sufficient, so that one can successfully navigate between the unfortunate outcomes of false alarms and missed events. Such sets of indicators are assembled through experience and accumulated knowledge of common indicators. Some standard indicators of impending military attack, for example, are a stockpiling of whole blood, recall of diplomatic personnel, recall of military personnel on leave and cancellations of leave, threats made in the press, and movement of warheads out of storage.

The point is that the indicators must exist for warning to be effective. And they must support alternative outcome models, as we will discuss in the following chapters.

Summary

Intelligence analysis must support operations and policy across the spectrum of conflict. The type of analysis and the speed with which it must be prepared and delivered to the customer vary accordingly. Analysis to support strategic intelligence tends to be long-term research focused on capabilities and plans and tends to consider many scenarios. Operational intelligence is more near term, involving support for the planning of specific operations. Tactical intelligence support tends to be rapid-response, or current intelligence, to support crisis management and plan execution; it is focused on the current situation and on indications and warning.

The number of potential model types is large; the next chapter discusses the major types that are used in intelligence analysis.

Notes

1. JCS Joint Publication 2-0, "Doctrine for Intelligence Support to Joint Operations" (Washington, D.C.: Department of Defense, Joint Chiefs of Staff, March 9, 2000), chap. 3.
2. Ibid.
3. Bill Fiora, "Moving from Tactical to Strategic Intelligence," *Competitive Intelligence Magazine* 4 (November–December 2001): 44.
4. JCS Joint Publication 2-0, chap. 3.
5. Ibid.
6. Geodesy is concerned with the size, shape, and gravitational field of the earth, its coordinate systems, and reference frames.
7. Andy Sullivan, "Attack of the Killer Bugs: Your Computer Could Be Hijacked by Scam Artists to Send Out Spam and Steal Your Bank Account," *Reuters Magazine,* January–February 2004.
8. John Arquilla and David Ronfeldt, "Looking Ahead: Preparing for Information-Age Conflict," in *In Athena's Camp: Preparing for Conflict in the Information Age,* ed. John Arquilla and David Ronfeldt (Santa Monica: RAND Corporation, 1997), 468. "Swarm" operations are a modern extension of the blitzkrieg concept—the application of coordinated and overwhelming force against an opponent using all available instruments of power: political, economic, military, and psychosocial, as appropriate.
9. Competent national leaders do think about long-term strategy, but they seldom want the help of strategic intelligence. In contrast, they are usually avid consumers of tactical intelligence.
10. John Rollins, "Fusion Centers: Issues and Options for Congress," CRS Report, January 18, 2008, www.fas.org/sgp/crs/intel/RL34070.pdf.
11. Harold P. Ford, *Estimative Intelligence* (Lanham, Md.: University Press of America, 1993), 3–5.
12. Roberta Wohlstetter, *Pearl Harbor: Warning and Decision* (Stanford: Stanford University Press, 1962). The difference between conflicting and contradictory evidence is discussed in chap. 7.
13. Michael R. Gordon and Bernard E. Trainor, *The General's War: The Inside Story of the Conflict in the Gulf* (London: Little, Brown, 1996).
14. Liam Fahey, *Competitors* (New York: John Wiley and Sons, 1999), 78.
15. Mark M. Lowenthal, *Intelligence: From Secrets to Policy,* 2nd ed. (Washington, D.C.: CQ Press, 2002), 87.
16. Michael Herman, *Intelligence Power in Peace and War* (Cambridge: Cambridge University Press, 1996), 233.

5

Overview of Models in Intelligence

One picture is worth more than ten thousand words.
Chinese proverb

The preceding chapters introduced the concept of models and provided some examples of how analysts use them. The process of creating the appropriate model is known as synthesis, a term borrowed from the engineering disciplines. *Synthesis* is defined as putting together parts or elements to form a whole—in this case, a model of the target. It is what intelligence analysts do, and their skill at it is a primary measure of their professional competence. In this chapter we review the types of models that are commonly used to describe intelligence targets, how they are created and used, and some strengths and weaknesses of each type.

Creating a Conceptual Model

The first step in creating a model is to define the *system* that encompasses the intelligence issues of interest so that the resulting model can answer the problem that has been defined (using the process described in chapter 2). The system could be something as simple as a new fighter aircraft, a data processing center, an opium poppy field, or a new oil pipeline. Many questions in the current or tactical intelligence area can be that narrowly focused. The example problem given earlier of the BMP in Afghanistan was narrowly focused on the BMP and its occupants. Problems coming into the Symantec war room are usually focused narrowly on the virus, hacker, or Trojan horse of immediate concern. However, few questions in strategic intelligence or intelligence research can be answered by using a narrowly defined system. For the complex targets that are typical of intelligence research, an analyst typically must deal with a complete system, such as the air defense system that will use the new fighter aircraft; a narcotics growing, harvesting, processing, and distribution network, of which the opium poppy field is but a part; or an energy production system that goes from oil exploration through drilling, pumping, transportation (including the oil pipeline), refining, distribution, and retailing. In law enforcement, an organized crime syndicate involves consideration of people, funds, communications, operational practices, movement of goods, political relationships, and victims. Many intelligence problems require consideration of related systems as well. The energy production system, for example, will give rise to intelligence questions about related companies, governments, suppliers and customers, and nongovernmental organizations such as environmental advocacy groups. The questions that customers pose should be answerable by reference to the target system only, without any need to reach beyond it.

A major challenge in defining the relevant system is exercising restraint: The definition must include *essential* subsystems or collateral systems but nothing more. Part of an analyst's skill lies in being able to include in a definition the relevant components, and only the relevant components, that will address the problem.

A system, as noted in chapter 1, can be examined structurally, functionally, or as a process. The systems model can therefore be structural, functional, process oriented, or any combination thereof. A structural model includes actors and objects and the organization of their relationships to each other. Process models focus on interactions and their dynamics. Functional models concentrate on the results achieved; models that simulate the combat effectiveness of a naval task force are one example.

Generic Models

After an analyst has defined the relevant system, the next step is to select the generic models, or model templates, to be used. These model templates then will be made specific, or "populated," using evidence. The generic biological weapons development model shown in Figure 3-3 is an example of a model template. Several types of generic models are commonly used in intelligence.

Lists

Lists and outlines are the simplest examples of a model. Benjamin Franklin favored a "parallel list" as a model for problem solving. He would list the arguments pro and con on a topic side by side, crossing off arguments on each side that held equal weight, to reach a decision. Lists continue to be used by analysts today for much the same purpose—to come up with a yes or no decision. The parallel list works well on a wide range of topics and remains very effective for conveying information to the customer. It also is often used in intelligence for comparative analysis, for example, comparing the performance of a Russian fighter aircraft with its U.S. counterpart or contrasting two cultures.

Curves

Curves are another simple model that can be synthesized both for analysis and for presenting the results of analysis. There will be more about curves in later chapters, but here I will discuss one of the most common, a curve that projects changes over time. When experts extrapolate future developments, they often concentrate on one or a few forces that affect an entity, such as the

Figure 5-1   Exponential (or Disaster) Curve

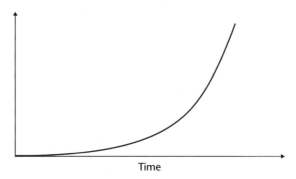

Population, pollution, child abuse, number of prisoners, or whatever phenomenon about which one wants to predict a disaster

Time

economy or the environment. They then usually posit some kind of disaster, based on models that use those variables, leading to the *exponential curve,* or *disaster curve,* shown in Figure 5-1. The creators of the disaster curve tend to ignore or discount the ability of other variables—especially such responsive or limiting factors as human adaptivity and technology—to change at the same rate or faster. A classic example is the extrapolation of exponential growth in telephones, made about 1900, which predicted that by 1920 the entire U.S. population would be working as telephone operators.[1]

Of course, the disaster curve never actually happens. An opposing reaction, feedback, contamination, or some other countervailing force steps in and retards the exponential growth curve so that an S curve results (see Figure 5-2). The occurrence of S curves is so frequent in synthesis that they are revisited in chapter 14.

Many phenomena can be modeled by the *Gaussian curve,* or *normal curve,* shown in Figure 5-3. The intelligence of a population, variation in imagery quality, atmospheric dispersion of a chemical release, variation in securities pricing—all these and more can be represented by the normal curve. To illustrate, take

Figure 5-2   S Curve

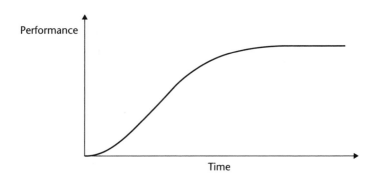

Performance

Time

Figure 5-3 Normal Curve

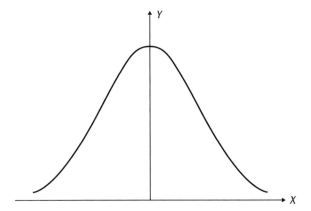

the quality of a photograph. The quality of a photograph has an average value, indicated by the zero axis where the curve in Figure 5-3 peaks. But if many (say, two hundred) photographs of a scene are taken with the same camera, and their quality is plotted, a curve like the one in Figure 5-3 results; a few photographs will be exceptional (falling on the far right side of the curve), and a few will be poor (falling on the far left side of the curve).

Comparative Modeling (Benchmarking)

Comparative techniques, like lists and curves, represent another simple but useful form of modeling that typically does not require a computer simulation. Comparative techniques are used in government mostly for weapons systems and technology analyses. Both governments and businesses use comparative techniques to evaluate a competitor's operational practices, products, and technologies. This is called *benchmarking.*

A powerful tool for analyzing a competitor's developments is to compare them with your own organization's developments. The analyst's own systems or technologies can provide a benchmark for comparison. One pitfall of comparative modeling is that analysts tend to rely on models that they are familiar with, such as their own country's organizational or industrial process models, instead of those of the target country. Such so-called mirror-imaging leads to many erroneous estimates. Other pitfalls of comparative techniques are discussed in chapter 7.

Comparative models have to be culture specific to avoid mirror-imaging. A classic example of a culture-specific organization model is the *keiretsu,* which is unique to Japan, although similar organization models exist elsewhere in Asia. A keiretsu is a network of businesses, usually in related industries, that own stakes in one another and have board members in common as a means of mutual security. A network of essentially captive (dependent on the keiretsu) suppliers provide the raw material for the keiretsu manufacturers, and the keiretsu trading companies and banks provide marketing services. Keiretsu have their roots in prewar Japan, which was dominated by four large conglomerates called *zaibatsu:* Mitsubishi, Mitsui, Sumitomo, and Yasuda. The zaibatsu were involved in areas such as steel, international trading, and banking and were controlled by a holding company.

Six keiretsu—Sumitomo, Mitsubishi, Mitsui, Dai Ichi Kangyo, Sanwa, and Fuyo—dominate Japan's economy. Most of the largest hundred Japanese corporations are members of one or another of these "big six" keiretsu.[2]

An intelligence analyst who mirror-images the keiretsu culture onto Western business practices would underestimate the close keiretsu cooperation between the supplier and manufacturer and the advantages it gives in continual product development, quality improvements, and reductions in costs. But the analyst also would miss the weaknesses inherent in a dependency relationship that shields the partners from competitive pressures, slows innovation, and eventually erodes the market position of all the keiretsu parties.

To avoid the problem of mirror-imaging, analysts sometimes create parallel models, side by side, for comparisons. This exercise helps to highlight the differences between one's own company or country model and that of the target and thus to catch potential areas of mirror-imaging.

Pattern Models

Many types of models fall under the broad category of *pattern models.* Pattern recognition is a critical element of all intelligence.[3] Most criminals and terrorists have a modus operandi, or standard operational pattern. Most governmental and industrial organizations (and intelligence services) also prefer to stick with techniques that have been successful in the past. An important aspect of intelligence synthesis, therefore, is recognizing patterns of activity and then determining in the analysis phase (a) whether the patterns represent a departure from what is known or expected and (b) whether the changes are significant enough to merit attention. The computer is a valuable ally here; it can display trends and allow the analyst to identify them. This capability is particularly useful in cases where trends would be difficult or impossible to find by sorting through and mentally processing a large volume of data. Pattern analysis is one way to effectively handle complex issues.

One danger in creating a pattern model is that the analyst may be tempted to find a pattern too quickly. Once a pattern has been settled on, it is easy to emphasize evidence that seems to support the pattern and to overlook, extenuate, or explain away evidence that might undermine it. (In the introduction we discussed how an intelligence analyst can avoid such missteps.)

Here are some of the main types of pattern models used by intelligence analysts:

Statistical. Much of pattern synthesis is statistical, and intelligence deals with a wide variety of statistical modeling techniques. Some of the most useful are easy to learn and require no previous statistical training.

Almost all statistical analysis now depends on the use of digital computers. The statistical software used should provide both a broad range of statistical routines and a flexible data definition and management capability. The statistical software should have basic graphics capabilities to display visually such data as trend lines.

Histograms, which are bar charts that show a frequency distribution, are one example of a simple statistical pattern. An example that might be used in intelligence analysis is shown in Figure 5-4; it permits an analyst to examine patterns of opium production over time in the major producing countries.[4]

Chronological. Patterns of activity over time are important for showing trends. Pattern changes are often used to compare how things are going now with how they went last year (or last decade). Predictive analysis often relies on chronological models.

Timing shapes the consequences of planned events. In sales campaigns, military campaigns, and political campaigns, among others, timing is critical to making an impact. An opponent's strategy often becomes apparent only when seemingly disparate events are placed on a timeline.[5] Consider, for example, the chronological model shown in Figure 5-5. The timeline shows the expected actions of a hypothetical European electronics manufacturer that is building a missile guidance system destined for shipment to a Middle Eastern country.

Figure 5-4   Histogram of Opium Production, 2000 to 2008

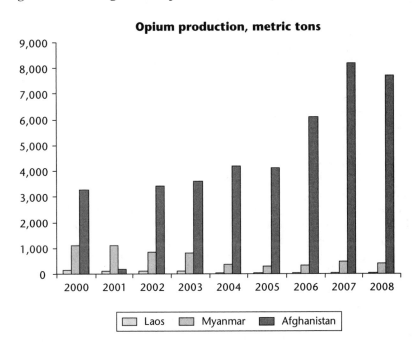

Figure 5-5   Chronological Model of Firm's Expected External Actions

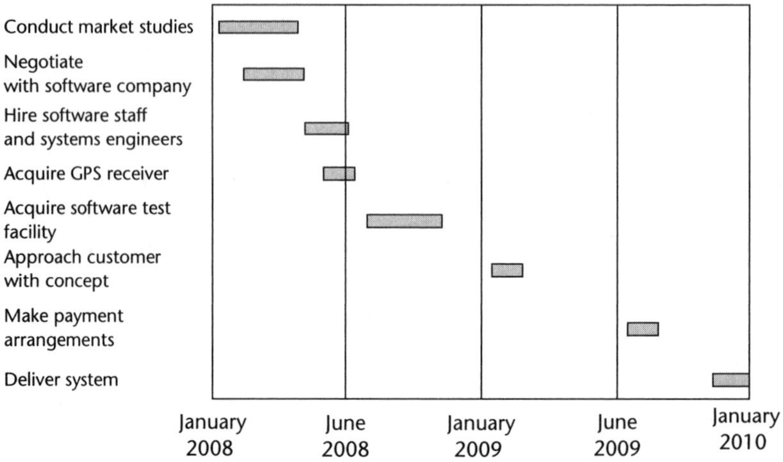

	January 2008	June 2008	January 2009	June 2009	January 2010
Conduct market studies	▨				
Negotiate with software company	▨				
Hire software staff and systems engineers		▨			
Acquire GPS receiver		▨			
Acquire software test facility			▨		
Approach customer with concept			▨		
Make payment arrangements				▨	
Deliver system					▨

Such a model can be used to predict an opponent's actions and to time future counteractions. In the example of Figure 5-5, the model could be used by the analyst's country's government to block shipment of the guidance system or to disrupt the payment arrangements.

Event-time patterns such as that depicted in Figure 5-5 tell analysts a great deal; they allow them to infer relationships among events and to examine trends. Activity patterns of a target network, for example, are useful in determining the best time to collect intelligence. An example is a plot of total telephone use over twenty-four hours—the plot peaks about 11 a.m., which is the most likely time for a person to be on the telephone.

Figure 5-6 shows an example of a type of time series data analysis that is useful in satellite-based SIGINT or imagery intelligence (IMINT) collection planning. The horizontal axis is calibrated in months over the period of one year; the vertical axis is calibrated in hours of the day over a twenty-four-hour period (Greenwich mean time). The dark areas show the visibility from a specific, low-orbiting satellite to Bermuda during the year, and the horizontal curved lines near 1100 and 2300 GMT show the points of sunrise and sunset in Bermuda during the year, establishing the limits of daylight. If the satellite was carrying a visible-imaging camera, the shaded areas during daylight would indicate opportunities for imagery collection (or conversely, the unshaded areas could indicate when operations in Bermuda could be carried out unobserved). Such time pattern correlations are best constructed with the help of computers. Several commercial software packages are well designed for computing and displaying time series data.

Spatial. Another way to examine data and search for patterns is to use spatial modeling—depicting the locations of objects in space. Spatial modeling can be used effectively on a small scale. Within a building, computer aided design/

Figure 5-6   Satellite Visibility and Set over Bermuda, Day versus Hour

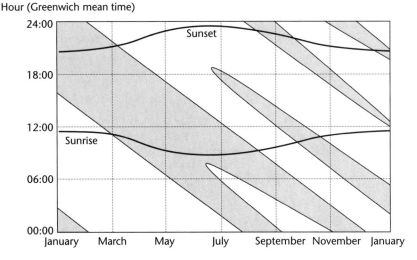

Note: Shaded areas mark days and times when activity over Bermuda is visible from a typical low-orbit satellite.

computer aided modeling, known as CAD/CAM, can be a powerful tool for intelligence synthesis. Layouts of buildings and floor plans are valuable both in physical security analysis and in assessing production capacity, for example. CAD/CAM models are useful both in collection and in counterintelligence analysis of a facility. CAD/CAM can be used to create a physical security profile of a facility, allowing an analyst to identify vulnerabilities by examining floor plans, construction details, and electronic and electrical connections.

Spatial models of local areas, such as city blocks, facilitate a number of analytic inferences. For example, two buildings located within a common security fence can be presumed to have related functions; whereas, if the two buildings were protected by separate security fences, no such presumption would follow. Spatial modeling on larger scales is usually called *geospatial modeling* and is discussed in more detail later in this chapter.

Relationship Models

Relationships among entities—organizations, people, places, things, and events—are perhaps the most common subject of intelligence modeling. There are four levels of such relationship models, each using increasingly sophisticated analytic approaches: hierarchy, link, matrix, and network models. The four are closely related, representing the same fundamental idea at increasing levels of complexity. The hierarchy model is a simple tree structure. A link model lets one view relationships in more complex tree structures. Matrix models show the interrelationship of two or more tree structures at a given level. A network model can be thought of as a flexible interrelationship of multiple tree structures at multiple levels.

Relationship models require a considerable amount of time to create, and maintaining the model (known to those who do it as "feeding the beast") demands much effort. But such models are highly effective for analyzing complex problems, and the associated graphical displays are very powerful in persuading customers to accept the results.

Hierarchy Models. Hierarchies are used extensively and almost intuitively in synthesis and analysis. Their primary application is to deconstruct a large or complex object—such as a project, an organization, or a weapons system—into its component parts. Figure 5-7 is an example of a hierarchy model of a project introduced earlier in this chapter—an electronics manufacturer developing a missile guidance system. The objective, to develop a missile guidance system, is indicated by the highest box. In the second tier are four major tasks that an intelligence analyst has identified as necessary for system development and its sale to the Middle Eastern country. Below that are a number of lower-level tasks that would be the subjects of intelligence collection and model synthesis.[6]

Organizational modeling naturally lends itself to the creation of a hierarchy, as anyone who ever drew an organizational chart is aware. A natural

Figure 5-7   Hierarchy Target Model of Missile Guidance System Development

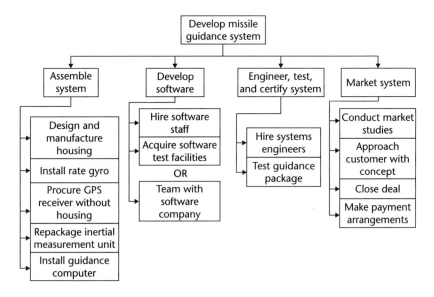

extension of such a hierarchy is to use a weighting scheme to indicate the importance of individuals or suborganizations in it.

A more sophisticated version of the hierarchy is the *relevance tree,* which is used in technology forecasting. Figure 5-8 shows an example of a relevance tree that subdivides chemical warfare agents according to their physiological effects. This particular type of relevance tree is referred to as *object oriented*—a term that is widely used in software programming and which has the same meaning in that discipline. *Object oriented* means that the tree is subdivided into distinct objects (in Figure 5-8, types of chemical warfare agents). Relevance trees have many varieties: objectives trees, decision trees, alternatives trees, and resource allocation trees.

Link and Social Network Models. One of the most powerful tools in the analyst's toolkit is link modeling and analysis, along with its more sophisticated cousin, network modeling and analysis. Link models have demonstrated their value for discerning the complex and typically circuitous ties between entities. Link models are closely related to hierarchy models; in fact, some types of link diagrams are referred to as *horizontal relevance trees.*[7] Their essence is the graphical representation of

- nodes and their connection patterns, or
- entities and relationships.

Link modeling has a long history; the Los Angeles police department reportedly used it first in the 1940s as a tool for assessing organized crime networks. Its primary purpose was to display relationships among people or between people and events. Today link modeling is routinely used in government intelligence and law enforcement to identify narcotics trafficking, terrorist, and espionage groups. It has been applied in sociology, anthropology, law enforcement, and the analysis of communications networks.

Figure 5-8   Chemical Warfare Agent Relevance Tree

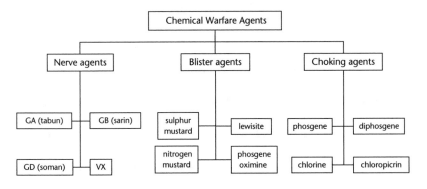

Most humans simply cannot assimilate all the information collected on a topic over the course of several years. Yet a typical goal of intelligence synthesis/ analysis is to develop precise, reliable, and valid inferences (hypotheses, estimations, and conclusions) from the available data for use in strategic decision making or operational planning. Link models directly support such inferences.

Before the 1970s, link modeling was an arduous and time-consuming endeavor because graphical trees had to be constructed on paper. Computer software has contributed to the recent expansion of link synthesis/analysis. Software tools simplify the process by allowing the relational storage of data as it comes in and by graphically displaying different types of relationships among the entities.

The primary purpose of link modeling is to facilitate the organization and presentation of data to assist the analytic process. A major part of many assessments is the analysis of relationships among people, organizations, locations, and things. Once the relationships have been created in a database system, they can be displayed and analyzed quickly in a link analysis program. Figure 5-9 illustrates part of a link display drawn from an actual case study of funds-laundering operations that involved Citibank private bank accounts belonging to Mohammed, Ibrahim, and Abba Sani Abacha. The three men are sons of General Sani Abacha, the dictator who controlled Nigeria from 1993 until his death in 1998. General Abacha is believed to have taken more than $3.5 billion from the Nigerian treasury during the five years that he was in power.[8] The figure illustrates some of the relationships involved in laundering the funds that were stolen. As with generalized network models, this is a generalized link model; it includes people, banks, companies, government organizations, and bank accounts.

Figure 5-9 shows the importance of being able to see second- and third-order links in pattern synthesis/analysis. Relationships that are not apparent when each piece of evidence is examined separately become obvious when link displays are used.

To be useful in intelligence analysis, the links should not only identify relationships among data items but also show the nature of the relationships. A subject-verb-object display has been used in the intelligence community for several years to show the nature of relationships, and it is sometimes used in link displays. A typical subject-verb-object relationship from Figure 5-9 would read, Mohammed Abacha (subject) owns (verb) Selcon Airlines (object). This is a positive relationship and needs to be distinguished from negative relationships, such as the one between Mohammed Abacha and Kudirat Abiola (Abacha was charged with Abiola's murder).

Quantitative relationships and time (date stamping) relationships are also used when the link software has a filtering capability. Filters allow the user to focus on relationships of interest and can simplify by several orders of magnitude the data that are shown in a link display. For example, the user could select "Morgan Procurement" in Figure 5-9 as the root (that is, the start, or left side, of the link diagram) and display a link chart of all the

Figure 5-9   Financial Relationships in a Link Model

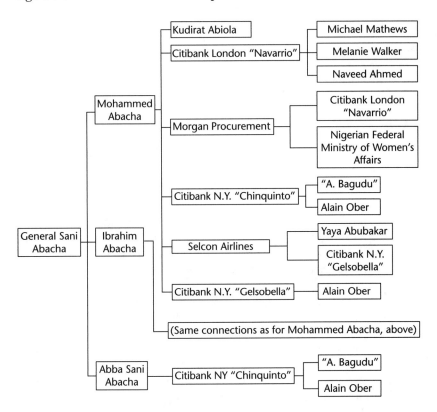

group and personal associations of Morgan Procurement. The user could then use the filters and display the Morgan Procurement network of associations for a specific time range (say, 1995–1998) and associations only with Swiss banks.

Matrix Models. When attempting to analyze the relationships between two hierarchies, one typically takes each hierarchy to the necessary level of detail and then arrays the two in a two-dimensional matrix. The result is the "interaction matrix," a valuable analytic tool for certain types of synthesis. It appears in various disciplines and under different names and is also called a *parametric matrix* or a *traceability matrix.*[9] An interaction matrix is shown in Table 5-1. In 2005 four proposed routes were under consideration for a South Asian gas pipeline project.[10] The interaction matrix summarizes in simple form the costs and risks of each proposal. The matrix is also a concise and effective way to present the results of analysis. Table 5-1 permits a view of the four proposals that could not easily or clearly be expressed by using plain text.

Table 5-1   Interaction Matrix, Gas Pipeline Proposals

Pipeline Proposals	Cost	Supporters	Risks
From South Pars field, Iran, to Karachi	$3 billion	Iran, Pakistan	Technical
From Iran to northern India	$4–5 billion	Iran, India	Political, security, cost
From Turkmenistan's Daulatabad field to Pakistan	$3.2 billion	Turkmenistan, Pakistan	Security
Underwater pipeline from Qatar to Pakistan	$3 billion	Qatar, Pakistan	Political, technical

An interaction matrix can be qualitative or quantitative, as Table 5-1 illustrates. A quantitative interaction matrix naturally fits into many of the commercially available decision-support software packages. It is typically used to ensure that all possible alternatives are considered in problem solving.

In economic intelligence and in scientific and technical intelligence, it is often important to assess the impact of an industrial firm's efforts to acquire other companies. One model for assessing the likely outcome of a merger or acquisition uses the five criteria that Cisco Systems uses to look at possible acquisitions. The criteria are listed in the first column of Figure 5-10.[11] In this interaction matrix model, the three candidates for acquisition are ranked on how well they meet each criterion; the darker the shading, the higher the ranking. This merger and acquisition model has potential applications outside the commercial world. In 1958 it would have been a useful tool to assess prospects for the success of the "merger" that year between Syria and Egypt that created the United Arab Republic. That proposal would not have fared well against any of the criteria in Figure 5-10, even the one on similar cultures, and in fact, the merger subsequently failed.

Network Models. The key limitation of the matrix model is that although it can deal with the interaction of two hierarchies at a given level, because it is a two-dimensional representation it cannot deal with interactions at multiple levels or with more than two hierarchies. Network synthesis is an extension of the link or matrix synthesis concept that can handle such complex problems. There are at least three types of network models:

- *Communications network models* are used by communications engineers to design and predict the performance of telecommunications networks. The nodes are communications terminals, and the links are channels through which data flow (for example, microwave point-to-point, fiber optic, or radio frequency cable lines).

Figure 5-10   **Matrix for Merger and Acquisition Analysis**

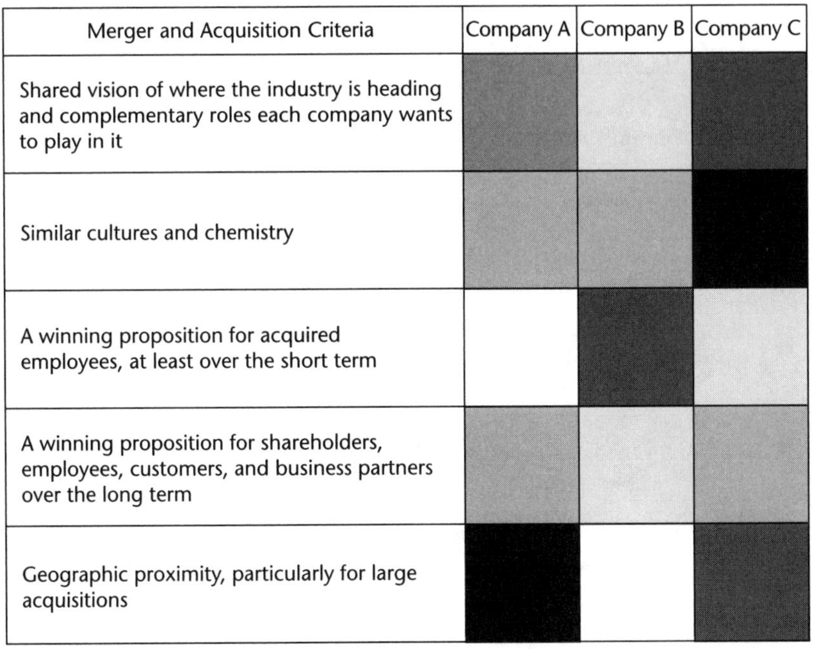

Merger and Acquisition Criteria	Company A	Company B	Company C
Shared vision of where the industry is heading and complementary roles each company wants to play in it			
Similar cultures and chemistry			
A winning proposition for acquired employees, at least over the short term			
A winning proposition for shareholders, employees, customers, and business partners over the long term			
Geographic proximity, particularly for large acquisitions			

Note: Three candidates for acquisition are ranked on how well they meet the criteria at left. The darker the shading, the higher the ranking.

- *Social network models* show patterns of human relationships. The nodes are people, and the links show that some type of relationship exists.

- *Generalized network models* are most useful in intelligence. Here the nodes can be any type of entity—people, places, things, concepts— and the links show that some type of relationship exists between entities.

Figure 5-11 is a modified version of the financial relationships model in Figure 5-9, redrawn as a network model with some additional information that has analytic value. Nodes are shaded to indicate type—bank accounts in dark gray, persons unshaded, and organizations in light gray. Relationships are shown as either positive (solid links) or negative (dashed links). Strength of relationship is shown by the thickness of the linkage line. Additional techniques can convey more information—making the links dotted to indicate a suspected relationship, for example, or making nodes larger or smaller to indicate relative importance. Of course, many of the same techniques can be used in link models, too.

Both link modeling and network modeling have been successfully applied in the U.S. intelligence community to assess problems of counterter- rorism, weapons of mass destruction, and counternarcotics, as well as to

Figure 5-11   Financial Relationships Network Model

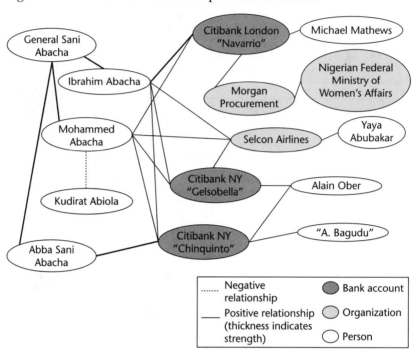

address clandestine arms traffic and weapons systems development. Link and network modeling is indispensable in military intelligence for targeting and for planning combat strategies and tactics. Simpler problems are appropriate for link modeling; complex problems usually demand network models.

Network models are used in law enforcement intelligence, especially in dealing with organized crime. Because most law enforcement concern is with persons and organizations, and their relationships, the law enforcement community uses an efficient method of drawing network diagrams to make relationships more apparent; it is illustrated in Figure 5-12.

Figure 5-12   Network Diagram Features Used in Law Enforcement Intelligence

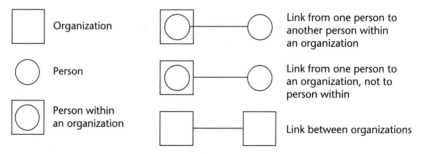

Profiles

Profiles are models of individuals—in national intelligence, the leaders of foreign governments; in business intelligence, the top executives in a competing organization; in law enforcement, mob leaders and serial criminals. The purpose of creating profiles usually is to help predict what the profiled person will do in a given set of circumstances.[12] Chapter 13 discusses the use of profiles for prediction.

The pattern of mental and behavioral traits that adult members of a society share is referred to as the society's *modal personality.* Several modal personality types may exist in a society, and their common elements are often referred to as *national character.* A recurring quip that reflects widely held—though tongue-in-cheek—views of national character goes:

Paradise is where the cooks are French, the mechanics are German, the police are British, the lovers are Italian, and it is all organized by the Swiss.

Hell is where the cooks are British, the mechanics are French, the police are German, the lovers are Swiss, and it is all organized by the Italians.

U.S. readers, after enjoying a laugh at this, might stop to reflect that in most countries, common stereotypes of U.S. national character include the quick-draw cowboy and the gangster—or in general, a macho figure carrying a gun.

Defining the modal personality type is beyond the capabilities of the journeyman intelligence analyst, and one must turn to experts. I offer here only a brief overview of the topic of behavioral profiles to indicate their importance in the overall decision-modeling problem, which is discussed in chapter 13. The modal personality model usually includes at least the following elements:

- Concept of self—the conscious ideas of what a person thinks he or she is, along with the frequently unconscious motives and defenses against ego-threatening experiences such as withdrawal of love, public shaming, guilt, or isolation
- Relation to authority—how an individual adapts to authority figures
- Modes of impulse control and of expressing emotion
- Processes of forming and manipulating ideas

Three model types are often used for studying modal personalities and creating behavioral profiles:

- *Cultural pattern models* are relatively straightforward to analyze (see chapter 13) and are useful in assessing group behavior. They have less value in the assessment of individuals. Cultural patterns are derived from political behavior, religious idea systems, art forms, mass media, folklore, and similar collective activities.
- *Child-rearing systems* can be studied to allow the projection of adult personality patterns and behavior. They may allow more accurate assessments of an individual than a simple study of cultural patterns,

but they cannot account for the wide range of possible pattern variations occurring after childhood.

- *Individual assessments* are probably the most accurate starting points for creating a behavioral model, but they depend on detailed data about the specific individual. Such data are usually gathered from testing, using techniques such as the Rorschach test, a projective personality assessment based on the subject's reactions to a series of ten inkblot pictures. However, test data are seldom available on individuals of interest to the intelligence business. Usually, fragmented data such as anecdotal evidence, handwriting analysis (graphology), or the writings and speeches of individuals (*Mein Kampf, The Thoughts of Chairman Mao*) must be used to construct a modal personality picture.

Another model template is the Myers-Briggs Type Indicator, which assesses individual personalities using sixteen categories or types. There are four different subscales of Myers-Briggs that purport to measure different personality tendencies. As with other test-based assessments, the trick is to get test results on the target individual.

Process Models

A process model is one that describes a sequence of events or activities that produce results. It can be an open or closed loop, with feedback being the difference, as Figure 5-13 illustrates. Most processes and most process models have feedback loops. Feedback allows the system to be adaptive, that is, to adjust its inputs based on the output. A simple system such as a home heating and air conditioning system provides feedback via a thermostat. For complex systems, feedback is essential to prevent the process from producing undesirable output. Feedback is such an important part of both synthesis and analysis that it receives detailed treatment in chapter 12.

Business process reengineering uses process models like the one shown in Figure 5-14. In this display, the process nodes are separated by

Figure 5-13   Simple Process Model

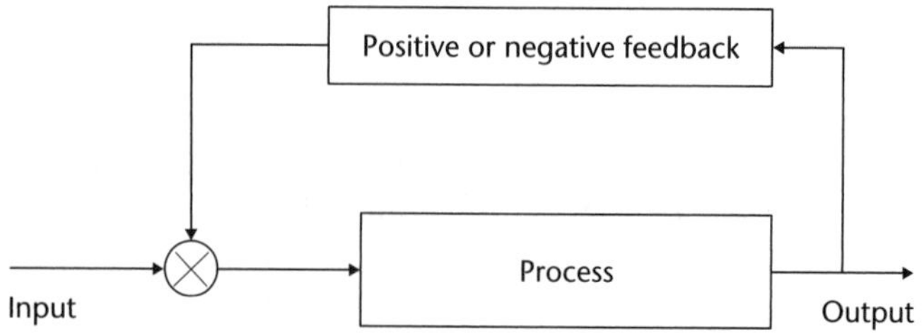

Note: The encircled *X* shows where the input and the feedback combine before they feed into the process.

Figure 5-14   **Business Process Model**

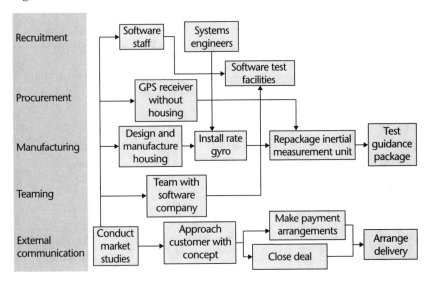

Note: GPS stands for global positioning system.

function into "swim lanes" to facilitate analysis. This model again is based on our example of an electronics manufacturer developing a missile guidance system.[13]

Chapter 2 introduced the iterative process of model improvement using new intelligence. Figure 5-15 shows a hypothetical example of this sort of iterative modeling using a business process. In this example, the model shown in Figure 5-14 envisions the electronics manufacturer hiring software staff to support software development and purchasing a global positioning system (GPS) receiver from an external source. Suppose that the analyst later receives evidence that the company is neither hiring software staff nor trying to acquire a GPS receiver. The analyst then revises the model, as shown in Figure 5-15, to delete those two blocks and adds a new one showing the analyst's estimate of internal manufacture of a GPS receiver. The analyst then must estimate whether software test facilities will be procured or whether the manufacturer will rely on those of its partner software company.

Simulation Models

Simulation models are mathematical descriptions of the interrelationships that are believed to determine a system's behavior. We have said that simulations differ from other types of models in that the equations they comprise cannot be solved simultaneously. One usually goes to simulation

Figure 5-15   Analysis Using the Business Process Model

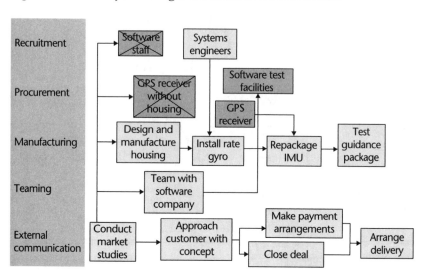

modeling when it is impossible or impractical to write or measure all of the variables necessary to solve the set of simultaneous equations that would fully describe a system.

In general, simulation models are most useful in making long-range forecasts where exact numerical estimates are not needed. Simulation models usually are most effective when used to compare the impact of alternative scenarios (of policy decisions or natural phenomena, for example).

Simulation may be used in either a stochastic or a deterministic situation. A simple spreadsheet is a deterministic model; the inputs are fixed by the numbers in the spreadsheet cells, only one solution appears, and the input numbers must be changed to get another answer. Where there is uncertainty about the proper input numbers, stochastic simulation is used. The computer rolls the dice to assign a value to each uncertain input and obtain an answer; then many repeated dice rolls are made to obtain a range of answers. The resulting simulation model has been named a *Monte Carlo model*, after the gambling capital of Monaco.

The challenge of the Monte Carlo simulation is to select the right type of uncertainty for the input variables. All uncertain variables have a probability distribution. A single roll of a six-sided die has what is called a *uniform distribution:* The chance of a 1 coming up is the same as the chance of a 2 or a 3. When two dice are rolled, the distribution is not uniform; 7 is much more likely to occur than 2 or 12. If the wrong probability distribution is chosen for the input, the stochastic simulation will produce the wrong answer.

Simulation models are typically classified as either a *continuous* or *discrete event,* or a hybrid of the two:

- In *continuous simulations* the system changes with time. An airplane in flight is an example of a continuous system; changes in the speed, altitude, and direction of the airplane occur continuously with time. This would also be a deterministic simulation, since the airplane's speed, altitude, and direction at any time can be predicted by inputs and standard equations.
- In *discrete event models,* the system changes state as events occur in the simulation. An airplane flight can be modeled as a series of discrete events. One discrete event would be at takeoff; another event occurs when the airplane reaches flight altitude, and another event occurs when it lands.
- *Hybrid models* are a combination of the two. A simple hybrid model of the airplane flight could have two discrete event simulations—the beginning and end of the flight—with a continuous event simulation of the travel in between.

Equations as Models. The most common modeling problem involves solving an equation. The equation is perhaps the simplest form of a simulation model. Most problems in engineering or technical intelligence are single equations of the form

$$f(x, y, z, t, \ldots, a, b, c, \ldots) = 0$$

or they are systems of equations of this form. Systems of equations are particularly prevalent in econometric synthesis/analysis; single equations are common in radar, communications, and electronic warfare performance analysis.

Most analysis involves fixing all of the variables and constants in such an equation or system of equations, except for two variables. The equation is then solved repetitively to obtain a graphic picture of one variable as a function of another. A number of software packages perform this type of solution very efficiently. For example, as a part of radar performance analysis, the radar range equation is solved for signal-to-noise ratio as a function of range, and a two-dimensional curve is plotted. Then, perhaps, signal-to-noise ratio is fixed, and a new curve plotted for radar cross-section as a function of range.

Often the requirement is to solve an equation, obtain a set of ordered pairs, and plug into another equation to obtain a graphic picture, rather than solving simultaneous equations.

The computer is a powerful tool for handling the equation-solution type of problem. Spreadsheet software has made it easy to create equation-based models. The rich set of mathematical functions that can be incorporated into a spreadsheet and the spreadsheet's flexibility make the spreadsheet a widely used model in intelligence.

Econometric Modeling. An econometric model is a quantitative description of an economic system. It incorporates a number of hypotheses on how economic systems function. Econometric models are sets of simultaneous linear equations used for macroeconomic analysis, and the number of equations can be very large. Such models are widely used in both the financial and intelligence communities. Intelligence applications include trade, balance of payments, and worldwide energy analysis models.

Economic modeling also makes use of input-output modeling, a procedure in which the output product of an industrial sector is set equal to the input consumption of that product by other industries and consumers. Input-output models are often disaggregated and can therefore show more cause-effect relationships than many other models. Input-output models can be interpreted in terms of block diagrams and matrix algebra techniques. Input-output modeling has been applied to a variety of economic policy analysis and forecasting problems.

Combination Models

Most of the models I have described can be merged into combination models, for example, a relationship-time display. This is a dynamic model in which link or network relationship lines become thicker (strengthen) or thinner (weaken) over time, and nodes change size or disappear. A commonly used combination model, and probably the most important for predictive intelligence purposes, is the scenario, a very sophisticated model, which is discussed in chapter 10. The following are some other examples of combination models that are frequently used in intelligence analysis.

Geospatial Models

The most widely used combination model in intelligence analysis undoubtedly is the geospatial model. Geospatial modeling combines imagery, geospatial information (e.g., maps and charts), and location information from multiple sources to describe, assess, and visually depict physical features and geographically referenced activities on Earth. But it is more than combining maps with imagery. It is sometimes considered a collection and processing discipline, but it really is an application of the target-centric approach to analysis.

Geospatial modeling typically uses electronically stored maps (of the world, of regions, of cities) to display geographically oriented data. The displays are valuable for visualizing complex spatial relationships. Networks often can be best understood by examining them in geospatial terms.

It is a very old analytic technique. Sun Tzu, in his *Art of War,* published about A.D. 500, advocated reliance on geospatial models in planning military movements. He observed, "We are not fit to lead an army on the march unless we are familiar with the face of the country—its mountains and forests, its pitfalls and precipices, its marshes and swamps."[14] Sherlock Holmes used geospatial modeling frequently in criminal investigations.

In practice, geospatial modeling is an all-source analysis method that often incorporates advanced technical collection methods, HUMINT, and COMINT. Every intelligence analysis group constructs geospatial models to solve analytical problems. The method is also increasingly used by tactical military and law enforcement units, and the processing part is automated; that is, it incorporates automated scene description and automated target recognition.

Geospatial models can be very complex and may have many associated submodels or collateral models. Figure 5-16 presents a geospatial model of a complex system—a South Asian gas pipeline that was proposed in 2005 to carry natural gas from fields in Iran and Turkmenistan to customers in Pakistan and India. The map in Figure 5-16 is a simple model showing one possible route. The pipeline itself is a complex system that includes a number of political issues (international agreements that have to be concluded; the requirement for an unprecedented level of cooperation among traditionally hostile powers in the region); technical issues (route selection; design and construction of the pipeline); security issues (the pipeline is an obvious target for terrorists); and economic and commercial issues (pricing terms for gas; agreements for which companies and middlemen get what benefits). Once in operation, the pipeline would significantly change the economies in the region.

The effects of such a pipeline would reach far beyond South Asia. European, Russian, and U.S. companies would compete to build it. When built, it would change the patterns of gas distribution worldwide—more gas would flow to customers in South Asia, and less to other regions. Many governmental intelligence services would have an interest in this very complex system, and each of them would have many customers in the political, economic, and military departments of their governments. Commercial firms that stand to gain or lose from the pipeline's construction would conduct their own intelligence efforts. A system for analysis of this example would be global and complex. Figure 5-16 shows a simple structural view of the system.[15] A functional view would deal with the economic changes that the pipeline would cause. A process view could show the patterns of gas extraction and delivery, the political processes to reach a pipeline agreement, or the security processes to protect it, among other things. As discussed in chapter 3, there would be many submodels or collateral models of the system.

Human Terrain Models

U.S. ground forces in Iraq and Afghanistan in the past few years have rediscovered and refined a type of geospatial model that was used in the Vietnam War. In combating an insurgency, military forces have to develop a detailed model of local situations that includes political, economic, and

Figure 5-16   Proposed South Asian Natural Gas Pipeline

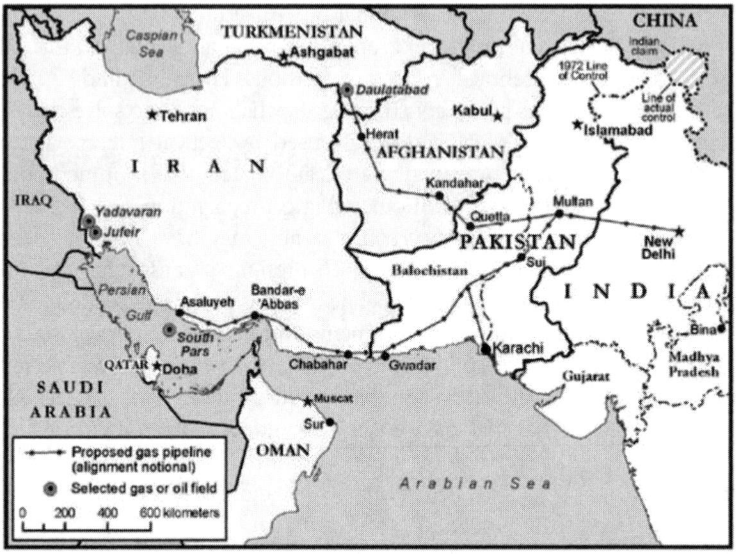

Source: Derived from "Iran Natural Gas," U.S. Department of Energy, Energy Information Administration, 2007. *www.eia.doe.gov/cabs/Iran/NaturalGas.html.*

sociological information as well as military force information. In Iraq and Afghanistan, this has been called "human terrain mapping." It involves acquiring the following information about each village and town:

- The boundaries of each tribal area (with specific attention to where they adjoin or overlap).
- Location and contact information for each sheik or village mukhtar and for government officials.
- Locations of mosques, schools, and markets.
- Patterns of activity such as movement into and out of the area; waking, sleeping, and shopping habits.
- Nearest locations and checkpoints of security forces.
- Economic driving forces, including occupations and livelihoods of inhabitants; employment and unemployment levels.
- Anticoalition presence and activities.
- Access to essential services such as fuel, water, emergency care, and fire response.
- Particular local population concerns and issues.[16]

Human terrain mapping, or more correctly human terrain modeling, is an old intelligence technique. Sun Tzu understood and advocated it. It was eloquently described by Rudyard Kipling in *Kim*, his novel about the "Great Game" in India in the nineteenth century. The Great Game involved competition for control of the balance of power and influence in the buffer states in central Asia between the British and Russian empires. In Kipling's book, the Ethnological Survey did the human terrain modeling. In actuality, beginning in 1878, the Intelligence Branch of the Quartermaster General's Department in India developed human terrain models from various sources, including gazetteers, route books, personality reports, political assessments, and intelligence reports submitted by political and military officials in the field, travelers, and locally engaged clandestine agents.[17]

The ability to do human terrain mapping and other types of geospatial modeling has been greatly expanded and popularized by Google Earth and Microsoft's Virtual Earth. These geospatial modeling tools provide multiple layers of information. The layers are in the form of collateral models (as discussed in chapter 3) that provide details about a location, such as building photographs, 3-D models of buildings, virtual tour videos that include interaction with locals, and textual material. It is an easy step to include detailed models of the building interiors including blueprints or CAD/CAM models. This unclassified online material has a number of intelligence applications. For intelligence analysts, it permits planning HUMINT and COMINT operations. For military forces, it supports precise targeting. For terrorists, it facilitates planning of attacks.

Space-Time Models

A dynamic variant of the geospatial model is the space-time model. Some intelligence practitioners describe it as *movement intelligence,* or MOVEINT, as if it were a collection INT instead of a target model. Many activities, such as the movement of a satellite, vehicle, ship, or aircraft, can best be shown spatially. A combination of geographic and time synthesis/analysis can show movement patterns, such as those of people or of ships at sea. For example, merchant ships radio their geographic positions at least daily. If a ship begins to transmit false position data, as revealed by independent means such as electronic intelligence (ELINT) or radar geolocation, it becomes a target of intelligence interest. If the ship's track does not fit a normal operating profile—for example, if it takes several days to move only a few miles—then alert analysts will begin to investigate whether the ship could have reached a nearby port for an unscheduled stop in that time.

Figure 5-17 shows an example of a ship-tracking display for the Russian ship *Akademik Tupolev* during part of a voyage in 1990. The *Tupolev* started its journey in the Dominican Republic and then moved north along the East Coast of the United States. Tracking was lost for about two days at the ship's northernmost point near Nova Scotia but resumed when the ship turned south toward

Figure 5-17   Ship Tracking: A Combination (Space-Time) Model

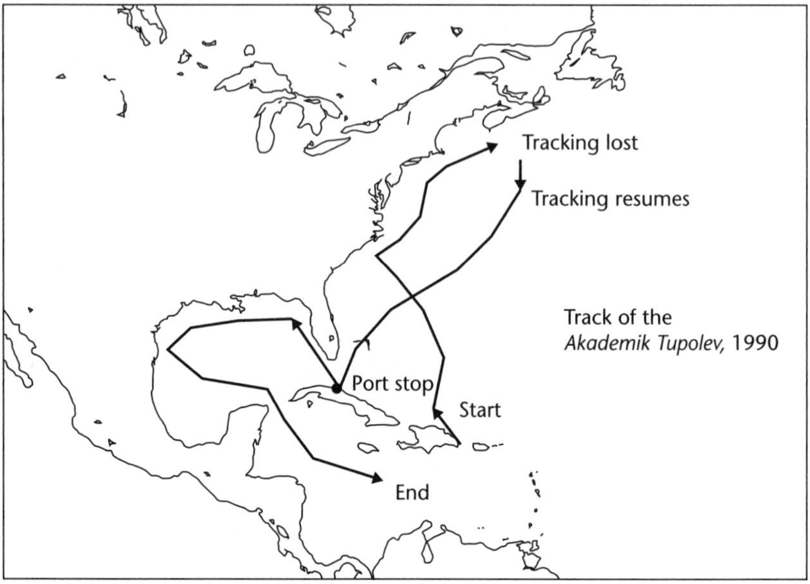

Havana for a port stop, then moved on to the Caribbean. The positions of the ship, taken alone, have no special significance; but the pattern of its movements close to the U.S. coastline, the delays in its progress, its disappearances, and a correlation of the ship's position with other intelligence reports might reveal much.

Geographic Profiling

Geographic profiling is a type of geospatial modeling, specifically, a space-time model for law enforcement that supports serial violent crime or sexual crime investigations. Such crimes, when committed against strangers, are difficult to solve. Investigating them can produce hundreds of tips and suspects, resulting in the problem of information overload. Geographic profiling gives police an effective method of managing and prioritizing the information they collect. The profiling process analyzes the locations connected to a series of crimes to determine the area where the offender probably lives. The result helps focus an investigation, prioritize tips and suspects, and suggest new strategies to complement traditional methods.

Summary

Creating a target model starts with defining the relevant system. The system model can be a structural, functional, or process model, or any combination. The next step is to select generic models or model templates.

Lists and curves are the simplest form of model. In intelligence, comparative models, or benchmarks, are often used; almost any type of model can be made comparative, typically by creating models of one's own system side by side with the target system model.

Pattern models are widely used in the intelligence business. Chronological models allow intelligence customers to examine the timing of related events and plan a way to change the course of those events. Geospatial models are popular in military intelligence for weapons targeting and to assess the location and movement of opposing forces.

Relationship models are used to analyze the relationships among elements of the target—organizations, people, places, and physical objects—over time. Four general types of relationship models are commonly used: hierarchy, link, matrix, and network models. The most powerful of these, network models, are increasingly used to describe complex intelligence targets.

Simulation models are also extensively used to describe complex targets. Simulation modeling can range in complexity from a simple equation to a sophisticated econometric model.

Profiles of leaders and key executives are used to predict decisions. Such profiles rely on the ability of the analyst to define the modal personality type. Process models, which describe a sequence of events or activities that produce results, are often used to assess the progress of a development project.

Many models are combinations of these generic model types. Predictive analysis, in particular, makes use of scenarios, and we will return to those. One of the most powerful combination models is the geospatial model, which combines all sources of intelligence into a visual picture (often on a map) of a situation. One of the oldest of analytical products, geospatial modeling has many names, such as human terrain mapping and geographic profiling. The space-time model is a dynamic variant of the geospatial model, used to observe how a situation develops over time and to extrapolate future developments.

The next two chapters discuss how to populate the model templates defined in this chapter.

Notes

1. In one sense this eventually turned out to be an accurate prediction. By the 1970s almost all telephones were either dial or pushbutton operated. As a result, almost all Americans over the age of ten are part-time telephone "operators" in the sense of the original extrapolation.
2. "Facts from the Corporate Planet: Ecology and Politics in the Age of Globalization," October 23, 2002, www.wired.com/news/business/0,1367,8918,00.html.
3. M. S. Loescher, C. Schroeder, and C. W. Thomas, *Proteus: Insights from 2020* (Utrecht, the Netherlands: Copernicus Institute Press, 2000), 25.
4. Statistics are taken from the United Nations Office on Drugs and Crime, http://www.unodc.org/unodc/en/crop-monitoring/index.html.
5. Loescher, Schroeder, and Thomas, *Proteus*, 24.
6. Michael C. O'Guin and Timothy Ogilvie, "The Science, Not Art, of Business Intelligence," *Competitive Intelligence Review* 12, no. 4 (2001): 15–24.

7. William L. Swager, "Perspective Trees: A Method of Creatively Using Forecasts," in *A Guide to Practical Technological Forecasting,* ed. James R. Bright and Milton E. F. Schoeman (Englewood Cliffs, N.J.: Prentice Hall, 1973), 165.

8. "Minority Staff Report for Permanent Subcommittee on Investigations—Hearing on Private Banking and Money Laundering: A Case Study of Opportunities and Vulnerabilities," November 9, 1999, www.senate.gov/~govt-aff/110999_report.htm.

9. Theodore J. Gordon and M. J. Raffensperger, "The Relevance Tree Method for Planning Basic Research," in *A Guide to Practical Technological Forecasting,* ed. James R. Bright and Milton E. F. Schoeman (Englewood Cliffs, N.J.: Prentice Hall, 1973), 134.

10. Ian Gill, "Gas Pipeline Race," *ADB Review,* October 2005, Asian Development Bank, Manila, www.adb.org/Documents/Periodicals/ADB_Review/2005/vol37-5/gas-pipeline.asp.

11. Michelle Cook and Curtis Cook, "Anticipating Unconventional M&As: The Case of DaimlerChrysler," *Competitive Intelligence Magazine,* January–February 2001.

12. Carolyn M. Vella and John J. McGonagle, "Profiling in Competitive Analysis," *Competitive Intelligence Review* 11, no. 2 (2000): 20.

13. O'Guin and Ogilvie, "The Science, Not Art, of Business Intelligence."

14. Sun Tzu, *The Art of War,* ed. James Clavell (New York: Dell, 1983), 9.

15. BBC News, "South Asia Gas Pipeline Talks End," July 13, 2005, http://news.bbc.co.uk/1/hi/world/south_asia/4674301.stm; Shamila N. Chaudhary, "Iran to India Natural Gas Pipeline," *TED Case Studies* (American University, Washington, D.C.) 11, no. 1 (January 2001).

16. Jack Marr, John Cushing, Brandon Garner, and Richard Thompson, "Human Terrain Mapping: A Critical First Step to Winning the COIN Fight," *Military Review* (March–April 2008): 18–24.

17. Penelope Tuson, "British Intelligence on Russia in Central Asia, c. 1865–1949," IDC Publishers, 2005, www.idc.nl/pdf/453_brochure.pdf.

6

Sources of Intelligence Information

Stand by your sources; they will repay you.
R. V. Jones, Assistant Director of Britain's Royal Air Force
Intelligence Section during World War II

Adding substance to the target models discussed in the previous chapter is a matter of information gathering and synthesis. This chapter focuses on the sources of data and how to use the information from those sources. It is included because, as the WMD Commission observed, "Analysts need to take full advantage of currently available and underutilized non-traditional technical intelligence capabilities."[1] Additionally, understanding of *all* collection assets is essential in planning collection strategies.

The automation of data handling has been a major boon to intelligence analysts. Information collected from around the globe arrives at the analyst's desk through the Internet or in electronic message form, ready for review and often presorted on the basis of keyword searches. A downside of the automation, however, is a tendency to treat all information in the same way. In some cases the analyst does not even know what collection source provided the information; after all, everything looks alike on the display screen. However, information must be treated differently depending on its source. Analytical success requires understanding where to acquire data and the limits and pitfalls of the information available from the sources discussed in this chapter.

A single data source seldom provides everything an analyst needs to synthesize a model of a complex target. Rather, a wide range of classified and unclassified sources must be called on, in part to reduce the chances of being misled by a single source.

Existing Reports

Information gathering begins with existing knowledge. Before starting an intelligence collection effort, analysts should ensure that they are aware of what has already been found on a subject. Finished studies or reports on file at an analyst's organization are the best place to start any research effort. There are few truly new issues. The databases of intelligence organizations include finished intelligence reports as well as many specialized data files on specific topics. Large commercial firms typically have comparable facilities in-house, or they depend on commercially available databases.

So a literature search should be the first step an analyst takes on a new project. The purpose is twofold: to define the current state of knowledge—that is, to understand the existing model of the intelligence target—and to identify the major controversies and disagreements surrounding the target model. This is an essential and yet a dangerous step. The existing intelligence should not be automatically accepted as fact. Few experienced analysts would blithely accept the results of earlier studies on a topic, though they would know exactly what the studies found. The danger is that in conducting the search, an analyst naturally tends to adopt a preexisting target model;[2] then premature closure, or a bias toward the status quo, leads the analyst to retain the existing model even when evidence indicates that a different model is more appropriate. In the business process model example in chapter 5, the analyst had to develop an alternate process model (Figure 5-15) when it became apparent that the existing model (Figure 5-14) would not work.

Once the finished reports are in hand, the analyst should review all of the relevant *raw* data that already exist. Few things can ruin an analyst's career faster than sending collectors after information that is already in the organization's files.

A Taxonomy of Intelligence Sources

For bureaucratic reasons or because of historical precedent, most texts organize their discussion of intelligence sources according to the current U.S. perspective on intelligence collection that is depicted in Figure 6-1. In this chapter I present an alternative view of the sources of intelligence, one that has more relevance for intelligence analysts.

Collection organizations in large intelligence communities (China, France, Russia, the United Kingdom, and United States) are of necessity specialized; that is, they are set up to collect information from one specific class of sources, such as imagery, radio signals, or human sources. Because of this specialization, collection organizations are often called *stovepipes,* invoking the metaphor of a tightly controlled channel that has only one function. The metaphor is best not followed too far because the only product that a stovepipe disgorges is smoke.

The U.S. intelligence community has divided the collection methods using the INT (short for *intelligence*) guilds to define the areas of collection responsibility of large collection organizations, such as the National Geospatial-Intelligence Agency (NGA) and the National Security Agency (NSA). As a result, INT names in the U.S. intelligence community are the result of bureaucratic initiatives, not proper INT descriptions. One current U.S. taxonomy is shown in Figure 6-1. The definitions of each INT are as follows:

Figure 6-1   U.S. Collection Taxonomy

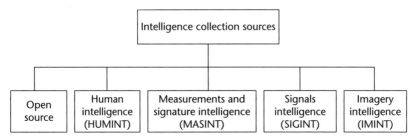

- *Open Source.* Information of potential intelligence value that is available to the general public.
- *Human Intelligence (HUMINT).* Intelligence derived from information collected and provided by human sources.
- *Measurements and Signatures Intelligence (MASINT).* Scientific and technical intelligence obtained by quantitative and qualitative analysis of data (metric, angle, spatial, wavelength, time dependence, modulation, plasma, and hydromagnetic) derived from specific technical sensors.
- *Signals Intelligence (SIGINT).* Intelligence comprising, either individually or in combination, all communications intelligence, electronics intelligence, and foreign instrumentation signals intelligence.
- *Imagery Intelligence (IMINT).* Intelligence derived from the exploitation of collection by visual photography, infrared sensors, lasers, electro-optics, and radar sensors, such as synthetic aperture radar, wherein images of objects are reproduced optically or electronically on film, electronic display devices, or other media.

Some taxonomies replace IMINT (in Figure 6-1) with geospatial intelligence, or GEOINT. The United States, in renaming the National Imagery and Mapping Agency the National Geospatial-Intelligence Agency, and a number of European nations that regularly conduct defence geospatial intelligence (DGI) conferences have given the term *GEOINT* some cachet. But as noted in the preceding chapter, geospatial intelligence is an all-source technique for synthesizing a target model, not a collection INT.

Although not shown in the taxonomy of Figure 6-1, signals intelligence (SIGINT) is divided into three distinct INTs: communications intelligence (COMINT), electronic intelligence (ELINT), and telemetry interception. The latter is typically called *foreign instrumentation signals intelligence,* or FISINT. The lumping of COMINT, ELINT, and FISINT together as SIGINT is usually defended as being logical because they have in common the interception of some kind of signal transmitted by the target. But some measurements and signatures intelligence (MASINT) and imagery intelligence (IMINT) sensors rely on a signal transmitted by the target, as well. *SIGINT* is in fact too general a term to use, when in most cases it means COMINT.

The taxonomy of Figure 6-1 is based on resource control ("turf") considerations and, from an analyst's standpoint, it is artificial. The taxonomy approach in this book is quite different. Instead of following the U.S. stovepipes, this book tries for a logical breakout that focuses on the nature of the material collected and processed, rather than on the collecti on means. Figure 6-2 illustrates this view of collection sources. It divides intelligence collection into two major source types and adds a new form of literal intelligence that has come into prominence: cyber collection.

Traditional COMINT, HUMINT, and open source collection are mainly concerned with *literal* information, that is, of information in a form that humans use for communication. The basic product and the general methods for collecting and analyzing literal information are usually well understood by intelligence analysts and the customers of intelligence. It requires no special exploitation after the processing step (which includes translation) to be understood. It literally speaks for itself.

Nonliteral information, in contrast, usually requires special processing and exploitation in order for analysts to make use of it. It is important to understand the nature and limitations of such processing and exploitation.

The rationale for this division is that analysts can challenge the interpretation of COMINT, HUMINT, cyber collection, or open source, if they are given access to the original material (and have language and cultural expertise). But if the processor/exploiter of nonliteral material makes a judgment, it is difficult for anyone else to contradict the judgment unless that person is also an expert in the field. Interpreting a hyperspectral image or an ELINT recording takes special expertise.

Figure 6-2   Analyst's View of the Collection Taxonomy

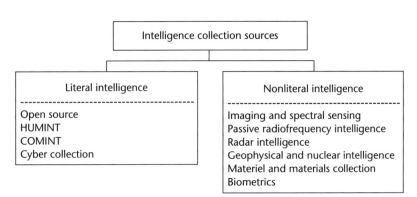

The logic of this division has been noted by other writers in the intelligence business. British author Michael Herman observed that there are two basic types of collection: one that produces evidence in the form of observations and measurements of things (nonliteral), and one that produces access to human thought processes (literal).[3]

This is not a completely satisfactory, or "clean," separation. An important part of COMINT—traffic analysis—is not literal information; it depends on processing and interpretation. HUMINT sources are used in materials and materiel collection, which provide nonliteral intelligence. But because of the way an analyst must treat the material, Figure 6-2 provides a more useful division than the one shown in Figure 6-1. Overlaps will occur no matter what taxonomy is selected. In the sections that follow, a number of these overlaps are identified.

Literal Intelligence Sources

The four literal intelligence sources dominate in volume and impact: open source, plus three classified sources—HUMINT, COMINT, and cyber collection. The first three of these have a history in intelligence that goes back hundreds of years. The use of open sources in intelligence probably dates back to the beginnings of written language. HUMINT efforts are described in the Old Testament ("Moses sent them to spy out the land of Canaan").[4] COMINT dates back at least to reading signal flags and smoke signals and deciphering written diplomatic communications. Cyber collection, which very much resembles COMINT, dates from the advent of computers.

Open Source

After exhausting the existing internal knowledge base, analysts can go to the easiest external sources (open literature, online databases). Open source information has traditionally meant published material that is publicly available—newspapers, books, and periodicals. As such it has been referred to as *literature intelligence* (LITINT) and more recently as *open source intelligence* (OSINT). Today OSINT includes much more than traditional published sources. Large volumes of imagery, for example, are becoming publicly available from commercial imaging satellites. Commercial databases hold vast quantities of economic data that are available for the price of a subscription. All fit the open source category, though they are not published in the traditional sense.

The largest single repository of open source material is that represented by the World Wide Web. Almost any subject of intelligence interest will have extensive coverage on the Web. The quality of material there, however, varies greatly. Much that is misleading or completely false resides on the Web, and the analyst must use Web sources with caution. But much valid material also resides on the Web, and commercial browsers and search engines make searching the material comparatively easy. Overall, the Web has become the most useful starting point for any intelligence analysis.

Open source material is perhaps the most valuable source of intelligence, and it is typically the most easily overlooked by government intelligence organizations in favor of classified information. Its chief value is that it is relatively easy to obtain. Analysts should not turn to more expensive collection resources until they have exhausted the potential of OSINT; and analysts should keep coming back to it as the expensive sources provide new leads.

Many analysts mistakenly consider "secret" data collected by covert means more meaningful or important than open or unclassified data and weigh it more heavily.[5] The WMD Commission observed that analysts "rely too much on secret information and use non-clandestine and public information too little. Non-clandestine sources of information are critical to understanding societal, cultural, and political trends, but they are underutilized."[6]

Political analysis draws heavily on open source intelligence. The statements of government leaders tell us much about their attitudes, their personalities (for personality profiling), the stresses that may exist within their government, and many other things. Their statements always have to be analyzed in context (whom they are talking to and what agendas they have, for example) and should be assessed with a good understanding of the leaders' national and organizational cultures. Fine nuances in public statements can convey much to an experienced political analyst. Economic analysis also relies heavily—in fact, primarily—on open source material, especially the very large databases on international trade and national economies that have been assembled by international organizations such as the United Nations. Scientific and technical (S&T) analysis makes extensive use of open literature in prediction, as discussed in chapter 14.

A common misconception is that open source material is less useful for military intelligence because the "good" material is classified. On the contrary, one of the major intelligence successes of World War II was based on the skillful use of open sources. Although the Germans maintained censorship as effectively as anyone else, they did publish their freight tariffs on all goods, including petroleum products. Working from those tariffs, a young U.S. Office of Strategic Services analyst, Walter Levy, used geospatial modeling to pinpoint the exact location of the German refineries, which were subsequently targeted by Allied bombers.[7] In more recent times, open source has been particularly effective in providing intelligence about terrorists and insurgent groups.[8]

As in other areas of intelligence, the general rule for open source is this: What is said is not as important as who said it. Statements by a head of government typically carry more weight than do those of a head of state. A finance minister's statements on budgetary issues carry more weight than do the same statements made by a minister of the interior.

Ironically, one problem of open source intelligence is that it is so abundant; an analyst cannot possibly take advantage of all the available material. In fact, an analyst cannot even learn about all of the available ways to obtain open source materials. Tracking the data sources is a full-time job. The solution is to turn to experts on research. Reference librarians can help search and retrieve documents from many different databases, including commercial ones. As those databases become available worldwide, almost any country or commercial company should have an excellent research capability available to its analysts.

Historically, most open source material came in printed ("hard") copy. Today, the most commonly used sources are online.

Online Databases. A wide variety of useful databases are now available through the Web. The number and availability of unclassified commercial databases are changing so rapidly that this book makes no attempt to catalog them. The rapid expansion of global information networks has opened to analysts large volumes of previously unavailable information.

A persistent problem with online data sources remains the difficulty of extracting relevant information from the mass of data. The analyst inevitably encounters information overload. Both government and commercial development projects continue to work toward the goal of creating a human-computer team that would dramatically improve the capability of human analysts to make inferences in complex, data-intensive domains. Such a team would vastly increase the ability to identify key facts hidden in immense quantities of irrelevant information, to assemble large numbers of disparate facts to reach valid conclusions, and to produce new patterns that assist in further analyses. We can reasonably expect to see steady progress in techniques for extracting relevant information from the morass.

In the interim, specialized databases offer some relief from the search problem. For example, one of the more useful sources of technology information for both government and business intelligence is in online patent databases. For many organizations that perform classified research, patents are the only way to publish their results openly.

Hard Copy Sources. Some open source material still is not available through the Web. Hard copy open source literature can be obtained from libraries and commercial databases and from scientists and businesspeople who have frequent dealings with their foreign counterparts. Valuable sources include newspapers, telephone books, monographs, journals, patents, and technical literature.

The most useful of such documents are the closed, restricted, and semiclassified journals known as *gray literature*. State ministries and large research and manufacturing organizations publish journals that contain sensitive or proprietary information. Some of them are classified. Most of them are controlled, and access is restricted; so it is a bit of a stretch to call them *open source*. However, some may be found in public libraries as a result of errors in document control or distribution, and they can often be obtained by clandestine collection (for example, by agents). The in-house publications of many research organizations, even when not restricted, are often more valuable than trade journals; they tend to present more detail on work being carried on within the organization. Conference proceedings, which also fit into the gray literature category, usually have more value than the widely distributed journals and magazines.

The Internet provides an equivalent to gray literature in Web sites and chat rooms that have password-protected content. Such sites often can have great intelligence value. The challenge, of course, is getting into them—a topic that is discussed in the cyber collection section of this chapter.

Human Intelligence

Human intelligence, or HUMINT, encompasses a variety of means for gathering information on foreign developments; its focus is people and their access to information on topics of interest. HUMINT is best used to provide information that is not available by other means. It typically is the best source on an adversary's plans and intentions. It usually is the best method of dealing with illicit networks.

Compared with the other INTs, HUMINT takes more time to collect because of the need to contact the source, even when that source has already been developed (that is, recruited). HUMINT is not always on target; collectors have to take their best shot working with the sources they have. But HUMINT is flexible—information that is not available from one source may be available from another, or from piecing together several sources. HUMINT is best used to go after targets such as an opponent's plans, trade secrets, indications of political instability, or for negotiation support. It also provides critical leads for further targeting by HUMINT or other INTs.

Governmental HUMINT activities include embassy officers' assessments, information elicited from contacts, information from paid agents, and documents or equipment clandestinely acquired by purchase or theft. The human sources can be diplomats and defense attachés, international conference attendees, defectors, émigrés, or refugees. (An attaché is a technical expert on the diplomatic staff of his or her country in a foreign capital. An émigré is a person who was forced to emigrate, usually for political or economic reasons.)

Cooperating private individuals and organizations also can supply privileged information that they encounter in the course of their work. Nongovernmental organizations have proliferated in recent years and are increasingly useful sources about foreign developments.

HUMINT is one of the primary collection methods in law enforcement. The American Mafia is only a shell of what it used to be, in no small part because of law enforcement's aggressive use of human sources—informers or "snitches" in the trade.[9]

HUMINT is a major source of intelligence information for many commercial organizations, and many governments also use HUMINT for commercial purposes. Most corporations do not use clandestine HUMINT (for example, agents in the employ of their competitors) for ethical reasons. If ethics does not constrain corporations, they nevertheless usually avoid clandestine HUMINT because of the costs associated with exposure. Two examples illustrate the exposure hazards of clandestine commercial HUMINT. In 2001 Proctor and Gamble engaged in information collection against rival Unilever that included the technique known informally as *dumpster diving* or *TRASHINT*—sifting through Unilever's off-property trash for documents. Once exposed, Proctor and Gamble reportedly agreed to pay Unilever $10 million as part of a settlement.[10] In 2000 Oracle Corporation admitted that it had hired an investigator to find documents embarrassing to Microsoft; the tactics used reportedly included covert searches of political organizations in Washington, D.C., and payment to janitors for trashed documents showing improper Microsoft activities.[11] Both incidents resulted in damaging media coverage of the offending companies.

Commercial espionage techniques developed rapidly during the Industrial Revolution, when Britain had an edge in many manufactures and was the target of the French, Germans, Dutch, and Swedes, who attempted to recruit skilled artisans (with their tools, if possible).[12] Of course, Britain returned the favor, targeting technologies where the others had an advantage. The defense often took the form of keeping their employees narrowly focused on a single part of any major process, such as steelmaking or industrial chemicals. No one person could give away the whole process.[13] The Soviet Union later refined this technique. Within the Soviet military industries, no single émigré, defector, or spy—unless he was a top-level executive—knew much of the overall picture. Everything was as compartmented as the Soviet system could make it. This system made for great security against HUMINT, but it came at a high price in thwarting adaptability and knowledge sharing among those who needed the information.

HUMINT collection can cover all phases of a development program, from concept to production or deployment and operations of systems. HUMINT sources have provided biographical information on research scientists, identified research institutes, and assessed systems under development. They have brought to light trends in research programs, identified key sites and equipment, and obtained photographs of sites and platforms. HUMINT data also make the data collected by COMINT, IMINT, and open source intelligence more comprehensible, and thus more effective, and yields important insights into data collected by the technical collection systems described later in this chapter. Access to equipment or technical documentation collected through HUMINT gives an analyst an inside view into performance capabilities or production techniques that supplement data collected by technical means.

The following sections outline HUMINT techniques that utilize liaison relationships, elicitation, émigrés and defectors, clandestine sources, sampling, and materiel acquisition. Their common theme is that the intelligence is collected by one person interacting with another person to obtain information.

Liaison Relationships. National intelligence organizations typically have liaison relationships with intelligence and law enforcement groups in other countries, sometimes even when official relationships between the two countries are cool. Corporate intelligence groups have their own liaison networks to share information about such things as terrorist threats to corporate executives abroad.

The nature and closeness of the liaison relationship is critically dependent on the level of mutual trust and confidence between the two organizations and, in turn, on their respective reputations for discretion and security. As Michael Herman observed, "National reputations for good or bad security are crucial elements in international intelligence standing."[14] During the cold war, the United States and other countries were reluctant to share information with West German intelligence, fearing that it had been penetrated by the East Germans (which turned out to be the case).

Intelligence liaison also is not uncommon among governmental and nongovernmental groups. Nongovernmental organizations provide many opportunities for governments or commercial firms to conduct liaison for intelligence gathering. Two well-known historical examples were the World War II liaisons set up by the U.S. Office of Naval Intelligence with Mafia groups for counterespionage operations, using dock workers' unions, and by the Office of Strategic Services for similar operations against the Fascist government in Sicily. Mafia chief "Lucky" Luciano was released from prison, reportedly for his assistance in counterintelligence and to help with the Sicilian operation.[15]

The ethics of the Mafia liaison has been hotly debated over the years, and many intelligence officers argue that intelligence groups should not cooperate with criminal organizations. Their reservations are often summed up with the adage, "If you go to bed with dogs, expect to wake up with fleas!" The contrary argument is that one should use a nonjudgmental approach when choosing liaisons—if they can help more than they hurt, use them.

Liaison entails a number of risks, one being the problem of false corroboration. It is not uncommon for several intelligence services to unwittingly use the same agent. (After all, if one service will pay you for what you know, others may also be willing to do so.) When the agent's information is shared among intelligence services through liaison, it will seem to come to the analyst from different sources—the liaison service and the analyst's own HUMINT service. As a result, a single agent's information will be given added credibility that it does not deserve.

Another problem with liaison is the necessity to rely on the liaison service to check out the source's credentials (known as vetting the source). Germany's federal intelligence service, the BND, provided the United States with intelligence about Iraq's alleged biological warfare program from a human source code-named Curveball. In that case, the Germans themselves apparently were suspicious of the source, but they did not allow U.S. intelligence officers to interview him. U.S. analysts nevertheless relied heavily on Curveball's information in reaching an erroneous judgment that Iraq had an active biological weapons program in 2002.[16]

Liaison with neutral or unfriendly powers comes with additional problems and risks. You cannot be certain what friendly services will do with the intelligence you provide. Things are even less certain with neutral or unfriendly services. Sweden, while pursuing a policy of nonalignment, had liaison with both Nazi and Allied intelligence services during World War II and with West-ern powers (primarily Britain and the United States) during the cold war. [17] The outcome benefited both Sweden and its liaison partners, but for both sides the risk that the Swedes would also help the opponents made for strained relationships.

Liaison relations with neutral or adversarial governments usually involve some form of quid pro quo that may not be worth the consequences. A repres-sive regime that is hiding terrorists might be willing to sell out the terrorists in exchange for intelligence about its domestic opposition. For many govern-ments, that is too high a price for intelligence. But it has been observed that liaison relationships between adversaries can exist for long periods of time. Israeli intelligence reportedly has long-term relationships with the intelligence services of several Arab states.[18] Reportedly, U.S. intelligence had liaison rela-tionships with Syria after the attacks of 9/11 because of Syria's interest in not being perceived as supporting the attacks.[19] The intelligence that is provided in these circumstances has to be viewed with great caution and at least cross-checked against other sources. There is a substantial risk that the liaison ser-vice will manipulate the intelligence to benefit its own interests.

Elicitation. Elicitation is the practice of obtaining information about a topic from conversations, preferably without the source knowing what is hap-pening. Elicitation is widely practiced in gatherings of diplomats and military attachés and in the commercial sector during business executives' social hours and sales conventions. Because the participants are all aware of the game, the information that is elicited may be tainted. But the gatherings are also valuable avenues for sending signals. Businesses in particular use this channel to signal competitors informally about their intentions, especially in cases when use of more formal channels would violate antitrust law.

Making direct contact with knowledgeable sources in their home country or organization is often difficult, and the setting can be unfavorable for elici-tation. However, these sources often publish their work or discuss it at inter-national conferences and during visits with other professionals. Elicitation is an effective tactic to use at such professional gatherings, particularly ones where economists, trade specialists, scientists, or engineers convene to pres-ent papers. These professionals are a valuable source of HUMINT, and the greater their egos, the more information—and the more valuable information—they are likely to impart. They are connected to others in their field in their home countries and in their organizations. Analysts, when they possess the appropriate credentials, often attend such meetings and do their own collec-tion by elicitation.

The challenge in getting information from an elicitation source is to ask the right questions. Experts have advantages in elicitation because of their knowledge of the subject matter and because the elicitation appears to be a natural part of their interaction with other experts. Experts, however, bring their own biases to the process.

A variation on elicitation is to trade for information, much as the liaison services do. While Peter Schwartz was at Royal Dutch Shell, he made regular use of scenarios (a sophisticated type of model) as a medium of exchange by presenting talks on them to selected groups—for example, insights on airline fuel futures to airline executives. In return, he received information from the executives on airline planning that he could use to refine his scenarios.[20]

Émigrés and Defectors. Government intelligence routinely makes use of émigrés and defectors. Émigrés have departed a country legally, but some countries would not have allowed them to leave if they had information of significant intelligence value. Defectors have departed the country illegally and often have information of value.

However, both émigrés and defectors have voluntarily cut their ties with their native lands, usually for economic or political reasons. As a consequence, their objectivity on such issues is in question, and their information must be carefully screened. As with elicitation sources, asking the right question is important; defectors want to please their new friends, and they may give answers that do that.

Corporate intelligence routinely makes use of a different type of émigré or defector—one who formerly worked for the competition—to get information about trade secrets such as marketing strategies, costs, and proprietary processes. Corporate émigrés and defectors typically have the same problems with objectivity as do governmental defectors. In addition, these people carry the added baggage of former employment agreements and legal issues that the traditional émigré or defector is not forced to carry. When changing corporate loyalties within a country, a corporate émigré or defector cannot expect governmental protection if he or she is accused of stealing trade secrets. Internationally, however, such protection may be available. During 1993 and 1994 the international automobile industry was the stage for the dramatic defection of J. Ignacio Lopez de Arriortua and six other senior managers from General Motors (GM) to Volkswagenwerk AG. Lopez and his colleagues apparently took a number of sensitive GM documents with them, as any defector should do if he wishes to increase his value to his new organization. Lopez was accused of masterminding the theft of more than twenty boxes of documents on research, planning, manufacturing, and sales when he left GM to become a Volkswagen executive in 1993. The German government followed the time-honored tradition of providing governmental protection for defectors; they at first refused to prosecute Lopez, and an eventual prosecution was dropped.[21] Volkswagen eventually paid GM damages in a civil suit. Corporate defectors to a country having less cordial relations with the United States would likely gain more protection, as would the company they defected to.

Clandestine Sources. Clandestine HUMINT sources (the classical spies, moles, or agents of spy fiction) are possibly the highest cost source for the quantity of information obtained. Therefore, targeting must be done carefully. Clandestine HUMINT may be the best way to determine plans and intentions.

Clandestine HUMINT is usually carried out by intelligence officers known as *case officers*. They normally work through a network of clandestine sources (agents) who are recruited from the local population.

In normal times the tight security that must surround and protect a clandestine source means that substantial time delays occur between the time the source finds out about something and the time the information reaches an intelligence analyst. Fast communication of perishable data is important in crisis or wartime, but speed tends to increase the risk that the source will be exposed.

Sampling Techniques. Sampling techniques are best known for their use in public opinion polls. They are valuable sources for creating the human terrain model discussed in chapter 5. When analysts need to know something about a large group of people (such as attitudes on Middle East issues among the Arab population), they do not undertake the difficult or impractical task of surveying each member of the group. Instead analysts make estimates based on a small subset, or sample, of the population. Sampling theory increases the efficiency of the estimative process by suggesting strategies for selecting the subset to be used in making an estimate, by defining alternative methods for making estimates from the subset data, by helping to reduce the cost of taking samples, and by providing techniques for quantifying (in a predictive sense) the size of the estimative error associated with a given sampling or estimation algorithm.

Communications Intelligence

Communications intelligence, or COMINT, is the interception, processing, and reporting of an opponent's communications. *Communications* in this definition includes voice and data communications, facsimile, Internet messages, and any other deliberate transmission of information. COMINT is collected by aircraft and satellites, overt ground-based sites, a limited number of seaborne collectors, and some covert and clandestine sites.

COMINT is traditionally considered the province of governments and is generally illegal when conducted by a private entity. But an increasing number of countries use COMINT for economic as well as political intelligence, targeting especially satellite communications, and some business enterprises do so as well. COMINT collection equipment is readily available in the commercial market worldwide. The best commercial units are not cheap, but they rival the best units that government COMINT organizations can supply.

COMINT collection, like HUMINT collection, can provide insights into plans and intentions. It can contribute information about people, organizations, financial transactions, equipment, facilities, procedures, schedules, budgets, operations, testing, deployment, and environmental conditions. COMINT gives clues about relationships and organizations, and perhaps about sensitive or classified projects. The chief constraint on its use today is that it is labor intensive, relying as it does on trained linguists. Eventually, machine translation of speech can be expected to ease this bottleneck. In the past, COMINT seldom provided much detail because it dealt primarily with brief conversations. That is no longer the case, as large volumes of material are now transmitted by data communications or facsimile.

Targets of COMINT for strategic intelligence could include government leadership, research and design organizations, test facilities, criminal enterprises, economic activities (such as international funds transfers), participants in test and operational activities, and executive policy discussions.

Military services conduct the bulk of COMINT activity worldwide, in which linguists monitor the mobile radio communications of opposing forces. COMINT that supports ongoing operations, known as tactical COMINT, is used heavily in law enforcement work and in countering illicit networks generally. The case of Pablo Escobar, to which we referred in chapter 1, is a typical example. Military COMINT is used extensively against air-to-ground, ground-to-ground, and naval communications. Most involve the intercept of radio communications, though the use of underwater sound communications by submarines has spurred the development of COMINT capabilities in underwater acoustics.

COMINT has achieved a number of successes in wartime. During World War II the United States scored its Midway victory over the Japanese navy largely because U.S. cryptanalysts had cracked the Japanese naval codes and were able to identify Midway as the Japanese target. In Europe the British success at breaking the German Enigma cipher codes contributed to several World War II successes, including the Normandy landing.[22]

One of the earliest and most significant successes for COMINT occurred at the Battle of Tannenberg, late in August 1914, during the opening moves of World War I. The Russian First and Second Armies were advancing through East Prussia toward the German Eighth Army. Communications among the Russian headquarters were handled by high-frequency radio, which can be received over a wide geographic region, and some of the messages were not enciphered. On the night of August 25, German radio units intercepted messages that gave the deployment and missions of the two Russian armies. Over the next few days, more intercepted messages gave away the strength, positions, and movements of the Russian armies. It quickly became apparent to the German commanders that General Samsonov's Second Army was being placed in an exposed position near the German town of Tannenberg and that Russian General Rennenkampf's First Army was not in a position to provide support if Samsonov's army was attacked.

General von Hindenberg, commander of the German Eighth Army, positioned his entire force for an attack on the Russian Second Army. On August 26 he began the attack, and over the next three days he deployed his units in response to Russian countermoves, being forewarned of them by additional intercepts of Russian radiograms. The result was a spectacular German victory. The Russian Second Army was decimated, General Samsonov committed suicide, and the eastern front ultimately settled into a stalemate.[23]

An interesting footnote to Tannenberg is the unanimous declarations by all of the key German participants that the intercepted information, although useful, was not critical to the outcome. Von Hindenberg himself, in his writings, gives the impression that he had no such information on the Russian disposi-tions.[24] In World War II, General Omar Bradley and Field Marshal Bernard Montgomery treated the intercepts of the German Enigma cipher machine in similar fashion, crediting their own operational skill for their victories.[25] Such statements deserve a certain amount of skepticism. They are the standard dis-claimers of successful generals, statesmen, and corporate executives who have good intelligence support. In the intelligence business, openly crediting sources can cause the loss of those sources. Moreover, a leader does not want to give too much credit to his intelligence information, because the logical inference is that the leader with the best intelligence—not the best leadership skills—will win. The truth probably lies somewhere in the middle.

Encryption technology has outpaced cryptanalysis in the decades since World War II, and it would be very difficult, if not impossible, to repeat the Allied successes of that war. The lessons of the war were learned by all coun-tries, and most cryptanalysis successes now come through radio operator mistakes, such as those that the Russians made at Tannenberg. Of course, a large amount of military and civilian radio traffic remains unencrypted, but the trend is to encrypt highly sensitive communications.

There are several techniques for COMINT collection.

Microphones and Audio Transmitters. The microphone-and-wire is an old technology still widely used by some intelligence services. It is cheap, reli-able, and long-lasting. Unfortunately, it is also relatively easy for counterintel-ligence units to find.

The audio transmitter, popularly known as the *bug,* also has been a useful technical intelligence tool for decades. Because it transmits a radio signal, rather than using a wire, it is simpler to put in place than the microphone-and-wire. It also is cheap and requires no great technical skill to use; so it is par-ticularly popular among the less-sophisticated intelligence organizations and in industrial espionage. The audio transmitter typically uses low radiated power to avoid detection, has its own power supply (unless it can tap into the building's power system), and is small enough to be effectively concealed. Increasingly, bugs can provide video as well as audio.

Advancing technologies in miniaturization, power sources, and transmis-sion techniques have provided these capabilities. Burst transmissions (very short radio signals, usually one second or less), spread spectrum (typically signals that look like noise), and other techniques are available to reduce the probability of signal intercept. Difficult-to-detect infrared links are also avail-able. Remote command and control techniques can switch transmitters on and off, reducing the probability of detection and conserving battery life.

Telephone Surveillance. Telephone conversations are perhaps the most common source of COMINT. The traditional approach is to monitor the tele-phone of interest through a tap. In addition to monitoring normal telephone conversations, some devices take advantage of the fact that telephone instru-ments can transmit room conversations (audio) along telephone lines when the telephone handset is resting in its cradle (on hook). Some telephone instruments, as designed, pass audio while on hook; others may do so inadvertently because of faulty installation or damage. The introduction of new and sophisticated computer-based telephone systems has greatly expanded the possibilities of this technical surveillance technique.

Telephone conversations also can be intercepted in bulk by COMINT equipment, if the equipment is properly positioned to collect microwave point-to-point transmissions from the telephone company's trunk lines. Unencrypted cellular telephone networks are also an easy target. A major problem with such intercepts on civil systems is that the quantity of conversation that must be processed can swamp the COMINT processors—especially if the language must be translated. Some means of specific telephone recognition must be found to allow selection of the conversations of interest. In modern telephone systems, that can be difficult indeed.

Much international telephone and data traffic is carried by communications satellites. This traffic can be intercepted by many unintended recipients. Such activity for commercial intelligence purposes is likely to increase in the future, though it is illegal under international law. A number of governments routinely intercept satellite communications, sifting them for information of value, including information that will permit their own companies to compete in international markets.

Other COMINT Techniques. If an intelligence service cannot gain access to a facility to install a microphone-and-wire or audio transmitter, it can sometimes use one of several remote acoustic monitoring techniques. All such techniques depend on the ability of structural or emplaced objects in a room to pick up sound and vibrate mechanically.

When used as a specialized type of microphone, the *accelerometer* picks up mechanical vibrations directly from the building structure and transmits the audio out of a facility by wire or a radio transmitter. Whether the vibrations are from voice or machine noise, the accelerometer can effectively receive sound from several rooms away. Typically, the accelerometer is placed in a structural beam that runs into the area to be monitored. The vibrations from conversations in the room travel along the structural beam and are picked up by the accelerometer.

Fluidics, as a method to surreptitiously collect audio information, exploits the way in which acoustic energy travels with relatively low loss in liquids, or in gases if channeled. Thus, if a water pipe picks up acoustic energy, the audio signal will travel long distances within the pipe. Electrical conduit or air ducts will also propagate audio over substantial distances. The old-style audio headsets that passengers used in many commercial airliners took advantage of this channeling effect in an air conduit.

Since the 1960s *radio frequency flooding* of installations has been used for intelligence data collection. The flooding signals usually operate in the microwave range and are used to collect data remotely, much as a radar senses its target. Flooding depends on the fact that objects, especially metal ones, vibrate slightly in response to audio in a room. A beam of microwave energy striking the metal object will be reflected from it with some weak modulation imposed by the audio vibrations. If the reflected energy can be collected and demodulated, conversations in the area can be monitored. Innocuous signals such as those emanating from a television or radio station can be used successfully to flood an installation. Flooding has also been directed at devices such as typewriters. Signals directed at the typewriters are modulated by the keystrokes, and the modulated signal is received by nearby antennas, thereby compromising the information typed.

Perhaps the best known instance of radio frequency flooding was that conducted by the Soviets against the U.S. Embassy in Moscow early in the cold war. The Soviets had concealed a passive sound pickup device in the Great Seal of the United States that they presented to the U.S. ambassador and that subsequently decorated the ambassador's study. The device was a small, U-shaped metal support for a strip of spring steel. The steel strip would vibrate slightly in response to sounds within the office. When the seal was illuminated with a strong microwave signal from a nearby Soviet-controlled building, the U-shaped support acted as an antenna and would pick up the microwave energy and reradiate it, modulated by the audio signal from within the room. A nearby receiver would pick up and demodulate the reradiated signal.[26]

Laser radar techniques have been used to exploit audio vibrations from windows or fixtures within an office since the 1960s. The principle is the same as for radio frequency flooding. An infrared laser (which is invisible to the human eye) can be aimed at an office window from distances ranging up to hundreds of yards. If the proper infrared band is selected for the laser, the window glass will reflect the energy. Conversations inside the office will cause the windowpane to vibrate slightly, and those audio vibrations will modulate the reflected laser energy. An optical receiver located near the laser transmitter can then pick up the backscattered energy, demodulate it, and recover the audio. The technology to use such laser devices is now widely available.[27]

Liaison Relationships. As with HUMINT, liaison relationships are important in COMINT. The United States has had formal liaison relations with the United Kingdom, Canada, Australia, and New Zealand that date back to World War II.[28] This so-called five-eyes relationship is an exception to the normal pattern of bilateral relationships. Bilateral relationships are usually preferred because the problems caused by intelligence sharing increase rapidly in multilateral arrangements. Bilateral U.S. liaison relations with Norway, Denmark, and Sweden provided valuable signals intelligence in the early years of the cold war. The geographic location of these three countries close to the northwestern border of the Soviet Union gave them unique advantages in signals collection.[29]

Cyber Collection

Collection that is undertaken against an information processing system or network does not fit under any of the traditional INTs. It typically has some connection with HUMINT, because it is often an extension of the technical collection efforts carried out by HUMINT operatives. Cyber collection also resembles COMINT, especially when collection from data communications networks is involved. Collection against publicly available information processing systems such as the Web falls into the category of open source. This section focuses on collection against protected systems, though the Web often is a channel for such attack.

Intelligence operations aimed at computers and networks may have become the most productive type of intelligence gathering. One reason is the sheer volume of useful information that is available on computers. This includes not only information of direct intelligence value—such as plans, equipment specifications, and economic data—but also information that can help in targeting other collection assets. Personnel data, for instance, can be acquired by targeting online employment search sites. The résumés on these sites often give details about classified programs and help in the targeting of individuals for COMINT operations or for recruitment as HUMINT sources.[30]

Another reason for the rising importance of cyber collection is the relatively low risk involved in obtaining it. The U.S. National Counterintelligence Executive (NCIX) reportedly has posed this question: "If you can exfiltrate massive amounts of information electronically from another continent, why risk running a spy?"

Most articles about cyber collection, or "hacking," are written from the defense point of view and consequently are pessimistic and full of warnings. I take a far more optimistic view because I am writing from the point of view of the attacker. The basic rule of strategic conflict cited elsewhere in this book—*the offense always wins*—applies full force in cyber collection. As in other areas of strategic conflict, the attacker has the advantage. The defense must defend against all possible forms of attack. The attacker needs to select only one vulnerability. The attacker has time working for him; patience and persistence are his keys to success. As former hacker Dustin Dykes has noted, "The security systems have to win every time; the hacker only has to win once."[31] The best that the defender can do is to make the attack more difficult and expensive or slow it down. Winning is not an option.

Attackers are helped in this process by the mindset of the defenders and by the complexity of computer networks:

- *Mindset.* Network administrators and network defenders just don't think like attackers.[32] The defenders want to believe that they have a secure system. The cyber collectors know better. The motto of the hacker is, "If there is a flaw in the security, we'll find it."[33] Because of mindset, the computer security programs intended to counter attacks usually focus on vulnerability because vulnerabilities are easier to think about than likely threats. Governments and private companies expend very little analysis effort in assessing how attackers view their targets: computers, networks, and databases. On the other hand, because of a lack of threat knowledge, companies and countries generally devote valuable resources to nonexistent threats simply because they are looking at the whole realm of the possible. Conversely, because the defenders have not done threat assessments from the attackers' viewpoints, defenders devote insufficient resources to areas under attack.

- *Complexity.* Large software programs and large networks always have more vulnerabilities than do smaller, less complex ones. Furthermore, new vulnerabilities appear every day, which is why time favors the attacker. The continual changing of system hardware and updating of system and applications software; the frequent installation of patches and upgrades; the introduction of new features, such as instant messaging, Internet relay chat, and Bluetooth—all provide a steady stream of new opportunities for attack. Poor configuration control of networks is common. Devices are improperly connected to the network. Every modification to the system creates a potential vulnerability. The constant changes form what Kevin Mitnick, a former hacker and now computer security expert, calls a "target-rich environment."[34]

There are two general types of cyber collection: computer network exploitation, or CNE, and direct or indirect exploitation of a single computer or an intranet (a privately maintained computer network that requires access authorization). The following sections describe some commonly used techniques for exploiting computer systems and networks in intelligence. Because this is a rapidly changing and highly technical field, these descriptions are cursory and omit some of the more sophisticated collection methods.

Computer Network Exploitation. There are numerous ways to exploit target networks. Collectors first must gain access to the target network, have tools to exploit it, and then remove any evidence of the operation. Collectors can exploit a vulnerability that occurs in the network or one that is presented by the supply chain. They can masquerade as authorized users of the target network or use human assets to gain physical access to the network. Once they have gained access, they usually leave behind a software implant called a *backdoor.* The implants communicate back to the controlling organization, allowing collectors to acquire data from the network. The process can be summed up in these four steps:

- *Passive network analysis and mapping,* which involves nonintrusive probing of the target network, confirms the presence of network devices and maps their connectivity. During this step, the attackers conduct analysis to understand the network from fragments of evidence about it and then create a model of the system, much as intelligence analysts must do.

- *Vulnerability scanning* makes contact with the target network and its components by using publicly available keys. Vulnerability scanning can be done both on and off the Internet, and it uses many of the tools that are used by top-tier hackers. It involves a wide range of specialized techniques with exotic names such as "pinging" and "port scanning."

- *Exploitation* is the step widely known as "hacking." The collector conducts a survey, establishes access to the target system, and installs software implants for future access. Most such implants, as noted above, are called backdoors—a form of software code that allows unauthorized access to a computer or network, ideally while remaining undetected.

- *Sustained collection* uses the backdoor to obtain useful intelligence information from the computer or network through continuing access.

In the initial two steps—network analysis and mapping, and vulnerability scanning—the main criterion for success is to be unnoticed. The scanner, in particular, has to be invisible to various types of intrusion detection systems, or "sniffers"—software programs or human administrators checking access or searching for intruders. These detection systems are increasingly dangerous to the attacker; formerly the presence of a sniffer was relatively easy to detect, but newer forms of sniffer software are much less visible. Once the attacker has alerted the defender, access to the network becomes very difficult to achieve.

The next two steps—exploitation and sustained collection—require the attacker to install the backdoor and keep its presence concealed. The backdoor (sometimes referred to as a trapdoor) permits easy continuing access to a computer's software or operating system. Legitimate backdoors, which are installed by systems development staff, allow staff to bypass security routines so that they can enter the system at any time to run tests, upgrade systems, or fix problems. Normally, these legitimate backdoors are eliminated when the system becomes operational. However, backdoors may be left open by mistake or by intention to permit continuing maintenance.

The best-known backdoor existed only in the movies. In *WarGames*, the hero (a computer hacker) discovers a backdoor called Joshua that allows him access to the North American Aerospace Defense Command's strategic defense software, starting a chain of events in which the war game becomes much too realistic.

The backdoor is perhaps the primary tool used by attackers for industrial computer espionage. In poorly defended systems a backdoor can give unlimited access to data in the system. Valuable corporate proprietary information has been acquired time and again from competitors through backdoors.[35]

Sustained collection can use a number of tools; four of the more widely known ones are Trojan horses (usually abbreviated "Trojans"), worms, rootkits, and keystroke loggers.

- A *Trojan horse* is a seemingly innocent program that conceals its primary purpose. In computer attacks, the purpose is to exfiltrate data from the target computer system. Operating systems software and almost any applications software package—screen savers, spreadsheets, word processors, database managers—could be Trojan horses. A simple Trojan in a word processor might, for example, make a copy of all files that the word processor saves and store the copies in a location where the horse's "master" can access them later. Another simple Trojan horse, once activated, waits until the user attempts to log off. It then simulates a real logoff while keeping the user online. When the user next attempts to log on, the Trojan captures the user's password for its master and simulates a logon.

- A *worm* can do many of the things that a Trojan horse does, and it can also do such things as install a backdoor. But in contrast to the Trojan horse, the worm is designed to be completely concealed instead of masquerading as an innocent program. Hackers have used worms to instruct a bank's computer to transfer money to an illicit account. Worms also are used to transmit controlled data to unauthorized recipients; this is how they are used in cyber collection.

- A *rootkit* is software code designed to take control of a computer while avoiding detection. The term comes from the expression in the Unix operating system for fundamental control of a computer ("root" access). The equivalent in Microsoft Windows is termed "administrator access." The rootkit is often concealed within a Trojan horse.

- *Keystroke loggers,* or keyloggers, can be hardware or software based. Their general purpose is to capture and record keystrokes. For cyber collection, they specifically are intended to capture passwords and encryption keys. Hardware keyloggers often are mounted in keyboards, requiring access to the keyboard at some point—though the advent of wireless keyboards has provided the option for attackers to collect keystrokes by monitoring the wireless signal from nearby. Software keyloggers usually are implanted in the computer's operating system.

The proliferation of computer capabilities around the world, and the development of commercial computer espionage capabilities, has resulted in the rapid expansion of computer network exploitation by governments, industrial spies, and hackers. Commercial computer espionage has continued to increase during this decade, and it has become difficult to distinguish such efforts from national security targeting. Many groups are interested in collecting commercial information, including competitors, hostile intelligence services, organized crime groups, and pranksters, or hackers. Increasingly these intelligence efforts are sponsored by governmental rather than nongovernmental groups.

When a hacker enters a system, as the following examples illustrate, the victim usually cannot identify the real source of the attack.

- In 1988 astrophysicist Clifford Stoll was working as a computer systems manager at a California laboratory. He noticed a 75 cent error in the billing logs and began investigating the logs to correct the error. Stoll discovered enough discrepancies to make him believe that someone was tapping into the lab's computer system illegally. He eventually tracked down a hacker who was attempting to access American computer networks involved with national security and who had broken into an estimated 30 of the 450 systems he had attacked. The hacker, twenty-five-year-old Markus Hess, of Hanover, Germany, and some others apparently provided their computer skills to the Soviet Union, which paid them for the information they discovered.[36]
- In 1999 and 2000 unidentified hackers downloaded scores of "sensitive but unclassified" internal documents from computers in the U.S. Department of Defense and in the Los Alamos and Lawrence Livermore Laboratories. The effort was traced to a foreign country whose officials denied being involved, but the intrusions suddenly stopped.[37]

Direct Access to a Computer or Intranet. A network that is physically isolated from the Internet (an intranet), or a single computer that never connects to the Internet, requires a different type of attack from that used in CNE. The attacker has to gain physical access to the computer or the intranet in some way. Once access has been gained—through a network jack or cable, a telephone closet, or some similar device—almost anything can be done. From the defense point of view, the game is over, and the defense has lost.

One of the simplest targets is a personal notebook computer that is carried on trips or to conferences. With a few minutes of uninterrupted access to the notebook, a collector can download the contents of the notebook's hard drive. Computers or any devices containing electronic storage—separate hard drives or thumb drives, for example—can legally be searched when they are taken across international borders, and they often are. Encrypting the material does not provide protection. Customs officials can demand the encryption key, deny the traveler entry to their country, or confiscate the computer. In many cases, customs officials are looking for terrorist material, pornography, or hate literature, but countries that have a reputation for commercial espionage also are likely to make intelligence use of the material acquired. Gaining entry to a notebook computer provides the attacker with one-time access. But if it is expected that the notebook later will be connected to an intranet, the attacker can place a backdoor on the computer.

In cases where computers and intranets never leave a secure facility, and where remote access is not possible, it is necessary to use field operations to access networks. This category encompasses deployment of any CNE tool through physical access or proximity. In intelligence, these are called HUMINT-enabled operations; in the world of hackers, they are usually referred to as "social engineering."[38] They encompass such classical HUMINT techniques as gaining access under false pretenses, bribery or recruitment of trusted personnel in a facility, and surreptitious entry. HUMINT-enabled operations are often facilitated by human error or carelessness; and complex intranets are particularly susceptible to human error and carelessness.

Even physical access to areas outside a protected area can help in either direct access or CNE. The TRASHINT (dumpster diving) technique mentioned earlier is sometimes a prelude to cyber attack. One can often obtain network information, system architecture, and passwords from trash.

Collecting Emanations. If a computer or network is not connected to the Internet, and if physical access is out of the question, it may be possible for an attacker to obtain intelligence by using short-range sensors to exploit equipment emanations. If a computer or an intranet component emits compromising electromagnetic signals, sensors placed close by can recover information being processed. Electronic and magnetic signals can radiate from the area both in space and through power lines or other conducting paths. The possibility of collecting keystroke emanations from wireless keyboards was previously noted, but even a conventional wired keyboard can emit a compromising signal.

These types of technical collection attacks are sensitive in detail and difficult to detect. They are a capability of sophisticated adversaries and require extensive HUMINT support. The U.S. government's attempts to improve protection against the collection of emanations some years back spawned a sizable industry known as TEMPEST. TEMPEST technology uses shielding and other electronic design techniques to reduce radiated electromagnetic signals that might be picked up by attackers.

Nonliteral Intelligence

There are many specialized techniques for collecting and processing nonliteral intelligence, most of which focus on specific classes of targets and provide specific intelligence answers. Most either use novel sensors or process raw data from conventional sensors in special ways. In the United States many of these techniques are lumped together under the name *measurements and signatures intelligence* (MASINT)—a term that embraces a diverse set of collection and processing techniques. Others are designated as IMINT or SIGINT. The range of specialized collection techniques is too large for a complete list, and the field is constantly changing, but the following describes some of them.

Nonliteral intelligence collection employs sensors such as radar, radio frequency antennas, lasers, passive electro-optical sensors, nuclear radiation detectors, and seismic or acoustic sensors for the purposes of gathering information. These instruments gather measurements such as radar cross sections, radiant intensities, or temperatures to characterize military operations and tactics; to assess missile, aircraft, and propulsion systems performance; to monitor research, development, testing and production facilities; and to understand cultural and economic activities, environmental effects, and naturally occurring phenomena. The collection sensors used divide broadly into either remote sensing or in situ sensing, though some sensors may blur the difference.

Remote and In Situ Sensing

Remote sensing is often defined as sensing of the earth's surface from satellites or aircraft using some part of the electromagnetic spectrum. It also includes the sensing of aircraft or satellites from the earth. Optical sensors work in the ultraviolet to infrared regions. Radars operate in the microwave and millimeter wave region.

As we move toward higher frequencies in the spectrum, moisture, clouds, and even darkness tend to decrease the sensor's effectiveness by reducing the amount of energy the sensor receives. For detection reliability, a sensor should operate under all weather and light conditions. But at higher frequencies the resolution of the sensor generally improves. Good resolution—the ability of the sensor to distinguish small objects—allows the identification of specific vehicles, for example. With poor resolution, the objects are blurred or indistinguishable.

The main advantage of remote sensors over other sensors is that they can cover a large area of the earth quickly. They achieve this because they can have a very wide swath width, allowing the sensor to search a wide area in one pass. Normally one faces trade-offs between swath width and resolution. Good resolution is essential for detecting small objects on the surface. However, sensors that have wide swath widths generally have poor resolution, and sensors with good resolution usually have small swath widths.

Remote sensors divide into two general classes: active and passive. Active sensors (radars) transmit a signal and then interpret the signals that are reflected off the target. Passive sensors exploit natural and human-made emissions or use an alternative illumination source, such as the sun. Most passive sensors operate in the microwave, millimeter wave, or optical bands. Most remote sensors used in Earth resources sensing create images, but a few do not. Each class and frequency band has unique advantages and disadvantages. And each class encompasses several specific sensor types that have advantages and disadvantages.

The alternative to remote sensing is to use devices that sense changes in the medium (air, water, earth) immediately surrounding the sensor. Such in situ sensors measure phenomena within an object or nearby and typically detect sound, electrical currents, temperature, contaminants, radiation, or magnetic fields. Air sampling equipment, carried aloft by reconnaissance aircraft to detect the debris from atmospheric nuclear tests, is an example of an in situ sensor. Telemetry equipment provides readings about the radiation belts from in situ sensors located on spacecraft. The number and variety of these sensors make it impractical to discuss the technical details of each.

Most in situ sensors do not have the broad-area search potential of the remote sensors. Compared with sensors mounted on air and space vehicles, they have either relatively slow search rates or relatively small ranges, or both. Consequently, all of them are limited to covering much smaller coverage areas than the remote sensors.

In situ sensors can be used to track ships or submarines. As ships or submarines move through the water, they leave behind trace chemicals. Metals are continuously deposited in the water by corrosion and erosion of the hull. Lubricants, waste flushed from sanitary tanks, hydrogen gas discharged from a submarine's life support system—all are deposited in a ship's wake. Neutron radiation from a nuclear power generator can cause detectable changes in seawater. All these contaminants leave a "track" in the ocean that can be followed by the appropriate sensors located on a trailing ship or submarine.

Two classes of in situ sensors—biosensors and chemical sensors—have become much more prominent as a result of the growing worldwide threat of biological or chemical warfare terrorism. Biosensors can identify specific pathogens such as anthrax and smallpox. Chemical sensors can identify all of the chemical warfare agents shown in Figure 5-8.

The following sections briefly describe some of the most important sensors used to collect nonliteral intelligence, their capabilities, and the uses of the intelligence they collect.

Imaging and Spectral Sensing

Imagery intelligence, or IMINT, is traditionally thought of as visible photography—whether with a handheld camera or from aircraft and spacecraft. Most imagery, in fact, is of this type. Increasingly, though, imagery from radar and from the infrared spectrum is important in intelligence.

IMINT can identify deployed military units, test facilities, and participants in exercises or operational missions. When used with COMINT and HUMINT, it has located research and development facilities and provided detailed information about the equipment used at the test areas. It can tip off other collectors when aircraft or ships have left their home bases, have arrived at their staging bases, or are participating in tests, operational exercises, or operational missions. That tip-off allows the coordinated use of non-IMINT collection, such as COMINT, or other types of nonliteral collection to cover the activity.

Commercial imagery—that is, images acquired by either government or commercial organizations that are sold to the general public—is taking over a role formerly reserved for government intelligence agencies. It is steadily improving in quality and availability. Commercial satellite imagery increasingly is being treated as open literature. Governments and commercial firms know of its existence, its coverage, and its quality. Almost anyone can buy it for any purpose; so imagery exploitation for a wide range of governmental and nongovernmental intelligence purposes has become an accepted practice.

In effect, this type of imagery—visible, radar, and spectral—is available as open source, and its quality is becoming good enough to be useful for a number of intelligence applications. The wide availability of satellite imagery has several effects, positive and negative:

- Fewer and fewer secrets are discovered by imagery. Its capabilities are well known, and the number of imagery satellites of all types is steadily increasing. Because of that, governments, terrorist groups, and organized crime groups are increasingly hiding sensitive activities underground, using concealment and deception, or scheduling sensitive activities to avoid imagery satellites.

- Wide availability may also be driving government imagery intelligence to new technical areas or new capabilities. Governments will likely push the resolution or nature of their classified imagery so as not to duplicate commercially available images.

- On the plus side, commercial imagery can be shared among coalition forces without revealing sources and methods.

Photography and Video. The important role that short-range imagery—handheld photography and video cameras—plays in intelligence is often overlooked because remote sensing technologies, especially satellite imagery, tend to get more attention. Handheld imagery is nevertheless still important in a wide range of intelligence. Handheld imagery has provided details about industrial products and allowed performance analysis of aircraft, tanks, ships, and submarines, as well as permitted thorough examination of the instruments on board the vehicles. It is useful in obtaining the size and characteristics of objects for technical evaluation, as well as personal photographs (mug shots) for counterintelligence and counternarcotics operations. Video is increasingly valuable for continuous surveillance of a target, and video shots of foreign leaders are useful in making physiological or behavioral assessments of them. It is used extensively in biometric identification, discussed later in this chapter.

Imaging Radar. When mounted on aircraft or spacecraft, radars can rapidly search large areas of Earth's surface. Microwave radars use frequencies that are not greatly affected by water vapor, and microwave radars are not affected by darkness; so they operate well at night and under most weather conditions. They have the added advantage of being able to see through vegetation and most camouflage netting, and sometimes even through the top layers of dry soil. They can penetrate nonmetallic walls and roofs of buildings.

Airborne or spaceborne imaging radars have the potential to detect and identify targets nearly as well as visible imagery can. Most such radars are called *synthetic aperture radars* (SARs). They take advantage of the Doppler (motion) effect of the moving vehicle and thereby produce high-resolution images with a small antenna. With an antenna beam the radar illuminates a patch on the ground off to the side of the satellite or aircraft platform. As the SAR moves past a ground target, the frequency of the radar return from the target shifts downward due to the Doppler effect, much as the sound frequency (pitch) of a locomotive whistle drops as the train passes by. By tracking this shift in its signal processor, the SAR is able to create an image of the target. The image will have the same resolution as it would if the antenna were as long as the distance traveled by the aircraft or spacecraft, within certain limits. Good quality SAR imagery is becoming widely available commercially.

Electro-optical Imaging. Electro-optical imaging systems are attractive because they can cover large areas of Earth's surface with resolution sufficient for imagery interpretation. However, their optics do not function through clouds, haze, fog, or precipitation. The original spaceborne imaging sensors were cameras using film that was returned to Earth by deorbiting "buckets." The U.S. KH-4 CORONA satellite used one such system. Today, electro-optical imagers use arrays of light-sensitive detectors that are much like those in digital cameras and transmit the images to a ground station.

Electro-optical images are taken in both the visible spectrum and the infrared spectrum. Infrared imaging uses wavelengths somewhat longer than that of visible light and can function at night as well as in daylight. At wavelengths near that of visible light (called *near infrared*), the image depends on light reflected from the earth's surface, in the same way that visible imaging does. Color infrared images using this near infrared light are often called *false-color* images. Objects that are normally red appear green, green objects (except vegetation) appear blue, and infrared objects, which normally are not seen at all, appear red. Vegetation studies rely heavily on color infrared imagery. Healthy green vegetation is a very strong reflector of infrared radiation and appears bright red in color infrared images.

Radiometry and Spectrometry. The electro-optical imagers discussed previously depend on reflected energy, usually from the sun. But all objects at temperatures above absolute zero also emit radio frequency energy. At longer wavelengths, further removed from those of visible light (far infrared), an image can be created by sensing heat radiated from the earth and objects on it, rather than from reflected light. Far infrared is useful for detecting human-made objects such as vehicles and power plants at night.

As the target becomes hotter, both the strength and the frequency of emissions increase. Very hot objects radiate in the visible range (a lamp filament, for example). Anyone who has ever watched iron being heated to red- or white-hot temperature has observed this phenomenon.

Different objects radiate differently. Rock, earth, seawater, and vegetation all have different emission patterns. Factories or vehicles, when in use, tend to radiate more strongly.

Radiometric sensors take advantage of this phenomenon to obtain information about ships, aircraft, missiles, and the environment (the natural background). These passive sensors receive and record the electromagnetic energy that objects naturally emit. The radiometer records the natural energy that is emitted in the radio frequency range by heated objects. The warmer the object, the more energy it radiates, and a good radiometer can sense temperature changes of less than one degree Celsius.

Radiometers are of two general types: microwave and infrared. Objects near room temperature are usually investigated by using microwave radiometers. Hotter objects, such as missile plumes and high explosive and nuclear detonations, tend to be investigated by using radiometers operating in the infrared bands.

Spectral Imaging. Spectral imaging combines electro-optical imaging and spectrometry to extract additional intelligence information by measuring the intensity of energy received in different spectral bands. Multispectral and hyperspectral sensors use the reflected or emitted light from the surface of an object or feature to identify the object or feature. They operate mostly in the infrared spectrum but may include the visible spectrum as well. Multispectral imagery permits analysts to examine moisture patterns and locate buried objects. Different surface features will show up prominently on different frequency bands of the multispectral images. If the proper wavelengths are selected, multispectral images can be used to detect camouflage, thermal emissions, and hazardous wastes, for example. Hyperspectral imaging uses the same technique but samples a much larger set of spectral bands (in the hundreds). A wide range of environmental intelligence and crop forecasting techniques use hyperspectral imaging. Detection of chemical or biological weapons, bomb damage assessment of underground structures, and foliage penetration to detect troops and vehicles are examples of the potential uses of hyperspectral imaging.

Passive Radiofrequency Intelligence

A wide variety of radiofrequency (RF) signals are emitted as a consequence of normal human activity. Some of these are unintentional emissions that are of intelligence interest. But two major classes of intentional emissions, in addition to communications signals discussed earlier, are of high intelligence interest. The collection and exploitation of these emissions is called either ELINT or FISINT.

Electronic Intelligence (ELINT). ELINT refers to the information gained from the remote sensing of noncommunications signals—including those emitted by radar, beacons, jammers, missile guidance systems, and altimeters. Although the acronym may be unfamiliar, ELINT is widely used. The detector that some motorists use to detect police radar is an ELINT device. ELINT divides broadly into two types: technical and operational.

Technical ELINT is used to assess a radar's capabilities and performance, to determine the level of technology used in building the radar, and to find weaknesses in the radar to help electronic warfare designers defeat it. Technical ELINT collection and processing typically concentrate on signals that already have been identified and on evolutionary modifications to the signals. However, the highest priority signals for ELINT collection are always new and unidentified signals because they presumably represent the most advanced capability. Newly developed radars would radiate only for short periods, in tests, and only during times when it was believed that hostile intercept potential was at a minimum. Therefore, short-duration intercepts are the best one can hope for on such radars.

Operational ELINT is primarily of interest to military field commanders and law enforcement officers for tactical intelligence. Operational ELINT involves locating deployed radars and determining their operational status; it is an important contributor to creating the geospatial intelligence models discussed in chapter 5. A ship, aircraft, or surface-to-air missile unit can often be tracked best by continuously pinpointing the location of the radar(s) it carries. Operational ELINT is used extensively in modern warfare to pinpoint targets for air attack and to locate threat radars so that attacking aircraft can avoid the defenses the radars control.

Operational ELINT can also use fine-grain signatures of radar signals to identify and track specific radars. This technique is called *specific emitter identification* or *fingerprinting* because, just as no two human fingerprints are identical, no two radars have identical signal parameters, even though they may be physically identical otherwise.

Foreign Instrumentation Signals Intelligence (FISINT). Vehicles that are undergoing testing—missiles, aircraft, and even farm tractors and earthmoving equipment—carry instruments called *transducers* that monitor pressures, temperatures, and subsystems performance. The instrument readings typically are recorded for later laboratory analysis. In vehicles in which the recorder might not survive a catastrophic failure (aircraft) or where recorder recovery is impracticable (missiles and satellites), the readings are transmitted via radio back to a ground site. Such transmissions are called *telemetry.* Their collection for intelligence purposes is called foreign instrumentation signals intelligence, abbreviated FISINT.

Complex and expensive systems such as missiles and satellites have a large number of instrument readings to transmit, and it is impractical to devote a separate transmission link to each reading. Telemetry systems therefore combine the signals from the readings in a process called *multiplexing* for transmission using a single transmitter. Each signal occupies a "channel" in the multiplex system. At the receiver, the channels are separated (demultiplexed) and sent to separate displays or recorders.

Interpretation of intercepted telemetry is difficult, in part because of the scaling problem. The engineers running the instrumentation know the scales for the readings they receive and which channels of telemetry come from which instrument. The intercepting party must often infer both the nature of the instrument and the scale of the readings from external evidence—correlating the readings with external events such as aircraft or missile altitude or speed.

Because telemetry involves the deliberate transmission of information, its interception could be considered a part of COMINT. But because it requires extensive processing, exploitation, and interpretation of the results, FISINT is included as part of nonliteral intelligence.

Unintentional RF Emissions. A variety of equipment emits radio frequency energy: internal combustion engines, electrical generators, and switches, for example. These emissions typically are weak, but sensitive equipment can detect the signals and locate the emitter or use the characteristic "signature" of the emission to identify the target. In addition to highly sensitive receiving equipment, processors need highly sophisticated signal processing equipment to deal with unintentional radiation signals and derive useful intelligence from them.

Specific pieces of equipment can often be identified by their unique radio frequency signatures. The functions being performed within a factory building and the rates of production, for example, can sometimes be determined by monitoring the radio frequency emission patterns.

Furthermore, because moving parts on the target can modulate a nearby radio frequency signal, intentional radiation can sometimes be used to obtain target signatures. The signal of a radar or radio mounted on an aircraft, for example, will be modulated by the aircraft propellers or jet turbine blades. The modulation, though weak, can identify both the aircraft type and the specific aircraft. The concept is similar to the use of microwaves or lasers to illuminate an object and pick up conversations as audio vibrations that modulate the signal.

Radar Intelligence

Radar traditionally is used to locate and track a target in space. One special type of radar sensing, usually called *RADINT,* uses radars to collect intelligence regarding the physical characteristics and capabilities of radar targets. RADINT targets have included satellites, missiles, ships, aircraft, and battlefield vehicles. RADINT can image the target, determine its radar cross-section, identify and discriminate among targets, precisely measure components, divine the motion of the target or its components, and measure the target's radar reflectance and absorption characteristics. Radar returns can be used to reconstruct the trajectories of missiles and convey the details and configuration of the missile reentry vehicle itself.

For several decades the United States and other countries have used high-resolution microwave radars for remote identification of targets. Such radars have particular advantages in aircraft or space object identification when compared with optical imaging devices. Microwave radars are able to operate through long atmospheric paths and in cloud or weather conditions that would render an optical system ineffective. Also, such radars offer a rich variety of waveforms and associated processing techniques, which can be used both to create images of and to observe operations of satellites and aircraft. Figure 6-3 shows a radar image of the Space Shuttle created using such techniques. The quality of radar imaging does not nearly match that of optical imaging. The image requires interpretation and an understanding of how satellites or aircraft are designed. The objects at the top and bottom of the image in Figure 6-3 are the wings, and the shuttle nose is at the left.

Figure 6-3   Radar Image of the Space Shuttle

Source: "A Sourcebook for the Use of the FGAN Tracking and Imaging Radar for Satellite Imaging," Federation of American Scientists Space Policy Project: Military Space Programs, December 18, 2008. *www.fas.org/spp/military/program/track/fgan.pdf.*

Geophysical and Nuclear Intelligence

Geophysical intelligence involves the collection, processing, and exploitation of environmental disturbances transmitted through the earth (ground, water, or atmosphere). Magnetic sensing can detect the presence or motion of vehicles and ships or submarines by the weak changes that they create in the earth's magnetic field. Magnetometers mounted on aircraft have been used to detect submerged submarines at short distances (on the order of a few hundred meters).

Unintentional emission or modulation of sound waves (acoustic energy) can provide the same types of intelligence information as those for radio frequency energy. This specialized area of unintentional emissions intelligence is called either *ACINT* (for underwater sound) or *ACOUSTINT* (sound in air). Acoustic energy collection works best in environments where sound carries well over long distances, as underwater sound does. The use of passive sonar to obtain the signatures of submarines is well known. The submarine's turbines, propellers, and other on-board machinery generate acoustic noise that can be detected and used for identification at ranges of many kilometers in water.

Closely related to acoustic intelligence is seismic intelligence, the measurement of seismic waves that travel through the earth as a result of a major disturbance, such as an underground or underwater explosion. If a number of appropriate in situ sensors are deployed around the globe, signal analysts can locate the source of such an explosion by comparing the times of the signal's arrival at each sensor.

All nuclear reactions result in the emission of particles and waves—gamma rays, X-rays, neutrons, electrons, or ions. The radiation is strongest from a surface or atmospheric nuclear detonation, but nuclear power reactors also emit. The strength and type of radiation allow one to characterize the emitter. A number of nuclear radiation detectors have been developed; some are capable of detecting concealed nuclear devices at substantial ranges, and some are quite small, the size of a shirt button.

Materiel and Materials Collection

Both materiel and materials collection rely heavily on HUMINT, because the acquisition is usually a clandestine effort that uses human sources. Although the two words sound much the same, they are different. The difference is in the nature of the substance or objects collected. Materials intelligence includes the collection and analysis of trace elements, particulates, effluents, and debris. Such materials are released into the atmosphere, water, or earth by a wide range of industrial processes. Materiel, in contrast, is a term used to describe equipment, apparatus, and supplies used by an organization or institution. Both materiel and materials collection have in common the need for extensive exploitation to produce useful intelligence.

Materials collection is important in making assessments of nuclear, chemical, and biological weaponry; factory production; and environmental problems. It has long been practiced in law enforcement, and one of its premier practitioners is fictional: Sherlock Holmes who, as he modestly admitted, could "distinguish at a glance the ash of any known brand either of cigar or of tobacco."[39]

Materiel acquisition has long been practiced in commercial intelligence. Throughout recorded history, manufacturers have acquired samples of a competitor's product for evaluation as part of planning sales tactics, to copy good ideas, or even for reverse engineering. The Hittites of Asia Minor were early targets of materiel acquisition efforts. Middle Easterners, at the time using bronze, acquired iron weaponry from the Hittites.[40] Many commercial firms (all automobile manufacturers, for example) purchase their competitors' new products for evaluation.

The Soviet intelligence services were very good at clandestine materiel acquisition. On one occasion they acquired a new IBM computer before it was officially on the market. The result must have been less than satisfactory for the Soviets, however, because none of the IBM sales or maintenance people they subsequently contacted knew how to make it work.

Materiel acquisition can also be done by special operations. One of the best known materiel acquisition efforts was the Bruneval raid of World War II.[41] In the fall of 1941, Dr. R. V. Jones, assistant director of Britain's Royal Air Force Intelligence Section, was zeroing in on a new German antiaircraft fire control radar that was believed to transmit on a frequency of 570 MHz. One of the more daring British reconnaissance pilots finally brought back a picture of a new radar located near Bruneval, France. The British quickly noted that the new radar was located less than two hundred yards from the coast. They settled on a commando raid to obtain detailed information about the radar and assembled a company of paratroops to make an airborne assault. A naval assault was too risky because of the high cliffs around Bruneval, but a light naval force was assembled to handle the commandos' evacuation. Jones, in the meantime, had identified the German radar by name—*Würzburg*—but he still could not confirm that the radar was the source of 570 MHz signals.

Jones specified in detail the parts he wanted his selected acquisition team—Royal Engineers and a radar mechanic—to bring back. They included the feed antenna for the radar dish, which would establish the operating frequency of the radar; and the receiver and display equipment, which would reveal whether any antijamming circuits existed. The transmitters would establish German technology for generating 570 MHz signals. Two radar operators were to be taken prisoner, if possible, so that they could be interrogated about the radar's operation. Finally, if equipment could not be removed, the labels and inspection stamps were to be taken, because they would provide valuable background information.

The raid, code-named Operation Biting, took place on the night of February 27, 1942. It was an unqualified success. The Bruneval force made off with the radar receiver, modulator, and transmitter, plus the feed element, which they sawed off the antenna. They brought back exactly what Jones had asked for, except that only one radar operator was captured.[42] With the knowledge gained from this raid the British were able to develop successful countermeasures to the Wüurzburg.

The Bruneval raid was a success because the British, like the Soviets during the cold war, knew exactly what they wanted. The acquisition team had an expert analyst intimately involved at every step. Most successes in materiel acquisition since that time have involved carefully focused teams closely tied to analytical expertise. Many failures have resulted when the acquirers, separated from the analysts, had no real idea what they were trying to get or why.

The most expensive single materiel acquisition effort may have been the *Glomar Explorer*'s effort to raise a sunken Soviet submarine. In April 1968 a Soviet Golf class submarine on patrol northwest of Hawaii exploded and sank in 17,000 feet of water, carrying all ninety men aboard down with it. Soviet salvage vessels were unable to locate the sunken craft, but the U.S. Navy pinpointed its location by using its more sophisticated search equipment. At that point the CIA entered the picture with a proposal to recover the submarine. That was the beginning of the project that reportedly was code-named Jennifer.

The CIA contracted with Howard Hughes's Summa Corporation to build a 620-foot-long deep-sea recovery vessel, equipped with huge derricks, and a companion barge to conceal the submarine when it was recovered. The *Glomar Explorer* was built under the cover of a deep-sea mining mission and was completed in 1973 at a cost of $200 million.

During July and August 1974 the *Glomar Explorer* located the submarine and began recovery operations. Cables were looped around the submarine, and winches began slowly pulling it up toward the barge. About halfway up, the hull broke apart, and two-thirds of the submarine fell back, to be lost on the bottom. The remaining third was recovered and yielded valuable intelligence, but the sought-after prizes—the code books and nuclear warheads—reportedly were lost.[43]

Although Project Jennifer did not totally succeed, it illustrates the combination that makes for collection success: innovating and doing the unexpected. U.S. intelligence collection's single biggest asset—and possibly its single biggest advantage over other collection services—is the innovativeness and unpredictability of Americans. In materiel acquisition, as in HUMINT generally, U.S. intelligence officers have tried things that other services are too unimaginative or too cautious to try, relying heavily on the U.S. edge in sophisticated technical collection. Of course, U.S. collection services also have taken more risks and consequently have gotten into more trouble than other services.

Biometrics

Biometrics is the use of a person's physical characteristics or personal traits for human recognition. Its current popularity belies its age. Morse code operators have long been able to recognize other operators by their characteristic patterns of keying the code, known as their *fist*. Digitized fingerprints and voiceprints have been used in human recognition for years, and their use is increasing. Iris and retinal scans, hand geometry, and keystroke dynamics are newer biometric technologies.

Today biometric facial recognition is probably the most rapidly growing area of biometrics. Facial recognition uses camera images, measuring distances and angles between points on the face—mouth extremities, nostrils, eye corners—to create a "faceprint" that can be recognized when a crowd of people is scanned. Biometric facial recognition currently is used to control access to facilities, to computers, to gaming casinos, and at border crossing points around the world.[44]

Summary

The traditional U.S. taxonomy of intelligence collection was created because of historical precedent or for bureaucratic reasons. It divides intelligence collection into open source, SIGINT, IMINT, HUMINT, and MASINT. This chapter presents an alternative view of the sources of intelligence, one that is more relevant for intelligence analysts. This alternative taxonomy divides sources by the nature of the intelligence produced into literal and nonliteral. Literal sources include open source, COMINT, HUMINT and cyber collection. Nonliteral sources involve several types of newer and very focused collection techniques that depend heavily on processing, exploitation, and interpretation to turn the material into usable intelligence.

In gathering information for synthesizing the target model, analysts start with the more readily available and inexpensive sources (internal files and open source material) and move to the more obscure and expensive ones (such as HUMINT, COMINT, and IMINT).

Open source material is perhaps the most valuable source of intelligence but is typically the most easily overlooked by government intelligence organizations in favor of classified information. Open source information has traditionally meant published material that is publicly available—newspapers, books, and magazines. Increasingly it includes the Internet and commercially available imagery sources.

HUMINT includes clandestine sources (the traditional spy) and liaison (the sharing of intelligence with other intelligence services or nongovernmental organizations). It also includes acquiring information from émigrés and defectors. Elicitation—the practice of obtaining information about a topic from conversations, preferably without the source knowing what is happening—is widely practiced in both governmental and commercial intelligence.

COMINT, or communications intelligence, is the interception, processing, and reporting of an opponent's communications. It includes bugs and the traditional microphone-and-wire, but also advanced technology, to collect voice, data, and facsimile communications.

Cyber collection is of two general types: network attacks, primarily conducted using the World Wide Web, and direct access attacks on computers or intranets, usually HUMINT-enabled. These attacks are conducted both by governments and by individuals or private entities. Both use techniques popularly known as "hacking" to obtain intelligence from computers and data networks.

Nonliteral intelligence collection relies heavily, though not exclusively, on remote sensing. The best known is imagery intelligence (IMINT), which includes short-range imagery—both still pictures and video—and remote sensing (from distances ranging from miles to thousands of miles). IMINT functions across the electromagnetic spectrum, producing radar, infrared, and visible spectrum images. Newer technology, such as multispectral and hyperspectral imaging, uses information about the spectral signature of a target to provide insights that are not available otherwise.

Electronic intelligence (ELINT) is the most widely used type of passive radiofrequency intelligence. It primarily supports the military and law enforcement. It divides broadly into operational ELINT, which is most common, and technical ELINT, used to assess radar performance. Telemetry collection, known as FISINT, is used to assess the performance of aircraft and missiles and the operational status of spacecraft. Active radiofrequency intelligence is called radar intelligence, or RADINT, and is used to obtain detailed signatures of aircraft and space vehicles.

For specialized intelligence requirements, a wide range of sophisticated technical collection techniques are available. They include geophysical intelligence (which involves sound, infrasound, and magnetic field sensing) and nuclear intelligence (which depends on sensing the emission of particles and electromagnetic energy from nuclear reactions). Materiel and materials collection (acquiring and exploiting equipment or material samples) is an old technique but still widely used. Modern forensic equipment allows valuable intelligence to be derived from minute samples of material. Finally, biometrics are used by intelligence, security, and law enforcement agencies, as well as private organizations such as casinos, for identifying individuals of interest.

We turn in the next chapter to how to evaluate the information that is gathered from these different sources and to fitting information into the target model, a discussion that will continue throughout the book.

Notes

1. *Report of the Commission on the Intelligence Capabilities of the United States Regarding Weapons of Mass Destruction*, March 31, 2005, www.wmd.gov/report/wmd_report.pdf, 400.
2. Rob Johnson, *Analytic Culture in the U.S. Intelligence Community* (Washington, D.C.: Center for the Study of Intelligence, Central Intelligence Agency, 2005), 22.
3. Michael Herman, *Intelligence Power in Peace and War* (Cambridge: Cambridge University Press, 1996), 82
4. The King James Bible, Numbers 13:17.
5. Johnson, *Analytic Culture,* 24.
6. *Report of the Commission,* 13.
7. Walter Laqueur, *The Uses and Limits of Intelligence* (Somerset, N.J.: Transaction Publishers, 1993), 43.
8. Susan B. Glasser, "Probing Galaxies of Data for Nuggets," *Washington Post,* November 25, 2005, A35.
9. Clarence Walker, "A Special Investigative Report: American Mafia Recruits Sicilian Mafia," August 2004, www.americanmafia.com.
10. Arthur Weiss, "How Far Can Primary Research Go?" *Competitive Intelligence Magazine,* November–December 2001, 18.
11. Ibid.
12. David S. Landes, *The Wealth and Poverty of Nations* (New York: W. W. Norton and Company, 1998), 276.
13. Ibid., 279.
14. Herman, *Intelligence Power in Peace and War,* 211.
15. Richard Eels and Peter Nehemkis, *Corporate Intelligence and Espionage* (Old Tappan, N.J.: Macmillan, 1984), 59; Charles D. Ameringer, *U.S. Foreign Intelligence* (Lanham, Md.: Lexington Books, 1990), 170.
16. *Report of the Commission,* 80.
17. Wilhelm Agrell, "Sweden and the Dilemmas of Neutral Intelligence Liaison," *Journal of Strategic Studies* (August 2006): 633–651.
18. Jennifer E. Sims, "Foreign Intelligence Liaison: Devils, Deals, and Details," *International Journal of Intelligence and Counter Intelligence* 19, issue 2 (Summer 2006): 195–217.
19. Ibid.
20. Peter Schwartz, *The Art of the Long View* (New York: Doubleday, 1991), 78.
21. Charlotte W. Craig, "Germany Drops Spy Case Against Lopez; Former GM Exec Must Give Money to Charity," *Detroit Free Press,* July 28, 1998, www.auto.com/industry/qlopez28.htm.
22. F. W. Winterbotham, *The Ultra Secret* (New York: Dell, 1974).
23. For more information, see Wilhelm Flicke, *War Secrets in the Ether* (Laguna Hills, Calif.: Aegean Park Press, 1994), 4–12.
24. Ibid.

25. Douglas H. Dearth and Thomas R. Goodden, *Strategic Intelligence: Theory and Application,* 2nd ed. (Washington, D.C.: U.S. Army War College and Defense Intelligence Agency, 1995), 111.
26. John Wingfield, *Bugging* (London: Robert Hale Ltd., 1984), 21–22.
27. Ibid., 52–53.
28. Duncan Campbell, "Interception Capabilities 2000," Report to the Director General for Research of the European Parliament, April 1999, www.fas.org/irp/eprint/ic2000/ic2000.htm.
29. Matthew M. Aid, "In the Right Place at the Right Time: US Signals Intelligence Relations with Scandinavia, 1945–1960," *Journal of Strategic Studies* 29, issue 4 (August 2006): 575–605.
30. Kevin G. Coleman, "Cyber Espionage Targets Sensitive Data", December 29, 2008, http://sip-trunking.tmcnet.com/topics/security/articles/47927-cyber-espionage-targets-sensitive-data.htm
31. Quoted in Kevin D. Mitnick and William L. Simon, *The Art of Intrusion* (Indianapolis: Wiley Publishing, 2005), 115.
32. Ibid., 43.
33. Ibid.
34. Ibid., 62.
35. John McAfee and Colin Haynes, *Computer Viruses, Worms, Data Diddlers, Killer Programs, and Other Threats to Your System* (New York: St. Martin's Press, 1989), 79.
36. Clifford Stoll, *The Cuckoo's Egg: Tracking a Spy Through the Maze of Computer Espionage* (New York: Simon and Schuster, 1989).
37. *Association of Foreign Intelligence Officers (AFIO) Weekly Intelligence Note 36-02,* September 9, 2002; available from the association by contacting afio@afio.com.
38. Mitnick and Simon, *Art of Intrusion,* chap. 10.
39. Sir Arthur Conan Doyle, "A Study in Scarlet," in *The Complete Sherlock Holmes* (London: Hamlyn, 1984), 26.
40. University of California at Davis, Department of Geology, "The Age of Iron," March 22, 2003, www.geology.ucdavis.edu/~GEL115/115CH5.html.
41. The full details of this real-life spy thriller can be found in Alfred Price's book *Instruments of Darkness* (London: William Kimber, 1967), 80–87.
42. Ibid.
43. "Project Jennifer," March 22, 2003, http://web.ukonline.co.uk/aj.cashmore/.features/articles/jennifer-text.html.
44. John D. Woodward Jr., "Super Bowl Surveillance: Facing Up to Biometrics," *Intelligencer: Journal of U.S. Intelligence Studies* (Summer 2001): 37.

7

Evaluating and Collating Data

What is truth?

Pontius Pilate

Most synthesis involves aggregating data or establishing data relationships in the target model by using the data sources discussed in the previous chapter. This step in the intelligence process is often called *collation:* the organizing of relevant information in a coherent way, looking at source and context. It involves evaluating the information for relevance, credibility, and inferential force and incorporating it into the target model.

The collation concept introduced here is further developed in succeeding chapters. The process normally starts with a model template, or template set, of the sort described in chapter 5. Next, the job is to fit the relevant information into the templates. We talk about templates in the plural because we wind up with several of them when dealing with complex problems—both collateral models, as discussed in chapter 3, and alternative models. As David Schum has noted, "The generation of new ideas in fact investigation usually rests upon arranging or juxtaposing our thoughts and evidence in different ways." [1] To do that we need multiple, alternative models.

This chapter describes how to establish the credentials of evidence. It continues with a discussion of widely used informal methods of combining evidence, followed by an introduction to structured argumentation methods (Wigmore's evidence charting and Bayesian analysis). A number of other structured argumentation methods are used in prediction: Scenario creation is covered in chapter 10; chapter 11 discusses influence nets and influence diagrams.

Evaluating Evidence

The fundamental problem in weighing evidence is determining its credibility. In the end, weighing evidence involves subjective judgments that the analyst alone must make. (Some helpful insights on reliability are contained in the preceding chapter—see the sections on COMINT and HUMINT for some analytical pitfalls.)

Weighing evidence entails three steps: (a) evaluating the source, (b) evaluating the communications channel through which the information arrived, and (c) evaluating the evidence itself. The communications channel is often ignored, but it is a critical piece of the reliability puzzle, as we shall see.

At the heart of the evaluation process is one of the oldest analytic principles, Occam's razor. The name comes from William of Occam, who said, "It is vain to do with more what can be done with fewer."[2] In modern-day English, we know this as the KISS principle: Keep it simple, stupid! Possibly the most common example of Occam's razor is the standard first step one is advised to take when a piece of electronic equipment doesn't work: Check to see if it is plugged in. Occam's razor is not an infallible principle; sometimes the correct explanation for a set of facts is very complex or convoluted. Conventional wisdom is often wrong. And counterintelligence, especially denial and deception, is a possibility that the sciences do not have to contend with. However, analysts can make data fit almost any desired conclusion, especially if they selectively discard inconvenient facts. So the razor is a valuable part of the analyst's toolkit (Analysis Principle 7-1).

Analysis Principle 7-1 ●————————————————————————

Occam's Razor

Explain your observations with the fewest possible hypotheses. In other words, choose the simplest explanation that fits the facts at hand.

Evaluating the Source

Accept nothing at face value. Evaluate the source of evidence carefully, and beware of the source's motives for providing the information. Evaluating the source involves answering three questions:

- Is the source competent (knowledgeable about the information being given)?
- Did the source have the access needed to get the information?
- Does the source have a vested interest or bias?

In the HUMINT business, this is called determining *bona fides* for human sources. Even when not dealing with HUMINT, one must ask these same three questions.

Competence. The Anglo-American judicial system deals effectively with competence: It allows people to describe what they observed with their senses because, absent disability, we are presumed competent to sense things. The judicial system does not allow the average person to interpret what he or she sensed, unless the person can be qualified as an expert in such interpretation.

Source evaluators must apply the same criteria. It is easy, in a raw intelligence report, to accept not only the source's observations but also the inferences that the source has drawn. Always ask, What was the basis for this conclusion? If no satisfactory answer is forthcoming, use the source's conclusions with caution or not at all.

A radar expert talking about an airborne intercept radar's performance is credible. If he goes on to describe the aircraft's performance, he is considerably less credible. An economist assessing inflation prospects in a country might have credibility, but if she goes on to assess the likely political impact of the inflation, one should be skeptical.

Access. Usually, source access does not come up, or is not an issue, because it is assumed that the source had access. Where there is reason to be suspicious about the source, however, check whether the source might not have had the claimed access.

In the legal world, checks on source access come up regularly in witness cross-examinations. One of the most famous examples was the so-called Almanac Trial of 1858, in which Abraham Lincoln conducted the cross-examination. It was the dying wish of an old friend that Lincoln represent his friend's son, Duff Armstrong, who was on trial for murder. Lincoln gave his client a tough, artful, and ultimately successful defense. In the trial's highlight, Lincoln consulted an almanac to discredit a prosecution witness who had claimed that he saw the murder clearly because the moon was high in the sky. The almanac showed that the moon was lower on the horizon, and the witness's access—that is, his ability to see the murder—was called into question.[3]

Access can be critical in evaluating a source. When CIA analysts prepared the National Intelligence Estimate concerning possible Iraqi weapons of mass destruction, they believed that the now-infamous source Curveball was reliable because his knowledge was detailed, technically accurate, and corroborated by another source's reporting. But, as a CIA group chief pointed out, the corroborating information simply established that Curveball had been to a given location, not that he had any knowledge of biological warfare activities being conducted there.[4]

Vested Interest or Bias. In HUMINT, analysts occasionally encounter the "professional source," who sells information to as many bidders as possible and has an incentive to make the information as interesting as possible. Even the densest sources will quickly realize that more interesting information gets them more money.

Official reports from government organizations have a similar vested interest problem. Be skeptical of this information; it deserves no automatic credibility because of the source. One seldom finds outright lies in such reports, but government officials occasionally distort or conceal facts to support their policy positions or to protect their personal interests. U.S. researchers have long provided U.S. government intelligence organizations with distorted information about their foreign contacts. The usual approach is to exaggerate the importance of their foreign counterparts' work, as a ploy to encourage more funding for their own work. A report does not necessarily have more validity simply because it came from a citizen of one's own country rather than from a foreigner. Vested interest and bias are also common problems for analysts who are dealing with experts when applying comparative modeling and benchmarking techniques (chapters 5 and 14).

When comparing systems or technologies, it is usual to compare system or technology performance, as measured in one's own test and evaluation programs, with estimates or data on the performance of the target's system. In assessing systems that use advanced technologies, test and evaluation results are especially important because many techniques work in theory but not in practice.

However, an intelligence organization faces a problem in using its own parent organization's (or country's) test and evaluation results because many of them have been contaminated. Some of the tests are faked; some contain distortions or omit key points. An honestly conducted, objective test may be a rarity. Several reasons for this problem exist: Tests are sometimes conducted to prove or disprove a preconceived notion and are thus unconsciously slanted. Some tests are faked because otherwise they would show the vulnerability or ineffectiveness of a system and because procurement decisions often depend on the test outcomes.

Although the majority of contaminated cases probably are never discovered, history provides many examples of this problem. Chapter 12 discusses the story of William Sims's continuous aim naval gunnery system, wherein the U.S. Navy tested a proposed new technique for naval gunnery. The test was designed to confirm the preconceived notion that the technique would not work, not to test a concept. During World War II both the British and the Germans conducted tests that were rigged to prove a point.[5] Another example of the problem is an electronics warfare test conducted a few years ago at one of the U.S. military test ranges. An airborne jammer was not performing as expected against a particular target-tracking radar. Investigation revealed that the radar had in fact been jammed, but the radar site personnel had tracked the jammer aircraft by using a second radar that was not supposed to be part of the test.

In addition to recognizing that your own organization's (or country's) test results may be contaminated, you also must deal with the parallel problem that the target organization may have distorted or faked its tests for the same reasons. It is unwise to rely on test reports alone; it may be necessary to monitor the tests as well. In examining any test or evaluation results, begin by asking two questions:

- Did the testing organization have a major stake in the outcome (such as the threat that a program would be canceled in the event of negative test results or the expectation that it would profit from positive results)?

- Did the *reported* outcome support the organization's position or interests?

If the answer to both questions is yes, be wary of accepting the test as valid. In the pharmaceutical testing industry, for example, tests have been fraudulently conducted or the results skewed to support the regulatory approval of the pharmaceutical.[6] The results could similarly be distorted in other industries.

A very different type of bias can occur when collection is focused on a particular issue. This bias comes from the fact that when you look for something in the intelligence business, you may find what you are looking for, whether or not it's there. In looking at suspected Iraqi chemical facilities prior to 2003, analysts concluded from imagery reporting that the level of activity had increased at the facilities. But the appearance of an increase in activity may have been a result of an increase in imagery collection.[7]

This section presents a top-level view of source credibility. David Schum and Jon Morris have published a detailed treatise on human sources of intelligence analysis.[8] They pose a set of twenty-five questions divided into four categories: source competence, veracity, objectivity, and observational sensitivity. Their questions cover in more explicit detail the three questions posed in this section about competence, access, and vested interest.

Evaluating the Communications Channel

A second basic rule of weighing evidence is to look at the communications channel through which the evidence arrives. In a large intelligence system, collection requirements must move through a bureaucracy to a requirements officer, from there to a country desk, a field requirements officer, a SIGINT collector or a HUMINT case officer (for instance), then to an agent; and the response then goes back through the reports chain. The message never gets through undistorted, and it is a wonder that it ever gets through at all. This distortion of the message is expressed in physics as the second law of thermodynamics (Analysis Principle 7-2). The law has been modified for the intelligence

---

Analysis Principle 7-2 ●————————————————————

The Second Law of Thermodynamics

The Second Law of Thermodynamics can be stated in several ways. Two of the simplest ways (they are equivalent) are,

—No physical process is perfectly reversible. There is no such thing as perpetual motion.

—Entropy always increases with time. This could also be stated as, The degree of randomness always increases in a physical system.

field: The accuracy of a message through any communications system decreases with the length of the link or the number of intermediate nodes.

The same principle applies in communications engineering; Claude Shannon described it in his communications theory exposition.[9] Just as heat always flows so that entropy (chaos, randomness) increases, so on a digital communications line the originally crisp pulses will gradually lose their shape over distance and disappear into the noise, as illustrated in Figure 7-1.

As is the case with an electronic communications channel that is analyzed by applying Shannon's communications theory, some nodes in the intelligence communications channel contribute more "noise" than others. A communications pulse traveling down a noisy or distorted channel loses its shape and finally disappears in noise. The signal disappears completely or emerges as the wrong signal.

The same communications problem occurs in organizations. Large and complex systems tend to have more entropy. The result is often described as "poor communication" problems in large organizations, and the effects can be observed in the large project curve discussed in chapter 13. Over a long chain of human communication, the equivalent of the process depicted in Figure 7-1 is that the original message eventually becomes little more than rumor.

In the business intelligence world, analysts recognize the importance of the communications channel by using the differentiating terms *primary sources,* for firsthand information, acquired through discussions or other interaction directly with a human source, and *secondary sources,* for information learned through an intermediary, a publication, or online. This division downplays the many gradations of reliability, and national intelligence organizations commonly do not use the primary/secondary source division. Some national intelligence collection organizations use the term *collateral* to refer to intelligence gained from other collectors, but it does not have the same meaning as the terms *primary* and *secondary* as used in business intelligence.

But neither the primary-versus-secondary distinction nor the collateral-evidence distinction serves a useful purpose; it is more important to look at the communications channel itself. Ask about the channel, What was it? Is this information being intentionally provided? If so, what part of it is true? Is it

Figure 7-1   Effect of Entropy on the Communications Channel

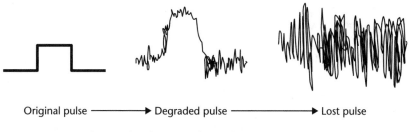

Original pulse ⟶ Degraded pulse ⟶ Lost pulse

Entropy (randomness, chaos) always increases.

deception, or is it a message or signal to the opponent? If it is a message or signal, what is the message, and what is the reason for it?

The hearsay rule as applied in judicial proceedings is a recognition of the application of Shannon's theory and of entropy in human affairs. Under the hearsay rule, a witness cannot testify about what a person said to prove the truth of what was said; in the court's view, the message has traveled through too many intermediate nodes to be credible. Entropy has an effect on the credibility of some intelligence, and credibility degrades in direct proportion to the number of nodes traversed.

Entropy has another effect in intelligence. An intelligence assertion that "*X* is a possibility" very often, over time and through diverse communications channels, becomes "*X* may be true," then "*X* probably is the case," and eventually "*X* is a fact," without a shred of new evidence to support the assertion. In intelligence, we refer to this as the "creeping validity" problem. The Iraqi WMD Commission noted this as a major analytical failing; the premise that Iraq had hidden weapons of mass destruction became, over time, a presumption and eventually an unrebuttable conclusion.[10]

Earlier we discussed bias in the source. Bias can also be a problem in the communications channel as well. Years back, one U.S. intelligence organization had the good fortune to obtain an audio tap into a highly classified foreign installation. The problem with the tap was that the audio was very weak and not in English. One could barely discern that it was speech. One translator with very sharp ears was able to produce transcripts, however, and the product was some exciting and very disturbing intelligence; several reports went to top levels of the U.S. government.

The transcribed material was very good—too good, in fact, and technically inconsistent. An investigation revealed that the translator wasn't translating; he was making it all up out of a fertile imagination and some knowledge of what was of current intelligence interest. The reports were withdrawn and the translator fired. On withdrawing them, we learned another basic rule of intelligence: The surest way to get a customer to read a report is to retract it.

Two lessons emerge from this example: First, if the source or a person in the communications channel has something to gain by providing interesting material, be wary. In this case the translator earned recognition and a promotion. Second, intelligence that sparks interest is more likely to be used. In this case the lesson comes from the customers, who cited the reports for years because they were so interesting and provocative. When the customers were told that the reports were not valid, their response was typically, "Well, they should be!"

Evaluating the Credentials of Evidence

The major credentials of evidence, as noted earlier, are credibility, reliability, and inferential force. *Credibility* refers to the extent to which we can believe something. *Reliability* means consistency or replicability. *Inferential force* means that the evidence carries weight, or has value, in supporting a conclusion. The credibility of tangible evidence depends on its authenticity, accuracy, and reliability. The credibility of testimonial evidence depends on the veracity, objectivity (and memory), and observational sensitivity of the testifier.[11]

U.S. government intelligence organizations have come up with a set of definitions to distinguish levels of credibility of intelligence:

- *Fact.* Verified information, something known to exist or to have happened.

- *Information.* The content of reports, research, and reflection on an intelligence issue that helps one evaluate the likelihood that something is factual and thereby reduces uncertainty.

- *Direct Information.* Information that can be considered factual because of the nature of the source (imagery, intercepts, observations).

- *Indirect Information.* Information that may or may not be factual because of some doubt about the source's reliability, the source's lack of direct access, or the complex (nonconcrete) character of the content (hearsay from clandestine sources, foreign government reports, or local media accounts).[12]

This division sounds suspiciously like the primary and secondary source division used in business intelligence. It downplays the real-world situation: that intelligence has a continuum of credibility and that direct information such as signal intercepts or imagery can be misleading or false as a result of denial and deception.

In weighing evidence, the usual approach is to ask the three questions that are embedded in the oath that witnesses take before giving testimony in U.S. courts:

- Is it true?
- Is it the whole truth?
- Is it nothing but the truth? (Is it relevant or significant?)

Is It True? Is the evidence fact or opinion (someone else's analysis)? If it is opinion, question its validity unless the source quotes evidence to support it.

How does it fit with other evidence? The relating of evidence—how it fits in—is best done in the synthesis phase. The data from different collection sources are most valuable when used together. The synergistic effect of combining data from many sources both strengthens the conclusions and increases the analyst's confidence in them.

- HUMINT and COMINT data can be combined with ELINT data to yield a more complete picture of a radar.

- HUMINT and open source are often melded together to give a more comprehensive picture of people, programs, products, facilities, and research specialties. This is excellent background information to interpret data derived from COMINT and IMINT.

- Data on environmental conditions during tests, collected by using specialized technical collection, can be used with ELINT and COMINT data obtained during the same test event to evaluate the capabilities of active sensor systems.

- Identification of research institutes and their key scientists and researchers can be made initially through HUMINT, COMINT, or open sources. Once the organization or individual has been identified by one INT, the other ones can usually provide extensive additional information.

- Successful analysis of COMINT data may require correlating raw COMINT data with external information, such as ELINT and IMINT, or with knowledge of operational or technical practices.

One of the best examples of synthesis comes from the extensive efforts U.S. intelligence made during the 1960s through the 1980s to assess the performance of Soviet ballistic missiles. Satellite photography was compared with telemetry to check hypotheses about the weight and size of missiles. Photographs of missiles on a launch pad could be used to alert telemetry collectors. Radar tracking of the boost phase could be cross-checked with telemetry to determine booster performance, and the same cross-checks on reentry vehicles could be used to estimate reentry vehicle size and weight more confidently.[13]

Is It the Whole Truth? Answering this question requires source analysis. In HUMINT, that means looking at such things as the source's reporting history or psychological profile. (Is the source loose-lipped? A conniver? Or a straight shooter?) We all have ad hoc profiles of the people we deal with, based on such things as first impressions or reputation. Sometimes we need more— a psychological profile, for example.

An incomplete picture can mislead as much as an outright lie. During the cold war, Soviet missile guidance and control experts regularly visited their counterparts in the United States to do some informal elicitation. Alerted to yet another impending Soviet visit, U.S. intelligence—working with a leading U.S. expert—set up an elaborate display of a new and highly accurate missile guidance system in the expert's office. The Soviet visitors were impressed with the new technology, and the entire visit centered on the details of the guidance system and how it was manufactured. What the U.S. expert did not mention was that for the system to work some components had to be machined to a precision that was beyond either U.S. or Soviet capabilities. It was a failed design, but the problem would not become apparent until (as we heard later) the Soviets had spent many months and much money trying to replicate it. The U.S. expert told no lies—he simply omitted a critical truth.

Is It Nothing but the Truth? It is worthwhile at this point to distinguish between data and evidence. Data become evidence only when the data are relevant to the problem or issue at hand. The simple test of relevance is whether the material affects the likelihood of a hypothesis about the target. Does it help answer a question that has been asked? Or does it help answer a question that *should* be asked? Customers seldom impart in their preliminary or initial guidance what they really need to know—another reason to keep them in the loop through the target-centric process.

Medical doctors often encounter the relevance problem. They must synthesize evidence (symptoms and test results) to make a diagnosis: a model of the patient's present state. Doctors encounter serious difficulties when they must deal with a patient who has two pathologies simultaneously. Some of the symptoms are relevant to one pathology; some to the other. If the doctor tries to fit all of the symptoms into one diagnosis, she is apt to make the wrong call. This is a severe problem for doctors, who must deal with only a few symptoms. It is a much worse problem for intelligence analysts, who typically deal with a large volume of data, most of which is irrelevant.

As a simple example of the relevance problem, suppose that port authorities in Naples, Italy, discover a cache of arms and explosive devices in a cargo container on the docks. COMINT reporting later indicates that six members of a known terrorist group had met in a Naples harbor café on the day that the illicit cargo was discovered. An analyst might be inclined to put the two facts together in the same target model of a planned terrorist act. But the two facts could be completely unrelated.

The converse problem in fitting evidence into the model is the risk of discarding relevant evidence. Avoid discarding evidence simply because it does not seem to fit the model. Anomalies may indicate that something is wrong with the model or that another model is more appropriate. Alternatively, as with the two-pathologies problem, the evidence should be partitioned and fit into two distinct models.

Pitfalls in Evaluating Evidence

There are at least seven pitfalls to avoid in weighing evidence.

Vividness Weighting. In general, the channel for communication of intelligence should be as short as possible; but when could a short channel become a problem? If the channel is too short, the result is *vividness weighting*—the phenomenon that evidence that is experienced directly is the most convincing ("Seeing is believing"). Customers place the most weight on evidence that they collect themselves—a dangerous pitfall that senior executives fall into repeatedly and that makes them vulnerable to deception. Strong and dynamic leaders are particularly vulnerable: Franklin Roosevelt, Winston Churchill, and Henry Kissinger are examples of statesmen who occasionally did their own collection and analysis, sometimes with unfortunate results. Michael Herman tells how Churchill, reading Field Marshal Erwin Rommel's decrypted cables during World War II, concluded that the Germans were desperately short of supplies in North Africa. Basing his interpretation on this raw COMINT traffic, Churchill pressed his generals to take the offensive against Rommel. Churchill did not realize what his own intelligence analysts could have readily told him: Rommel consistently exaggerated his shortages in order to bolster his demands for supplies and reinforcements.[14]

There is danger in judging any evidence by its presentation, yet we continue to do so. Statistics are the least persuasive form of evidence; abstract (general) text is next; concrete (specific, focused, exemplary) text is a more persuasive form; and visual evidence, such as imagery or video, is the most persuasive. Of course, vividness can work for the analyst. She can use the persuasive force of certain types of evidence to make the presentation of her conclusions more effective.

An example of the powerful impact that vivid evidence can have is the murder of *Wall Street Journal* reporter Daniel Pearl in Pakistan in February 2002. The videotape of the murder and decapitation of Pearl evoked strong public reaction. Sometimes decision makers can be unduly affected by such vivid evidence.

Weighting Based on the Source. One of the most difficult traps for an analyst to avoid is that of weighing evidence based on its source. HUMINT operatives repeatedly value information gained from clandestine sources—the classic spy—above that from refugees, émigrés, and defectors. COMINT gained from an expensive emplaced telephone tap is valued (and classified) above that gleaned from high-frequency radio communications (which almost anyone can monitor). The most common pitfall, however, is to downplay the significance of open source material; being the most readily available, it is deemed to be the least valuable. Using open sources well is a demanding analytic skill, but it can pay high dividends to those who have the patience to master it. Collectors may make the mistake of equating source with importance. Having spent a sizable portion of their organization's budget in collecting a body of material, they may believe that its value can be measured by the cost of collecting it. No competent analyst should ever make such a mistake.

Favoring the Most Recent Evidence. Analysts often give the most recently acquired evidence the most weight. The danger of doing that is implied by our application of the second law of thermodynamics to intelligence, discussed earlier. As the representation in Figure 7-1 suggests, the value of information or the weight given to it in a report tends to decrease with time. The freshest intelligence—crisp, clear, and the focus of the analyst's attention—often gets more weight than the fuzzy and half-remembered (but possibly more important) information that has had to travel down the long telephone lines of time. The analyst has to remember this tendency and compensate for it. It sometimes helps to go back to the original (older) intelligence and reread it to bring it more freshly to mind.

Favoring or Disfavoring the Unknown. Most analysts find it hard to decide how much weight to give to answers when little or no information is available for or against each one. Some analysts give an answer too much weight when evidence is absent; some give it too little. Former CIA analyst Richards J. Heuer Jr. cites this "absence of evidence" problem in the example of two groups of automobile mechanics who were given a choice of reasons why a car would not start, with the last choice on the list being "other." The mechanics were told to estimate what percentage of failures was attributable to each reason. One group received a shortened list that omitted several of the reasons. That group tended to overweight the remaining reasons on the list and underweight the category "other." [15]

Trusting Hearsay. The chief problem with HUMINT is that it is hearsay evidence. As noted earlier, the courts long ago learned to distrust hearsay for good reasons, including the biases of the source and the collector. Sources may deliberately distort or misinform because they want to influence policy or increase their value to the collector. Moreover, the analyst lacks the non-verbal details of the conversation—the setting, the context, facial and body expressions—to aid judgment. The hearsay problem had severe consequences in the case of Curveball's reporting on Iraqi BW programs that was discussed earlier in this chapter. If U.S. analysts had been able to observe Curveball's demeanor during interrogation, they would have reached quite different conclusions about the validity of his reporting.

COMINT, like HUMINT, is hearsay, for two reasons: First, much interpretation goes into a COMINT report, and the COMINT analyst who translates and interprets the conversation may not do so objectively. COMINT analysts, like HUMINT sources, know that exciting or provocative reports are more likely to be published than mundane ones. Second, some COMINT targets know that they are being monitored and deliberately use the collector as a conduit for information. Intelligence analysts have to use hearsay, but they must weigh it accordingly.

Unquestioning Reliance on Expert Opinions. Expert opinion is often used as a tool for analyzing data and making estimates. Any intelligence community must often rely on its nation's leading scientists, economists, and political and social scientists for insights into foreign developments. These experts can and do make valuable contributions, and calls have been made to increase the U.S. intelligence community's use of outside experts. [16] But outside experts often have problems in being objective. With experts, an analyst gets not only their expertise but also their biases—the axes the experts have to grind and the ego that convinces them that there is only one right way to do things (their way). British counterintelligence officer Peter Wright once observed, "On the big issues, the experts are very rarely right." [17] The fallibility of experts has been noted in many cases. They can be useful in pointing out flaws in logic, and their understanding of political, social, and economic situations in other countries often is superior to that of their intelligence community counterparts. But studies have found that experts are no better than simple statistical models at making predictions.[18]

Both analysts and HUMINT collectors have a long history of dealing with experts, especially scientists, who inflate reports on foreign developments to further their own research work. More than a few scientific experts consulted by intelligence organizations have been guilty of report inflation at one time or another. When experts are used as evaluators, the same problem can arise. Analysts should treat expert opinion as HUMINT and be wary when the expert makes extremely positive comments ("That foreign development is a stroke of genius!") or extremely negative ones ("It can't be done").

The negative comments frequently stem from what former British intelligence officer R. V. Jones, whom we met in chapter 6, described as "principles of impotence." An expert will find it more reassuring to decide that something is impossible than to conclude that it is possible but he or she failed to accomplish it. Having made such a judgment, an expert will always defend it vigorously, for the same reasons that intelligence analysts find it difficult to change their conclusions, once made (Analysis Principle 7-3).

Analysis Principle 7-3 ●───────────────────────────

Principles of Impotence

Fundamental limits are well known and valid in physics: It is generally accepted that one can neither travel faster than the speed of light nor reduce the temperature of an object to absolute zero. R. V. Jones described such postulates as "principles of impotence" and pointed out that they pose a special danger for scientific experts. Having tried an experiment or development and failed, the expert is strongly tempted to invoke a principle of impotence and say, "It can't be done."

Jones encountered several examples of principles of impotence during his tenure, such as, "It is impossible to make a bulletproof fuel tank"; "Radio waves cannot be generated in the centimeter band (above 3,000 MHz)"; and "Photoconductive materials cannot be made to detect wavelengths longer than two microns."[19] All of these "impossibilities" later became realities.

During 1943 to 1944, aerial photography of the German rocket test center at Peenemunde revealed the existence of a rocket about forty-five feet long and six feet in diameter. As was the case with many other interesting analytic problems of World War II, this one fell to R. V. Jones to puzzle through.

British experts of the time were familiar only with rockets that burned cordite in a steel case. A simple calculation showed that a cordite-burning rocket of that size would weigh approximately eighty tons and would have to have a warhead weighing on the order of ten tons to be worthwhile. To the

British cabinet, the prospect of rockets as heavy as railroad locomotives, carrying ten tons of high explosives and landing on London was appalling.

In June 1944 a V-2 rocket crashed in Sweden, and British intelligence officers had an opportunity to examine the fragments. They reported that two liquids fueled the rocket, one of them liquid oxygen. Armed with this evidence, Jones was able to sort through the volumes of conflicting HUMINT reports about the German rocket and to select the five reports that mentioned liquid oxygen. All five were consistent in attributing light weights to the rocket and warhead. Jones subsequently and correctly reported to the British war cabinet—over the objections of British rocket experts—that the V-2 weighed twelve tons and carried a one-ton warhead.[20]

Although experts have frequently led us astray, their contribution has on the whole been positive. Some say that experts are harder to deceive. In the words of one author, "It is hard for one specialist to deceive another for very long."[21] By this view, deception can be beaten more easily with expert help. Maybe. On the other hand, many experts, particularly scientists, are not mentally prepared to look for deception, as intelligence officers should be. Some are naïve—even gullible. A second problem, as in the examples of the "principles of impotence," is that experts often are quite able to deceive themselves without any help from opponents.

Varying the way expert opinion is used is one way to attempt to head off the problems cited above. Using a panel of experts to make analytical judgments is a common method of trying to reach conclusions or to sort through a complex array of interdisciplinary data. Yet such panels have achieved mixed results at best. A former CIA office director has observed that "advisory panels of eminent scientists are usually useless. The members are seldom willing to commit the time to studying the data to be of much help."[22] The quality of the conclusions such panels reach depends on several variables, including the panel's

- expertise,
- motivation to produce a quality product,
- understanding of the problem area to be addressed, and
- effectiveness in working as a group.

A major advantage of the target-centric approach is that it formalizes the process of obtaining expert opinions. It also lends itself readily to techniques, such as the Delphi method, for avoiding negative group dynamics. Delphi is a systematic version of the panel consensus designed to eliminate some of the traditional panel shortcomings. It uses anonymous inputs to help obtain an objective consensus from initially divergent expert opinion. One objective of the Delphi method is the encouragement, rather than the suppression, of conflicting or divergent opinions—specifically, the development of alternative target models. Participants explain their views, and others review the explanations absent the personality, status, and debating skills that are brought to bear in conferences. The Delphi method arrives at a consensus by pooling the two separate items involved in any estimate:

- expert information or knowledge
- good judgment, analysis, and reasoning

Although a Delphi participant may not initially be well informed on a given question, that person still can contribute judgment, analysis, and reasoning concerning the information and arguments that other respondents advance.

When panels are used, several other techniques are available to make the panel input more effective. In general, the techniques apply whenever collaborative analysis is used, as it inevitably will be if the target-centric approach is applied.

If the analysis is a group effort and qualitative, a method for combining the various opinions must be determined in advance and approved by the participants. The analysis may be as simple as creating a list of all the participants' comments, or as difficult as reducing variance among opinions to the point that one combined opinion can be generated. If the analysis is quantitative, it has to be decided whether all the participants' votes will be averaged or whether the group will be asked to come to consensus.

In determining a voting method, consider the level of expertise of each voter. Often, analyses include persons from different organizations with varying viewpoints and levels of expertise. But it is rarely feasible politically to accord greater weight to those voters who are better informed. Instead, seek consensus among voters. In this process, each person's vote is posted before the group. All votes are then viewed to determine a median or mode. If there appears to be great dispersion among the votes, a mediator intervenes and asks the voters on opposing ends to explain their positions to each other. In many cases a disparity in knowledge is the cause of the polarized opinions.

Premature Closure and Philosophical Predisposition. In the introduction, we discussed the failures caused by premature closure. Premature closure violates several tenets of good problem-solving procedures, in particular the tenet of postponing evaluation and judgment until all relevant data are available. Both single-source and all-source analysts fall into the trap of reaching conclusions prematurely. ELINT, COMINT, and IMINT analysts too often focus on one explanation for an intercept or an image and exclude the others.

Premature closure has also been described as "affirming conclusions." This description is based on the observation that people are inclined to verify or affirm their existing beliefs rather than to modify or discredit those beliefs. It has also been observed that "once the Intelligence Community becomes entrenched in its chosen frame, its conclusions are destined to be uncritically confirmed."[23] This outcome has been repeatedly demonstrated in practice.

The primary danger of premature closure is not that one might make a bad assessment because the evidence is incomplete. Rather, the greater danger is that when a situation is changing quickly or when a major, unprecedented event occurs, the analyst will become trapped by the judgments already made. Chances increase that he or she will miss indications of change, and it becomes harder to revise an initial estimate, as intelligence analysts found during the Cuban missile crisis.

Few intelligence successes make headlines. Failures make headlines. One exception was the Cuban missile crisis, in which U.S intelligence services obtained information and made assessments that helped policymakers act in time to make a difference. The assessments would have been made sooner, except for the difficulty of changing a conclusion once reached and the tendency that existed to ignore the Cuban refugees who "cried wolf" too often.

For some time before 1962, Cuban refugees had flooded Western intelligence services, embassies, and newspapers with reports of missiles being hidden in Cuba. When the reports about the deployment of medium-range ballistic missiles began to sift into the CIA and the Defense Intelligence Agency in 1962, they were by and large disregarded—intelligence analysts had heard false reports too many times. Only as the weight of evidence from several independent sources, including photographic evidence and ship movement patterns, began to grow was it possible to change the collective mind of the intelligence community.[24]

The way the Cuban missile crisis unfolded illustrates the problem that Princeton University professor Klaus Knorr described as "philosophical predisposition," meaning a situation in which expectations fail to apply to the facts.[25] Before 1962 the Soviets had never deployed nuclear weapons outside their direct control, and U.S. analysts assumed that they therefore would not deploy nuclear warhead-equipped missiles in Cuba. They discounted information that contradicted this assumption. The counterintelligence technique of deception thrives on this tendency to ignore evidence that would disprove an existing assumption (a subject to which we will return in chapter 9). Furthermore, once an intelligence agency makes a firm estimate, it has a propensity in future estimates to ignore or explain away conflicting information. Denial and deception succeed if one opponent can get the other to make a wrong initial estimate.

The Iraqi WMD Commission identified what it described as a "textbook example" of premature closure. Iraq was attempting to acquire aluminum tubes for its Medusa rocket, and a CIA officer suggested that the CIA try to learn the precise rocket dimensions, so as to determine if the tubes were in fact intended for the rockets. The CIA rejected the request because analysts had already concluded that Iraq was acquiring the tubes for gas centrifuges to support its nuclear weapons program.[26]

Fortunately, there are several problem-solving approaches that help to prevent premature closure and overcome the bias of philosophical predisposition in the sifting of data. We will return to this point in the discussion of alternative models later in this chapter. Understanding the ways to combine different types of evidence also helps.

Combining Evidence

To draw conclusions from evidence, an analyst must weigh the evidence in some way and then make a judgment as to what conclusions the evidence supports and to what extent. In most cases, and for most analysts, this is a qualitative judgment that involves combining disparate types of evidence.

Convergent and Divergent Evidence

Two items of evidence are said to be conflicting or divergent if one item favors one conclusion and the other favors a different conclusion. Two items of evidence are said to be converging if they favor the same conclusion.

For example, a HUMINT cable reports that the Chinese freighter *Kiang Kwan* has left Shanghai bound for the Indian Ocean. A COMINT report on radio traffic from the *Kiang Kwan* as it left port states that the ship's destination is Colombia. Ships seldom sail from Shanghai to Colombia via the Indian Ocean, so the two reports point to two different conclusions; they are divergent. Note that both items of divergent evidence can be true (for example, the ship could make an intermediate stop at an Indian Ocean port); they simply lead to differing conclusions. The evidence that Iraq was acquiring aluminum tubes that fit the dimensions of its Medusa rocket, cited earlier, diverged from the conclusion that the tubes were for gas centrifuges, but both conclusions nevertheless could have been true. The Iraqis could have purchased the tubes for both purposes.

In contrast, two items of evidence are *contradictory* if they say logically opposing things. A COMINT report says that the *Kiang Kwan* left Shanghai yesterday at 1800 hours; a HUMINT report says that the ship was in Singapore this morning. Given the distance between these ports and the maximum speed of merchant ships, only one report can be true.

Redundant Evidence

Convergent evidence can also be redundant. To understand the concept of redundancy in evidence, it helps to understand its importance in communications theory. Information comes to an analyst by several different channels. It often is incomplete, and it sometimes arrives in garbled form. As stated in Analysis Principle 7-2, entropy takes its toll on any information channel. In communications theory, redundancy is one way to improve the chances of getting the message right.

Redundant, or duplicative, evidence can have corroborative redundancy or cumulative redundancy. In both types, the weight of the evidence piles up to reinforce a given conclusion. A simple example illustrates the difference.

Corroborative Redundancy. An analyst following clandestine arms transfer networks receives two reports. A COMINT report indicates that a Chinese freighter carrying a contraband arms shipment will be at coordinates 05-48S, 39-52E on June 13 to transfer the arms to another boat. A separate HUMINT report says that the Chinese freighter *Kiang Kwan* will rendezvous for an arms transfer south of Pemba Island on June 13. Both reports say the same thing; a quick map check confirms that the coordinates lie near Pemba Island, off the Tanzanian coast, so no new information (except the ship's name) is gained from the second report. The second report has value for confirmatory purposes and helps establish the validity of both sources of information.

In communications theory, an analogous situation might be a noisy teletype channel. Message errors are not a concern when one is dealing with text only, because text has inherent redundancy: If the message "Chinese freighter will rendezvous" is sent, but the recipient gets the printout "Chinese frei3hter will rentezvous," the message will probably be understood in spite of the errors. The coordinates of the rendezvous point, however, have less inherent redundancy. Some redundancy does exist in geographical coordinates—a message that has the coordinates "5 degrees 88 minutes South," clearly has an error, since minutes of latitude and longitude never exceed 59. However, it is unclear what the correct latitude should be. It is common practice to spell out or repeat numbers in such a message, or even to repeat the entire message, if a chance of a garble exists; that is, the sender introduces corroborative redundancy to ensure that the correct coordinates are received.

Cumulative Redundancy. Now, suppose instead that the HUMINT report in the previous example says that a Chinese freighter left port in Shanghai on May 21, carrying AK-47 rifles and ammunition destined for Tanzanian rebels. The report does not duplicate information contained in the COMINT report, but it adds credibility to both reports. Furthermore, it leads to a more detailed conclusion about the nature of the illicit arms transfer.

The second report, in this case, adds cumulative redundancy to the first report. Both reports are given more weight, and a more complete estimate can be made than if only one report had been received.

Structured Argumentation

The preceding section discussed some qualitative and intuitive approaches for combining evidence. It often is important to combine the evidence and demonstrate the logical process of reaching a conclusion based on that evidence by careful argument.[27] The formal process of making such an argument is called *structured argumentation.*

Formal graphical or numerical processes for combining evidence are time-consuming to apply and are not widely used in intelligence analysis. They are usually reserved for cases in which the customer demands them, whether because the issue is critically important, because the customer wants to examine the reasoning process, or because the exact probabilities associated with each alternative are important to the customer. Two such formal processes of structured argumentation are Wigmore's charting method and Bayesian analysis.

Wigmore's Charting Method

John Henry Wigmore (1863–1943) was the dean of the Northwestern University Law School and author of a ten-volume treatise commonly known as *Wigmore on Evidence.* In that treatise he defined some principles for rational inquiry into disputed facts and methods for rigorously analyzing and ordering possible inferences from those facts.[28]

Wigmore argued that structured argumentation brings into the open and makes explicit the important steps in an argument and thereby makes it easier to judge both their soundness and their probative value.[29] One of the best ways to recognize any inherent tendencies one may have to make biased or illogical arguments is to go through a body of evidence using Wigmore's method.

The method is complex and is not detailed here. It is, however, a very powerful tool for comparing alternative models or hypotheses. It requires the construction of elaborate diagrams that incorporate all important evidence and that have the following main features (a few of which are illustrated in Figure 7-2):

- Different symbols are used to show different kinds of evidence—explanatory, testimonial, circumstantial, corroborative, undisputed fact, and combinations.

- Relationships between symbols (that is, between individual pieces of evidence) are indicated by their relative positions (e.g., evidence tending to prove a fact is placed below the fact symbol).

- The connections between symbols indicate the probative effect of their relationship and the degree of uncertainty about the relationship. For example, a double arrowhead on the connector indicates that strong credit is given to the relationship; a question mark next to the connector signifies doubt about the probative effect of the connection; a zero on the connector indicates a negating effect.[30]

Wigmore intended his approach to be used by trial lawyers. But the trial lawyers basically ignored him because his diagrams were too hard to prepare.[31] The approach has fared no better with intelligence analysts, as even proponents admit that it is too time-consuming for most practical uses, especially in

Figure 7-2   **Example of Wigmore's Charting Method**

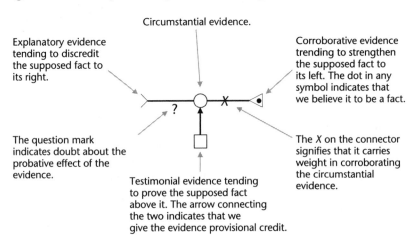

Circumstantial evidence.

Explanatory evidence tending to discredit the supposed fact to its right.

Corroborative evidence trending to strengthen the supposed fact to its left. The dot in any symbol indicates that we believe it to be a fact.

The question mark indicates doubt about the probative effect of the evidence.

Testimonial evidence tending to prove the supposed fact above it. The arrow connecting the two indicates that we give the evidence provisional credit.

The X on the connector signifies that it carries weight in corroborating the circumstantial evidence.

intelligence analysis, where the analyst typically cannot afford the luxury of such a formal approach.

Recognizing this shortcoming, Wigmore proposed a narrative form, listing rather than charting the evidence, to simplify the process and make it more readily usable by a novice.[32] But even the narrative approach runs into trouble when one is dealing with the large mass of data that is typical of complex problems. Efforts have been made in recent years to incorporate a structured argumentation process into software to aid intelligence analysts. Those efforts show promise of making structured argumentation a usable analytic tool, even for dealing with complex intelligence problems.[33] Making Wigmore's approach, or something like it, widely usable in intelligence analysis would be a major contribution. His method brings into the open and makes explicit the important steps in an argument and thereby makes it easier to evaluate the soundness of any conclusion.

Bayesian Techniques for Combining Evidence

By the early part of the eighteenth century, mathematicians had solved what is called the "forward probability" problem: What is the probability of a given event happening when all the facts about a situation are known? For example, if you know the numbers of black and white balls in a bag, it is easy to determine the probability of drawing a black ball from the bag. In the middle of the eighteenth century, Thomas Bayes, a British mathematician and Presbyterian minister, dealt with the "inverse problem": Given that an event has occurred, what can be determined about the situation that caused the event? Continuing our bag of balls example, if you draw three black balls and one white ball from a bag, what estimate can you make about the relative number of black and white balls in the bag? And how does your estimate change if you then draw a white ball? Intelligence analysts find this problem of far more interest than the forward probability problem, because they often must make judgments about an underlying situation from observing the events that the situation causes. Bayes developed a formula for the answer that bears his name: Bayes's rule.

Bayesian analysis is the best known of the formal numerical processes. Based on Bayes's rule, it is a formal method for using incoming data to modify previously estimated probabilities. It therefore can be used to narrow the error bounds on both estimates and predictions. Each new piece of information can be evaluated and combined with prior historical or subjective assessments of the probability of an event, to determine whether its occurrence has now been made more likely or less, and by how much. Bayesian analysis can also be used to compute the likelihood that the observed data are attributable to particular causes. One advantage claimed for Bayesian analysis is its ability to blend the subjective probability judgments of experts with historical frequencies and the latest sample evidence.

To explain Bayes's rule, let us assume that we know how often a given event normally occurs. We can assign that event a probability: P(event). Assume also that we have previously made an intelligence conclusion and given it a likelihood, or probability, of P(conclusion). Finally, we are fairly sure that if our conclusion is true, it changes the probability P(event). We call this changed probability P(event | conclusion), which is read as "probability that the event will occur, given that the conclusion is true."

Now, suppose that the event does occur. Its occurrence changes the probability of our conclusion to a new probability P(conclusion | event), which is read as "probability that our conclusion is true, given that the event has occurred." The new probability is given by Bayes's rule, which is expressed by the formula,

$$P(\text{conclusion} \mid \text{event}) = \frac{P(\text{event} \mid \text{conclusion}) \, P(\text{conclusion})}{P(\text{event})}$$

A simple illustration will help make Bayes's rule clear. Suppose an analyst has previously made an estimate based on existing evidence that a particular bank is laundering narcotics funds and has given the estimate a probability P (conclusion) = .4. The analyst knows that the probability of similar banks making profits in excess of 12 percent is .2 if the bank operates legally. The bank in question, however, recently made a profit of 20 percent, which certainly looks suspicious. The analyst concludes that there is a 30 percent (.3) chance of the bank making this much profit if it is in the fund-laundering business. The probability that the bank is laundering funds has increased:

$$P(\text{conclusion} \mid \text{event}) = \frac{(.3)\,(.4)}{(.2)} = .6$$

One problem with Bayesian analysis is that it does not deal well with ignorance. That is, if the analyst assigns probabilities to either conclusions or events based on very little knowledge, contradictions can result. The solution to this problem in Bayes's rule is to use a more formal methodology called the Dempster-Shafer approach to combining evidence. The Dempster-Shafer approach is mathematically complex and is not described in detail here.[34]

Both Bayes's rule and Dempster-Shafer rely on placing a numerical weight on bits of evidence. There are three approaches to numerical weighting: ordinal scale, interval scale, and ratio scale weighting. Ordinal scales simply indicate rank or order, but no mathematical operations are possible. Interval scales have equal intervals between numbers, but the lack of an absolute zero reference does not allow multiplication or division. The Fahrenheit and Celsius scales are interval scales for measuring temperature because both scales have a somewhat arbitrary zero reference. Only ratio scaling, which has an absolute zero reference, allows the multiplication and division required for Bayesian or Dempster-Shafer analysis. The Kelvin temperature scale is an example of a ratio scale; it has an absolute zero reference—the temperature where all motion of atomic particles stops.

Alternative Target Models

Alternative models are an essential part of the synthesis process. In studies describing the analytic pitfalls that hampered past assessments, one of the most prevalent is failure to consider alternative scenarios, hypotheses, or models.[35] Analysts seem to be addicted to single-outcome scenarios. One national intelligence officer has observed that "analysts . . . rarely engage in systematic testing of alternative hypotheses."[36] The Iraqi WMD Commission noted, "The disciplined use of alternative hypotheses could have helped counter the natural cognitive tendency to force new information into existing paradigms."[37] There are a number of reasons why analysts do not make use of alternative models, either initially or as new evidence comes in to suggest that a different target model is more appropriate:

- Analysts are usually facing tight deadlines. The temptation is to go with the model that best fits the evidence, without considering alternatives.

- Presented with two or more target models, customers always pick the one that they like best, but that may or may not be the most likely model. Analysts know this.

- Maintaining a corporate judgment is a pervasive and often an unstated norm in the intelligence community.[38] Customers tend to view a change in judgment as indicating that the original judgment was wrong, not that new evidence forced the change.

- It has been noted that it serves the interest of any intelligence agency to be perceived as decisive rather than academic and contradictory,[39] and that message quickly becomes embedded in any analysis culture. A similar motivation long ago led judicial systems to adopt the principle of *stare decisis:* Let previous decisions stand, wherever possible. Both analysts and judges face the same tension: Do you want to be consistent, or do you want to come up with the right answer?

The problem has at times been so serious that the U.S. intelligence community has been directed to empower independent groups to provide alternative target models. In 1976 the President's Foreign Intelligence Advisory Board and Director of Central Intelligence George H. W. Bush created an independent analysis team, known as Team B, to provide an alternative National Intelligence Estimate on Soviet strategic objectives and capabilities.[40] The effort engendered considerable resentment among analysts who had prepared the Team A estimate.

Building alternative models takes time. Analysts, always rushed, don't want to do it. Also, as former DNI Mike McConnell has observed, analysts inherently dislike alternative, dissenting, or competitive views.[41] But it is important to keep more than one possible target model in mind, especially as conflicting or contradictory intelligence information is collected.

Sometimes the policymakers provide an alternative target model. For example, in 1982 the United States committed U.S. Marines to Lebanon in an ambitious attempt to end a civil war, force occupying Israeli and Syrian armies out of Lebanon, and establish a stable government. The U.S. administration withdrew from Lebanon eighteen months later, its policy discredited and its reputation damaged, with more than 250 Americans dead, most of them marines killed in a terrorist bombing. The U.S. intelligence community had one assessment of the Lebanon situation; the Washington policymaking community had a strikingly different assessment that envisioned Lebanon as a role model for future Middle East governments.[42] Table 7-1 shows a parallel list comparing these two alternative models of the Lebanon situation.

Note that this is far from a complete picture of Lebanon, which today, as in 1982, has all the elements of a complex problem as defined in chapter 2. The table also is more than a target model; it contains a number of analytical judgments or hypotheses that were drawn from two competing target models.

It is best to be inclusive when defining alternative models, especially when dealing with intelligence enigmas—a subject discussed in chapter 8. During the 1970s and early 1980s the United States expended considerable intelligence and scientific research effort in the suspicion that the Soviet Union was building a particle beam weapon capable of destroying ballistic missile warheads in flight. The source of this suspicion was one of several competing models of an unidentified facility in the Soviet Union located near the Semipalatinsk nuclear testing area. The U.S. Air Force called it PNUT—possible

Table 7-1   Alternative Models of the Lebanon Situation in 1982

Policymakers	Analysts
We can negotiate speedy Israeli and Syrian withdrawals from Lebanon.	President Assad won't pull Syrian troops out unless convinced that he will be attacked militarily.
Lebanon can be unified under a stable government.	Lebanon in effect has no borders, and you can't say what a citizen is.
President Gamayel can influence events in Lebanon.	President Gamayel doesn't control most of Beirut, and even the Christians aren't all behind him.
We have five military factions to deal with: the Christian Phalange, Moslem militia, Syrian forces, the PLO, and Israeli forces.	There are 40 militias operating in West Beirut alone.
The marines are peacekeepers.	The marines are targets.

nuclear underground test facility, and the CIA called it URDF-3—unidentified research and development facility three. Some air force officials argued that the facility was a test site for a particle beam weapon. The air force position was supported by U.S. researchers who had a vested interest in funding for particle beam weapons research.[43]

While a number of alternative hypotheses were proposed for PNUT/URDF-3, the real explanation apparently was not seriously considered: It was a nuclear rocket testing program. The major reason for this oversight appears to have been that the United States, which had previously dropped its own nuclear rocket program, simply did not include the nuclear rocket hypothesis in considering the facility.[44] If analysts had included the nuclear rocket model hypothesis, an application of Occam's razor to the available evidence would have made it the leading contender to explain the facility's purpose.

Summary

Once a model template has been selected for the target, it becomes necessary to fit the relevant information (collected from the sources discussed in the previous chapter) into the template. Fitting the information into the model template requires a three-step process:

- Evaluating the source by determining whether the source (a) is competent, that is, knowledgeable about the information being given; (b) had the access needed to get the information; and (c) had a vested interest or bias regarding the information provided.

- Evaluating the communications channel through which the information arrived. Information that passes through many intermediate points becomes distorted. And it is important to recognize that processors and exploiters of collected information can also have a vested interest or bias.

- Evaluating the credentials of the evidence itself. This involves evaluating (a) the credibility of evidence, based in part on the previously completed source and communications channel evaluations; (b) the reliability; and (c) the relevance of the evidence. Relevance is a particularly important evaluation step; it is too easy to fit evidence into the wrong target model.

As evidence is evaluated, it must be combined and incorporated into the target model. Multiple pieces of evidence can be convergent (favoring the same conclusion) or divergent (favoring different conclusions and leading to alternative target models). Convergent evidence can also be redundant, reinforcing a conclusion.

Structured argumentation is a formal process of combining evidence graphically or numerically. It brings into the open and makes explicit the important steps in an argument and thereby makes it easier to evaluate the soundness of the conclusions reached. But it is time-consuming to apply and therefore is too often ignored in favor of informal evidence combination methods. Two of the best-known formal methods are Wigmore's evidence charting method and Bayesian analysis.

Alternative target models are an essential part of the process. Properly used, they help the analyst deal with denial and deception and avoid being trapped by analytic biases. But they take time to create; analysts are reluctant to change or challenge existing judgments; and alternative models can play into the hands of policymakers who want support only for preconceived notions.

In the ongoing target-centric process, the picture will always be incomplete after the available information is incorporated into the target model. That means that gaps exist, and new collection must be undertaken to fill the gaps.

Notes

1. David A. Schum, "On the Properties, Uses, Discovery, and Marshaling of Evidence in Intelligence Analysis," lecture to the SRS Intelligence Analysis Seminar, Tucson, Ariz., February 15, 2001.
2. Bertrand Russell, *A History of Western Philosophy* (New York: Simon and Schuster, 1945), 472.
3. John Evangelist Walsh, *Moonlight: Abraham Lincoln and the Almanac Trial* (New York: St. Martin's Press, 2000).
4. *Report of the Commission on the Intelligence Capabilities of the United States Regarding Weapons of Mass Destruction,* March 31, 2005, www.wmd.gov/report/wmd_report.pdf, 97.
5. Alfred Price, *Instruments of Darkness* (London: William Kimber, 1967).
6. John Braithwaite, *Corporate Crime in the Pharmaceutical Industry* (London: Routledge and Kegan Paul, 1984).
7. *Report of the Commission,* 125.
8. David A. Schum and Jon R. Morris, "Assessing the Competence and Credibility of Human Sources of Intelligence Evidence: Contributions from Law and Probability," *Law, Probability and Risk,* 6 (March/December 2007): 247–274.
9. Claude E. Shannon, *The Mathematical Theory of Communication* (Urbana: University of Illinois Press, 1963).
10. *Report of the Commission,* 10, 49.
11. Schum, "On the Properties."
12. "The Skills of an Intelligence Analyst," North Carolina Wesleyan College, March 29, 2003, http//faculty.ncwc.edu/toconnor/392/spy/analskills.htm.
13. John Prados, *The Soviet Estimate* (Princeton: Princeton University Press, 1987), 203.
14. Michael Herman, *Intelligence Power in Peace and War* (Cambridge: Cambridge University Press, 1996), 96
15. Richards J. Heuer Jr., *Psychology of Intelligence Analysis* (Washington, D.C.: Center for the Study of Intelligence, Central Intelligence Agency, 1999), 119.
16. William J. Lahneman, *The Future of Intelligence Analysis,* Center for International and Security Studies at Maryland, vol. I (March 10, 2006): iii.
17. Peter Wright, *Spycatcher,* (New York: Viking Penguin, 1987), 12.
18. Rob Johnson, *Analytic Culture in the U.S. Intelligence Community* (Washington, D.C.: Center for the Study of Intelligence, Central Intelligence Agency, 2005), 64.
19. R. V. Jones, "Scientific Intelligence," *Research* 9 (September 1956): 350.
20. Ibid.
21. Roy Godson, *Intelligence Requirements for the 1990s* (Lanham, Md.: Lexington Books, 1989), 17.
22. David S. Brandwein, "Maxims for Analysts," *Studies in Intelligence* 22 (Winter 1978): 31–35.
23. Matthew Herbert, "The Intelligence Analyst as Epistemologist," *International Journal of Intelligence and CounterIntelligence,* 19 (June 2006): 678.

24. Prados, *The Soviet Estimate,* 133.
25. Klaus Knorr, "Failures in National Intelligence Estimates: The Case of the Cuban Missiles," *World Politics* 16 (April 1964): 455–467.
26. *Report of the Commission,* 68.
27. David A. Schum, *The Evidential Foundations of Probabilistic Reasoning* (Evanston: Northwestern University Press, 1994), 161.
28. Terence Anderson and William Twining, *Analysis of Evidence* (Evanston: Northwestern University Press, 1991), xxiv.
29. Ibid., 119.
30. Ibid., 112.
31. William Twining, *Theories of Evidence: Bentham and Wigmore* (Stanford: Stanford University Press, 1985), 164–166.
32. Anderson and Twining, *Analysis of Evidence,* 156.
33. See, for example, the description of SEAS, the Structured Evidential Argumentation System, at www.ai.sri.com/project/GENOA.
34. Glenn Shafer, *A Mathematical Theory of Evidence* (Princeton: Princeton University Press, 1976), 3–34.
35. Willis C. Armstrong, William Leonhart, William J. McCaffrey, and Herbert C. Rothenberg, "The Hazards of Single-Outcome Forecasting," in *Inside CIA's Private World,* ed. H. Bradford Westerfield (New Haven: Yale University Press, 1995), 241–242.
36. *Report of the Commission,* 507.
37. Ibid., chap. 1.
38. Johnson, *Analytic Culture,* 23.
39. Ibid., 23–24.
40. Douglas H. Dearth and R. Thomas Goodden, *Strategic Intelligence: Theory and Application,* 2nd ed. (Washington, D.C.: U.S. Army War College and Defense Intelligence Agency, 1995), 305.
41. Lahneman, *The Future of Intelligence Analysis,* E-6.
42. Kennedy School of Government, Harvard University, Case Program, "Lebanon and the Intelligence Community," C15-88-859.0, 1988.
43. John Pike, "The Death Beam Gap: Putting Keegan's Follies in Perspective," e-Print, October 1992, www.fas.org/spp/eprint/keegan.htm.
44. Ibid.

8

Collection Strategies

Whereas information enters the intelligence machine by source, it has to leave it by subject; it is this changeover inside the machine that causes all the difficulty.
R. V. Jones, Assistant Director of Britain's Royal Air Force Intelligence Section during World War II

Equipped with a problem breakdown and a target model, the intelligence analyst moves to identify gaps in knowledge of the target model. Having identified where the gaps are, the analyst is ready to go to the collection sources described in chapter 6 for help in filling them in.

For collectors of intelligence, as for those in many other fields, the key to success is to *ask the right question.*[1] But how do you, the analyst, know what the right question is? You don't have the knowledge that a collector has. He or she always can do things that you cannot imagine. So the collector has to understand what you really want (and therefore he or she is in the same position with respect to you that you are with respect to the customer). The solution is to share not only what you need but also why you need it. Sharing the problem and target models is the best way to begin. Collection strategies proceed from having a well-developed target model *and* a problem breakdown; understanding the relationship between the two; and sharing both with the collectors. The problem breakdown helps you ask the right questions. The existing target model provides the context. Armed with this information and their unique knowledge of what their collection assets can do, collectors can then ask the right questions of their assets.

As an introduction to collection strategies, it is worth looking back to how Sir Francis Walsingham, spymaster to Queen Elizabeth I, planned for collection. His "Plat for Intelligence out of Spain" in preparation for the Spanish Armada reads:

1. Sir Ed. Stafford to draw what he can from the Venetian Amb.
2. To procure some correspondence of the Fr. K. agent in Spain.

3. To take order with some in Rouen to have frequent advertisements from such as arrive out of Spain at Nantes, Newhaven [i.e., Le Havre] and Dieppe.

4. To make choice of two especial persons, French, Flemings, or Italians, to go along the coast to see what preparations are a making there. To furnish them with letters of credit.

5. To have two intelligencers in the court of Spain—one of Finale, another of Genoa. To have intelligence at Brussels, Leyden, Bar.[2]

Clearly Walsingham had a target model, one focused on England's most important strategic target, Spain, and its plans to attack England. He also had a strategies-to-task problem breakdown. He knew what the gaps were in his knowledge and what collection assets were available. So he gave very specific guidance on how to fill the gaps. Things were so simple then. (Walsingham's problem was not collection; it was getting his leaders to believe his intelligence, a subject for chapter 15.)

The U.S. Collection Management Problem

Contrast Walsingham's plan with the collection challenges facing a large intelligence service, such as that of the United States, which has many collection assets and many targets. Management of information acquisition is a major effort in large intelligence communities, where high-volume collection is based on a formalized process of defining requirements, needs, and information gaps. The U.S. intelligence community has for decades attempted to create structures for handling requirements. As a result, there are thirteen separate processes and systems in the U.S. intelligence community to initiate collection activity (counting just the major ones, excluding special access programs).

Collection requirements form a hierarchy. Chapter 2 illustrated some requirements hierarchies that result from the strategies-to-task problem breakdown. Lower elements in the hierarchy are more specific and, in a well-drafted requirements hierarchy, are linked to the higher elements by some measures that indicate their relative value in the overall scheme of things. The number of specific lower level targets will be in the dozens for targeting a business firm, in the hundreds for even a small country or a consortium, and in the thousands for a targeted illicit network such as an international narcotics operation. A typical requirement at the lower levels might read, "Locate all armored vehicles in the battlefield area"; "Obtain a copy of Ambassador Smythe's negotiating notes for tomorrow's trade negotiations"; or "Determine the intentions of the Cuban leadership on seaborne migration."

The collection requirements problem stems in part from the success that the United States has had in developing collection assets. Intelligence literature often makes a point of criticizing U.S. intelligence collection capabilities as being cumbersome and inefficient.[3] It is true that some small government intelligence services, such as Israel's Mossad, and a number of multinational corporations can be successful within the areas where they have concentrated their intelligence expertise. They also have all of the advantages that accrue to a small, tightly knit organization. However, U.S. government collection capabilities are unquestionably the best in the world. The U.S. intelligence community has the most resources and does the best systems planning. It innovates constantly and attempts things few other services would try. In breadth and depth of coverage, the United States remains the best, and therein lies its problem. Because U.S. intelligence can do so much, it is asked to do too much. Expensive collection assets are used all too often where cheaper ones might suffice.

As a result, the U.S. intelligence requirements structures have received considerable criticism, and repeated attempts to define such a structure over decades suggest that something may be fundamentally wrong with the concept. One critic said of the requirements process as it has been practiced in recent years,

> Analysts themselves often thought that too many people were employed and too much activity was oriented solely to generating "intelligence requirements"; a better job could probably have been done by a few experienced people, working with the available data, and therefore aware of what was missing. Instead intelligence requirements were the object of repeated studies and reorganization efforts.[4]

Analysts believe that the existing requirements process is a bureaucratic beast that consumes resources but adds little value. In spite of that view, formal requirements structures are necessary in dealing with high-volume satellite IMINT and COMINT and with open source material, where many potential targets exist and where a large customer suite with competing priorities wants more collection than could be accomplished with the entire national budget. There are several things wrong with this requirements structure, however.

First, as one senior U.S. intelligence official noted, everyone tasks the system, but no one prioritizes.[5] No one is willing to fight the special interests and say, We don't need this badly enough to spend resources on it. In contrast, businesses tend to watch their overhead costs closely and are willing to cut low-payoff functions. Second, if information is available from unclassified sources, intelligence collection assets should not be used to get it, except where cross-checking is essential, for example, in countering suspected deception. Increasingly, commercial sources such as commercial imaging satellites can do collection that once required national intelligence assets and can do it more cheaply. Third, formal requirements structures tend to focus on bean counting. Content, not quantity, is the critical measure, and formal requirements structures do not handle content evaluation well. Only analysts and customers can evaluate content and thereby place a value on collection. Furthermore, a complex requirements system tends to be cumbersome and slow, looking backward rather than forward. Michael Herman has observed that "a requirements system necessarily lags behind reality and following it is no guarantee of success." [6]

When these problems are not addressed, then the bulk of raw data collected by the INTs is irrelevant. For example, most new overhead (aircraft- or satellite-based) imagery contains information that is already known; natural terrain features and fixed structures change little, if at all, in the course of a year. Most COMINT traffic, which consists of personal telephone conversations and unusable (encrypted) traffic, must be discarded as irrelevant. And most open source information winds up in the wastebasket.

However, all of the data that are collected must be processed to some extent, and the handling of this volume of irrelevant data chokes the processing and exploitation systems and often chokes the analyst as well. The problem derives from trying to force a process that is based on the idea of an intelligence cycle instead of using the shared target process described in chapter 1. To come closer to the effectiveness of the target-centric paradigm, it is essential to make the hierarchical requirements structure efficient and responsive, and doing that is a continuing challenge for U.S. intelligence.

Even a large and bureaucratic collection network such as that of the United States can be responsive. But the intelligence analyst has to play a more significant role in making it so. The WMD Commission had severe criticism of the intelligence community's effectiveness in developing collection strategies. [7] Specifically, it noted the following:

> You can't analyze intelligence that you don't have. . . . the Intelligence Community has not developed the long-term, coordinated collection strategies that are necessary to penetrate today's intelligence targets. (p. 12)
>
> [The Intelligence Community] rarely adopts integrated strategies for penetrating high-priority targets. (p. 17)

But the WMD Commission also noted that analysts have a major role to play:

> Analysts must be willing to admit what they don't know in order to focus future collection efforts. (p. 12)
>
> Analysts missed opportunities to drive collection or provide collection targeting. (Overview)

Helping to focus collection can place a substantial burden on the analyst. But the payoff for the analyst can be high, and there is a way to ease the burden. As an analyst, you have to create both the problem breakdown model and the target model, as we have discussed in previous chapters. By sharing these models with collectors so that they can identify gaps in knowledge, you better equip them to fill the gaps. Tracking the status of collection requests; finding out who else is asking for the same information (and thereby is part of a community of interest); and obtaining access to others' research results are all facilitated by a common system.

Collectors tend to resist analysts' efforts to be involved in the collection systems development and collection strategies processes. Their mantra is "Tell me what you need, and I'll handle the collection." But senior intelligence community leaders with a broad understanding of the entire process, such as former DNI Mike McConnell, have come to this conclusion:

> The analyst plays a critical role in advising the collectors in not only collection targeting, but on the design and capabilities of future collection systems. For an analyst to perform these crucial tasks well, sophisticated understanding … of the functions of collector agencies is essential.[8]

In carrying out this complementary responsibility, analysts must (a) identify what is known about the intelligence issue and what is not known; (b) determine how collection and analysis are currently done; and (c) decide how both can be improved. The collection strategy part of this process proceeds through four steps:

- examining the relationship between the problem breakdown and the target model;
- identifying gaps in the analyst's knowledge of the target—an analyst's responsibility, but one where collectors can help;
- defining a collection strategy to use existing assets to deal with the gaps—a shared responsibility with collectors; and
- planning for future collection systems development, including planning to deal with denial and deception—a collector's responsibility, but analysts can provide valuable help.

The reason for the structured approach to dealing with the problem (strategies-to-task) breakdown and the target model is to facilitate managing collection against complex problems. Let us consider each step in turn.

The Problem Breakdown and Target Model Relationship

At this point we have covered the idea of a target model and a customer problem breakdown (which is a hierarchical model). At times the two have looked almost identical; but in general, the *target model and the problem breakdown are separate;* and it's best to keep them that way. Although they often look very similar, it is important to remember which is which and to use them both.

- Using only a target model gives customers unwanted information and forces them to select what is relevant from a mass of detail. For example, a tactical commander is very interested in the combat forces model of a target country but usually does not want to delve into the country's political and economic models.

- In contrast, using only a problem breakdown model results in too narrow a focus; the analyst tends to develop tunnel vision and to miss things that the customer needs to know about important related issues. The tactical commander might be quite interested, for example, in religious shrines that are located close to opposing military forces or nongovernmental organizations that are operating in the area—things that could well be missing in the problem breakdown.

Understanding how the problem breakdown relates to the target model allows the analyst to deal with the difficulty that R. V. Jones cited in the passage quoted at the beginning of this chapter. We therefore focus here on using the interrelationship for planning collection strategies, or as Jones would say, "having the information enter the machine by source." In chapter 15, we'll return to this process and discuss its use in preparing finished intelligence, or "getting the material to leave the machine by subject." For now, we are dealing with the difficult changeover that Jones referred to.

Although the target model and the problem breakdown are separate concepts, they are closely related to each other. Let us illustrate the relationship with a simple example. Take the problem of money laundering—the movement of illicit proceeds into mainstream commerce and other funds transactions designed to conceal the source, ownership, or use of the funds. Criminal organizations, terrorist groups, and pariah states use money laundering to evade international sanctions. Money laundering can be thought of as a process having three distinct stages—placement, followed by layering, followed by integration—as shown in the simple process model of Figure 8-1.[9]

Figure 8-1   Model of a Money-Laundering Process

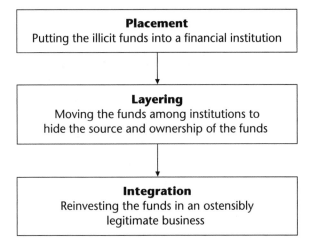

The problem of putting constraints on money laundering divides naturally into dealing with the three stages, and the three stages form the first level of the problem breakdown. But different customers of intelligence will be interested in different stages. Countermeasures, it turns out, have been most effective when aimed at the placement stage. It is easier to detect money laundering in that first stage, and most law enforcement and regulatory work has concentrated on detecting the placement of illicit funds.[10] Therefore, law enforcement organizations, such as Interpol or the U.S. Financial Crimes Enforcement Network, might focus on the placement stage, though they would want intelligence from all three stages. Financial regulatory customers, such as the United Kingdom's Financial Services Authority, focus on both placement and layering. Business regulatory customers, such as the U.S. Securities and Exchange Commission or state regulatory agencies, might focus on the integration stage. As indicated in Figure 8-2, each of these customers has interests in specific parts of the overall problem.

The first step an analyst takes is to interrelate the customer's problem model and the target model for both information-gathering and analysis purposes. Veteran analysts do this naturally, seldom making the interrelationships explicit. For simple problems, explicit definition may be unnecessary. However, when we deal with complex (nonlinear) problems, the target model or scenario should be made explicit. Even when dealing with simple problems, analysts can easily omit important points or fail to take full advantage of the information sources unless they have an explicit interrelationship diagram. An explicit representation of the interrelationship, following the examples given in this chapter, is useful for the veteran analyst and essential for the novice.

Figure 8-2 features a generic, top-level problem breakdown for money laundering. But the money laundering problem has many associated target models. There are many independent networks engaged in money laundering worldwide. Consider one target that we discussed in chapter 3: the Abacha family's laundering of stolen Nigerian government funds. The Abachas placed money in a Citibank London account; "layered" the funds by

Figure 8-2   Customer Connections to the Problem Breakdown

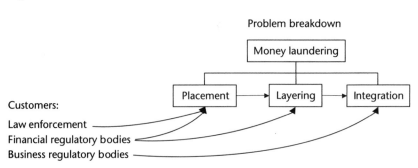

moving them among different Citibank London and Citibank New York accounts (shown in Figure 5-9), as well as through Citibank AG Frankfurt and Swiss banks; and "integrated" the funds using individuals and the shell (dummy) companies Morgan Procurement and Selcon Airlines.[11] So a model of the Abacha funds-laundering target might look like the one in Figure 8-3 (which only shows part of the Abacha network) overlaid on the top-level problem breakdown.

If we did no more, collectors could use this as a starting point for collection. HUMINT collection is likely to be most useful against the placement and integration stages, where well-placed human sources can monitor and report on unusual transactions. COMINT collection is well positioned to help in tracking the financial transactions associated with layering because such transactions are typically made through international data transmission. Open source intelligence can be useful in analyzing the business activities involving integration. But we can do more to help the collector.

Identifying Gaps

When the analyst has defined the problem, as discussed in chapter 2, he must ask questions such as, How do I pull information out of the target model to address the problem that is before me? Does the target model, in its present form, give me everything I need to answer my customer's questions? If not, where are the gaps in knowledge of the target, and how can I fill those gaps? This section describes a formal process that an analyst might go through in considering those questions. Veteran intelligence analysts do follow the process described here, though they do so intuitively and seldom in such a formal way.

Figure 8-3 Abacha Funds-Laundering Target Model

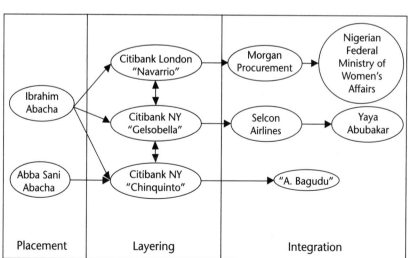

For some collectors (open source and IMINT are examples), the analyst may need to identify the gaps and give specific collection guidance. Some collectors (typically, HUMINT and COMINT collectors) can do a better job of identifying collection opportunities, once they understand the gaps, because of their superior knowledge of their assets.

A target model is never complete enough to satisfy the intelligence customer. After a problem hierarchy is defined and interrelated with the target model as described above, it will become obvious that there are gaps in knowledge of the target. Those gaps have to be made explicit, and intelligence collection has to fill in the missing pieces of the model to answer customers' questions.

After reviewing existing data and incorporating them into the target model, as discussed in chapter 7, the next step is to identify the gaps in data, information, or knowledge. A gap is a missing element that, if found, allows one to choose among alternatives with greater confidence. These gaps always exist in the intelligence business. The skill we have in organizing thoughts and evidence influences how well we are able to generate or discover new thoughts and evidence.

Analysts have a natural tendency to draw conclusions from the information available, rather than determine what policy questions must be answered and then go after the needed information. Lazy analysts, faced with a new project, will simply sift through their carefully kept files, add a few items that are within easy reach, and write a report. They never get to gap analysis. The opposite and equally poor approach is to keep looking for the one last scrap of information that makes the other pieces fall into place. An analyst almost never gets that last piece of the puzzle. So gap analysis (and filling gaps) has to be done but not overdone; the analyst needs to know when to stop.

Identifying data gaps is a continual and iterative process—as new data comes in and is fitted into the model, new gaps can be identified. Gap analysis is the process of

- identifying and prioritizing gaps, based on the importance of the underlying need and size of the gap;
- classifying gaps as to their nature: Do they occur in collection, processing, analysis, or dissemination? and
- sorting gaps as either short term, for current collection systems "tuning," or long term, for new capabilities development.

Consider some examples of gap analysis in a tactical situation. In the example of the Afghan BMP (in chapter 3), the problem was to determine when the BMP would reach the village where staff from Doctors without Borders were working. If the intelligence officer did not know how fast the BMP could travel on the road, she would have a collection gap in knowledge to fill. In the Symantec war room example of chapter 4, the analyst might have to deal with several gaps. He might come upon a familiar virus that could be easily countered, but have a critical need to know where it started and what

Internet service provider (ISP) to call—a collection gap. In the process of defeating the virus, the analyst would learn about a need to improve the collection system to identify the ISP more quickly—a long-term gap. The analyst could encounter a new type of virus, one that could not be examined effectively from his existing knowledge—an analysis gap.

Figure 8-4 illustrates possible gaps that could have occurred at some point in developing the target model in Figure 8-3. The analyst might determine that laundered funds were somehow getting from the Citibank London "Navarrio" account to the Nigerian Federal Ministry of Women's Affairs but not know what the intermediate integration entity was. Or she might know that funds were getting to "A. Bagudu" but not know which of the Citibank accounts was the source.

Developing the Collection Strategy

At this point in the analysis process, the problem has been defined and the gaps in information about the target have been identified. It is time for the analyst to plan a collection activity to fill the gaps and to follow up by offering guidance to collection sources and organizations. As chapter 6 described, a rich set of collection INTs is available to help an analyst acquire information.

Before designing a collection strategy to fill a gap, it is important to understand the nature of the gap. Some intelligence gaps exist because analysis of the problem has been nonexistent or inadequate, not because of lack of collection. Other gaps need research to determine what part collection can play. An analyst should not treat all gaps as collection gaps; the collector will simply

Figure 8-4   Abacha Funds-Laundering Gaps

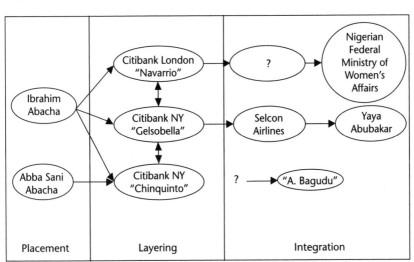

collect again without solving the problem, in some cases compounding the problem by adding more unneeded data to be analyzed.

Using Existing Collection Assets

Acquiring new data to fill gaps is a matter of making good use of existing collection assets. These assets are the agents already in place, the open literature that is coming in and being translated, the collection satellites or aircraft currently flying, and so on. The process of asking for use of these assets to fill gaps is called "tasking."

Analysts rely on their judgment in putting together the best collection strategy for tasking to fill gaps. Analysts traditionally initiate the tasking and must pull together the incoming information to form a coherent picture. In the collaborative environment envisioned in chapter 1, formulating a collection strategy would be a team effort, with input from collectors and processors. The following describes how it would proceed.

Basic Collection Strategy Development. Most collection strategies are developed as a result of past experience. Making use of existing methods is a good way to save effort, time, and cost. Stated another way, most collection problems are old ones; only the specific questions to be answered are new. It is prudent to avoid re-creating solutions that already have been tried at least once before. Begin by looking at what has succeeded in the past.

Start with a review of the collection strategies previously used against similar targets and look at their results. Each specialized substantive area of intelligence has its own collection techniques that have been tested over the years. Political intelligence traditionally has relied on a combination of open source and HUMINT, with some COMINT thrown in. Military intelligence relies heavily on COMINT and IMINT, along with some specialized technical collection. Weapons systems intelligence, discussed in chapter 14, uses all sources but relies most heavily on specialized technical collection, IMINT, and open source. Analyzing previous strategies and their results will illuminate the prospects for future strategies.

An analyst cannot rely only on previous strategies, however. As chapter 9 will note, a predictable collection strategy can be defeated. Also, simply shifting tasking from one target to another usually opens gaps in other areas.[12] If possible, develop innovative approaches to using existing assets. Collectors must be encouraged not to repeat collection that does not obtain the needed information but instead to try new ideas. Techniques that work in economic or political intelligence problems may be applied to problems in other areas, such as military or scientific and technical intelligence.

In identifying collection strategies, be sure to distinguish collectors' current contributions from their potential contributions. In some cases, gaps can be closed by applying collection resources where they now contribute very little. A HUMINT source that reports on political affairs may also be able to obtain economic information. A COMINT source that provides order of battle information may also have insights into the personalities of enemy field commanders.[13]

However, major reorientation of collection assets often requires considerable planning and may have to be considered a long-term solution.

For straightforward collection problems, collection planning can be done quickly and efficiently by using the approach that is summarized in Figure 8-5, continuing with the Abacha case model. Starting with a given target model and a detailed problem breakdown, the analyst and collectors identify gaps in knowledge of the target that must be filled to satisfy the customers' needs. After reviewing their collection assets and capabilities, they define a collection strategy and ask specific INTs to go after specific elements of the target to fill the gaps.

On more complex collection problems, the general approach is the same, but a formal process may be needed to develop and compare alternative collection strategy packages. This is a resource allocation step—an effort to fill short-term gaps (immediate needs) by identifying possible collection mechanisms and selecting the most promising combination of collection assets. The collection plan illustrated in Figure 8-5, for example, represents one possible combination of collection assets, or one strategy, to fill the gaps identified in Figure 8-4 and to gain more information. Let us look in detail at how it was developed, recognizing that this is a hypothetical example.

- First, the detailed problem breakdown may have indicated a need for more information about the banks involved. A HUMINT source connected to any of the banks involved with the Abachas could have identified the suspicious transactions that indicated placement and integration. In fact, bank personnel were aware of and concerned about a sudden influx of more than $20 million

Figure 8-5 Abacha Funds-Laundering Collection Plan Overlaid on the Target Model

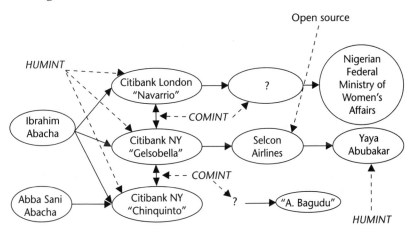

Note: Solid lines indicate connections; broken lines show intelligence collection targeting.

into the New York accounts, a transfer of $5 million to an unfamiliar person, and the discovery that the Abacha sons were conducting business in Libya, which had no apparent connection to the supposed source of funds in the accounts. These transactions were out of line with the account history.

- From past collection experience, an analyst knows that COMINT has the potential to identify the patterns of funds movements among banks that are a sign of layering activity and also may be able to fill the two gaps in knowledge indicated by question marks in Figure 8-5. So the analyst would provide the diagram with a request to COMINT collectors.

- U.S. Department of Transportation records and similar open sources are a good first place to look for details on the use of Selcon Airlines as a shell company for the funds integration stage.

- From previous HUMINT reporting about Yaya Abubakar, the analyst knows that a HUMINT source has access to Abubakar. The analyst would logically turn first to HUMINT for additional intelligence, as indicated in Figure 8-5, requesting more details on the path of funds to Abubakar and amounts he received.

In developing collection strategies, the analyst should time the collection so that it occurs when the probability of getting desirable content will be highest. For example:

- Missile range testing has consistent patterns. When a pattern of vehicle deployments indicates that a missile test is about to take place, it is the right time to task collection assets.

- People consistently use the telephone heavily at certain times of day. Ask for COMINT collection during those times.

- Questioning technical staff at professional conferences elicits more useful information than questioning them at other times.

An analyst can also obtain synergistic benefits by intelligently timing collection by different resources. Coordinated collection by different INTs at the same time can provide insights that those INTs could not provide individually. In the missile range testing example, IMINT collection of the missile on its launch pad should take place just before the telemetry collection of the missile in launch phase, and technical collection, such as radar collection of the missile in flight and during reentry, should be timed to follow the launch phase. The combination of all these collection activities can tell far more about the missile's performance than can any one of them alone.

The key to success with any collection strategy is a close and enduring relationship with the collectors. Simply writing collection requirements and "throwing them over the wall" doesn't work. If collectors have access to—and understand—the target model and the problem breakdown, they can respond much more effectively than they could if they do not have knowledge of these elements. Imparting this information usually requires the analyst to develop and maintain personal contacts with collectors. Analysts in business intelligence, law enforcement intelligence, and tactical military intelligence are much closer to their sources and are able to provide detailed, explicit collection guidance. It is difficult to do at the national level for large communities such as the U.S. intelligence community. But it can be done and increasingly is being done on high-priority problems.

Advanced Collection Strategy Development: Cost-Benefit Analysis. The result of the effort discussed thus far should be a strategy package—a combination of strategies for closing the gaps. On very large and high-priority efforts, alternative strategies can be compared and the best alternative selected. This is seldom done in practice because it takes much planning and a high level of understanding of the various available sources. Topics such as locating mobile ballistic missiles or assessing weapons of mass destruction, for example, are important enough to merit developing and comparing alternative strategies. The most straightforward and accepted method of comparison is cost-benefit or cost-utility analysis:

- Estimate the benefit or utility of each strategy (option) and combination of options.
- Estimate the costs or risks of each strategy and combination.
- Select a package that has a high ratio of benefits (or utility) to costs (or risks).

The first step is to estimate the benefit or utility of each collection option. At this point we have determined the importance of the requirement and the value if the gap is filled. Now focus on the probability of success. Which asset has the best chance to get the needed information? Determine the value of the information that could be provided. Also examine ways to increase the probability of success and to maximize the value of the information collected. Establish the probability of success for each category of collection or for fusion of sources, if appropriate. Factor in the possibility that the opponent will use denial and deception against any collection.

Distinguish contingent collection from certain collection. A broad area search for mobile missile sites has high payoff if a successful hit occurs, but success is stochastic (controlled by probabilities), and the probabilities are low. A fixed intercontinental ballistic missile site is an almost certain hit for IMINT collection (assuming no cloud cover), since its location is known, but the value of the intelligence gathered may be low. The evaluation ought to incorporate the probability of obtaining the desired content (a relevance issue) and the ability to beat denial and deception.

In summary, closing the short-term gaps against high-priority targets involves efficiently allocating existing collection resources based on

- the importance of the requirement or specific task;
- the value of the information collected, if successful; and
- the probability of success of the collection effort.

Next, determine the resource cost or risks of the options. One way of doing that is to produce a resource cost estimate that identifies the opportunity costs associated with using collection assets as proposed. The term *opportunity costs* means that if a collection asset is being used against one target, it probably will not be available to use against other targets. Actual costs of collection may be difficult to come by; collection organizations guard such information zealously.

Risk may be more important than cost as a factor against which to measure benefit. When Dwight D. Eisenhower's administration decided to conduct aerial reconnaissance over the Soviet Union during the 1950s, the costs of the U-2 program were a relatively minor factor in its decision-making process. A much larger factor was the risk of a shoot-down and the consequent damage to the U.S. image and to U.S.-Soviet relations. A U-2 was indeed shot down, and the subsequent political fallout might suggest that risk was in fact a better measure than program cost, though the benefits gained by the U-2 program were sufficiently great that the decision to overfly was a good one.[14]

Measuring the Right Things. Know what to measure and how to measure it. Measures of user satisfaction can be taken after collection to evaluate how well the intelligence process performed against a need or closed a gap. Expressed another way, the measurement is a quantification of how well a particular requirement or condition has been satisfied. Meaningful measures of user satisfaction could include questions such as, What percentage of all Iranian mobile missiles were located? Where are the petroleum industry's planned oil exploration regions? What is the expected size of the 2009 opium crop in Pakistan, Laos, Mexico, Thailand, Afghanistan, and Burma? Where are the opium processing centers in those countries, and how much can they process? Where are the concealed weapons of mass destruction production centers in Syria? All of these questions call for analytic conclusions, but all lead to more specific definitions of measures of user satisfaction. A poor example of a measure of user satisfaction is, How much of the target area was searched in imagery at a given resolution? One hundred percent of the target area could be searched without turning up a single item of useful intelligence. Collectors are fond of using such quantitative measures because they provide a firm and technically computable measure.

Intelligence organizations such as those in the United States and Russia do not have an efficient feedback loop connecting collectors and analysts, in part because they are so large. Instead, these organizations operate as open-loop systems, meaning they don't have feedback. The U.S. agencies, in particular, have become fixated on numbers—both on quality and quantity of collection—and insufficiently concerned with content. For example:

- If the COMINT collectors obtain continuous copy of a high-priority communications channel for six hours, they probably will get credit, even if no conversations of substance were carried on the channel during that time or if the entire channel was encrypted.
- If the IMINT collectors take one hundred pictures of a critical installation, they get credit for each image in their collection performance ratings, even if the last ninety-nine pictures contain nothing new.
- HUMINT collectors typically have their performance rated by the number of reports submitted, encouraging the submission of many short reports instead of a few complete ones.

A target-centric approach to the intelligence process forces collection performance to focus on content, not on quantity. If collected material does not belong in any target model—that is, if it has no intelligence value—it quickly becomes obvious to all concerned, and the collector is more likely to take action to make future intelligence relevant to the targets.

Dealing with Enigmas

While identifying knowledge gaps in the target model, an analyst will occasionally encounter a type of gap that is common in the intelligence business: the unidentified entity, or enigma.

An enigma is a different type of thing for the analyst than for the collector. For analysts, the enigma is something that the analyst knows exists but of which there is no physical evidence. Examples include a communications link that has to exist from narcotics suppliers to distributors, a fabrication facility that must exist somewhere if cell phones are being produced, or an unnamed terrorist organization that must be responsible for recent acts of violence. The gap may be in identifying the communications link, in finding evidence that the facility exists, or in naming the terrorist organization and identifying its leader.

For collectors, the enigma is a physical object that cannot be fit into existing models. Among IMINT collectors, it occurs as the mysterious facility observed in imagery whose purpose cannot be determined. Among ELINT collectors, it is the strange new radar signal. Among COMINT collectors, it is the encrypted communications link between two unidentified organizations. The gaps here may be in identifying the function of the radar or in establishing the identities of the organizations.

One of the better-known current enigmas is a large underground complex that Russia is building at Yamantau Mountain in the Urals. The complex, under construction for the past thirty years, has been the subject of attention and speculation in Congress and the press, but its purpose remains an enigma.[15]

Dealing with enigmas requires analyst-collector teamwork in using the target model. The target model must identify entities that, in the analyst's view, have to exist. The collector's input to the model must note potentially relevant, unidentified facilities and signals and communications links, and the analyst must respond by helping the collector—typically by finding a model into which the collector's unidentified entities fit.

Planning for Future Collection: Filling the Long-Term Gaps

A distinctly separate problem arises when the need is not to task existing collectors but to fill gaps that no existing collector is able to fill. Then the requirement is either to develop new capabilities—recruit a new agent with the necessary access, acquire new open source publications, develop a new SIGINT or IMINT collection system, and the like—or to find a new way to use existing systems.

This planning is normally the responsibility of the collectors. Developing new capabilities is a long-term process. In developing new HUMINT sources, the lead time can be one to five years or more. New satellite SIGINT or IMINT collection systems take ten years to develop and deploy during peacetime, though experience indicates that they can be deployed much faster in crisis or wartime. Planning the development requires time and expertise that analysts do not have. Thus the analyst has to depend on the collectors to do the long-range planning.

The analyst's normal contribution to the long-term gap problem is to define long-term requirements and leave the rest to the collector. One problem with filling long-term gaps is that a formal requirements system tends to focus on today's needs and gaps. Major intelligence problems, such as proliferation of weapons of mass destruction, terrorism, and international criminal activity, tend to endure. But they change in relative importance, and new problems arise. At the end of 2008 and the beginning of 2009, a worldwide economic crisis suddenly became the most important intelligence issue for most governments. By 2020 new environmental problems, pandemics, mass migrations, and basic resource (food and water) shortages might be more important than today's problems. The existing U.S. collection requirements structure is not well suited to dealing with the future, and it has difficulty dealing with denial and deception. Chapters 10 to 12 deal with the predictive problem generally. The next chapter deals with the denial and deception problem.

Summary

A large intelligence community such as that of the United States experiences considerable difficulty in planning for and managing collection. Although analytic shortfalls are responsible for most failures, analysts cannot analyze intelligence that they don't have. A large intelligence community needs a carefully planned set of collection strategies against high-priority targets. Analysts have to help make the collection process work effectively. They can do so by being heavily involved in developing collection strategies.

Four steps are commonly used in developing collection strategies: The customer problem breakdown of chapter 2 and the target model of chapter 7 are used together, first in identifying gaps in knowledge and later in producing finished intelligence. Step 1 is to interrelate the target model with collection sources so that you can plan collection to fill gaps in knowledge, making use of the best available sources.

Step 2 is identifying gaps in your knowledge of the target. The gaps usually become fairly obvious when the target model and problem breakdown are compared, but they have to be made explicit. Collectors can help with this and the following steps, if they have access to the target model and problem breakdown.

Defining a collection strategy, step 3, involves using existing assets to deal with the gaps. Past experience with collection against similar targets can help in this step. Looking at the sources that were used in populating the existing target model can help identify the sources that are best positioned to fill gaps. Having a good understanding of the target so that you can time collection improves the chances that the effort will obtain useful information. The most success in collection strategy comes from having a close relationship with collectors. On large collection efforts against high-priority targets, it may be worthwhile to develop and compare alternative strategies by using cost-benefit analysis.

Planning for future collection systems development, step 4, is primarily the collectors' responsibility. It involves assessing both existing and likely future needs and gaps, including planning to deal with denial and deception.

These steps form an iterative process. They are listed in sequential order to facilitate understanding, but in practice they tend to be worked in varying orders, and several iterations of the process will occur over time.

Notes

1. Steven D. Leavitt and Stephen J. Dubner, *Freakonomics* (New York: HarperCollins, 2005), 89.
2. Stephen Budiansky, *Her Majesty's Spymaster* (New York: Viking Penguin, 2005), 199.
3. See, for example, Roy Godson, *Intelligence Requirements for the 1990s* (Lanham, Md.: Lexington Books, 1989).
4. John Prados, *The Soviet Estimate* (Princeton: Princeton University Press, 1987), 181.
5. Godson, *Intelligence Requirements,* 68.
6. Michael Herman, *Intelligence Power in Peace and War* (Cambridge: Cambridge University Press, 1996), 292.
7. *Report of the Commission on the Intelligence Capabilities of the United States Regarding Weapons of Mass Destruction,* March 31, 2005, www.wmd.gov/report/wmd_report.pdf.
8. Lahneman, William J., *The Future of Intelligence Analysis,* University of Maryland, Center for International and Security Studies at Maryland, final report, vol. I, March 10, 2006, E-8.
9. Joseph M. Myers, "International Strategies to Combat Money Laundering," speech to the International Symposium on the Prevention and Control of Financial Fraud, Beijing, October 19–22, 1998.
10. Ibid.

11. "Minority Staff Report for Permanent Subcommittee on Investigations—Hearing on Private Banking and Money Laundering: A Case Study of Opportunities and Vulnerabilities," November 9, 1999, www.senate.gov/~govt-aff/110999_report.htm.

12. In response to the attacks of September 11, the United States shifted a large segment of its intelligence collection and analysis capability onto the terrorism target. The knowledge gaps that have been opened in other areas will take years to close. Unfortunately, the shifted resources could not be used efficiently, for reasons that are explained by the Brooks curves (see chapter 13).

13. The U.S. Department of Defense defines "order of battle" as "the identification, strength, command structure, and disposition of the personnel, units, and equipment of any military force." See DOD Dictionary of Military Terms, amended October 17, 2008, www.dtic.mil/doctrine/jel/doddict.

14. Prados, The Soviet Estimate, 96–102.

15. U.S. Congress, Congressional Record, June 19, 1997, H3943.

9

Denial, Deception, and Signaling

All warfare is based on deception.

Sun Tzu

In evaluating evidence and developing a target model, an analyst must constantly take into account the fact that evidence may be deliberately shaped by an opponent's actions. That is, the analyst is seeing (or not seeing) what the opponent wants him to see (or not to see). This usually means considering the possibility of denial and deception. Denial and deception (called D&D) are major weapons in the counterintelligence arsenal of a country or organization. They may be the only weapons available to many countries against highly sophisticated technical intelligence (especially against IMINT and SIGINT).

At the opposite extreme, the opponent may be shaping what the analyst sees to send a message or signal. It is important to be able to recognize signals and to understand their meaning.

Denial and Deception

Denial and deception come in many forms. Denial is somewhat more straightforward:

- Communications and radar signals can be denied to SIGINT by operational practices such as intermittent operation or use of land lines instead of radio—practices commonly known as emissions control (EMCON). More technically sophisticated opponents use encryption or a wide range of technical approaches known collectively as low-probability-of-intercept (LPI) techniques. Signals can also be denied by the more aggressive tactic of jamming the SIGINT system with interfering signals.

- Denial against IMINT may take the form of camouflage netting, obscuring or masking techniques, or placing sensitive operations in underground facilities (protecting them against attack at the same time); blinding sensors with lasers; conducting operations during darkness or cloud cover to hide military force movements or illegal activity; and moving units frequently to prevent their being targeted.

- Denial of hyperspectral imagery collection could include scrubbing gas emissions (cleaning them up by removing telltale chemicals) and processing effluents to conceal the nature of the process at a plant.

Deception techniques are limited only by our imagination. Passive deception might include using decoys or having the intelligence target emulate an activity that is not of intelligence interest—making a chemical warfare plant look like a medical drug production facility, for example. Decoys that have been widely used in warfare include dummy ships, missiles, and tanks.

Active deceptions include misinformation (false communications traffic, signals, stories, and documents), misleading activities, and double agents (agents who have been discovered and "turned" to work against their former employers), among others.

Illicit groups such as terrorists conduct most of the deception that intelligence must deal with. Illicit arms traffickers (known as "gray" arms traffickers) and narcotics traffickers have developed an extensive repertoire of deceptive techniques to evade international restrictions. They use intermediaries to hide financial transactions. They change ship names or aircraft call signs en route to mislead law enforcement officials. One airline changed its corporate structure and name overnight after its name became linked to illicit activities.[1] Gray arms traffickers use front companies and false end-user certificates.[2] The following are some of the standard deception techniques that illicit arms carrier aircraft use:

- registering the aircraft in one country, then chartering it by companies registered in another, with crews that are hired in yet other countries, and basing the aircraft somewhere else;
- using another aircraft's call sign;
- flying into an airport with one registration number and then flying out with a different one;
- making an unscheduled landing on the way to the approved destination and unloading illicit cargo; and
- making an unscheduled landing to load illicit cargo en route and then shipping the additional load under cover of the legal cargo.

In another, actual example, a pilot was told to give the destination of his aircraft as N'Djamena in Chad, but when he arrived in Cairo he was told to file a new flight plan giving his destination as Muscat, Oman. Once the plane was on its way to Oman, the crew were told to divert to Mukalla Airport, near Riyan, in southern Yemen, and then to fly a specific, circuitous route over Saudi Arabian airspace.[3]

Commercial entities also engage in deception to mislead competitors, but a company must usually tread a fine line in conducting such deception. The objective is to mislead the competitor without misleading the public (which in countries such as the United States can result in lawsuits) and without doing anything illegal. In a number of areas, however, such as positioning for competitive contract bidding and in mergers and acquisitions, deception is a common and accepted part of the game.

Defense against denial and deception starts with one's own denial effort, that is, the protection of sources and methods of collecting and analyzing intelligence.

Defense against D&D: Protecting Intelligence Sources and Methods

In the intelligence business, it is axiomatic that if you need information, someone will try to keep it from you. And we have repeatedly noted that if an opponent can model a system, he or she can defeat it. So your best defense is to deny your opponent an understanding of your intelligence capabilities. Without such understanding, the opponent cannot effectively conduct D&D.

For small governments, and in the business intelligence world, protection of sources and methods is relatively straightforward. Selective dissemination of, and tight controls on, intelligence information are possible. But a large government has too many intelligence customers to justify such tight restrictions. Those bureaucracies therefore have established an elaborate system simultaneously to protect and disseminate intelligence information. This protection system is loosely called *compartmentation*, because it puts information in compartments and restricts access to the compartments.

There are two levels of protection for intelligence information. The levels distinguish between the *product* of intelligence and the *sources and methods;* usually the product is accorded less protection than the sources and methods. Why? The product, if lost, reveals only itself and not how it was obtained. Information about the product is typically classified "Secret" or below, though "Top Secret" reports are used to protect especially sensitive information. Information that might reveal the identity of the source (such as the identity of an agent) is given the highest level of protection. Loss of that information usually results in someone being imprisoned or killed; the source is lost permanently, and other potential sources are discouraged from coming forward.

In the U.S. intelligence community, the intelligence product, sources, and methods are protected by the sensitive compartmented information (SCI) system. The SCI system uses an extensive set of code words to protect sources and methods. Usually only the collectors and processors have access to the code word materials. The product is generally protected only by standard markings such as Secret and Top Secret, and access is granted to a wide range of people.

Under the SCI system, protection of sources and methods is extremely high for two types of COMINT. Clandestine COMINT—usually acquired through taps on telecommunications systems—is heavily protected because it is expensive to set up and provides high-quality intelligence, and its loss has a severe and often permanent impact. COMINT based on decryption is the second highly protected type. Successes at breaking encryption are tightly compartmented because an opponent can readily change the encryption code, and breaking the new code is laborious.

Most IMINT, on the other hand, has no special controls because the information needs to be made available quickly to field commanders. Very little protection of its sources and methods is needed anyway, because when a reconnaissance aircraft flies overhead, it is obvious to the enemy that you are taking their picture. Most aerial photography has been classified Secret or below, and a substantial amount of satellite photography is now unclassified. High security protection is reserved for unusual IMINT—unique capabilities that are not obvious to the opponent.

Open source intelligence has little or no protection because the source material is unclassified. However, the techniques for exploiting open source material and the specific material of interest can tell an opponent much about an intelligence service's targets. For this reason, intelligence agencies that translate open source often restrict its dissemination, using markings such as "Official Use Only." A restrictive marking also allows a government to avoid copyright laws while limiting use of the material. Corporations make use of similar restrictive markings on material that is translated or reproduced for in-house use for the same reasons—concealment of their interest and avoidance of copyright problems.

A more serious reason for protecting open source methods is that if an opponent knows what the intelligence target materials are, it is easier for the opponent to take deceptive countermeasures. For example, the United States has long been aware that many intelligence services translate and avidly read *Aviation Week and Space Technology*. When the Defense Department wishes to mislead or deceive another country about U.S. aerospace capabilities and intentions, this magazine would be a logical place to plant a misleading story.

The protection given to specialized technical collection varies greatly across the many INTs involved. ELINT is classified Secret or below. When opponents use a radar, they have to assume that someone will intercept it, and denial is very difficult. In contrast, the value of FISINT depends upon concealing any successes in identifying the purpose of each telemetry channel that is collected. FISINT therefore resembles COMINT—the processing part is accorded tight compartmentation protection. Information operations are given a high degree of protection for a similar reason; they are easily defeated if their success becomes known to an opponent.

Higher Level Denial and Deception

An earlier section illustrated some straightforward examples of denial and deception. Deception must follow a careful path; it has to be very subtle (too-obvious clues are likely to tip off the deception) but not so subtle that your opponent misses it. It is commonly used in HUMINT, but in the modern world it frequently has to be multi-INT, or a "swarm" attack, to be effective. Increasingly, various countries are using carefully planned and elaborate, multi-INT D&D. Such efforts even have been given a different name—*perception management*—that focuses on the result that the effort is intended to achieve.

Perception management can be very effective against an intelligence organization that, through hubris or bureaucratic politics, is reluctant to change its initial conclusions about a topic. If the opposing intelligence organization makes a wrong initial estimate, then long-term deception is much easier to pull off. If denial and deception are successful, the opposing organization faces an *unlearning* process: Its predispositions and settled conclusions have to be discarded and replaced. Highly adaptive organizations have the capacity to unlearn and are therefore less vulnerable to denial and deception than are more structured organizations. Large, bureaucratic organizations find unlearning very difficult.

The best perception management results from highly selective targeting, intended to get a specific message to a specific person or organization. This requires knowledge of that person's or organization's preferences in intelligence—a difficult feat to accomplish, but the payoff of a successful perception management effort is very high. It can result in an opposing intelligence service making a miss-call or cause it to develop a false sense of security. If you are armed with a well-developed model of the three elements of a foreign intelligence strategy described in chapter 3—targets, operations, and linkages—an effective CI counterattack in the form of perception management or covert action is possible, as the following examples show.

The Man Who Never Was

During World War II the British had a very good model of German intelligence, including a good understanding of German operations in Spain and the close linkages between German and Spanish intelligence. Armed with this knowledge, the British were able to plant on the Spanish coastline a body that apparently was that of a British staff officer carrying documents that indicated the targets of the next Allied invasion. The deception succeeded because the British had an excellent model of how the German and Spanish services worked together, and they knew what form of information the Germans were likely to believe. A fake operations plan probably would have aroused German suspicions. Instead, the key document was a masterpiece of subtlety in the form of a personal letter hinting that the next invasions would hit Sardinia and Greece and that Sicily (the actual invasion target) was a feint. The Germans were completely deceived. The story of the deception has been told in a book and a motion picture, both titled *The Man Who Never Was*.[4]

The Cuban Missile Crisis

In early 1962 the Soviets decided to place nuclear-equipped SS-4 and SS-5 ballistic missiles in Cuba to counter the increasing U.S. edge in ballistic missiles aimed at the Soviet Union. The deployment was to be hidden from U.S. intelligence by an elaborate denial and deception program that combined HUMINT, IMINT, open source, and diplomatic deception.

- Soviet military units designated for the Cuban assignment were told that they were going to a cold region. They were outfitted with skis, felt boots, fleece-lined parkas, and other winter equipment.
- Officers and missile specialists traveled to Cuba as machine operators, irrigation specialists, and agricultural specialists.
- Missiles were shipped from eight Soviet ports to hide the size of the effort; the missiles were loaded under cover of darkness.
- The missile crates and launchers were shielded with metal sheets to defeat infrared photography.
- Ordinary automobiles, tractors, and harvesters were placed on the top decks to convey the impression that the ships were carrying only agricultural equipment.
- The ships made false declarations when exiting the Black Sea and the Bosporus. They altered the cargo records and declared tonnage well below what was being carried. They often listed Conakry, Guinea, as their destination.
- In Cuba, anything that resembled agricultural equipment was unloaded in the daytime. Weaponry was unloaded only at night and was moved directly to the missile bases along back roads at night.
- Radio Moscow regularly reported that the Soviet Union was supplying Cuba with "machine tools, wheat, and agricultural machinery . . . and fertilizer."
- In what proved to be a brilliant move, the Soviets leaked accurate information about the deployment to mask it. They funneled accurate details through counterrevolutionary Cuban organizations in the United States. The CIA discounted the information, because they did not regard the groups as credible, and dismissed the subsequent stream of reports from Cubans, tourists, and foreign diplomats in Cuba—some of which were valid—as simply more of the same.
- During September, Soviet diplomats gave repeated assurances to top U.S. officials that they had no intention of putting offensive weaponry in Cuba.[5]

The deception was not perfect. There were some slips:

- The Soviets used the freighter *Poltava* to carry missiles. Some U.S. experts speculated that the ship might be carrying ballistic missiles because the Soviets used large-hatch ships such as the *Poltava* to deliver such missiles.

- Had a vessel experienced mechanical failure en route, the captains were told to explain to any ships offering assistance that they were exporting automobiles. If such an encounter had occurred, it would have been a tip-off to analysts that something was amiss because the Soviet Union was not an automobile exporter at the time.

- Once deployed, the units were not well concealed from aerial reconnaissance. They had a characteristic imagery signature that the Soviets did not change and that led to the U.S. discovery of the San Cristobal missile site in October—and the beginning of the Cuban missile crisis.[6]

In summary, the deception was a remarkably well crafted, multi-INT denial and deception effort that succeeded for a long time because the Soviets had a very good understanding of U.S. intelligence capabilities.

The Farewell Dossier

Detailed knowledge of an opponent is the key to successful counterintelligence, as the "Farewell" operation shows. In 1980 the French internal security service, Direction de la Surveillance du Territoire (DST), recruited a KGB lieutenant colonel, Vladimir I. Vetrov, code-named "Farewell." Vetrov gave the French some four thousand documents, detailing an extensive KGB effort to clandestinely acquire technical know-how from the West, primarily the United States. In 1981 French president François Mitterrand shared the source and the documents (which DST named "the Farewell Dossier") with U.S. president Ronald Reagan.

The documents revealed a far-reaching and successful intelligence operation that had already acquired highly sensitive military technology on radars, computers, machine tools, nuclear weaponry, and manufacturing techniques. But the specific targets on the list provided the guidance for an effective counterstrike.

In early 1982 the Defense Department, the FBI, and the CIA began developing a counterattack. Instead of simply improving U.S. defenses against the KGB efforts, the U.S. team used the KGB shopping list to feed back, through CIA-controlled channels, the items on the list—augmented with "improvements" that were designed to pass acceptance testing but would fail randomly in service. Flawed computer chips, turbines, and factory plans found their way into Soviet military and civilian factories and equipment. Misleading information on U.S. stealth technology and space defense flowed into Soviet intelligence reporting. The resulting failures were a severe setback for major segments of Soviet industry. The most dramatic single event resulted when the United States provided gas pipeline management software that was installed in the Soviets' trans-Siberian gas pipeline. The software had a feature that would at some point cause pressure in the pipeline to build up to a level far above its tolerance. The result was the Soviet gas pipeline explosion of 1982, described as the "most monumental non-nuclear explosion and fire ever seen from space."[7]

Mounting a deception campaign often requires extensive effort, but sometimes the payoff is worth it. The Farewell deception exacted high costs but produced many benefits; it may have hastened the end of the cold war.

In many ways, the Farewell deception was the perfect counterintelligence response. Even its subsequent exposure did not reduce the effectiveness of the deception, since the exposure called into question all of the successful KGB technology acquisitions and discredited the KGB's technology collection effort within the Soviet Union.[8] The deception would not have been possible without the detailed knowledge that Col. Vetrov provided, which allowed the United States to create detailed models of the KGB targets, the nature of the KGB operations, and the linkages—that is, the use of other Warsaw Pact country intelligence services in the technology acquisition effort.

The Indian Nuclear Test

Other intelligence services often learn of U.S. collection capabilities through the actions of policymakers. Demarches[9] and public statements that are based on intelligence results inevitably reveal something about intelligence capabilities. India used such knowledge in developing a strategic deception plan to cover its test of a nuclear device on May 11, 1998. On that date, the Indians conducted three underground nuclear tests at their Pokharan nuclear test site in the country's northwestern desert. The test came as a complete surprise to the U.S. government.

The deception succeeded because the Indian government had an excellent understanding of the keys that U.S. imagery analysts used to detect test preparations. The U.S. government had succeeded in deterring an earlier plan by India to stage the tests. In December 1995 U.S. reconnaissance satellites observed test preparations at the Pokharan site, including the movement of vehicles and the deployment of testing equipment. The U.S. ambassador to India showed the imagery to top Indian officials in a successful demarche to persuade them not to test.[10]

Using the knowledge they gained from that demarche, the Indians planned an elaborate denial and deception campaign to conceal preparations for the 1998 tests. The denial campaign involved, among other things, burying the cables and wires running into the test shaft.[11] The deception campaign had at least two major elements:

- The Indian government issued a number of public statements just prior to the test, designed to reassure Washington that no nuclear test was contemplated and to focus U.S. attention on a possible ballistic missile test.

- At the same time, Indian leaders began preparations for a missile test at their Chandipur missile test range, more than a thousand miles from the Pokharan site. The Indians actually tested a surface-to-air missile, but they moved additional equipment into the test range so that the test appeared to be an intermediate-range ballistic missile test.[12]

As a result, U.S. reconnaissance satellites reportedly were focused on the Chandipur missile site, with only minimal coverage of the nuclear test site at the time of the test.[13] The deception was helped along by the U.S. government's mindset that because India wanted to improve trade relations, the country would not provoke a crisis by testing a nuclear weapon.[14]

Countering Denial and Deception

Many of the standard techniques for countering denial and deception were developed during World War II, and they continue to work, with new twists and new technologies. However, when collection becomes too predictable—as can happen in large intelligence organizations—tactics for countering denial and deception no longer work. If opponents can model the collection process, they can defeat it. U.S. intelligence learned that lesson in HUMINT against numerous Soviet targets after some painful losses. There is a tendency to believe that overhead (satellite) IMINT and SIGINT are less vulnerable to countermeasures. However, critics have pointed out that not only denial but also effective deception is possible against both IMINT and SIGINT if the opponent knows enough about the collection system.[15] The effectiveness of hostile denial and deception is a direct reflection of the predictability of collection.

The best way to defeat denial and deception is for all of the stakeholders in the target-centric approach to work closely together. The two fundamental rules of collection form a complementary set: One rule is intended to provide incentive for collectors to defeat denial and deception, and the other suggests ways to defeat it.

The first rule is to establish an effective feedback mechanism. *Relevance* of the product to intelligence questions is the correct measure of collection effectiveness, and analysts and customers—not collectors—determine relevance. The system must enforce a content-oriented evaluation of the product because content is the measure of relevance. This implies that a strong feedback system exists between analyst and collector and generally that collectors have established close links to the analysts. The link has to work both ways. Collectors need to see clearly how their product was used to modify the target model.

At one point in history, intelligence services did very well at countering denial and deception. During World War II both the British and the Germans had efficient systems for identifying D&D techniques and countering them. (The successful Allied deception that covered the 1944 Normandy invasion was a notable exception.) Few denial and deception tactics worked for very long. Britain and Germany owed their World War II successes to a tight feedback loop in their intelligence processes. Intelligence analysts interacted constantly with IMINT and SIGINT collectors to develop counter-countermeasures. As a result, there existed a constant action–counteraction process, much like the one that has existed in the electronic warfare and radar communities during the past sixty years.

The second rule is to make collection smarter and less predictable. Don't optimize systems for quality and quantity; optimize for content. One might, for example, move satellite-based collectors to less desirable orbits to achieve surprise or to keep opponents off balance. At the opposite extreme in sophistication, in collecting discarded papers (TRASHINT), don't keep coming back to the same dumpster every day at the same time.

Apply sensors in new ways. Analysis groups often can help with new sensor approaches in their areas of responsibility. Also, techniques for defeating denial and deception that have been developed for one problem (counternarcotics, for example) may be applicable to others (weapons proliferation).

Consider provocative techniques against D&D targets. In U.S. Air Force reconnaissance programs dating back to the 1950s, provocation was used effectively to overcome the practice of emissions control by the Soviets. In emissions control, one keeps all nonessential signals off the air until the SIGINT collector has left the area. The U.S. response was to send an aircraft on a penetration course toward the Soviet border, for example, and turn away at the last minute, after the Soviets had turned on their entire air defense network to deal with the threat. Probing an opponent's system and watching the response is a useful tactic for learning more about the system. Even so, probing may have its own undesirable consequences: The Soviets would occasionally chase and shoot down the reconnaissance aircraft to discourage the probing practice.

Hit the collateral or inferential targets. If an opponent engages in denial or deception about a specific facility, then supporting facilities may allow inferences to be made that would expose the deception. Security measures around a facility and the nature and status of nearby communications, power, or transportation facilities may provide a more complete picture. A sequel to the successful British commando raid on the Bruneval radar, described in chapter 6, was that the Germans protected all of their Würzburg radars near the coast with barbed wire entanglements. The barbed wire showed up clearly on aerial photography and made it relatively easy for British photo interpreters to locate all of the radars that the Germans had successfully concealed up until then.

Finally, use deception to protect a collection capability. Military tacticians claim that the best weapon against a tank is another tank, and the best weapon against a submarine is another submarine. Similarly, the best weapon against denial and deception is to mislead or confuse opponents about intelligence capabilities, disrupt their warning programs, and discredit their intelligence services. Chapter 6 discussed Project Jennifer, the U.S. use of the *Glomar Explorer* to raise a sunken Soviet submarine. Project Jennifer was protected by an elaborate deception program. Its intent was to convince Soviet intelligence that the *Glomar Explorer*'s purpose was deep-sea mining, and the ship's operations were carefully planned to support that impression. The deception apparently succeeded, in part because U.S. intelligence knew that Moscow would pay very little attention to a ship having only a commercial purpose.

In analysis, the first defense against D&D involves maintaining alternative target models, as discussed in chapter 7. Another important step is constantly to develop new techniques for sensor fusion or synthesis of intelligence data. An analyst can often beat denial and deception simply by using several types of intelligence—HUMINT, COMINT, and so on—in combination, simultaneously, or successively. It is relatively easy to defeat one sensor or collection channel. It is more difficult to defeat all types of intelligence at the same time. Hyperspectral imaging, for example, is a valuable weapon against IMINT deception because it can be used to measure so many different aspects (signatures) of a target. Increasingly, opponents can be expected to use swarm D&D against several INTs in a coordinated attack like the one the Soviets orchestrated in the Cuban missile crisis. Such complex operations, however, as in that example, inevitably have their weak points. The analyst has to find them.

Signaling

Signaling is the opposite of denial and deception. It is the process of deliberately sending a message, usually to an opposing intelligence service. It is included here because, like D&D, its use depends on a good knowledge of how the opposing intelligence service obtains and analyzes knowledge. Recognizing and interpreting an opponent's signals is one of the more difficult challenges an analyst must face. Depending on the situation, signals can be made verbally, by actions or displays, or by very subtle nuances that depend on the context of the signal.

In negotiations, signals can be both verbal and nonverbal. True signals often are used in place of open declarations to provide information while preserving deniability. False signals are used to mislead, usually to gain a negotiating advantage.

One signal that has gained use with the increase in satellite imagery is the display of items in an imaged area to send a message. Massing troops on a frontier as an intimidation tactic is one example of signaling. It is such a well-known tactic that in July 1990 Saddam Hussein's massing of troops on the Kuwait border initially was interpreted as a signal, putting pressure on Kuwait to obtain economic concessions.

In business, signals are often conveyed by actions rather than by words. A competitor's product price increase or decrease, an acquisition, a new product line, or a major reorganization, among other things, can be a signal of the company's future intentions in the market.

Analyzing signals requires examining the content of the signal, its context, its timing, and its source. Statements made to the press are quite different from statements made through diplomatic channels—the latter usually carry more weight. As an example of context, a statement that the Egyptian ambassador makes to a U.S. military attaché at an embassy function could easily be a signal; the ambassador knows that he is speaking to an intelligence officer.

Signaling between members of the same culture can be subtle, with high success rates of the signal being understood. Two U.S. corporate executives can signal to each other with confidence; they both understand the rules. A U.S. executive and an Indonesian executive would face far greater risks of misunderstanding each other's signals. The cultural differences in signaling can be substantial. Cultures differ in their reliance on verbal and nonverbal signals to communicate their messages. The more people rely on nonverbal signals and context, the greater the complexity. For instance, the Japanese and Chinese rely heavily on nonverbal signals, and the context of a signal is highly significant. As Figure 9-1 indicates, the Swiss are at the opposite extreme; their messages are verbal, explicit, and independent of context.

Figure 9-1   Cultural Differences in Signaling

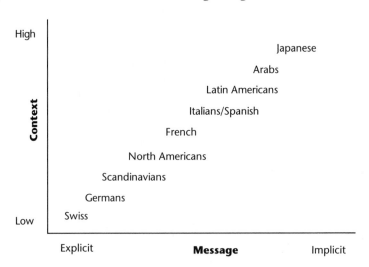

Source: Edward T. Hall, *Beyond Culture* (Garden City, N.Y.: Anchor Press, 1976).

Signaling is an art, and interpreting signals is an art. Failure to understand the signals can have severe consequences.

> During the Korean War, as U.S. and U.N. forces advanced North of the 38th parallel, China decided that a North Korean defeat was unacceptable. China's leaders moved aggressively on several fronts to signal their intention to inter- vene militarily if the advances continued. Diplomatic notes, press releases, and overt troop movements all were used to send the signal. U.S. policymak- ers and military leaders either dismissed or failed to understand the signals, and the Chinese intervention came as a surprise.[16]

In July 1990 the U.S. State Department unintentionally sent several signals that Saddam Hussein apparently interpreted as a green light to attack Kuwait. State Department spokesperson Margaret Tutwiler said, "We do not have any defense treaties with Kuwait. . . ." The next day, Ambassador April Glaspie told Saddam Hussein, "We have no opinion on Arab-Arab conflicts like your border disagree- ment with Kuwait." And two days before the invasion, Assistant Secretary of State John Kelly testified before the House Foreign Affairs Committee that there was no obligation on our part to come to the defense of Kuwait if it was attacked.[17]

The Kuwait example illustrates the other side of signaling—that intelli- gence analysts need to support the customer. Clearly, it is important to be able to tell a policymaker what the opponent's signals are and interpret them. But it is equally important to let policymakers know how their signals, whether intentional or not, are likely to be interpreted by the opponent.

Analytic Tradecraft in a World of D&D

Analysts tend to view intelligence analysis as an art or a craft, not as a formal discipline with a tested and validated methodology.[18] And, in fact, intelligence professionals refer to the techniques of analysis as *tradecraft*. The argument has been made that intelligence analysis should become a profession—which means instituting a repeatable, standardized process, with established best practices. Writers often make the analogy that intelligence analysis is like the medical profession.[19] Analysts and doctors weigh evidence and reach conclusions in much the same fashion. In fact intelligence analysis, like medicine, is a combina- tion of art, tradecraft, and science.[20] Different doctors can draw different conclu- sions from the same evidence. Different analysts do likewise.

And intelligence analysts have a different type of problem than doctors typically have. Scientific researchers and medical professionals do not rou- tinely have to deal with denial and deception. They typically do not have an opponent who is trying to deny them knowledge. In medicine, once doctors have a process for treating a pathology, it will in most cases work as expected. The human body won't develop countermeasures to the treatment.[21] But in intelligence, the opponent may be able to identify the analysis process and counter it. If analysis becomes standardized, an opponent can predict how you will analyze the available intelligence, and then denial and deception become much easier to pull off. Consider, for example, the effect of the Soviet "leak" during the Cuban missile crisis that was discussed previously. Intelligence collection and analysis, by their nature, have to evolve. One cannot establish a process and blithely retain it indefinitely.

Intelligence analysis is in fact analogous to poker, especially Seven Card Stud or Texas Hold 'Em. You have an opponent. Some of the opponent's resources are in plain sight; some are hidden. You have to observe the opponent's actions (bets, timing, facial expressions, which incorporate art and tradecraft) and do pattern analysis (using statistics and other tools of science). Revisiting Sun Tzu's quote that begins this chapter, poker, like warfare, is based on deception. And intelligence, like poker, is about warfare. There are lots of poker "methodologies," just as there are lots of intelligence methodologies. No single one works universally, and all can be defeated once they are understood.

Some underlying principles are common to poker and intelligence analysis. In poker, you create a model of your opponents, based on observations of their past behavior; and you create a model of the current hand, based on the model of your opponents, evidence of their behavior during the current hand, and a statistical analysis of what can be observed (e.g., the exposed cards). You analyze those models and make judgments. In intelligence analysis, you do the same.

Summary

In evaluating raw intelligence, analysts must constantly be aware of the possibility that they are seeing material that was deliberately provided by the opposing side. Most targets of intelligence efforts practice some form of denial. Deception—providing false information—is less common than denial because it takes more effort, and it can backfire.

Defense against D&D starts with your own denial of your intelligence capabilities to opposing intelligence services. Some collection sources and methods have to be heavily protected or they will become vulnerable to D&D. Names of HUMINT sources, the nature of COMINT or many types of technical collection, and the decryption of encrypted messages all fall into this category. In contrast, the information that a source provides is accorded less protection than details about the source itself because the information provided needs to go to many intelligence customers. IMINT and open sources usually receive less source protection than do HUMINT, COMINT, or specialized technical collection.

Where one intelligence service has extensive knowledge of another service's sources and methods, more ambitious and elaborate D&D efforts are possible. Often called *perception management,* these involve developing a coordinated, multi-INT campaign to get the opposing service to make a wrong initial estimate. Having done so, the opposing service faces an unlearning process, which can be very difficult. A high level of knowledge also permits covert actions to disrupt and discredit the opposing service.

A collaborative, target-centric process helps to stymie denial and deception by bringing in different perspectives from the customer, the collector, and the analyst. Collectors can be more effective in a D&D environment with the help of analysts. Working as a team, they can make more use of deceptive, unpredictable, and provocative collection methods that have proved effective in defeating D&D.

The opposite of D&D, yet closely related to it, is the practice of signaling: deliberately sending a message to the opposing intelligence service. Like D&D, its success depends on a good understanding of the opponent to whom a signal is sent. Signals can be verbal or can be actions or displays. Analysts have to be alert to the presence of signals and adept at interpreting their meaning. When signals must be sent between different cultures, they often are missed or misinterpreted.

Intelligence analysis is a combination of art, tradecraft, and science. In large part the reason is that analysts must constantly deal with denial and deception, and dealing with D&D is primarily a matter of artfully applying tradecraft.

Notes

1. Brian Wood and Johan Peleman, *The Arms Fixers* (Oslo: International Peace Research Institute [PRIO], 1999), www.nisat.org/publications/armsfixers, chap. 5.
2. International legal protocol surrounding the shipment of lethal weapons requires that the shipper have a certificate of "end use," in which the buyer declares that the weapons are for its use only and will not be trans-shipped.
3. Wood and Peleman, *The Arms Fixers,* chap. 5.
4. Ewen Montagu, *The Man Who Never Was* (Annapolis: Naval Institute Press, 1953).
5. James H. Hansen, "Soviet Deception in the Cuban Missile Crisis," *Central Intelligence Agency: Studies in Intelligence* 46, no.1 (2002), www.cia.gov/csi/studies/vol46no1/article06.html.
6. Ibid.
7. Thomas C. Reed, *At the Abyss: An Insider's History of the Cold War* (Novato, Calif.: Presidio Press, 2004).
8. Gus W. Weiss, "The Farewell Dossier," *Central Intelligence Agency: Studies in Intelligence* 39, no. 5 (September/October1996), www.cia. gov/csi/studies/96unclass.
9. A *demarche* is a political or diplomatic step, such as a protest or diplomatic representation made to a foreign government.
10. Tim Weiner and James Risen, "Policy Makers, Diplomats, Intelligence Officers All Missed India's Intentions," *New York Times,* May 25, 1998.
11. Ibid.
12. "Strategic Deception at Pokharan Reported," *Delhi Indian Express in English,* May 15, 1998, 1.
13. Weiner and Risen, "Policy Makers, Diplomats, Intelligence Officers."
14. Ibid.
15. Angelo Codevilla, *Informing Statecraft* (New York: Free Press, 1992), 159–165.
16. P. K. Rose, "Two Strategic Intelligence Mistakes in Korea, 1950," *Central Intelligence Agency: Studies in Intelligence* (Fall/Winter 2001), www.cis.gov/csi/studies/fall_winter_2001/article06. html.

17. Jude Wanniski, "Where Did Saddam Hussein Come From?" *Wall Street Journal,* February 19, 1998.

18. Rob Johnson, *Analytic Culture in the U.S. Intelligence Community* (Washington, D.C.: Center for the Study of Intelligence, Central Intelligence Agency, 2005), 20.

19. Steven Marin, "Intelligence Analysis: Turning a Craft into a Profession," May 2, 2005, http://analysis.mitre.org/proceedings/ Final_Papers_Files/97_Camera_Ready_Paper.pdf.

20. Johnson, *Analytic Culture,* 43.

21. This analogy has its limits, of course. Doctors must routinely deal with patients who conceal embarrassing information; but the patient seldom if ever is trying to lead the doctor to an incorrect diagnosis. And microbes do develop resistance to antibiotics over time.

10

Prediction

Your problem is that you are not able to see things before
they happen.
Wotan to Fricka, in Richard Wagner's opera *Die Walküre*

Describing a past event is not intelligence analysis; it is history. The highest form of intelligence analysis requires structured thinking that results in a prediction of what is likely to happen. True intelligence analysis is always predictive.

However, policymaking customers tend to be skeptical of predictive analysis unless they do it themselves. They believe that their own opinions about the future are at least as good as those of intelligence analysts. So when an analyst offers a prediction without a compelling supporting argument, he or she should not be surprised to have the policymaker ignore it.

On the other hand, policymakers and executives will accept and make use of predictive intelligence if it is well reasoned and if they can follow the analyst's logic. Former national security adviser Brent Scowcroft observed, "What intelligence estimates do for the policymaker is to remind him what forces are at work, what the trends are, and what are some of the possibilities that he has to consider."[1] A predictive intelligence assessment that does those things will be readily accepted. This chapter and the two following chapters discuss how to prepare such assessments.

Introduction to Prediction

Intelligence can handle predictions of routine developments. Extrapolation—the act of making predictions based solely on past observations—serves us reasonably well in the short term for events that involve established trends and organizational actions.

Long-term prediction is considerably more challenging because it is constrained by the second law of thermodynamics, as introduced in chapter 7: Entropy (chaos, randomness) always increases with time. And when you reach a turning point, a major shift of some kind, then prediction becomes highly uncertain. We do not readily grasp fundamental changes, and we are skeptical of those who claim to have done so. To go beyond description to prediction, an analyst must be able to bring multidisciplinary understanding to the problem and apply a proven prediction methodology. Understanding a narrow technical specialty may be useful for simple target modeling, but it is insufficient beyond that.

Intelligence predictions can also affect the future that they predict. Often the predictions are acted on by policymakers—sometimes on both sides. CIA reports released to the press by Congress and by President Jimmy Carter warned that Soviet oil production was likely to plateau by the early 1980s and then decline, to the point where the Soviet Union would become a net importer of oil. Production did in fact fall, but the Soviets—perhaps warned by the published CIA estimate—shifted investment to their energy sector and changed their extraction and exploration policies to avert the worst.[2] As another example, the publication of the Yugoslavia National Intelligence Estimate in 1990 (see the appendix) hastened the breakup of Yugoslavia that it predicted.

The first step in making any prediction is to consider the phenomena that are involved to determine whether prediction is even possible.

Convergent and Divergent Phenomena

In chapter 7 we discussed convergent and divergent evidence. Items of evidence were convergent if they tended to reinforce the same conclusion and divergent if they pointed to different conclusions. In considering trends and events for predictive purposes, we use the same terminology: Convergent phenomena make prediction possible; divergent phenomena frustrate prediction.

A basic question to ask at the outset of any prediction attempt is, Does the principle of causation apply? That is, are the phenomena we are to examine and make predictions about governed by the laws of cause and effect? One of the basic principles of classical physics was that of causation. The behavior of any system could be predicted from the average behavior of its component parts. Scientist Irving Langmuir defined such behavior as *convergent* phenomena.

The events leading up to World War I, which Barbara Tuchman superbly outlines in *The Guns of August,* had an inevitable quality about them, as befits convergent phenomena.[3] World War I was predictable—it had been predicted, in fact, by many astute observers at the time. No one person or event actually "started" World War I; the assassination of Archduke Francis Ferdinand and his wife, Sophie, in Sarajevo merely triggered a process for which groundwork had been laid over many years. Likewise, a war between the United States and Japan was predictable (and both sides had predicted it) throughout most of 1941. The Japanese aggression in China and Indochina, the consequent U.S. imposition of a petroleum embargo on Japan, the freezing of funds by both sides, the steady deterioration in American-Japanese relations during the fall of 1941—all events converged toward war.[4] Also, a pattern of continued al Qaeda terrorist attacks on U.S. interests worldwide was predictable and had been predicted before September 11, 2001, when terrorists flew airplanes into the Pentagon and the World Trade Center. In the 1940s and 1950s Ambassador George

Kennan identified perhaps the most significant convergent phenomenon of the last century when he defined his "containment" policy for the United States to pursue against the Soviet Union. He argued that, if contained, the Soviet Union would eventually collapse because of its overdeveloped military and underdeveloped economic system.

In contrast, many phenomena are not governed by the laws of cause and effect. Quantum physics deals with the individual atom or basic particles and has found that their behavior is as unpredictable as the toss of a coin; they can be dealt with only by the laws of probability.[5] Such behavior can, from a small beginning, produce increasingly large effects—a nuclear chain reaction, for example. Langmuir described those phenomena as *divergent*. In the terms of chaos theory, such phenomena are the result of what are called *strange attractors*— those creators of unpredictable patterns that emerge out of the behavior of purposeful actors.[6] When dealing with divergent phenomena, we have almost insurmountable difficulty in making predictions.

To contrast the predictability of the two types of phenomena, consider three CIA predictions: CIA analysts warned policymakers of Russia's looming economic crisis two months before the August 1998 ruble crash; they also subsequently identified the economic rebound in the Russian economy long before business and academic experts did.[7] Both events involved convergent phenomena and were predictable. In contrast, the CIA was unable to predict the rise of Vladimir Putin to the Russian presidency until his handling of the Chechen war dramatically increased his popularity. But in early 1999 Putin himself probably did not foresee that happening.[8] It was a divergent phenomenon.

A good example of a divergent phenomenon in intelligence is the *coup d'état*. Policymakers often complain that their intelligence organizations have failed to predict coups. But a coup event is conspiratorial in nature, limited to a handful of people, and dependent on the preservation of secrecy for its success. If a foreign intelligence service knows of the event, then secrecy has been compromised and the coup is almost certain to fail—the country's internal security services will probably forestall it. The conditions that encourage a coup attempt can be assessed, and its likelihood estimated by using probability theory, but the timing and likelihood of success are not "predictable."

The failed attempt to assassinate Hitler in 1944, for example, had more of the "what if?" hypothetical quality that characterizes a divergent phenomenon. Assassinations, such as that of Israeli prime minister Yitzhak Rabin in 1995, are simply not predictable. Specific terrorist acts, such as those on September 11, 2001, similarly are not predictable in detail, though some kind of terrorist attempt was both predictable and predicted. In all such divergent cases, from the Sarajevo assassination to the World Trade Center bombing, some tactical warning might have been possible. An agent within the Serbian terrorist organization the Black Hand could have warned of the Sarajevo assassination plan. An agent within al Qaeda might have warned of the planned World Trade Center attack. But tactical warning is not the same as prediction. All such specific events can be described by probabilities, but they cannot be predicted in the same fashion as the larger events they were immersed in—World War I, the collapse of Nazi Germany, and increasing conflict between the United States and al Qaeda.

One of the watershed moments in personal computing was clearly a divergent phenomenon. In 1980 IBM was searching for software to run on its planned personal computer (PC) and had zeroed in on a small start-up company named Microsoft Corporation, located in Bellevue, Washington. Microsoft could provide the languages that programmers would use to write software for the PC, but IBM wanted more; it needed an operating system. Microsoft did not have an operating system and was not positioned to write one, so Bill Gates, Microsoft's president, steered IBM to Digital Research Intergalactic (DRI).

An intelligence analyst assessing the likely future of personal computing in 1980 would have placed his bets on DRI. DRI built the CP/M operating system, at that time the most popular operating system for computers using the Intel processor. It had the basic features IBM needed. Gates arranged an appointment between the IBM team and Gary Kildall, DRI's president, in Pacific Grove, California.

Instead of meeting with the IBM team, however, Kildall chose to take a flight in his new airplane. Miffed, the IBM team told Gates to find or write an operating system himself. Gates found one from a small software company in the Seattle area and called it the Disk Operating System (DOS), which later became the most widely used personal computer operating system and a major contributor to Microsoft's dominance of the personal computer business. A single event, a decision by one man not to keep an appointment, shaped the future of personal computing worldwide.[9]

In summary, the principles of causation apply well to convergent phenomena, and prediction is possible. Divergent phenomena, such as the actions of an individual person, are not truly predictable and must be handled by different techniques, such as those of probability theory. Where prediction is possible, analysts typically use force synthesis/analysis, which we will discuss in this chapter.

The Predictive Approach

The target-centric analytic approach to prediction follows a pattern long established in the sciences, in organizational planning, and in systems synthesis/analysis. In intelligence analysis, we are concerned with describing the past and the current states of the target to make a prediction about its future state.

Prediction is as old as engineering. No large projects—temples, aqueducts, pyramids—were undertaken without some type of predictive process. Many prediction techniques have evolved over the past five centuries as mathematics and science have evolved.[10] They frequently reappear with new names, even though their underlying principles are centuries old.

The predictive synthesis/analysis process discussed in this chapter and the next is derived from a predictive approach that has been formalized in several professional disciplines. In management theory, the approach has several names, one of which is the Kempner Tregoe Rational Management Process.[11] In engineering, the formalization is called the Kalman Filter. In the social sciences, it is called the Box-Jenkins method. Although there are differences among them, all are techniques for combining complex data and incorporating new data to estimate the present state, or predict the future state, of an entity.

The approach is a method of combining data to estimate an entity's present state and evaluating the forces acting on the entity to predict its future state. The concept—to identify the forces acting on an entity, to identify likely future forces, and to predict the likely changes in old and new forces over time, along with some indicator of confidence in the judgments—is the key to successful prediction. It takes into account redundant and conflicting data, as well as the analyst's degree of confidence in those data. It can be made quantitative if time permits and if confidence in the data can be quantified. But the concept can be applied qualitatively by subjectively assessing the forces acting on the entity. Figure 10-1 shows an overview of this predictive methodology. The key is to start from the present target model (preferably along with a past target model) and move to one of the future models, using an analysis of the forces involved as a basis. Other texts on predictive analysis describe these forces as issues, trends, factors, or drivers.[12] All of the terms have the same meaning: They are the entities that shape the future.[13] In most cases, the future target models will be in the form of scenarios, as Figure 10-1 indicates.

Figure 10-1   Prediction Methodology

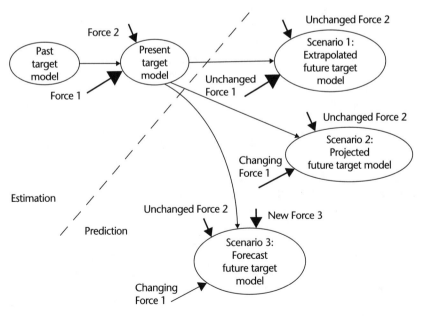

Note: Arrows vary in thickness to indicate the strength of their respective forces. Thicker arrows represent stronger forces; thinner arrows, weaker ones.

The methodology uses three predictive mechanisms that will be discussed in detail in chapter 11: extrapolation, projection, and forecasting. All three predictive mechanisms follow the approach of assessing forces that act on an entity. An *extrapolation* assumes that those forces do not change between the present and future states; a *projection* assumes that they do change; and a *forecast* assumes that they change and that new forces are added. The methodology follows these steps:

- First, estimate at least one past state and the present state of the entity. In intelligence, this entity is the target model, and it can be a model of almost anything—a terrorist organization, a country, a clandestine trade network, an industry, a technology, or a ballistic missile.

- Determine the forces that acted on the entity to bring it to its present state. In the figure, these forces (Forces 1 and 2) are shown graphically, with the thickness of the arrow indicating strength. These same forces, acting unchanged, would result in the future state shown as an extrapolation (Scenario 1).

- In making a projection, estimate the changes that are likely to occur in the existing forces. In the figure, a decrease in one of the existing forces (Force 1) is shown as causing a projected future state that is different from the extrapolation (Scenario 2).

- In making a forecast, start from the projection, and then identify the new forces that may act on the entity and incorporate their effect. In the figure, one new force is shown as coming to bear, resulting in a *forecast* future state that differs from the *projected* future state (Scenario 3).

- Determine the likely future state of the entity based on an assessment of the forces. Strong and certain forces are weighted most heavily in this prediction. Weak forces and those in which the analyst lacks confidence (high uncertainty about the nature or effect of the force) are weighted least.

Figure 10-2 shows how the process of Figure 10-1 works in practice: It is iterative. In this figure we are concerned with some target (technology, system, person, organization, industry, country, situation, or some combination) that changes over time. We want to describe or characterize the entity at some future point. We might want to establish the future performance of an aircraft or missile, the future state of a country's economy, the future morale and effectiveness of a terrorist organization, or the future economic health of an industry. The models are created in an iterative process, each one building on the results of the previous ones. They become more difficult to create as one moves upward in the figure.

Designing good predictive scenarios requires an iterative process such as Figure 10-2 indicates. Iteration is the key to dealing with complex patterns and complex models.[14] The basic analytic paradigm is to create a model of the past and present state of the target, followed by predictive models of its

Figure 10-2   Applying an Iterative Approach to the Prediction Methodology

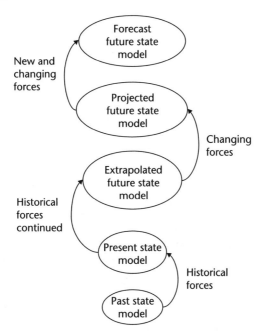

possible future states, usually created in scenario form. Following are two examples of its use in practice.

The CIA's Office of Soviet Analysis predicted in late 1987 that Moscow could not effectively counter the U.S. Strategic Defense Initiative (SDI) without severely straining the Soviet economy, discounting Moscow's assertions that it could do so quickly and cheaply. The prediction was made by a straightforward extrapolation of the state of the Soviet economy without its attempting to counter SDI, followed by a projection in which a new force—the burden on the economy of countering SDI—was added. The analysts correctly predicted the alternative outcome: that Moscow instead would push arms control measures to gain U.S. concessions on SDI.[15]

A CIA assessment of Soviet leader Mikhail Gorbachev's economic reforms in 1985 to 1987 correctly predicted that his proposed reforms risked "confusion, economic disruption, and worker discontent" that could embolden potential rivals to his power.[16] That projection was based on assessing the changing forces in Soviet society along with the historical forces that would resist change.

Introduction to Force Synthesis/Analysis

Force synthesis/analysis has many names—*force field analysis* and *system dynamics* are two.[17] It is a technique for prediction that involves finding out what the existing forces are, how they are changing, in what direction, and how rapidly (see Analysis Principle 10-1). Then, for forecasting, the analyst must identify new forces that are likely to come into play. Most of the following chapters focus on identifying and measuring those forces. One of the most important comes from the feedback mechanism, which is discussed in chapter 12. An analyst can (wrongly) shape the outcome by concentrating on some forces and ignoring or downplaying the significance of others.

Analysis Principle 10-1 ●─────────────────────────────────────

Force Analysis According to Sun Tzu

Factor or force synthesis/analysis is an ancient predictive technique. Successful generals have practiced it in warfare for thousands of years, and one of its earliest known proponents was a Chinese general named Sun Tzu. He described the art of war as being controlled by five factors, all of which must be taken into account in predicting the outcome of an engagement. The five factors he called Moral Law, Heaven, Earth, the Commander, and Method and Discipline. In modern terms, the five would be called social, environment, geospatial, leadership, and organizational factors.

Four factors, or instruments of national power, are usually cited as the "levers" that a policymaker can pull in international relations. Three are well established: political (or diplomatic), economic, and military instruments. The fourth was once called *psychosocial* but more commonly is called a *social instrument*. Some authors divide *social* into psychological and informational.[18] Others, reflecting the current stress on information, call the four instruments diplomatic, economic, military, and information. In the business world, they are almost the same: political, economic, environmental, and social. The argument can be made that technology is a fifth major instrument of national power, or of business power, on the same level as the other four. Technology certainly is a factor (and often the critical factor) in intelligence assessments.

Note that these factors of national power or industrial power can be external, internal, or feedback forces. For instance, regulatory forces, discussed in chapter 12, are a political feedback force—that is, they result from monitoring the state of an economy or an industry, for example, and taking regulatory actions to change that state. Contamination, also in chapter 12, is an internal force that can be social, environmental, or both.

Qualitative Force Synthesis/Analysis

Qualitative force synthesis/analysis is the simplest approach to both projection and forecasting and the easiest to do. It usually is done by an analyst who is an expert in the subject area and who begins the process by answering the following questions:

1. What forces have affected this entity (organization, situation, industry, technical area) over the past several years?[19]
2. Which five or six forces had more impact than others?
3. What forces are expected to affect this entity over the next several years?
4. Which five or six forces are likely to have more impact than others?
5. What are the fundamental differences between the answers to questions 2 and 4?
6. What are the implications of these differences for the entity being analyzed?

Those answers give the changes in direction of the projection shown in Figure 10-1. At more sophisticated levels of qualitative synthesis/analysis, the analyst examines adaptive forces (feedback forces) and their changes over time.

This section has introduced some fairly advanced prediction concepts. An example may help to clarify how the predictive methodology works in practice.

Predicting Organizations' Behavior and Future

To illustrate the prediction process for organizations, let us attempt a predictive assessment of the al Qaeda terrorist organization, starting from the organization's historical states and going forward in time to alternative predictive states. The example is highly simplified; it considers only a few of the forces involved, for illustrative purposes, and does not represent all of the possible future scenarios. Figure 10-3 shows the rise of al Qaeda and some possible future directions; movement upward indicates increasing power and ability of al Qaeda to achieve its goals; movement downward indicates the opposite.

Figure 10-3   **Predictive Model of Possible Future States of al Qaeda**

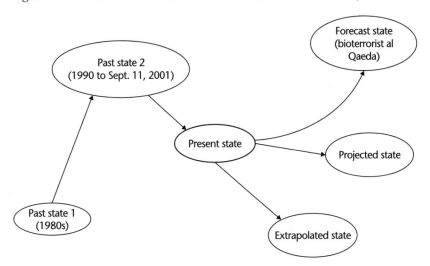

Note: Nodes are elevated to indicate strength and lowered to indicate weakness.

The figure illustrates two past states of al Qaeda. Past state 1 is the earlier of the two. In the mid-1980s Osama bin Laden and Palestinian Muslim Brotherhood leader Abdallah Azzam cofounded the Maktab al-Khidamat (MAK) to fight against the Soviet occupation of Afghanistan. The effort funneled fighters and money (military and economic forces) into the combat. In the late 1980s bin Laden split from MAK to form al Qaeda, and his organizational focus turned from Afghanistan to global promotion of Islamic fundamentalist goals.

Past state 2 covers the period when the organization grew stronger as a result of continuing positive economic, military, and social forces. Funding came in from many parts of the Islamic world, more terrorist "cells" were formed, military training was expanded and improved, and recruits were attracted to the increasingly extreme fundamentalist Islamic message of bin Laden. Political forces constrained the growth of the organization, as Middle Eastern governments and United Nations pressure drove bin Laden out of Saudi Arabia to Sudan and then to Afghanistan. The political pressure and opposing military forces (continuing U.S. military presence in the Persian Gulf region and attempts to attack bin Laden in Afghanistan) drove al Qaeda to more aggressive terrorist attacks, culminating in the attack on the United States on September 11, 2001.

The figure then moves to the present state of al Qaeda, which we define as the state since September 11, 2001. Al Qaeda fortunes have taken a turn for the worse, as a combination of powerful new military, political, and economic forces worldwide degrades the organization's capabilities by closing cells, hunting down leaders, and shutting down sources of funding. The result is an organization in disarray and much weaker compared with its powerful position before September 11. It is under pressure in the military, economic, and political arenas, and no government wants to be identified as a safe harbor for al Qaeda cells. Social forces are both positive and negative; al Qaeda continues to have strong popular support in the Islamic world because it continues to fight the United States, but it is viewed negatively in much of the rest of the world and in parts of the Arab world as well.

From the present state the analyst devises three future states: extrapolated, projected, and forecast. In the extrapolated state, al Qaeda continues to decline under the combination of unchanging military, economic, and political pressures. Remaining cells are hunted down, but followers continue to be recruited (social force continues unchanged). Funding to the group decreases as governments continue to close down the sources of funding, and the organization eventually cannot train or equip its cells to carry out significant terrorist activity.

In the projected state, changes occur in the political and economic forces that allow al Qaeda to arrest its decline. Most governments turn to other concerns, such as an economic crisis, or perceive that they have done enough to deal with the terrorism threat, and funding and recruitment resume. Al Qaeda continues to lose cells through U.S. and British efforts, but new cells are created as new followers, attracted to the cause by admiration of the group's willingness to fight the United States (a pro-growth social force), join.

The forecast state is much the same as the projected state, except that new technology forces are added to the target model, and the result affects the other forces. Specifically, new methods of terrorism are developed and employed, as al Qaeda uses its new funding to develop a genetic engineering capability. With that capability it creates a series of virulent and deadly bioorganisms and uses them in attacks on the United States and allied countries. Political and military forces against al Qaeda weaken, as public sentiment in the United States and elsewhere changes from a desire to battle al Qaeda to a wish for an accommodation that would end the bioterrorist attacks. The resulting negotiations with al Qaeda strengthen its position as the defender of Islam against the infidels worldwide.

Note that the three outcomes—extrapolated, projected, and forecast—represent alternative scenarios, and the fact that the forecast state incorporates both new and changing forces does not make it the most likely outcome. None of the three scenarios could happen, or all three could happen in turn. Because most intelligence predictions, like this example, are in scenario form, the next section discusses how to develop scenarios.

Scenarios

Intelligence scenarios are descriptions in story form of a future target model. Scenarios are used primarily for planning and decision making. Scenario planning is normally used to explore possible future conditions, if given a set of assumptions. Each scenario represents a distinct, plausible picture of a segment of the future.

Because it is impossible to know the future precisely, the solution is to create several scenarios. These are essentially specially constructed stories about the future, each one modeling a distinct, plausible outcome. The scenarios establish the boundaries of our uncertainty and the limits to plausible futures.

Why Use Scenarios?

The purpose of scenario planning is to highlight large forces that shape the future. Scenario planning makes those forces visible so that if they do happen, the intelligence officer will at least recognize them.[20] Scenario planning helps the intelligence officer and the customer anticipate the future and better respond to events.

Scenarios have great power to communicate the sense or feel of situations that do not and may never exist, a power that is at once an asset and a danger. They give users a feel for what might happen if they pursue a certain course of action in a complex situation that cannot be quantified. An example would be a scenario that describes the likely pattern of daily life in the future under specified assumptions about nuclear power plant regulation. Depending on the views of the scenario planner, the scenario could be used to support or oppose increased regulation. A supporter of regulation would likely develop scenarios that included a series of Three Mile Island or Chernobyl disasters absent regulation. An opponent of regulation would be more likely to devise scenarios that showed a world of high electric power costs, atmospheric pollution from smokestack power plants, and declining economies resulting from the increasing energy costs of regulation. An intelligence analyst must have the objectivity to avoid such slanted scenarios.

Scenarios are used in strategic planning in business, for instance, to examine merger candidates or consider a new product line. These are often global scenarios. Scenarios are used also in tactical or operational planning— for example, for interdicting illicit traffic such as narcotics. In narcotics interdiction, the scenario would include a geospatial target model of narcotics growing and processing areas and drug trans-shipment routes, possibly with timeline models showing when trans-shipments take place. The scenario would also include relationship models (link or network diagrams) showing the pattern of funds laundering. For operational planning, the scenario would then be modified to show the effect of specific narcotics interdiction actions— for example, deployment of radar surveillance aircraft into the Caribbean or a program to pay farmers not to grow the crop. Because of the analyst's knowledge of the target, she is a key participant in incorporating such effects into the scenario.

Once scenarios are created, the job of the intelligence analyst is to track indicators that point toward a specific one of them (for example, favorable consumer reaction to the new product line or the increased flow of narcotics through a specific location). How the analyst does this is discussed later.

In an alternative future as depicted by a scenario, a decision maker can identify relationships among forces, the probable impacts of those forces on an organization or situation, the key decision points for taking action, and foundations for decisions and strategies. By providing a realistic range of possibilities, the set of alternative scenarios helps the decision maker to identify common features likely to have an impact on the organization no matter which alternative occurs.

Predicting the future in detail is no more possible than predicting the weather in detail. The details tend to be controlled by divergent phenomena, such as an assassination in Sarajevo. But the dominant forces and trends tend to be convergent phenomena that allow the creation of a few "most likely" outcome scenarios, with indicators that can tell which is more likely. Scenario synthesis/analysis is used to create these scenarios.

Types of Scenarios

Analysts use four basic types of scenarios.[21] Demonstration scenarios, driving-force scenarios, and system-change scenarios move through time, enabling the user to understand the forces and decision points that lead to the final "scene" of the scenario. The slice-of-time scenario is a snapshot; it dwells on the final scene. Science fiction writers (who, after all, write scenarios about alternative futures) use all four types. Some science fiction writers simply drop the reader into the final scene; others explain the history and developments that led to the final scene.

Demonstration Scenario. The demonstration scenario was pioneered by Herman Kahn, Harvey DeVeerd, and others at RAND Corporation in the early days of systems analysis. In this kind of scenario, the writer first imagines a particular end state in the future and then describes a plausible path of events that could lead to that state. The *branch point* version of this type of scenario identifies decisive events along the path (events that represent points at which key choices determine the outcome). The branch points serve as indicators that a particular scenario is happening. The idea is to focus attention on the branch points rather than on the final outcome. As Kahn and Anthony Wiener, of the Hudson Institute, pointed out, this kind of scenario answers two questions: First, how might some hypothetical situation come about, step by step? And, second, what alternatives exist at each step for preventing, diverting, or facilitating the process?[22] The major weakness of the demonstration scenario is that it depends on the idiosyncrasies and experiences of the scenario creators.

Driving-Force Scenario. This scenario is most commonly used in governmental and business planning and is most useful in predictive intelligence. It is basically an implementation of the force synthesis/analysis approach: Examine the major forces acting on the target, determine how they are changing and what new forces are expected to come into play, and assess the resulting state of the target over time.

One approach to creating multiple driving-force scenarios is to identify a set of key factors or forces, specifying at least two distinctly different levels of each factor or force, and developing a matrix that interrelates each factor at each level with each other. For example, two commonly used driving forces in economic scenarios are growth in gross national product and growth in population. If each is set to "high," "medium," and "low," there are nine possible combinations, each of which defines the context of a possible future. The scenario planner's task is to describe each of these futures, assuming that the driving forces remain constant. Another alternative, discussed in *Proteus*, a book of possible future scenarios sponsored by the U.S. National Reconnaissance Office, is to select different dominant forces for each scenario. In *Proteus*, for example, the scenario "Amazon.plague" has a single dominant force: a series of highly contagious, deadly viruses that sweep the globe.[23]

The purpose of the driving-force scenario is to clarify the nature of the future by contrasting alternative futures with others in the same scenario space. It might be that certain policies would fare equally well in most of the futures or that certain futures might pose problems for the organization. In the latter case, decision makers will know where to direct their monitoring.

A flaw in driving-force scenarios is that they assume that the forces, once specified, are fixed. This assumption is consciously made in order to simplify the problem, but it ignores potential events that would affect the strength of forces or introduce new ones.

System-Change Scenario. The system-change scenario addresses the flaw in driving-force scenarios. It is designed to explore systematically, comprehensively, and consistently the interrelationships and implications of a set of trend and event forecasts, including significant social, technological, economic, and political forces. Thus this scenario type varies both from the demonstration scenario (which leads to a single outcome and ignores most or all the forces that might lead to other outcomes) and from the driving-force scenario (which takes account of a full range of future developments but assumes that the driving forces do not change). Typically, there is no single event that caps the system-change scenario, and there are no dominant driving forces.

The system-change scenario depends on cross-impact analysis (discussed later in this chapter) to identify interactions among events or developments and then from those interactions to develop the outline of alternative futures. This is a very difficult scenario to develop because it includes changing forces and their interrelationships.

Slice-of-Time Scenario. The slice-of-time scenario jumps to a future period in which a synthesis of explicit or assumed forces shapes the environment and then describes how those involved think, feel, and behave in that environment. George Orwell's *1984* and Aldous Huxley's *Brave New World* create scenarios like these. The objective is to show that the future may be more (or less) desirable, fearful, or attainable than is now generally thought. A slice-of-time scenario is the same as the environmental assumptions found in many business plans; environmental assumptions describe a specific future environment—a world of reduced tariffs or of combined high unemployment and inflation—without explaining how the environment came to be. Slice-of-time scenarios are not generally useful in intelligence because they give short shrift to the driving forces that led to the scenario. They therefore provide few indicators for intelligence analysts or their customers to monitor.

Scenario Perspectives

Scenarios are models, and like the models discussed in chapter 2, they can be either descriptive or normative. Descriptive scenarios are usually described as *exploratory.* Scenario planners using the exploratory perspective adopt a neutral stance toward the future, attempting to be objective, scientific, and impartial. The scenario usually begins in the present and then unfolds to some future time. A simple exploratory scenario is the straight-line extrapolation; it assumes that only current forces and policy choices are allowed to be felt in the future (no technological discoveries or revolutions, for example, are permitted). These extrapolation scenarios are "momentum" scenarios—they are dominated by inertia, and no countervailing forces arise to slow the observed trend.[24] Inertia is the tendency for organizations and other bodies to stay their course and resist change. Most China scenarios tend to be momentum scenarios based on the country's recent spectacular growth. They don't contemplate a weak, divided China-of-the-future (for example, a China ruled by economic or military warlords), in spite of the Soviet example and of Chinese history. Scenarios about Japan created in the early 1980s had a similar momentum pattern and proved inaccurate. Because momentum scenarios are straight-line extrapolations, it is prudent not to use them for long-term assessments. An analyst can start with extrapolation but should then look at new and changing forces that create projection and forecast scenarios.

Scenario planners using the *normative* perspective focus on the question, What kind of future might we have? As with a normative model, the purpose is to indicate a preferred course of action. The scenario planner therefore describes a "favored and attainable" end state, such as a stable international political environment and the sequence of events by which that ideal could be achieved. An alternative normative approach is to define a "feared but possible" end state (for example, increasing international terrorism and governmental instability) and show the sequence of events that could lead to that end state.

How to Construct Scenarios

Scenario planning is really a variant of the well-known modeling, simulation, and gaming methods. It is an art, not a standardized or systematic methodology. The assumptions on which a scenario is based must be made explicit because of its great potential for misuse.

Numerous approaches can be taken in writing scenarios, ranging from a single person writing a description of a future situation to the use of an interactive computer model. A common technique is to create three scenarios: a "most likely" future (exploratory, driving-force), a "worst case" future (normative-feared but possible, driving-force), and a "best case" future (normative-desired and attainable, driving-force).

Peter Schwartz, former head of global planning for Royal Dutch Shell, has described a four-step process of scenario construction: Define the problem, identify factors bearing on the problem, identify possible solutions, and find the best (most likely) solutions.[25]

Define the Problem. Scenario planning begins by identifying the focal issue or decision. Rather than trying to explore the entire future, ask yourself, What question am I trying to answer? There are an infinite number of stories that we could tell about the future; our purpose is to tell those that matter, that lead to better decisions. So we begin by agreeing on the issue that we want to address. Sometimes the question is broad (What are the future prospects in the Middle East?); sometimes it is specific (Is a terrorist attack on the U.S. railroad industry likely in the next year?). Either way, the point is to agree on the issues that will be used as tests of relevance as we plan the scenario.[26]

Identify Factors Bearing on the Problem. This step is basically an extension of the strategies-to-task approach to a problem breakout that was discussed in earlier chapters. In this step, the analyst identifies the key forces in the local environment. Because scenarios are a way of understanding the dynamics shaping the future, we attempt to identify the primary driving forces at work in the present. These fall roughly into four categories:[27]

- *Social Dynamics.* Quantitative, demographic issues (What will be the ethnic mix of country *X* in 2015? Will immigration increase or decrease?); softer issues of values, lifestyle, demand, or political activism (How is the United States likely to be regarded in Western Europe if it builds a missile defense shield? What is the political and economic impact of a large retiree population?)

- *Economic Issues.* Macroeconomic trends and forces shaping the economy as a whole (What are the effects of international trade barriers and exchange rates on raw material costs? What are economic sanctions likely to do to our markets?); microeconomics (What might industrial competitors do? How will the defense industry's fundamental structure change?); and forces at work on or within an organization (What is its level of debt, and what are those of potential partners? Is the organization facing a loss of skilled employees? Does it have an up-to-date computer network?)

- *Political Issues.* Electoral (Will the prime minister be reelected?); legislative (Will further safety restrictions be imposed on handguns?); regulatory (How will U.S. Customs interpret the new immigration laws?); and litigable (Will the courts accept any new theories on the criminality of terrorist acts?)

- *Technological Issues.* Direct (How will the genome map affect existing DNA testing?); enabling (Will biochips enable a new cell phone revolution?); and indirect (Will new World Wide Web technologies expand the need for security consultants?)

Next the analyst isolates the driving forces. Which driving forces are critical to this outcome? Some driving forces affect everyone the same way. Most companies, for instance, are driven by the need to cut costs and incorporate new technologies. But unless one of the target organizations is markedly better or worse than others at doing these things, the differences will not affect the end result. The important thing is to identify any asymmetric forces that may be present.

Then the analyst should rank the driving forces by importance and uncertainty. Some forces are more important than others. Whether a market will grow may not be as important as whether new players will enter the market. And some forces are far more certain than others. Local housing and population patterns usually change fairly slowly. The aging of the U.S. population is fairly predictable over the coming decades and will have a similar effect in any scenario. On the other hand, other questions are highly uncertain. The most critical driving forces will be those that are both very important and highly uncertain.[28]

Identify Possible Solutions. This is probably the most important step. First, the analyst identifies the scenario types to be considered. Three distinct scenario types are typical: The *emergent* scenario (which evolves from an opponent's current strategy); the *unconstrained what-if* scenario (which comes from asking unconstrained questions about completely new strategies); and the *constrained what-if* scenario (which asks what the opponent might do under different environmental conditions or forces).[29]

The analyst then works with the issues, reshaping and reframing them and drawing out their less obvious elements until a consensus emerges about which two or three underlying issues will make a difference in the outcome. This step involves differentiating the scenarios: identifying inconsistencies, finding underlying similarities, and eliminating scenarios that are redundant or implausible.

Now the analyst goes back to all the driving forces and trends that were considered in steps 2 and 3 and uses those to flesh out the scenarios. For instance, degree of risk; access to capital; and ability to control costs, raise quality, or extend functionality all might be critical in some scenarios and not so important in others.

There are three commonly used techniques for building scenarios. *Case-based models* are the foundation for a type of analysis called case-based reasoning. This technique might be considered reasoning by analogy or reasoning by history.

Case-based reasoning means using old experiences to understand and solve new problems. An analyst remembers a previous situation similar to the current one and uses that to solve the new problem. It can mean adapting old solutions to meet new demands, using old cases to explain new situations, using old cases to critique new solutions, or reasoning from precedents to interpret a new situation (much as lawyers do) or create an equitable solution to a new problem (much as labor mediators do).[30] The analyst makes inferences based directly on previous cases, rather than by the more traditional approach of using general knowledge. He or she solves a new problem by remembering a previous, similar situation (a similar model) and reusing information and knowledge of that situation (duplicating the model).

We can illustrate case-based reasoning by looking at some typical situations having intelligence implications:

- In 1984 reports indicated that the Soviets were systematically destroying Afghan irrigation systems to drive resistance supporters out of the countryside. This paralleled a Soviet army practice of destroying the irrigation systems in Central Asia during their war against the Basmachi rebels in the 1920s.[31]

- An analyst of the defense industry, monitoring the possible merger of two defense companies, might be reminded of a recent merger between two competing companies in the pharmaceutical industry. She recalls that the merged companies had problems because of dramatically different marketing approaches, similar to the situation in the merger she is monitoring. She commissions a case study of the pharmaceutical merger to obtain details on the potential problems and to determine how they might apply in the situation she is studying.

- A financial consultant, hired by the defense industry analyst to examine financial aspects of the same merger, is reminded of a combination of financial indicators in a previous merger that resulted in serious financial difficulties for the merged companies. He uses this past case to identify likely difficulties in the present one.

- An engineer responsible for the health of a reconnaissance satellite has experienced two past losses of satellite control. He is quickly reminded of the past situations when the combination of critical measurements matches those of the past system breakdowns. He also remembers a mistake he made during both previous failures and thereby avoids repeating the error.

A second common technique for building scenarios is *contextual mapping*. This technique is used to identify plausible sequences of development in a given field and to relate those sequences to potential developments in a different field. The method is at least as useful for forcing a fresh perspective as it is for predicting actual developments. Its use requires experienced experts familiar both with the method and with the topic of inquiry.

Contextual mapping has been used largely in technological forecasting applications. As an example, one might specify expected future developments in miniaturized chips, combined with a projection of future sensor and wide radio frequency bandwidth transmitter technologies, to define a unique small, cheap video surveillance device of the future. Such future developments are then treated as external forces that alter the likely future state of a system—for example, a crime deterrence system. The output is usually a graphic display, often with timelines, showing the interconnecting paths that lead to the projected development.

The third common technique, *cross-impact analysis,* supports system-change scenarios. It usually shows interactions among events or developments, specifying how one event will influence the likelihood, timing, and mode of impact of another event in a different but associated field. As a simple example, the development of the Global Positioning System (GPS) enabled the development of relatively cheap and highly precise munitions (bombs and missiles). These developments in turn required increased emphasis on providing the military with very precise, real-time geospatial intelligence, driving a demand for continuous battlefield reconnaissance from, for example, unmanned aeronautical vehicles (UAVs). And the combination of all these developments forced opposing military organizations into creating highly mobile force units that constantly move during combat to avoid being hit. It also increased the value of denial and deception.

The essential idea behind a cross-impact model is to examine all of the pairwise connections within a set of forecast developments. Specifically, the analyst might ask how the prior occurrence of one event would affect other events or trends in the set. When those relationships have been specified, the analyst creates a scenario by letting events "happen"—either randomly, in accordance with their estimated probability, or in some prearranged way—and assessing how each development affects others in the sequence. Repeating the process with different event sequences creates contrasting scenarios.

Cross-impact analysis has been used extensively to model the interaction of future events and trends. In the 1970s the Futures Group developed a version of it called *trend impact analysis* that became well established and is still in use.[32] Network analysis methodologies, described in chapter 13, naturally support cross-impact analysis.

Find the Best (Most Likely) Solution(s). Having built a set of potential future scenarios, the analyst must examine them in light of the original question. Does the idea of paying farmers not to grow coca crops have favorable outcomes in all of the counter-narcotics scenarios? Perhaps a common outcome in the scenarios is that new groups of farmers start growing coca crops to qualify for the payments, or a bidding war starts between the drug cartels and the government. The customers of intelligence, the operations people who are informed by the scenarios, need to understand these possible outcomes and prepare their options accordingly.

The final scenarios need to describe relationships among objects or entities (tanks, missiles, airplanes, and units in a military scenario; companies, governments, technologies, and weapons systems in a nonproliferation scenario; governments, farmers, drug cartels, banks, and drug users in a counter-narcotics scenario). In a dynamic scenario, the objects must then change in space and time according to known rules (patterns of business competition; military doctrine in military scenarios; past patterns of clandestine trade and of systems development in a nonproliferation scenario). A military scenario, which can be well defined by existing scenario definition tools, is quite different from a nonproliferation or counter-narcotics scenario. It is not the same in format, content, event descriptions, or the types of objects being manipulated. However, the basics remain the same; relationship analysis, for example, is pretty much the same in all scenarios.

Indicators and the Role of Intelligence

The final step in Peter Schwartz's process comes after the scenarios are completed. The job of the intelligence officer becomes one of monitoring. The analyst has to look for the leading indicators that would tell which of the scenarios—or which combination of scenarios—is actually taking place. As Babson College professor Liam Fahey has pointed out, indicators will also give important insights into what scenarios are *not* taking place.[33]

The monitoring job may involve watching trends. An intelligence analyst might monitor demographic and economic trends, the spread of infectious diseases, changes in pollution levels, or proliferation of terrorist cells. A political or economic analyst might look at the questions that opponents ask and the positions they take in trade negotiations. A military intelligence analyst might monitor troop movements and radio traffic for signals as to which scenario is developing.

These indicators suggest movement toward a particular scenario.[34] They provide a means to decide which options should be the focus of a customer's decisions. Specifically, they help identify which outcomes should be prepared for, possibly by use of some of the instruments of national power, and which potential outcomes can be disregarded.

Scenarios, like target models, serve different purposes for different participants. The purpose of scenarios for executives and intelligence customers is to inform decision making. For intelligence analysts, they serve the additional purpose of helping to identify needs, that is, to support intelligence collection.

Intelligence can have one of two roles in scenarios. If an organization has a planning group that develops scenarios, the intelligence officer should participate in the scenario development. Then the role of intelligence is to draw the indicators from the forces and to tell the planner or decision maker how the scenarios are playing out. We want to know which forces and indicators need to be monitored to give an early signal of approaching change and point to more likely outcomes. The planning culture in many organizations is still heavily biased toward single-point forecasting. In such cases, the intelligence customer is likely to say, Tell me what the future will be; then I can make my decision. The customer is likely to complain that several "forecasts" are more confusing, and less helpful, than a single one. If no scenario-planning group exists, the intelligence officer must develop the scenarios herself to address the questions posed by the decision maker. In this case, intelligence synthesis/analysis generally will focus on more narrowly drawn scenarios than planners use, and they are likely to be more tactical than strategic. For example, an intelligence-generated battlefield scenario would probably involve looking only at enemy forces and predicting what their actions will be, while ignoring the actions that friendly forces might be taking.

Summary

Intelligence analysis, to be useful, must be predictive. Some events or future states of a target are predictable because they are driven by convergent phenomena. Some are not predictable because they are driven by divergent phenomena.

Analysis involves predicting the future state of a target by using one of three means—extrapolation (unchanging forces), projection (changing forces), and forecasting (changing and new forces). The task is to assess, from the present state of the intelligence target, the transition process that takes the target to its future state and the forces that shape that transition. Chapter 11 discusses in more detail how extrapolation, projection, and forecasting are done in the intelligence business.

Most predictive analysis results in some form of scenario—a description of the future state of the target. Typically, the analyst will create several alternative scenarios based on different assumptions about the forces involved. Two scenarios most used in intelligence are the driving-force scenario, a type of projection, and the system-change, a forecast. Chapters 12 to 14 describe some of the forces to consider in creating a driving-force scenario. System-change scenarios are very demanding to construct; they require cross-impact analysis—that is, looking at how events or developments in one area will affect events or developments in a different area.

Creating a scenario involves four steps that are very similar to the traditional problem-solving process. The first step is problem definition; the focus here is to create a scenario that will be useful to the intelligence customer. The next step is to identify the factors or driving forces that bear on the problem and that will be a part of the scenario. These include social dynamics and economic, political, and technological forces. The factors and forces then must be ranked according to their importance in the scenario. The final steps are to identify the possible outcome scenarios and select the most likely ones to present to the customer.

Once the scenarios are completed, intelligence analysts have to monitor incoming intelligence. The new intelligence provides indicators that help determine which scenario appears to be developing.

Notes

1. Quoted in Woodrow J. Kuhns, "Intelligence Failures: Forecasting and the Lessons of Epistemology," in *Paradoxes of Strategic Intelligence: Essays in Honor of Michael Handel*, ed. Richard K. Betts and Thomas G. Mahnken (London: Frank Cass Publishers, 2003), 96.
2. Center for the Study of Intelligence, Central Intelligence Agency, "Watching the Bear: Essays on CIA's Analysis of the Soviet Union," conference, Princeton University, March 2001, www.cia.gov/cis/books/watchingthebear/article08.html, 6.
3. Barbara W. Tuchman, *The Guns of August* (New York: Random House, 1962).
4. Roberta Wholstetter, *Pearl Harbor: Warning and Decision* (Stanford: Stanford University Press, 1962).
5. Irving Langmuir, "Science, Common Sense, and Decency," *Science* 97 (January 1943): 1–7.
6. Jamshid Gharajedaghi, *Systems Thinking: Managing Chaos and Complexity* (Boston: Butterworth-Heinemann, 1999), 52.
7. Center for the Study of Intelligence, "Watching the Bear," 11.
8. Ibid.
9. Paul Carroll, *Big Blues* (New York: Crown, 1993), 18.
10. George Likourezos, "Prologue to Image Enhanced Estimation Methods," *Proceedings of the Institute of Electrical and Electronics Engineers* 18 (June 1993): 796.
11. Thomas Kempner and B. B. Tregoe, *The New Rational Manager* (Princeton: Princeton Research Press, 1981).

12. M.S. Loescher, C. Schroeder, and C.W. Thomas, *Proteus: Insights from 2020* (Utrecht, the Netherlands: Copernicus Institute Press, 2000), A-iv.
13. Andrew Sleigh, ed., *Project Insight* (Farnborough, U.K.: Centre for Defence Analysis, Defence Evaluation and Research Agency, 1996), 17.
14. Gharajedaghi, *Systems Thinking*, 51.
15. Center for the Study of Intelligence, "Watching the Bear," 4.
16. Ibid., 5.
17. Gharajedaghi, *Systems Thinking*, 122.
18. David Jablonsky, "National Power," *Parameters,* Spring 1997, 34–54.
19. The time frame for most predictions extends over years. On a fast-developing situation, the appropriate time frame for force analysis may be months or even days, rather than years.
20. T.F. Mandel, "Futures Scenarios and Their Use in Corporate Strategy," in *The Strategic Management Handbook,* ed. K.J. Albert (New York: McGraw-Hill, 1983), 10–21.
21. W.I. Boucher, "Scenario and Scenario Writing," in *Nonextrapolative Methods in Business Forecasting,* ed. J.S. Mendell (Westport, Conn.: Quorum Books, 1985), 47–60.
22. Herman Kahn and Anthony Wiener, *The Year 2000* (New York: Macmillan, 1967).
23. Loescher, Schroeder, and Thomas, *Proteus.*
24. Inertia and countervailing forces are discussed in detail in chapter 12.
25. Peter Schwartz, *The Art of the Long View* (New York: Currency Doubleday, 1996).
26. Lawrence Wilkinson, "How to Build Scenarios," February 12, 2002, www.wired.com/wired/scenarios/build.html.
27. Ibid.
28. Liam Fahey, *Competitors* (New York: John Wiley and Sons, 1999), 452.
29. Ibid., 453.
30. Janet L. Kolodner, "An Introduction to Case-Based Reasoning," *Artificial Intelligence Review* 6 (1992): 3–34.
31. Angelo Codevilla, *Informing Statecraft* (New York: Free Press, 1992), 217.
32. T.J. Gordon, "The Nature of Unforeseen Developments," in *The Study of the Future,* ed. W.I. Boucher (Washington, D.C.: U.S. Government Printing Office, 1977), 42–43.
33. Fahey, *Competitors,* 415.
34. Sleigh, *Project Insight,* 13.

11

Predictive Techniques

It's hard to make predictions, especially about the future.
Attributed to Yogi Berra and physicist Neils Bohr, among others

The value of a prediction lies in the assessment of the forces that will shape future events and the state of the target model. If the analyst accurately assesses those forces, she has served the intelligence customer well, even if the prediction she derived from that assessment is wrong. A competent customer will probably make his own predictions anyway, but the force assessments help him to make a more reasoned prediction and to refine it as new events unfold. In the best cases, the analyst's prediction will not come true because the customer will act on the intelligence to change the predicted outcome to a more favorable one.

In this chapter we develop the three approaches introduced in chapter 10 for predicting the future state of a target—extrapolation, projection, and forecasting. Different authors use different terms for these. Babson College professor Liam Fahey uses the terms *simple projection* to refer to extrapolation and *complex projection* to refer to both projection and forecasting.[1] I treat projection and forecasting separately, to emphasize the differences in the forces involved. An extrapolation predicts future events by assuming that the current forces influencing the target go unchanged. A projection assumes that those forces will change, and a forecast assumes the same, with the addition of new forces along the way.

Two types of bias exist in predictive analysis: pattern, or confirmation, bias—looking for evidence that confirms rather than rejects a hypothesis; and heuristic bias—using inappropriate guidelines or rules to make predictions.[2] In this chapter we address how to deal with both—the first, by having alternative models for outcomes; the second, by defining a set of appropriate guidelines for making predictions, amplified on in succeeding chapters.

Two points are worth noting at the beginning of the discussion:

- One must make careful use of the tools used in synthesizing the model, as some will fail when they are applied to prediction. Expert opinion, for example, is often used in creating a target model, but experts' biases, egos, and narrow focuses tend to make their subjective predictions wrong. (A useful exercise for the skeptic is to look at trade press or technical journal predictions that were made more than ten years ago and that turned out to be way off base—stock market predictions and popular science magazine predictions of automobile designs are particularly entertaining.)

- Time constraints work against the analyst's ability to consistently employ the most elaborate predictive techniques. Veterans tend to use analytic techniques that are relatively fast and intuitive. They view scenario development, red teams (teams formed to take the opponent's perspective in planning or assessments), competing hypotheses, and alternative analysis as being too time-consuming to use in ordinary circumstances.[3] Extrapolation is most often used because it is the easiest to do. But it is possible to use shortcut versions of many predictive techniques. This chapter and the following one contain some examples of shortcuts.

Extrapolation

An extrapolation is a statement based only on past observations of what is expected to happen. Extrapolation is the most conservative method of prediction. In its simplest form, an extrapolation, using historical performance as the basis, extends a linear curve on a graph to show future direction. When there is little uncertainty about the present state of a target model, and when an analyst is confident that she knows what forces are acting on the target, the prediction begins from the present and propagates forward along the direction of an unchanged system (straight-line extrapolation). In this low-uncertainty, high-confidence situation, new information is given relatively low weight. But when uncertainty about the state of the model is high, new information is accorded high value in prediction; when uncertainty about the forces acting on the target is high, prediction uncertainty is high.

Extrapolation is usually accurate in the short run, assuming an accurate starting point and a reasonably accurate understanding of the direction of movement. The assumption is that the forces acting on the target do not change. Inertia (the tendency to stay on course and resist change, discussed in chapter 12) is what typically causes a straight-line extrapolation to work. Where inertial effects are weak, extrapolation has a shorter lifetime of accuracy. Where they are strong, extrapolation can give good results over time.

Extrapolation Techniques

Figure 11-1 shows the simplest type of extrapolation. This example is a trend extrapolation in the aircraft industry from the DC-3 aircraft to the C-17. The graph shows a remarkably consistent growth in performance of the aircraft (measured as cargo load times distance traveled over time) from the 1930s to 1970, when technology shifted from piston engines to jets and electronic

Figure 11-1   Trend Extrapolation for Productivity of Civil and
Military Transport Aircraft

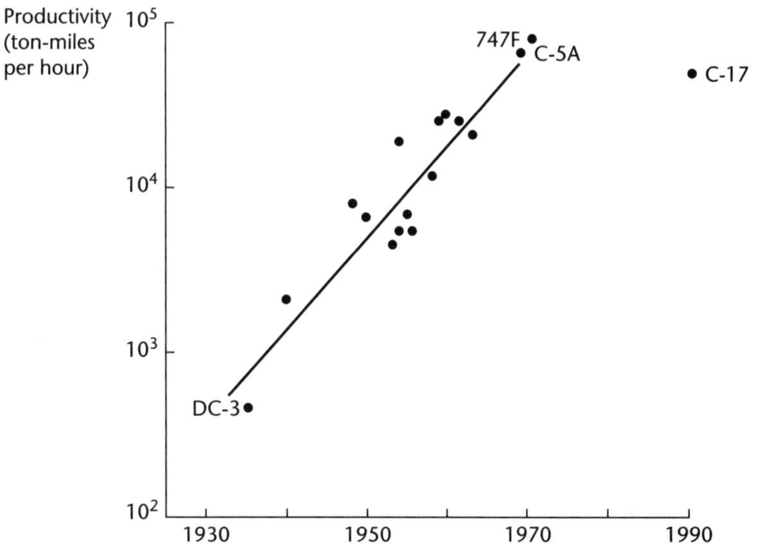

Note: Each dot represents a different type of aircraft. *Ton-miles per hour* is the cargo load times the distance traveled over time.

operations took over for manual ones.[4] However, the graph also shows one pitfall of a straight-line trend extrapolation. The straight segment of an S curve can look like a straight line. In such a case, the curve will not continue its climb indefinitely but will level off, as it did in this example; the more recent C-17 did not match the performance of the older C-5A and 747F. Chapter 14 has a section on S curves that offers some clues to help select the right type of extrapolation.

Figure 11-2 shows a type of extrapolation that is used to predict periodic (repeating) phenomena. The technique used, called *autocorrelation,* works well when one is dealing with a cyclical (sinusoidal) behavior such as wave action. Prediction of sunspot number (the number of "spots" or dark areas observed on the sun, shown in Figure 11-2), economic cycles, and automobile and lawnmower sales are examples.

Adaptive techniques are more sophisticated methods of extrapolating that are based on new observations. The Box-Jenkins is one such technique. Box-Jenkins is useful for quickly spotting changing forces in a target model. It uses a variable's past behavior, such as the sunspot occurrences shown in Figure 11-2, to select the best forecasting model from a general class of models. Box-Jenkins provides some of the most accurate short-term forecasts. However, it requires a very large amount of data, and it is complex and time-consuming to apply.

Figure 11-2   Trend Extrapolation for Repeating Phenomena: The Sunspot Cycle

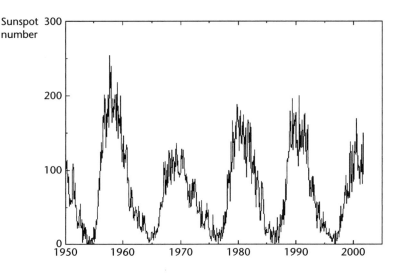

Note: *Sunspot number* is the number of "spots" or dark areas observed on the sun.

Correlation and Regression

Correlation is a measure of the degree of association between two or more sets of data, or a measure of the degree to which two variables are related. Regression is a technique for predicting the value of some unknown variable based only on information about the current values of other variables. Regression makes use of both the degree of association among variables and the mathematical function that is determined to best describe the relationships among variables. If values from only one independent variable are used to predict values for another dependent variable, the process is referred to as bivariate regression. Multivariate regression involves using values from more than one independent variable to predict values for a dependent variable.

Figure 11-3 shows an example of a correlation analysis that was used to project the number of telephones that various countries might install. The correlation with gross national product, as the figure shows, is high, so a straight-line extrapolation would allow one to predict the changes in numbers of telephone sets as a function of predicted changes in a country's gross national product.

The graph can be used simply for straight-line extrapolation; it bears a striking similarity to the straight-line extrapolation of Figure 11-1, except that time is not a variable. But an extrapolation would probably not account for major technological changes, such as the subsequent proliferation of cellular

Figure 11-3 Correlation of Number of Telephones with Gross National Product (GNP), 1998

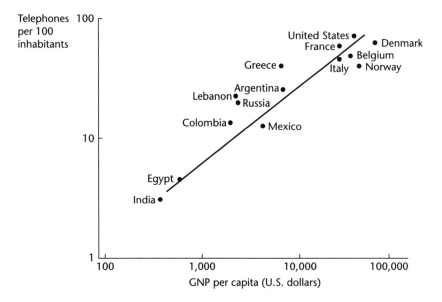

telephone systems in many of the countries listed. To do that we have to abandon the correlation graphic and deal with the more sophisticated analytical tools of projection or forecasting.

Limitations of Extrapolation

Extrapolation has two major shortcomings. First, it is inaccurate in the long run because it is narrowly focused and assumes that the static forces that operate on the model will continue unchanged, with no new forces being added. As noted earlier, this method depends on inertia. Second, extrapolation will be inaccurate if the original target model was inaccurate. If the extrapolation starts from the wrong point, it will almost certainly be even farther off as it is extended forward in time. Both problems were present in every National Intelligence Estimate predicting the future development of Soviet military forces from 1974 to 1986. They all overestimated the rate at which Moscow would modernize its strategic forces.[5] All of those estimates relied on extrapolation, without fully considering restraining forces, and used starting points that were, at best, shaky.

Projection

Before moving on to projection and forecasting, we need to differentiate them from extrapolation. An extrapolation is a simple assertion about what a future scenario will look like. In contrast, a projection or a forecast is a *probabilistic* statement about some future scenario. The underlying form of such statements is, If *A* occurs, plus some allowance for unknown or unknowable factors, then we can expect *B* or something very much like *B* to occur, or at least *B* will become more probable.

Projection is more reliable than extrapolation. It predicts a range of likely futures based on the assumption that the forces that have operated in the past will change, whereas extrapolation assumes that the forces do not change. The changing forces produce a change from the extrapolation line, as shown by the C-17 entry in Figure 11-1.

Both projection and forecasting make use of two major analytical techniques. One technique, force synthesis/analysis, was discussed in chapter 10. After a qualitative force synthesis/analysis has been completed, the next step in projection and forecasting is to apply probabilistic reasoning to it. Probabilistic reasoning is a systematic attempt to make subjective estimates of probabilities more explicit and consistent. It can be used at any of several levels of complexity (each successive level of sophistication adding new capability and completeness). But even the simplest level, generating alternatives, helps to prevent premature closure and serves to add structure to complicated problems.

Generating Alternatives

The first step to probabilistic reasoning is no more complicated than stating formally that more than one outcome is possible. One can generate alternatives simply by listing all possible outcomes of the problem under consideration. As we discussed in chapter 10, the possible outcomes can be defined as alternative scenarios.

Ideally the alternatives should be mutually exclusive (only one can occur, not two or more simultaneously) and exhaustive (nothing else can happen; one of the alternates listed must occur).[6] For instance, suppose that an analyst is tracking an opponent's research and development on a revolutionary new technology. The analyst could list two outcomes only:

- The technology is used in producing a product (or weapons system).
- The technology is not used.

This list is exhaustive and the alternatives are mutually exclusive. If a third option, "The technology is used within two years," were added, the mutually exclusive principle would have been violated (unless the first outcome had been reworded to "The technology is used after two years").

This brief list of outcomes may or may not be very useful, with just two alternative outcomes. If the analyst is interested in more details, the outcome can (and should) be broken down further. A revised list containing four alternative outcomes might be as follows:

- The technology is used:
—successfully.
—but the result is a flawed product.

- The technology is not used:
—and no new technology is introduced into the process.
—but a variant or alternative technology is used.

This list illustrates the way that specifying all possible (and relevant) outcomes can expand one's perspective. The expanded possibilities often can generate useful insights into problems. For example, the alternative that a different technology is used in lieu of the technology in question suggests that intelligence analysis should focus on whether the target organization has alternative research and development under way.

The key is to list all the outcomes that are meaningful. It is far easier to combine multiple outcomes than it is to think of something new that wasn't listed, or to think of separating one combined-event outcome into its subcomponents. The list can serve both as a reminder that multiple outcomes can occur and as a checklist to decide how any item of new intelligence might affect an assessment of the relative likelihoods of the diverse outcomes listed. The mere act of generating a complete, detailed list often provides a useful perspective on a problem.

When generating a set of outcomes, one should beware of using generic terms (such as "other"). As the story of the automobile mechanics in chapter 7 illustrates, we do not easily recall the vast number of things that could fall under that seemingly simple label. A catchall outcome label should be included only when complete list of all alternatives cannot be generated first. In intelligence, it is rare that all possible future states can be included. Also, one should not overlook the possibility of nothing happening. For instance, if an analyst is creating a list of all the things that the French government might do regarding a tariff issue, one item on the list should be "Nothing at all."

Influence Trees or Diagrams

A list of alternative outcomes is the first step in projection. A simple prediction might not go beyond that. But for more formal or rigorous analysis, the next step typically is to identify the things that influence the possible outcomes and indicate the interrelationship of those influences. This process is frequently done by using an influence tree. Influence trees and diagrams represent a systematic approach to the force analysis introduced in chapter 10.

For instance, let us assume that an analyst wants to assess the outcome of an ongoing African insurgency. There are three obvious possible outcomes: The insurgency will be crushed, the insurgency will succeed, or there will be a continuing stalemate. Other outcomes may be possible, but we can assume that they are so unlikely as not to be worth including. The three outcomes for the influence diagram are then:

- Regime wins.
- Insurgency wins.
- Stalemate.

The analyst now describes those forces that will influence the assessment of the relative likelihood of each outcome. For instance, the insurgency's success may depend on whether economic conditions improve, remain the same, or become worse during the next year. It also may depend on the success of a new government poverty relief program. The assumptions about these "driver" events are currently described as *linchpin premises* in U.S. intelligence practice, and these assumptions need to be made explicit.[7]

After listing all of the influencing, or driver, events, the analyst next focuses on two questions:

- Do any of the influencing events influence each other?
- Is it possible to assess the relative likelihood of the outcomes of the influencing events directly, or do the outcomes of those events depend in turn on other influencing events (and outcomes)?

If the answer to the first question is that the events influence each other, the analyst must define the direction of influence. In the case at hand, we have two influencing events—economic conditions and the poverty relief program. One can argue that each event influences the other to some extent, but it seems reasonable that the poverty relief program will have more influence on economic conditions than the converse. So we are left with the following relationship:

Poverty relief program influences economic conditions, which influence the outcome of the insurgency.

Having established the uncertain events that influence the outcome, the analyst proceeds to the first stage of an influence tree, which is shown in Figure 11-4. This tree simply shows all of the different outcomes in the hierarchy of dependency.

The thought process that is invoked when generating the list of influencing events and their outcomes can be useful in several ways. It helps identify and document factors that are relevant in judging whether an alternative outcome is likely to occur. The analyst may need to document the process (create an "audit trail") by which she arrived at the influence tree. The audit trail is particularly useful in showing colleagues what the analyst's thinking has been,

Figure 11-4 Influence Tree for an Insurgency

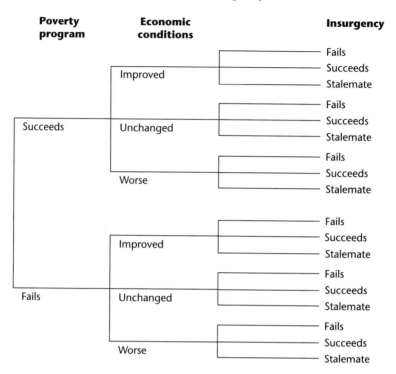

especially if she desires help in upgrading the diagram with things that she may have overlooked. Software packages for creating influence trees allow the inclusion of notes that create the audit trail.

In the process of generating the alternative lists, the analyst must address the issue of whether the event (or outcome) being listed actually will make a difference in the assessment of the relative likelihood of the outcomes of any of the events being listed. For instance, in the economics example, if the analyst knew that it would make no difference to the success of the insurgency whether economic conditions improved or remained the same, she would have no need to differentiate those as two separate outcomes. She should instead simplify the diagram.

The second question, having to do with additional influences not yet shown on the diagram, allows the analyst to extend this pictorial representation of influences to whatever level of detail she considers necessary. Note, however, that an analyst should avoid adding unneeded layers of detail. Making things more detailed than necessary can degrade, rather than improve, the usefulness of this diagramming technique.

The thought process also should help identify those events that contain no uncertainty. For example, the supply of arms to both government and insurgent forces will have a strong influence on the outcomes. We assume that, in this problem, these are not uncertain events because intelligence officers have high confidence in their estimates of the future arms supply. They are not linchpins. The analyst will undoubtedly take these influences into account in her analysis. In fact, she would make use of this information when assessing the relative likelihoods of the main event (the insurgency) outcome, which will be done next; but she does not need to include it in her diagram of uncertain events.

Probabilistic reasoning is used to evaluate outcome scenarios. A relative likelihood must be assigned to each possible outcome in the tree in Figure 11-4. We do this by starting at the left and estimating the likelihood of the outcome, given that all of the previous outcomes in that branch of the tree have occurred. This is a subjective process, done by evaluating the evidence for and against each outcome using the evaluative techniques discussed in chapter 7. Figure 11-5 shows the result. Note that the sum of the likelihoods for each branch point in the tree equals 1.00, and that the cumulative likelihood of a particular outcome (on the far right) is the product of the probabilities in the branches that reach that point. (For example, the outcome probability of the poverty program succeeding, economic conditions improving, and the insurgency failing is .224 = 0.7 × 0.4 × 0.8.)

The final step in the evaluation is to sum the probabilities on the right in Figure 11-5 for each outcome—"fails," "succeeds," and "stalemate." When we do this we get the following probabilities:

Insurgency fails	.631
Insurgency succeeds	.144
Stalemate	.225

This influence tree approach to evaluating possible outcomes is more convincing to customers than would be an unsupported analytic judgment about the prospects for the insurgency. Human beings tend to do poorly at such complex assessments when they approach them in a subjective manner, totally unaided; that is, when the analyst mentally combines the force assessments in an unstructured way. On the other hand, numerical methods such as the influence tree have the inherent disadvantage of implying (merely because numbers are used) a false degree of accuracy. The numbers are precise and unambiguous in meaning, but they are no more accurate than the subjective feelings they represent.

The probability calculations and the tree structuring technique demand that no feedback loops exist or that the feedback is so small that it can be ignored. A feedback loop would exist, for example, if economic conditions significantly affect the poverty relief program, or if a continuing

Figure 11-5   Influence Tree with Probabilities

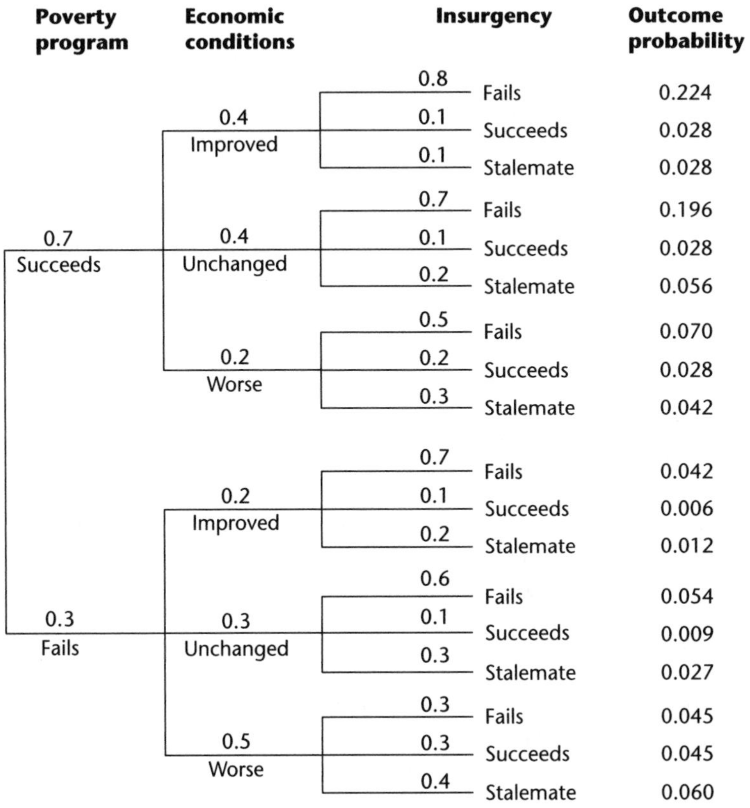

Poverty program	Economic conditions	Insurgency		Outcome probability
0.7 Succeeds	0.4 Improved	0.8	Fails	0.224
		0.1	Succeeds	0.028
		0.1	Stalemate	0.028
	0.4 Unchanged	0.7	Fails	0.196
		0.1	Succeeds	0.028
		0.2	Stalemate	0.056
	0.2 Worse	0.5	Fails	0.070
		0.2	Succeeds	0.028
		0.3	Stalemate	0.042
0.3 Fails	0.2 Improved	0.7	Fails	0.042
		0.1	Succeeds	0.006
		0.2	Stalemate	0.012
	0.3 Unchanged	0.6	Fails	0.054
		0.1	Succeeds	0.009
		0.3	Stalemate	0.027
	0.5 Worse	0.3	Fails	0.045
		0.3	Succeeds	0.045
		0.4	Stalemate	0.060

insurgency stalemate affects economic conditions. If feedback loops emerge and are needed in influence diagrams, the analyst will need to use techniques designed to handle dynamic feedback situations, such as simulation modeling.

Influence Nets

Influence net modeling is an alternative to the influence tree. It is a powerful tool for projection and forecasting of complex target models where the influence tree would be too cumbersome for practical use. Influence net modeling is a combination of two established methods of decision analysis: Bayesian inference net analysis, originally employed by the mathematical community, and influence diagramming techniques, such as the insurgency example, which were originally employed by operations researchers. Influence net modeling is an intuitive, graphical method.

To create an influence net, the analyst defines *influence nodes,* which depict events that are part of cause-effect relations within the target model. They also create "influence links" between cause and effect that graphically illustrate the causal relation between the connected pair of events. The influence can be either positive (supporting a given decision) or negative (decreasing the likelihood of the decision), as identified by the link "terminator." The terminator is either an arrowhead (positive influence) or a filled circle (negative influence). The resulting graphical illustration is called the *influence net topology.* An example topology, showing some of the influences on Saddam Hussein's decision whether to withdraw from Kuwait in 1990, is pictured in Figure 11-6. The decision is stated as, Saddam Hussein decides to withdraw from Kuwait peacefully. The arrows come from boxes that support that decision; the filled circles come from boxes that support the opposite decision, that is, not to withdraw.

Making Probability Estimates

Probabilistic projection and probabilistic forecasting are used to predict the probability of future events for some time-dependent random process, such as the health of the Japanese economy. A number of these probabilistic techniques are used in industry for projection and forecasting. Two that we use in intelligence analysis are the following:

- *Point and interval estimation.* This method attempts to describe the probability of outcomes for a single event. An example would be a country's economic growth rate, and the event of concern might be an economic depression (the point where the growth rate drops below a certain level).

Figure 11-6   Example Influence Net Model

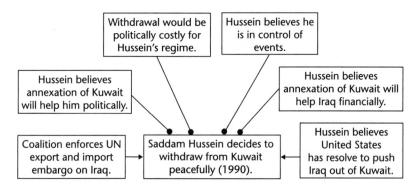

Note: The arrows come from boxes that support the decision for Saddam Hussein to withdraw from Kuwait peacefully. The filled dots come from boxes that do not support the decision.

Source: Julie A. Rosen and Wayne L. Smith, "Influencing Global Situations: A Collaborative Approach," *Air Chronicles,* Summer 1966.

- *Monte Carlo simulation*. This method simulates all or part of a process by running a sequence of events repeatedly, with random combinations of values, until sufficient statistical material is accumulated to determine the probability distribution of the outcome. The probability of intercepting a weak radar signal in ELINT, for example, is often estimated using a Monte Carlo simulation. Monte Carlo simulations are frequently used in estimating the costs of new intelligence programs.

Generally, these techniques and others of their genre require modeling of events and estimations of probability functions.

Most of the predictive problems we deal with in intelligence use subjective probability estimates. Formal probability estimates, such as Monte Carlo simulations, are used infrequently, either because we do not have enough data or because the value of a formal process is not worth the time involved. We routinely use subjective estimates of probabilities both in snap decision making and in the broad issues for which no objective estimate is feasible. An estimate about the probability of a major terrorist attack occurring somewhere in the United Kingdom next week, for example, would inevitably be subjective; there would not be enough hard data to make a formal quantitative estimate. An estimate of the probability that the Chinese economy will grow by more than 5 percent next year could be made by using formal quantitative techniques because quantitative data are available.

Even if a formal probability estimate is used, it will always have a strong subjective element. A subjective component is incorporated into every estimate of future probability; it is a basis for the weighting of respective outcomes to which no numerical basis can be assigned.

Sensitivity Analysis

When a probability estimate is made in projection or forecasting, it is usually worthwhile to conduct a sensitivity analysis on the result. For example, the occurrence of false alarms in a security system can be evaluated as a probabilistic process. The effect of introducing alarm maintenance procedures can be included in the evaluation by means of sensitivity analysis.

The purpose of sensitivity analysis is to evaluate the relative importance or impact of changes in the values assigned to influencing-event outcomes. The inputs to the estimate are varied in a systematic manner to evaluate their effects on possible outcomes. This process lets an analyst identify variables whose variation has little or no effect on possible outcomes.

A number of tools and techniques are available for sensitivity analysis. Most of them are best displayed and examined graphically. Figure 11-7 shows the results of an analysis of the likelihood of a manufacturer successfully creating a new biological warfare virus. Three possibilities are assumed to exist: The process will create the new virus; the process will fail; or the manufacturer will

Figure 11-7 Sensitivity Analysis for Biological Warfare Virus Prediction

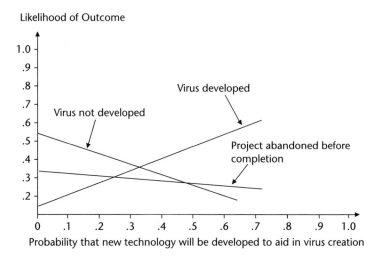

abandon the project before it is conclusive. These three possibilities add up to a likelihood of 1.0 at any point on the graph in Figure 11-7. One of the elements in the analysis is the probability that a new genetic engineering technology will emerge to aid the development of the biological warfare virus (the horizontal axis in the figure). The sensitivity analysis indicates that success in producing the virus is relatively sensitive to the genetic engineering technology (the success line goes up sharply as the probability increases that the technology works). If the probability of success for the new technology is above .55, the process is more likely to succeed (likelihood of new virus creation above .5 on the vertical scale); it is more likely to fail if the probability of success is less than .55. The graph also indicates that the manufacturer's possible decision not to complete the project is relatively insensitive to the technology's success, because the likelihood of project abandonment does not change much as the probability of technology success increases; such a decision might be made for political or economic reasons, for example, rather than technical reasons. The chart is simplistic, of course; in fact, the straight lines would typically be curves with sharp "knees" at points where the probabilities start changing at different rates.

Forecasting

Projections usually work out better than extrapolations over the short to medium term. But even the best-prepared projections often seem very conservative when they are compared to the reality years later. New political, economic, social, technological, or military developments will create results that were not foreseen even by experts in a field. Typically, these new developments are described as disruptive technologies or disruptive events. To take these disruptive developments into account, we are forced to go to forecasting techniques.

A major objective of forecasting in intelligence is to define alternative futures of the target model, not just the most likely future. These alternative futures are usually scenarios, as discussed in the preceding chapter. The development of alternative futures is essential for effective strategic decision making. Since there is no single predictable future, customers need to formulate strategy in the context of alternative future states of the target. To that end, it is necessary to develop a model that will make it possible to show systematically the interrelationships of the individually forecast trends and events. A forecast attempts to identify new forces that will affect the target—to consider the possible effects of new developments in distantly related fields, such as new technologies in the realm of plastics, or new constraints posed by the sociological impact of pollution, or new forms of life created through genetic engineering—and to present them all to the customer as possibilities. In forecasting, one also must look at forces such as synergy, feedback, inertia, contamination, and countervailing forces—all discussed in chapter 12.

Customers generally prefer that the highest possible level of predictive analysis (forecasting) be provided so that they can have confidence in it. "Confidence" for some customers might mean that the analysis is conducted according to some sort of accepted (preferably quantitative) methodology. For other customers, it might mean confidence in the person producing the analysis.

A forecast is not a blueprint of the future, and it normally starts from extrapolations or projections. Forecasters then must expand their scope to admit and juggle many additional forces or factors. They must examine key technologies and developments that are far afield but that nevertheless affect the subject of the forecast.

The Nonlinear Approach to Forecasting

A forecasting methodology requires analytic tools or principles. It also requires analysts who have significant understanding of many technologies and disciplines and the ability to think about issues in a nonlinear fashion. As with the intelligence process discussed in chapter 1, an analyst cannot effectively approach forecasting in a linear manner—gathering data, analyzing it, and formulating a solution. Such a linear and mechanistic view of the universe has never served us well for forecasting, and it is inappropriate for dealing with complex targets. The natural pattern of thinking about the future appears chaotic on the surface, but it is chaos with a purpose. Futuristic thinking examines deeper forces and flows across many disciplines that have their own order and pattern. In predictive analysis we may seem to wander about, making only halting progress toward the solution. That nonlinear process is not a flaw; rather it is characteristic of a natural learning process when individuals deal with complex and nonlinear matters.

The sort of person who can do such multidisciplinary analysis—analysis of what will happen in the future—has a broad understanding of the principles that cause a physical phenomenon, a chemical reaction, or a social reaction to occur. People who are multidisciplinary can pull together concepts from several technical fields and assess political, economic, and social factors, as well as technical ones. Such breadth of understanding recognizes the similarity of these principles and the underlying forces that make them work. It might also be called "applied common sense," but unfortunately it is not very common. Analysts instead tend to specialize because in-depth expertise is highly valued by both intelligence management and the intelligence customer. The CIA, for example, once had a Soviet canned-goods analyst and a Soviet timber analyst.[8]

In 1950 U.S. intelligence had two major failures in prediction in six months, resulting from a combination of mindset and failure to do multidisciplinary analysis. On June 25 of that year, the North Korean People's Army invaded South Korea. United Nations forces intervened to defend South Korea and pushed the invading forces back into the North. In October and November, responding to the impending defeat of the North Koreans, the Chinese People's Liberation Army attacked and drove the UN forces back into South Korea. Both the North Korean and the Chinese attacks were surprises.

The mindset in Washington that permeated political, military, and intelligence thinking at the time was that the Soviet Union was the dominant Communist state, exercising near-absolute authority over other Communist states. The resulting perception was that only the Soviet Union could order an invasion by its client states and that such an act would be a prelude to a world war. Washington was confident that Moscow was not ready to take such a step; so no attack was expected. This mindset persisted after the invasion, with the CIA Daily Summary reporting that the invasion was a "clear-cut Soviet challenge to the United States." As evidence mounted of a subsequent Chinese intervention, CIA analyses continued to insist that the Soviets would have to approve any Chinese action in Korea.[9]

In fact, quite the opposite was true. Moscow opposed Chinese intervention fearing that it could lead to a general war involving the Soviet Union. The U.S. mindset of Soviet decision-making supremacy was abetted by the failure of the CIA to consider the multidisciplinary factors that led to both invasions. Cultural, historical, and nationalistic factors in fact dominated North Korean and Chinese decision making. Kim Il Sung, North Korea's leader, was determined to unify Korea under his leadership; he apparently believed that the South Korean population would rise up to support the invasion and that the United States would not intervene.[10] After the U.S. advance into North Korea, China's strategic interests were threatened by the possibility of a hostile Korea on its border. The CIA analyses took none of this into account.

Techniques and Analytic Tools of Forecasting

Both projection and forecasting use the tools described in this and succeeding chapters. In chapter 2 we introduced the idea of a conceptual model. The conceptual model on which projection and forecasting are based is an assessment of the dynamic forces acting on the entity being studied. Forecasting is based on a number of assumptions, among them the following:

- The future cannot be predicted, but by taking explicit account of uncertainty, one can make probabilistic forecasts.
- Forecasts will be misleading if they do not sweep widely across possible future developments in such areas as demography, values and lifestyles, technology, economics, law and regulation, and institutional change.
- Alternative futures, including the "most likely" future, are defined primarily by human judgment, creativity, and imagination.[11]

For executives and policymakers, the purpose of defining alternative futures is to try to determine how to create a better future than the one that would materialize if we merely kept doing what we're doing. In intelligence, the aim often is to predict an opponent's actions so that a response can be formulated.

Forecasting starts from our experiences or with examination of the changing political, military, economic, and social environments. We identify issues or concerns that may require attention. These issues or concerns are then defined in terms of their component forces. Forecasts of changes to those forces (mostly in the form of trends and events) are generated and subsequently interrelated using techniques such as cross-impact analysis. A "most likely" forecast future is written in scenario format from the trend and event forecasts; outlines of alternatives to that future are generated by synthesis/analysis. In complex forecasts a technique called cross-impact modeling, discussed in chapter 10, is sometimes used.

If the forecast is done well, these scenarios stimulate the customer of intelligence—the executive—to make decisions that are appropriate for each scenario. The decisions can be analyzed for their robustness across scenarios. The purpose is to arrive at a set of decisions that effectively address the issues and concerns identified in the initial stage of the process. The decisions are then implemented in action plans.[12]

Evaluating Forecasts

Forecasts are judged on the following criteria:

- *Clarity.* Are the objects of the forecast and the forecast itself intelligible? Is it clear enough for practical purposes? Users may, for example, be incapable of rigorously defining "gross national product" or the "strategic nuclear balance," but they may still have a very good ability to deal with forecasts on those subjects. On the other hand, they may not have the least familiarity with the difference between households and families and thus be puzzled by forecasts in that area. Most users have difficulty interpreting the statistics used in forecasting (for example, medians and interquartile ranges).

- *Intrinsic credibility.* To what extent do the results make sense to the customer? Do the results appear valid on the basis of common sense?

- *Plausibility.* To what extent are the results consistent with what the customer knows about the world outside the scenario and how that world *really* works or may work in the future?

- *Relevance.* If the forecasts are believed to be plausible, to what extent will they affect the successful achievement of the customer's mission or assignment?

- *Urgency.* To what extent do the forecasts indicate that, if action is required, time is of the essence in developing and implementing the necessary changes?

- *Comparative advantage.* To what extent do the results provide a better foundation for investigating decision options than do other sources available to the customer *today*? To what extent do they provide a better foundation now for future efforts in forecasting and policy planning?

- *Technical quality.* Was the process that produced the forecasts technically sound? To what extent are the basic forecasts consistent with one another?[13]

These criteria should be viewed as filters. To reject a forecast requires showing that the scenario cannot pass through all or most of these filters. A "good" forecast is one that survives such an assault; a "bad" forecast is one that does not. It is important to communicate to customers that forecasts are transitory and need constant adjustment to be helpful in guiding thought and action. It is not uncommon for customers to criticize forecasts. Common complaints are that the forecast is obvious; that it states nothing new; that it is too optimistic, pessimistic, or naïve; or that it is not credible because obvious trends, events, causes, or consequences were overlooked. Such objections, far from undercutting the results, facilitate strategic thinking. The response to them is simple: If something important is missing, add it. If something unimportant is included, strike it. If something important is included, but the forecast seems obvious, or the forecast seems highly counterintuitive, probe the underlying logic. If the results survive, use them. If not, reject or revise them.

Summary

Predictions may not come true. But a good prediction—one that accurately describes the forces acting on a target model and the assumptions about those forces—has lasting value for the intelligence customer. As a situation develops, the customer can revise the prediction, if the intelligence analyst gets the forces right. Three predictive techniques are used in intelligence.

Extrapolation is the easiest of the three because it simply assumes that the existing forces will not change. Over the short term, extrapolation is usually reliable, but it seldom gives an accurate picture over the medium-to-long term because forces do change. Extrapolation can be used to predict both straight-line and cyclic trends. Correlation and regression are two frequently used types of extrapolation.

Projection assumes a probability that the forces will change, and it uses several techniques to evaluate the probabilities and the effects of such changes. This probabilistic reasoning relies on techniques such as influence trees and influence nets. Sensitivity analysis can help the customer to identify the significance of changes in the probabilities that go into a projection.

Forecasting is the most difficult predictive technique. It must include the probabilities of changing forces, as for projection. It must also identify possible new forces from across the political, economic, social, and technical arenas and assess their likely impact. Because of the resulting complexity, most forecasting relies on the use of scenarios. Forecasting, like projection, also takes into account the effects of shaping forces, which are discussed in the next chapter.

Notes

1. Liam Fahey, *Competitors* (New York: John Wiley and Sons, 1999), 448.
2. Rob Johnson, *Analytic Culture in the U.S. Intelligence Community* (Washington, D.C.: Center for the Study of Intelligence, Central Intelligence Agency, 2005), 66.
3. Ibid., 15.
4. Joseph P. Martino, "Trend Extrapolation," in *A Practical Guide to Technological Forecasting*, ed. James R. Bright and Milton E. F. Schoeman (Englewood Cliffs, N.J.: Prentice-Hall, 1973), 108.
5. Center for the Study of Intelligence, Central Intelligence Agency, "Watching the Bear: Essays on CIA's Analysis of the Soviet Union," conference, Princeton University, March 2001, www.cia.gov/cis/books/watchingthebear/article08.html, 5.
6. This will permit later extension to more sophisticated analyses, such as Bayesian analysis, discussed in chap. 7.
7. Jack Davis, *Intelligence Changes in Analytic Tradecraft in CIA's Directorate of Intelligence* (Washington, D.C.: Central Intelligence Agency, 1995), 8.
8. Center for the Study of Intelligence, "Watching the Bear," 7.
9. P. K. Rose, "Two Strategic Intelligence Mistakes in Korea, 1950," *Studies in Intelligence*, (Fall/ Winter 2001), www.cis.gov/csi/studies/fall_winter_2001/article06.html.
10. William Stueck, *The Korean War: An International History* (Princeton: Princeton University Press, 1995).
11. James L. Morrison and Thomas V. Mecca, "Managing Uncertainty: Environmental Analysis/ Forecasting in Academic Planning," January 12, 2003, http://horizon.unc.edu/courses/papers/Mang.asp.
12. Ibid.
13. W. I. Boucher, *Technical Advisors' Final Report: Chapters Prepared by Benton International, Inc.*, prepared for the Futures Team of the Professional Development of Officers Study, Office of U.S. Army Chief of Staff (Torrance, Calif.: Benton International, 1984).

12

Shaping Forces

We build too many walls and not enough bridges.
Isaac Newton

We introduced the idea of force synthesis/analysis in chapter 10. The forces that have to be considered—technological, economic, political, social, environmental, and military—vary from one intelligence problem to another. I do not attempt to catalog them in this book—there are too many. However, some broad-based forces apply to most types of predictive analysis. They tend to shape or temper both events and other forces. They are mostly social or environmental. An analyst should start a predictive effort by asking which of these forces are relevant to the problem under consideration.

Inertia

One force with broad implications is inertia, the tendency to stay on course and resist change. Newton's first law (Analysis Principle 12-1) says that bodies at rest tend to stay at rest and bodies in motion tend to remain in motion.

Opposition to change is a common reason for organizations coming to rest. Opposition to technology in general, for example, is an inertial matter; it

---

Analysis Principle 12-1 ●────────────────────────

Inertia

Newton's first law (liberally translated) says that

1. Bodies at rest tend to remain at rest, and
2. Bodies in motion tend to remain in motion,

unless you place them in the real world, where friction applies. Then,

3. Bodies in motion tend to come to rest; and then you go back to rule 1.

---

results from a desire by both workers and managers to preserve society as it is, including its institutions and traditions. The price of inertia is illustrated in the history of the Bessemer steelmaking process in America.

The Bessemer process was invented at about the same time (1856) by two men, each working independently—Henry Bessemer, an Englishman, and William Kelly, an American. The process involved blowing air under pressure into the bottom of a crucible of molten iron. Within a few years the Bessemer process almost completely replaced the conventional, crucible method of steelmaking. It lowered the price of producing steel and was the basis for the modern steel industries. It was one of the foundations of the Industrial Revolution.

Between 1864 and 1871, ten companies in the United States began using the Bessemer process to make steel. All but one of them imported English workers familiar with the process. By 1871 that one, the Cambria Company, dominated the industry. Although Cambria had begun at a disadvantage, its workers were able to adapt to changes and improvements in the process that took place between 1864 and 1871. The British steelworkers at the other companies, secure in the tradition of their craft, resented and resisted all change, and their companies did not adapt.

The most common manifestation of the law of inertia is the "not-invented-here," or NIH, factor, meaning that an organization opposes pressures for change from the outside. It was powerful in the old Soviet technical bureaucracies and in the U.S. defense industry. The Soviet system developed a high level of stability as a result of central economic planning. But all societies resist change to a certain extent. The societies that succeed seem able to adapt while preserving that part of their heritage that is useful or relevant.

A textbook example of resistance to innovation is the story of the U.S. Navy and Lt. William Sims. One century ago the standard gunnery method used a highly trained gun crew to manipulate the heavy set of gears that aimed naval guns at an opposing ship. Because both ships would be moving, and the gun platform would also move with the pitch and roll of the ship, naval gunnery became an art, and accuracy depended on professionalism and teamwork.

In the early 1900s a young naval officer, William Sims, developed a new method that made use of the inertial movement of the ship. He was able to simplify the aiming gear set and remove the gunnery sight from the gun's recoil so that the operator could keep his eye on the gunsight and move the gears at the same time. His tests demonstrated that the new method would markedly improve the accuracy of naval gunnery.

Sims then attempted to attract the attention of U.S. Navy headquarters and was told that the navy was not interested. Sims persisted, however, and the navy finally consented to a test with some conditions: Sims's aiming device had to be strapped to a solid block in the Washington Naval Yard. Deprived of the ship's inertial movement, the aiming device failed, proving to the navy that continuous-aim firing was impractical.

Sims, however, was as persistent and bold as the person he next contacted with his idea—President Theodore Roosevelt. Roosevelt forced the navy to take the device and give it a fair test. Sims's device was subsequently adopted and significantly improved naval gunnery accuracy.[1]

The organizational resistance to change that Sims encountered is common. The U.S. Navy is a highly organized society, and Sims's innovation directly threatened that society by making some skills less essential. The navy resisted his innovation, and it took someone outside the society—the president of the United States—to force the change. Organizations are societies just as a U.S. Navy ship's crew is a society. They possess a basic antipathy to changes that threaten their structure. Most research and development groups restrict their members' freedom to innovate: Ideas that don't fit the mold of the group are unwelcome.

From an analyst's point of view, inertia is an important force in prediction. Established factories will continue to produce what they know how to produce. In the automobile industry, it is no great challenge to predict that next year's autos will look much like this year's. A naval power will continue to build ships for some time even if a large navy ceases to be useful.

Countervailing Forces

All forces are likely to have countervailing or resistive forces that must be considered. The principle is summarized well by another of Newton's laws of physics: For every action there is an equal and opposite reaction (Analysis Principle 12-2).

This analysis principle indicates that no entity (country, organization, initiative, or project) can expand unopposed. Opponents will always arise. Harvard historian David S. Landes writes that "all innovations of thought and practice elicit an opposite if not always equal reaction."[2] If the force reaction is initially not equal, as Landes posits, then a change in momentum (in physics) or in the situation (in the social sciences) occurs until the action and reaction balance. Thus every action ultimately creates an equal and opposite reaction.

Analysis Principle 12-2 ●─────────────────────────

Newton's Third Law (the Dialectic)

Newton's third law of physics states that whenever one body exerts a force on another, the second always exerts on the first a force that is equal in magnitude but oppositely directed. In the social sciences, Hegel's dialectic is the philosophical equivalent of Newton's third law. Hegel described a process of thesis-antithesis-synthesis, by which views of one type lead, by their internal contradictions, to the creation of views of the opposite type.

Applications of this principle, called Newton's third law, are found in all organizations and groups—commercial, national, and civilizational. As Samuel P. Huntington notes, "We know who we are . . . often only when we know who we are against."[3] The rallying cry of Japan's Komatsu Corporation, and the definition of its being, was summed up in its slogan, "Beat Caterpillar!"— Caterpillar Inc. being Komatsu's chief competitor worldwide.

In Isaac Asimov's brilliant short story *The Last Trump,* the Archangel Gabriel sounds the last trumpet and Judgment Day arrives (on January 1, 1957, to be precise). Earth's residents (and former residents, who are coming back to life in their last corporeal form) slowly realize that boredom, not the fire and ice of Dante's *Inferno,* is the ultimate Hell. Etheriel, Earth's guardian angel, meanwhile is appealing to a higher court—the Almighty—for an ex post facto reversal of the Judgment Day order. Finally Etheriel, realizing who has actually won the final battle for the souls of humankind, asks, "Is then the Adversary your servant also?" God invokes Newton's third law in his reply: "Without him I can have no other . . . for what is Good but the eternal fight against Evil?"[4]

A predictive analysis will always be incomplete unless it identifies and assesses opposing forces. All forces eventually meet counterforces. An effort to expand free trade inevitably arouses protectionist reactions. One country's expansion of its military strength always causes its neighbors to react in some fashion. If laws bar access to obscenity onine, you can count on offshore evasion of restrictions and growing pressures for free speech.

Counterforces need not be of the same nature as the force they are countering. A prudent organization is not likely to play to its opponent's strengths. Today's threats to U.S. national security are asymmetric; that is, there is little threat of a conventional force-on-force engagement by an opposing military, but there is a threat of an unconventional yet highly lethal attack by a loosely organized terrorist group, as the events of September 11, 2001, demonstrated.[5] Asymmetric counterforces are common in industry as well. Industrial organizations try to achieve cost asymmetry by using defensive tactics that have a large favorable cost differential between their organization and that of an opponent.[6] Any intelligence assessment of the consequences of a policymaker's or field commander's decision should take countervailing forces into account because the opponents will react and are likely to react asymmetrically.

Contamination

Contamination is the degradation of any political, social, economic, or technical entity through an infectionlike process (Analysis Principle 12-3). Corruption is a form of social contamination. Money laundering is a form of economic contamination.

Nobel Laureate Irving Langmuir described the contamination phenomenon in this story about a glycerin refinery:

Analysis Principle 12-3 •—————————————————————————

Gresham's Law of Currency

Gresham's law of currency is based on the observation that when currencies of different metallic content but the same face value are in circulation at the same time, people will hoard the more valuable currency or use it for foreign purchases, leaving only the "bad" money in domestic circulation. The law explains a major disadvantage of a bimetallic currency system. Gresham's law is generally summarized as, "The bad drives out the good."

Glycerin is commonly known as a viscous liquid, even at low temperatures. Yet if crystals are once formed, they melt only at 64 degrees Fahrenheit. If a minute crystal of this kind is introduced into pure glycerin at temperatures below 64 degrees Fahrenheit, the entire liquid gradually solidifies.

A glycerin refinery in Canada had operated for many years without having any experience with crystalline glycerin. But suddenly one winter, without exceptionally low temperatures, the pipe carrying the glycerin from one piece of apparatus to another froze up. The whole plant and even the dust on the ground became contaminated with nuclei, and although any part of the plant could be temporarily freed from crystals by heating above 64 degrees, it was found that whenever the temperature anywhere fell below 64 degrees crystals would begin forming. The whole plant had to be shut down for months until outdoor temperatures rose above 64 degrees.[7]

Contamination phenomena can be found throughout organizations as well as in the scientific and technical disciplines. Once such an infection starts, it is almost impossible to eradicate. It keeps poisoning its host, and there are too many little bits to stamp out entirely—like the crystals of glycerin or metastasizing cancerous cells. For example, in the U.S. electronics industry, a company's microwave-tube production line suddenly went bad. With no observable change in the process, the tubes no longer met specifications. Somehow, the line had become contaminated. Attempts to find or correct the problem failed, and the only solution was to close down the production line and rebuild it completely.

Contamination phenomena have analogies in the social sciences, organization theory, and folklore. Folklore tells us, "One bad apple spoils the barrel." At some point in organizations, contamination can become so thorough that only drastic measures will help—such as shutting down the glycerin plant or rebuilding the microwave-tube plant. Predictive intelligence has to consider the extent of such social contamination in organizations because contamination is a strong restraint on an organization's ability to deal with change.

The effects of social contamination are hard to measure, but they are often highly visible. Large sectors of industry in Russia reached a level of hopeless contamination some time ago, and recovery is proving to be very difficult. Indications of contamination can be seen in the production results, but there are also other visible symptoms. For example, most Japanese plants are clean and neat, with grass and flowers even in unlikely areas, such as underneath drying kilns. A Russian factory is likely to have a dirty, cluttered environment, buildings with staggering losses of energy, and employees with chronic absenteeism and alcohol problems. The environment in the Japanese plant reinforces the positive image. The environment in the Russian plant reinforces and prolongs the contamination. Such contamination can be reversed—the cleanup of New York City in the 1990s is an example—but a reversal normally requires a massive effort.

The contamination phenomenon has an interesting analogy in the use of euphemism in language. It is well known that if a word has or develops negative associations, it will be replaced by a succession of euphemisms. Such words have a half-life, or decay rate, that is shorter as the word association becomes more negative. In older English, the word *stink* meant "to smell." The problem is that most of the strong impressions we get from scents are unpleasant ones; so each word for olfactory senses becomes contaminated over time and is replaced. *Smell* has a generally unpleasant connotation now, and words such as *scent, aroma,* and *bouquet* are replacing it, to fall in their turn. Similarly, words that denote any socially, mentally, or physically disadvantaged group seem to become contaminated over time; words such as *deaf, blind,* and *retarded* were replaced by *handicapped,* and then by *mentally/physically challenged,* or sometimes *people with disabilities,* reflecting the negative associations that attach to the words as contamination sets in.

The phenomenon of contamination in language can be especially useful for the intelligence analyst in assessing the effectiveness of programs, whether social, political, or technical—and of hardware also. *We don't rename our successes.* Ford Motor Company since 1964 has kept the name "Mustang" for its most beloved automobile, but there will never be another Edsel. And no one names a cruise ship the *Titanic.* The renaming of a program or project is a good signal that the program or project is in trouble—especially in Washington, but the same rule holds in any culture.

Synergy

Predictive intelligence analysis almost always requires multidisciplinary understanding. Therefore it is essential that the analysis organization's professional development program cultivate a professional staff that can understand a broad range of concepts and function in a multidisciplinary environment. Synergy is a fundamental concept: The whole can be more than the sum of its parts because of interactions among the parts. Synergy is therefore, in some respects, the opposite of the countervailing forces discussed earlier.

Synergy is not really a force or a factor so much as it is a way of thinking about how forces or factors interact. Synergy can result from cooperative efforts and alliances among organizations (synergy on a large scale). It can be the consequence of a combination of social, economic, political, and technological forces on a grand scale, such as those that sparked the Industrial Revolution.[8] Netwar, as discussed in chapter 1, is an application of synergy. Synergy can also result from interactions within a physical system, as the following example shows.

When the U.S. Nike-Hercules surface-to-air missile system was deployed in the 1950s, its target-tracking radar proved to be very difficult for attacking aircraft to defeat in combat training exercises. The three standard techniques for defeating such radars at the time were rapid maneuvers, radar decoys, and noise jamming. None of the three techniques worked very well against the Nike-Hercules radar:

- Maneuvers had no effect.

- The radar could not be pulled off target by releasing the radar decoy material known as chaff (thin strips of aluminum foil that cause a radar signal resembling an aircraft), because the radar range rate tracking system could discriminate between slow-moving chaff and a fast-moving aircraft.

- The radar's antijam circuits eliminated conventional noise jamming.

The U.S. Air Force's Strategic Air Command (SAC) put its electronic warfare planners on the problem because the Nike-Hercules capabilities could be expected to appear in future radars that SAC's B-52s would face. SAC's planners found that a combination of the three techniques—noise jamming, with an S maneuver in which chaff was dropped when the aircraft track was perpendicular to the radar bearing—consistently defeated the tracking radar. The secret to the success of what became called the "sidestep" maneuver was synergy.

In electronics warfare, it is now well known that a weapons system may be unaffected by a single countermeasure; however, it may be degraded by a combination of countermeasures, each of which fails individually to defeat it. The same principle applies in a wide range of systems and technology developments: The combination may be much greater than the sum of the components taken individually.

An example of synergy on a large scale is that between the fields of computers and communications. These once-distinct technical areas have been merging over several decades, as we expand our ability to use one to enhance performance of the other. Managing the merger of these two required technical knowledge in both, plus an understanding of political issues (regulation in communications) and economic issues (cost-performance trade-offs of central versus distributed computing). It also required a keen market sense that determined the willingness of large numbers of people to take advantage of the merger, as people have done in using networks such as the Internet.

Synergy is the foundation of the "swarm" approach that military forces have applied for centuries—the coordinated application of overwhelming force. The massed English longbows at the Battle of Crécy in 1346 were more lethal than the sum of many single longbows might indicate. In planning a business strategy against a competitive threat, a company will often put in place several actions that taken alone would not succeed. But the combination can be very effective. As a simple example, a company might use several tactics to cut sales of a competitor's new product: start rumors of the release of its own improved product, circulate reports on the defects or expected obsolescence of the competitor's product, raise buyers' costs of switching from their own to the competitor's product, and tie up suppliers by using exclusive contracts. Each action, taken separately, might have little impact, but the synergy—the "swarm" effect of the actions taken in combination—might shatter the competitor's market.

In intelligence support to policymakers, the same rule holds. A combination of policy actions may be much more effective than any single action. The policymaker or executive usually identifies the possible combinations and, in the end, selects one combination. The usual job of the intelligence analyst is to evaluate the likely effects of a given combination, though in some cases he may also formulate likely combinations for the executive.

Most of the major innovations and changes that make straight-line extrapolation obsolete occur because of some form of synergy. Synergy was a major factor in the spread of television, CB radio, and personal computing. It should be constantly on the analyst's mind as he or she evaluates the factors going into a forecast.

Feedback

In examining any complex system, it is important for the analyst to evaluate the system's feedback mechanism. Feedback is the mechanism whereby the system adapts—that is, learns and changes itself. Feedback was introduced as a third class of force (along with internal and external forces) in chapter 10; the following discussion provides more detail about how feedback works to change a system.

Many techniques for prediction depend on the assumption that the process being analyzed can be described, using systems theory, as a closed-loop system. Under the mathematical theory of such systems, feedback is a controlling force in which the output is compared with the objective or standard, and the input or process is corrected as necessary to bring the output toward a desired state, as shown in Figure 12-1. The results (the output) are evaluated, and the result of the evaluation fed back as an input to the system at the point shown in the figure. The feedback function therefore determines the behavior of the total system over time. Only one feedback loop is shown in the figure, but many feedback loops can exist and usually do in a complex system.

The model shown in Figure 12-1 is a generalized one that is used extensively in electrical engineering to describe the operation of mechanical and

Figure 12-1   Feedback Process

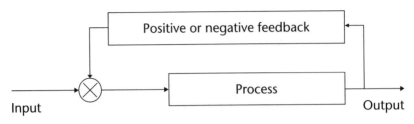

Note: The circled X shows where the input and the feedback combine before they flow into the process.

electrical control systems. It also has been found to represent many social processes, especially adaptation by organizations. Although its general validity has not been tested, the model is accepted here as having some validity in predicting the future state of the system.

An analyst should not consider a prediction complete until she has assessed the potential effects of feedback. Such an assessment requires the analyst to predict the nature and extent of feedback. Feedback can be positive and encourage more output, or it can be negative and encourage less output. Feedback can also be strong and have a greater effect on output, or be weak and have a lesser effect. Finally, feedback can be immediate and thus reflected immediately in the output, or its effect can be delayed so that it changes the output at some future time.

Strength

Most systems are adaptive. Feedback causes changes in the input and should also cause the management assessment and innovation parts of a process to change. The measure of this adaptivity is the strength of feedback. In most systems, a change in the output (type, quantity, and so on) changes the input as the result of an evaluatory process. In positive feedback systems, where benefits outweigh costs, the output causes a reinforcement of the input, and the output therefore tends to grow at a rate determined in part by the amount of positive feedback. In negative feedback systems, where costs outweigh benefits, output is fed back in such a manner as to decrease input, and the output tends to stabilize or decrease.

The rate of change in forces that is due to feedback is a result of weighing the observed benefits of a development (positive feedback) against the costs (negative feedback). This is the evaluation, or decision-making, step.

Organizations tend to act to reduce the strength of feedback in two ways. First, because few organizations can readily cope with the uncertainty that comes from adaptivity, organizations try to hold things constant so that they can deal with them. This tendency is a powerful constraint on feedback.[9] Sims's problem with introducing his gunnery innovation is one of many examples of the problem.

Second, feedback must reach decision makers or action takers to be effective. Only when it is accepted by the appropriate people in an organization can it shape future actions. But the organization itself—its administrative layers and staff—diffuses, weakens, misdirects, and delays feedback, effectively reducing its strength. A large bureaucratic organization or a centralized economy, with its relative inflexibility and numerous layers of administrators, keeps feedback at a feeble level. Funding is set through political processes that have only an indirect relation to previous industrial successes and failures. The market provides poor feedback in a centralized or command economy.

Time Delay

All feedback loops, whether in technological or social systems, have inherent delay. The time lag causes a problem when it results in the feedback's sending the wrong signal. Sometimes feedback of positive benefits comes more slowly than does feedback of a negative kind. So in the early stages the system may receive only negative feedback, though more positive information may be coming later. The benefits of deregulation or free trade agreements, for example, may be much more difficult to identify and take longer to observe than the costs.

It is fairly common, on the other hand, for benefits to be perceived more quickly than costs. The drug industry has provided us with examples of this phenomenon, one of the most dramatic of which occurred with the drug thalidomide. First introduced in Europe in 1956 for use as a sedative and to combat morning sickness in pregnant women, thalidomide was withdrawn from the market in 1961, but only after it was found to have caused severe birth defects in thousands of infants.[10]

The delayed effects of environmental pollution have provided other examples of such "false positive" feedback. The nuclear power industry, however, has probably provided the most spectacular examples. The industry benefited for some years from extensive government-supported efforts to advance the technology. The resulting pace of nuclear power technology development was too rapid to allow adequate mitigation of the risks.[11] As a result, in 1979 the United States suffered from the Three Mile Island reactor incident, which released radioactive material into the air near Harrisburg, Pennsylvania, creating widespread panic, and in 1986 Russia had its Chernobyl disaster—a reactor meltdown that contaminated a wide area in the Ukraine and caused several deaths.

As the examples suggest, delays in negative feedback are a continuing problem in areas of rapid technological advance. The rapid advances depend on technology diffusion mechanisms that work extremely well in the United States, with its efficient communications networks and high mobility of workers. Multinational corporations are also a powerful technological diffusion mechanism. The advance of technology is fast, compared with the technology evaluation process, leading to examples of "technology driven" systems in which the constraining effects of regulatory, human resources, organizational, and management factors are too slow to exert much power.

The pharmaceutical, communications, and computer industries have displayed this technology drive in action for several decades. Genetic engineering is a current technology-driven field that could produce serious problems worldwide in coming decades.

Regulation

Any analysis of an industry or organization must take into account the role of government regulatory forces. Some such forces are positive, but more government support does not necessarily mean that the industry or organization will succeed. An examination of protected industries yields some examples.

European governmental ownership of, and participation in, European businesses increased in the 1970s. A driving force was the need to rescue European businesses from failure or foreign takeover, especially in the aftermath of the 1973 oil shortage. When the computer industry merger of Honeywell-Bull was being negotiated in France in the 1970s, the French government agreed to the merger on the conditions that no employees would lose their jobs and no plants would be closed. Because the merger created an estimated 15,000 surplus employees, those conditions placed a heavy burden on the new firm. The result was low plant utilization, and Honeywell-Bull was not competitive in France in spite of a guaranteed market in French government-controlled firms.

The Honeywell-Bull case illustrates also that government bureaucracies learn slowly and all too often forget with time the lessons they do learn. When France, in the eighteenth century, wanted to make steel of the same quality as English steel, the French government subsidized British experts to form a company for that purpose—but the subsidy required the company to use French-made wrought iron. Cursed by the terms of the subsidy to use an inferior raw product, the company never succeeded in producing high-quality steel.[12]

Over the past century, governments have increased their regulatory influence over industrial decisions worldwide. In some countries, the intervention has been predominantly to monitor worker safety and health, protect the environment, and so forth. Other governments have intervened primarily to protect jobs and promote the economy. In some countries the intent has been to benefit the government leadership financially.

Governments are at a disadvantage in this kind of intervention: They seem to look at things one facet at a time, in a relatively simplistic manner. In part because of slower feedback processes and a more cumbersome structure, governments are generally not as quick on their feet as the corporations they deal with. And in their interventions, governments continually encounter the law of unintended consequences; that is, actions taken to change a complex system will have unintended, and usually adverse, consequences (Analysis Principle 12-4).

The classic illustration of the law of unintended consequences dates back to Tudor England. In England before 1535, real property passed by descent to the oldest son at his father's death. At that transfer, a tax was owed to the king.

Analysis Principle 12-4 ⬤─────────────────────────────

The Law of Unintended Consequences

The law of unintended consequences, simply stated, says that:

*   Any deliberate change to a complex (social or technical) system will have unintended (and usually unforeseen) consequences, and
*   The consequences are normally undesirable.

Over the years, feudal lawyers had created a device called the *Use,* which allowed trustees to hold legal title to land in trust for the true owner so that, unless all of the trustees died at once, the land could be repeatedly passed from father to son without the requirement that a tax be paid.

The story goes that King Henry VIII, as his financial needs increased, "contemplated the state of his exchequer with great dismay."[13] A survey of the kingdom's assets revealed to Henry how England's landowners were avoiding his taxes through the device of the Use. In 1535 Henry prevailed upon a reluctant Parliament to pass the Statute of Uses.[14] The statute was simple and direct: It vested legal title in the land's true owner, not in the trustee, so that taxes would be due upon the death of the true owner.

The statute is remarkable for two reasons: First, it totally failed in its revenue-raising purpose. Within a few years British lawyers, who were no less clever then than tax lawyers are today, had found enough loopholes in the statute to thwart it. Second, the *unintended* consequences of this tax-raising statute were vast, so much so that it has been called the most important single piece of legislation in the Anglo-American law of property. Specifically, the law gave rise to the modern law of trusts and to modern methods of transferring real estate. The British Parliament's reaction to the Statute of Uses also led to the Law of Wills as we know it.

The Statute of Uses also is one of the few known exceptions to the rule that unintended consequences are usually undesirable. It had highly beneficial results for succeeding generations, though not for Henry VIII.

The law of unintended consequences has an analogy in the world of data processing. In a modern, distributed processing network, or in a very complex software package, one cannot predict all the effects of changes. But it is predictable that most of the unintended consequences—system crashes, lockouts, and so forth—will be undesirable ones.

The law of unintended consequences may be merely an elegant expression of Murphy's law (which states that anything that can go wrong, will) or simply an expression of human inability to foretell the outcome of a complex social process. One facet of the law has been described as "counterintuitiveness." One generic model of a welfare system demonstrated that expanding a welfare system to reduce the number of poor families in a community actually (and counterintuitively) increases their numbers.[15] Another model indicated that making drugs illegal as a way to curb drug abuse and reduce other societal problems had the opposite effect.[16] As another example, Soviet secrecy during the cold war forced U.S. defense planners to assume the worst-case scenario and provoked a military buildup that the Soviets did not want.

The impact of regulation is difficult to measure—not only are the consequences unexpected but they are often difficult to trace back to the regulations that spawned them. One measure of these consequences occurs when an industry is deregulated, as when the United States deregulated the telecommunications industry. The effect in telecommunications was dramatic: new industries sprang up. Spurred by the competitive threat, AT&T became more innovative and market oriented than it had been in the past. The application of new technologies, such as packet switching for data communications, got a boost.

Just as government support does not mean automatic success, so government opposition does not mean automatic failure. Worldwide, the narcotics industry marches on in spite of strong opposition from many governments. During the Prohibition era in the United States, the liquor industry thrived.

Summary

Predictive analysis relies on assessing the impact of forces that shape organizations, lead to new developments, and motivate people:

- *Inertia,* or resistance to change, is common in established organizations. Organizations naturally seek to establish and maintain a stable state.

- *Countervailing forces* will always appear to oppose any significant force, and the countervailing force may be of an asymmetric type.

- *Contamination* phenomena can dilute the effectiveness of national or organizational instruments of power (political, economic, social, or technical).

- *Synergy*—the combination of forces to achieve unexpected results—is behind many social and technical advances. Synergy determines the effectiveness of the "swarm" attack that organizations increasingly use to win conflicts.

- *Feedback* is an adaptive force that can be beneficial or detrimental, depending on strength and delay. Rapid advances in technology, along with significant time delays in negative feedback about the technology, can cause problems.

- Government *regulatory forces* often constrain technical or social evolution and often have unintended consequences.

These shaping forces should be a first stop in any predictive analysis about a target model. The following two chapters give some examples of their application in organizational and systems analysis.

Notes

1. Elting Morrison, *Men, Machines, and Modern Times* (Cambridge: MIT Press, 1966).
2. David S. Landes, *The Wealth and Poverty of Nations* (New York: W. W. Norton and Company, 1998), 201.
3. Samuel P. Huntington, *The Clash of Civilizations and the Remaking of World Order* (New York: Simon and Schuster, 1996), 21.
4. Isaac Asimov, "The Last Trump," in *Isaac Asimov: The Complete Stories*, vol. 1 (New York: Doubleday, 1990), 106–119.
5. Another thoughtful perspective on the use of asymmetric attack against the United States is presented in the book *Unrestricted Warfare*, by Chinese People's Liberation Army colonels Qiao Liang and Wang Xiangsui (Beijing: PLA Literature and Arts Publishing House, February 1999).
6. Michael E. Porter, *Competitive Advantage* (New York: Free Press, 1985), 500.
7. Irving Langmuir, "Science, Common Sense, and Decency," *Science* 97 (January 1943): 1–7.
8. Landes, *The Wealth and Poverty of Nations*, chaps. 13 and 14.
9. Donald A. Schon, *Organizational Learning* (Boston: Addison-Wesley, 1978).
10. Crohn's and Colitis Foundation of America, "Thalidomide and IBD," March 10, 2003, www.ccfa.org/weekly/wkly828.htm.
11. Ibid.
12. Landes, *The Wealth and Poverty of Nations*, 287.
13. John E. Cribbet, *Principles of the Law of Property* (New York: Foundation Press, 1975).
14. Ibid.
15. Jamshid Gharajedaghi, *Systems Thinking: Managing Chaos and Complexity* (Boston: Butterworth-Heinemann, 1999), 49.
16. Ibid., 48.

13

Organizational Analysis

I do not rule Russia—ten thousand clerks do.

Tsar Nicholas I

One can use a number of analytical techniques to assess the major forces that shape most entities. We apply the techniques to answer questions about force impact, as discussed in chapter 10, and to construct influence trees. Most forces can be analysis targets, as well as forces in another analysis. A country's information technology, for example, might be the target of a technology assessment. The results of that assessment would be a force to be considered in an analysis of the country's information warfare capability. The results would also be a force to consider in an organizational assessment, such as an assessment of an industrial concern located in the country. An organizational assessment of the country's software development firms would be a significant input into an analysis of the country's information technology. Organizational and technological forces are important in predictive analyses of many targets, and that is why they are the subjects of this chapter and the next.

The typical organization is a system that, as noted in chapter 1, can be viewed (and analyzed) from three perspectives: structure, function, and process. *Structure* refers to the components of the organization, especially people and their relationships. *Function* refers to the outcome or results produced and tends to focus on decision making. *Process* describes the sequences of activities and the expertise needed to produce the results or outcome. Babson College professor Liam Fahey, in his assessment of organizational infrastructure, describes four perspectives: structure, systems, people, and decision-making processes.[1] Whatever their names, all three perspectives (or four, following Fahey's example) must be considered.

For the analyst, one goal of organizational analysis is to understand the strengths and weaknesses of the target organization. Another goal is predictive: to forewarn of change in the target organization's structure, function, or process that arise from changing forces. Policy-oriented customers can use the analysis in planning strategy; operations units can use it to adversely affect the target, possibly with information warfare. Depending on the goal, an analyst may need to assess the organization's mission, its power distribution, its human resources, and its decision-making processes. The analyst might ask questions such as, Where is control exercised? Which elements provide support services? Are their roles changing? Network analysis tools, discussed later in this chapter, are valuable for this sort of organizational analysis.

An analyst identifies vulnerable points in the target organization so that intelligence customers—the decision makers—can select the appropriate target to act on, that is, to identify where perception management or coercive techniques would be most effective. For example, the analyst's customers may want to know when and how to convey to the opponent that it can expect strong retaliatory actions if it behaves in a certain way.

Structure

There are many ways to analyze an organization's structure, but three approaches are more common than others. The first is to examine the size and capabilities of the organization along with its mission. Do the size and capabilities fit well with the mission? The second way is to assess the effectiveness of the structure itself. A structure that works for one group may be disastrous if applied to another. The third approach is to analyze the relationships among groups in the organizational hierarchy. These three approaches can complement one another to give a more complete structural picture.

Organizational Size and Capabilities

The usual way to measure whether an organization's size and capabilities facilitate its mission is to compare the organization with other organizations that have a similar mission—a technique called *benchmarking*. If size and capability hinder the mission, rather than promote it, the organization will have problems, as illustrated by a curve popularized in economic circles as the "Laffer curve."[2] The Laffer curve, depicted in Figure 13-1, illustrates an observation that many governments have made about tax policies. If tax rates are low, increasing the rate increases the total revenue generated. At some point, diminishing returns set in, and each taxation increment generates less new revenue than the previous increment did. If rates rise even higher, revenue actually begins to drop, as taxation drives people away from the activity being taxed.

The Laffer curve has a similar application for organizations. For organizations the vertical axis would be mission effectiveness, and the horizontal axis would describe how well the organizational structure is matched to its mission and environment. The organization must have a mission that it can accomplish but one that is not too narrowly defined. If the organization's size and capabilities are inadequate for the mission and environment (the left side of the graph in Figure 13-1) the result is frustration and loss of focus. A mission that is too narrowly defined for organizational size and capabilities can result in stagnation and loss of opportunities, or worse.

Figure 13-1   Laffer Curve for Tax Rates

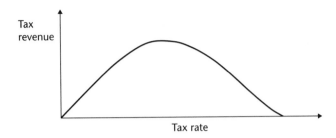

Type of Structure

One of the most challenging areas of organizational analysis is assessment of structural effectiveness. Some questions to ask include these: Where does the power lie? Does the organizational structure encourage reaching and executing good decisions? Does it fit with the culture?

But the first question is, Does the target organization make sense in its environment? Any form of government or economic structure can work—socialism, capitalism, dictatorship, democracy, theocracy—if it suits the people affected by it. Democracy, a preferred structure in Japan, Western Europe, and English-speaking countries, has not fared well in Africa or the Middle East because of a cultural mismatch. In business, the structures that work for an Internet start-up culture, a traditional bricks-and-mortar company, a research and development firm, a microelectronics device company, a food products company, or a natural gas pipeline company are not interchangeable. In fact, the different types of groups may have dramatically different structures.

One way to analyze organizational structure is to look at the trends in an organization and its management toward decentralization (devolving authority and responsibility to the lowest possible level) or centralization (keeping authority at the top level). Decentralization is not necessarily better as an organizational approach; it may be a great thing in a U.S. or European company, but it probably will fail in an Arab country because it does not fit the culture. Historical examples of successes and failures help such an analysis. Decentralization historically has worked if done according to the "colony" principle: Give maximum autonomy to the "colony" chief, but ensure that he is a company loyalist in training, belief, and tradition.[3] Both the Roman Empire and the Roman Catholic Church successfully applied the colony principle to decentralize.

Network Analysis

Network analysis, sometimes referred to as *relationship analysis,* is a well-developed discipline for analyzing organizational structure. The traditional hierarchical description of an organizational structure does not sufficiently portray entities and their relationships. *Social network analysis,* in which all the network nodes are persons, is widely used in the social sciences, especially in studies of organizational behavior. In intelligence we more frequently use *generalized network analysis*, in which the nodes can be persons, organizations, places, or things. The Abacha funds-laundering network in chapter 5 (Figure 5-9) illustrates the need to include entities such as banks, airlines, and bank accounts as nodes. However, the basic techniques of social network analysis apply to generalized network analysis as well.

Network analysis has been used for years in the U.S. intelligence community for targets such as terrorist groups and narcotics traffickers, and it is becoming increasingly important in business intelligence. As Fahey notes, competition in many industries is now as much competition between networked enterprises (companies such as Cisco and Wal-Mart that have created collaborative business networks) as it is between individual, stand-alone firms.[4] The netwar model of multidimensional conflict between opposing networks, described in chapter 1, is more and more applicable to all intelligence, and network analysis is our tool for examining the opposing network.

Social Network Analysis. A social network is a set of individuals, referred to as *actors* (shown graphically as nodes on Figure 13-2), that are connected by some form of relationship (shown as lines on Figure 13-2). Such networks can comprise few or many actors and many kinds of relations between pairs of actors. To build a useful understanding of a social network, a complete and rigorous description of a pattern of social relationships is a necessary starting point for analysis. Ideally, we should know about all of the relationships between each pair of actors in the population.

We prefer to use mathematical and graphical techniques in social network analysis to represent the descriptions of networks compactly and systematically. These techniques also enable us to use computers to store and manipulate the information quickly and more accurately than we could by hand. Suppose we had information about trade flows of fifty different commodities (coffee, sugar, tea, copper, bauxite, and so on) among 170 or so nations during a given year. The 170 nations can be thought of as nodes, and the amount of each commodity exported from each nation to each of the other 169 can be thought of as the strength of a direct tie from the focal nation to the other. An intelligence analyst might be interested in how the networks of trade in mineral products differ from networks of trade in vegetable products. To answer this fairly simple (but important) question, a huge amount of data manipulation is necessary. It could take years to do by hand; a computer can do it in a few minutes.

Another reason for using "formal" methods (mathematics and graphs) for representing social network data is that the techniques of graphing and the rules of mathematics themselves suggest things that we might look for in our data—things that might not have occurred to us if we presented our data by using descriptions in words. It is fairly easy to see, in Figure 13-2, that taking out node A will have the most impact on the network. It might not be so obvious if all the relationships were described textually.

Figure 13-2   Social Network Analysis Diagram

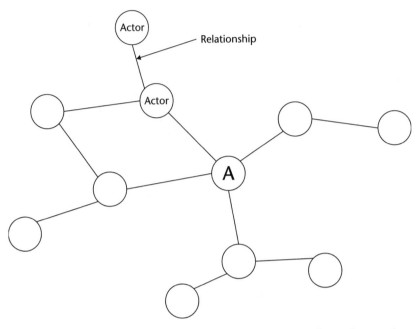

Note: The letter *A* marks the node whose removal will have the greatest effect on the network.

Several analytic concepts come along with social network analysis, and they also apply to generalized network analysis. The most useful concepts are *centrality* and *equivalence*. These are used today in the analysis of intelligence problems related to terrorism, arms networks, and illegal narcotics organizations.

Centrality refers to the sources and distribution of power in a social structure. The network perspective suggests that the power of individual actors arises from their relations with others. Whole social structures may be seen as displaying high levels or low levels of power, as a result of variations in the patterns of ties among actors. Furthermore, the degree of inequality or concentration of power in an organization and among organizations can be estimated.

Power arises from occupying advantageous positions in social networks. An actor's position in the network tells us much about the extent to which that actor may be constrained by, or may constrain, others. The extent to which an actor can reach others in the network may be useful in describing the actor's opportunities. Three basic sources of advantage are *high degree, high closeness,* and *high betweenness*.

The more ties an actor has to other actors, the more power (the higher degree) that actor has. In Figure 13-3, actor A has degree five (ties to five other actors); all other actors have degree one (ties to just one other actor). Actor A's high degree gives him more opportunities and alternatives than other actors in the network. If actor D elects to not provide A with a resource, A has other places to go to get it; but if D elects not to exchange with A, then D will not be able to exchange at all. Actors who have more ties have greater opportunities because they have choices. Their rich set of choices makes them less dependent than others and hence more powerful.

The second reason why actor A is more powerful than the others in the "star network" depicted in Figure 13-3 is that actor A is closer (high closeness) to more actors than any other actor. Power can be exerted by direct bargaining and exchange, but power also comes from being a center of attention whose views are heard by more actors. Actors who are able to reach other actors by shorter paths, or who are more reachable by other actors by shorter paths, have favored positions. Such a structural advantage can be translated into power.

The third reason that actor A is advantaged is that he lies between all other pairs of actors (high betweenness), and no other actors lie between A and other actors. If A wants to contact F, A may do so directly. If F wants to contact B, she must do so by way of A. This gives actor A the capacity to broker contacts among other actors—to extract "service charges" and to isolate actors or prevent contacts.

In simple structures such as the star, the advantages all tend to accrue to one actor. In more complex and larger networks, an actor may be located in a position that is advantageous in some ways and disadvantageous in others.

Let us look at a terrorist network to illustrate the concept of centrality. In seeking to disrupt terrorists, one obvious approach is to identify the central players and then target them for assessment, surveillance, or removal. The degree of network centrality of the individuals removed will determine the extent to which their removal impedes continued operation of the activity. Thus, centrality is an important ingredient (but by no means the only one) in considering the identification of network vulnerabilities.

Figure 13-3   Social Network Analysis: A Star Network

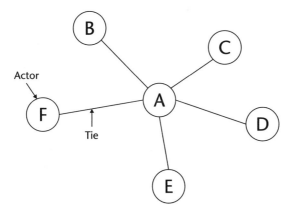

The second analytic concept that accompanies social network analysis is *equivalence*. The disruptive effectiveness of removing one individual or set of individuals from a network (for example, by making an arrest or by hiring a key executive away from a business competitor) depends not only on those individuals' centrality but also on some notion of their uniqueness—that is, on whether or not they have equivalents. The notion of equivalence is useful for strategic targeting and is closely tied to the concept of centrality. If nodes in the social network have a unique role (no equivalents), they will be harder to replace. The most valuable targets are both central and without equivalents. Continuing the example of a terrorist network, the network leader may have equivalents—for example, a strong subordinate who can take over. But the accountant, with his unique expertise and knowledge, may be the irreplaceable part of the network by virtue of his centrality and lack of equivalents.

Network analysis literature offers a variety of conceptions of equivalence. Three in particular are quite distinct and seem to capture among them most of the important ideas on the subject. They are *substitutability, stochastic equivalence,* and *role equivalence.* Each can be important in specific analysis and targeting applications.

Substitutability is easiest to understand; it could best be described as "interchangeability." Two objects or persons in a category are substitutable if they have identical relationships with every other object in the category. If a target individual has no substitute, her removal will cause more damage to the operation of the network than it would if a substitute existed. If another individual can take over the same role and already has the same connections, an opponent who wanted to damage the network would have to remove or incapacitate not only the target individual but all other substitutable individuals as well. Individuals who have no available network substitutes make more worthwhile targets.

Substitutability also has relevance to detecting the use of aliases. The use of an alias by a criminal might show up in a network analysis as the presence of two or more substitutable individuals (who are in reality the same person, with an alias). The interchangeability of the nodes actually indicates the interchangeability of the names.

Stochastic equivalence is a slightly more sophisticated idea. Two network nodes are stochastically equivalent if the probabilities of their being linked to any other particular node are the same. Narcotics dealers working for one distribution organization could be seen as stochastically equivalent if they, as a group, all knew roughly 70 percent of the group, did not mix with dealers from any other organizations, and all received their narcotics from one source.

Role equivalence means that two individuals play the same role in different organizations, even if they have no common acquaintances at all. Substitutability implies role equivalence, but not the converse. For example, the chief financial officer (CFO) of company A can be mapped onto the CFO of company B, if companies A and B are similar enough (the two CFOs have similar roles and responsibilities). Or an explosives expert in terrorist group A can be mapped onto a biological weapons expert in terrorist group B, if group A specializes in the use of explosives against its target and group B specializes in the use of biological terrorism. Stochastic equivalence and role equivalence are useful in creating generic models of target organizations and in targeting by analogy—for example, the explosives expert is analogous to the biological weapons expert in planning collection, analyzing terrorist groups, or attacking them.

Generalized Network Analysis. As we have said, in intelligence work we usually apply an extension of social network analysis that retains its basic concepts. But whereas all of the entities in social network analysis are people, in generalized network analysis they can be anything—organizations, places, and objects, for example. If we are charting a generalized network diagram for a terrorist organization, it will be important to include associated organizations, weapons, locations, and means of conducting terrorist activities (vehicles, types of explosives). The purpose of such generalized network displays is usually to reveal such things as the patterns of operations, likely future targets, and weaponry. Generalized network analysis thereby includes some aspects of functional analysis and process analysis.

In intelligence, generalized network analysis tends to focus on networks in which the nodes are organizations or people within organizations. Fahey has described several such networks and defined five principal types:

- *Vertical networks:* networks organized across the value chain; for example, 3M Corporation activities go from mining raw materials to delivering finished products.

- *Technology networks:* alliances with technology sources that allow a firm to maintain technological superiority, such as the Cisco Systems network.

- *Development networks:* alliances focused on developing new products or processes, such as the multimedia entertainment venture DreamWorks SKG.

- *Ownership networks:* networks in which a dominant firm owns part or all of its suppliers, as do the Japanese keiretsu.

- *Political networks:* those focused on political or regulatory gains for their members, for example, the National Association of Manufacturers.[5]

Hybrids of the five are possible, and in some cultures, such as in the Middle East and East Asia, family can be the basis for a type of hybrid business network.

Generalized network analysis may become one of the principal tools for dealing with complex systems, thanks to new, computer-based analytical methods. Prospects include future systems that can learn from the analysts and create models from data. But any system that purports to organize massive amounts of data will produce many false alarms. The analyst still will have to do cognitive correlation and evaluate sources.[6]

As implemented in software, generalized network analysis tools have to convey dynamic information to be of the most value to intelligence analysts. That is, links should appear and disappear, expand or contract in size, change intensity, change color—all to convey additional information to the user. Nodes should move up or down, closer or farther away (or have size changes) on the display to indicate importance.

Function

Functional analysis of an organization tends to focus on behavioral analysis, specifically on predicting decisions. The purpose of behavioral analysis is always predictive: How will the target react to a given situation? In all behavioral analysis, but especially in decision prediction, three aspects of the decision process have to be considered—rational, cultural, and emotional.[7] We will discuss each of these in this section as well as how the decision-making process is played out in groups.

Rational Aspect

Wharton business school professor Russell Ackoff, in his entertaining book *The Art of Problem Solving: Ackoff's Fables,* tells the story of a household appliance manager who claimed that consumers are often irrational. The manager cited the example of an improved dishwasher that had been poorly received, whereas new cooktops and ovens that offered no new features and were more expensive had been very successful. Ackoff and the manager agreed to an experiment—they would put the failed products on one side of a room, the successes on the other, and the two would tour the room together with a fresh eye. Within a minute after entering the room, the manager retracted his assertion about consumers' irrationality. He saw that consumers could use all of the successful appliances without bending or climbing, but all of the failed products required bending or climbing.[8]

The opponent is seldom irrational, and consumers are almost never irrational, but both are often misunderstood. Rational decision making is broadly defined as a logical and normally quantitative procedure for thinking about difficult problems. Stated formally, rational decision making requires the systematic evaluation of costs or benefits accruing to courses of action that might be taken. It entails identifying the choices involved, assigning values (costs and benefits) to possible outcomes, and expressing the probability of those outcomes being realized.

Predictive intelligence analysis often attempts to identify the option that a decision maker is most likely to select in a given situation. The approach is based on the assumption that decisions are made on an explicit or implicit cost-benefit analysis, also known as "expected utility theory." The theory's origins are in the study of economic decision making and behavior, notably in the work of John von Neumann and Oskar Morgenstern.[9] The theory views decision making as behavior that maximizes utility. An individual faced with a decision will, consciously or subconsciously, identify the available options, the possible outcomes associated with each option, the utility of each option/ outcome combination, and the probability that each option/outcome combination will occur. The decision maker will then choose an option that is likely to yield, in her own terms, the highest overall utility.

Rational decision prediction, based on expected utility theory, is the place to start any predictive analysis, but it is not the end point. In chapter 7 we introduced R. V. Jones's "principles of impotence"—a false assumption that a particular problem is unsolvable. Principles of impotence have been applied in intelligence to unnecessarily constrain thinking, but fundamental limits do exist, and one such limit applies in physics and in the analogous field of behavioral analysis. In physics, we know it as Heisenberg's uncertainty principle, which states that it is impossible to measure accurately both the velocity and the position of a single elementary particle. It is therefore impossible to predict with certainty the movement of a single particle. The limitation occurs because the act of measurement affects the object being measured.

This principle applies to a wide range of phenomena in both the physical and the social sciences. Although physicists can predict the average behavior of large groups of particles, the behavior of any one particle, as Heisenberg said, cannot be predicted with certainty. The analogy for human behavior is that it is possible to predict the behavior of groups of people (as political pollsters know well) but not the behavior of an individual.

A second fundamental principle from Heisenberg has to do with feedback. In chapter 12 we discussed feedback as a basic shaping force. It is also a significant factor in decision prediction. Heisenberg's uncertainty principle says that the process of measurement alters the quantity being measured. In other words, the more precisely you try to measure a phenomenon, the more you affect the result. When pollsters take a sample of public opinion, the questions they ask tend to alter the opinions of the group polled. A thermometer, measuring the temperature of an object, alters that temperature slightly.[10] Attempts to measure an employee's performance skew that employee's behavior. The problem is one of unintentional feedback. In management theory, the principle was perhaps first documented in the Hawthorne Experiment.

In 1927 the Western Electric Company began an investigation into the effectiveness of lighting on the productivity of factory workers. Western Electric chose its Hawthorne Works facility, in Illinois, for the experiment. The test involved varying the illumination levels within the plant and observing the effect on production. The researchers were surprised to observe that production increased whether the lights were made brighter, dimmed, or left constant. Only by reducing the lighting to levels approaching darkness could the researchers cause production to drop.

The researchers followed up with a more carefully designed study of the effects of rest periods and length of the work day. The study lasted five years, from 1927 to 1932. Again, the work teams whose performance was being measured steadily increased their production independent of changes in rest period timing and workday length. Furthermore, major increases in worker morale and health, along with decreases in absenteeism, were observed throughout the test period.[11]

The Hawthorne Experiment became a management science classic because of the insights it gave into motivating workers. For our purposes, the important point is that the workers knew they were being measured and thus changed their behavior to affect the measurement. In short, the attempt to measure changed the behavior being measured.

The uncertainty principle has several applications in intelligence analysis. In any analysis, the result tends to affect the entity being measured. The publication of economic trend predictions affects those trends. A broker's "strong buy" rating on a stock causes people to buy the stock and the price to rise, making it a self-fulfilling prediction. As noted in chapter 10, intelligence predictions shape the future because both sides often act based on the predictions.

In summary, the utility theory (rational) approach is useful in decision prediction, but it must be used with caution for two reasons. First, people will seldom make the effort to find the optimum action in a decision problem. The complexity of any realistic decision problem dissuades them. Instead, they select a number of possible outcomes that would be "good enough." They then choose a strategy or an action that is likely to achieve one of the good-enough outcomes.[12] Second, the social sciences version of the uncertainty principle places limits on how well we can predict decisions based on rationality. To improve the decision prediction, we have to include cultural and emotional factors. They are the factors that often cause an opponent's decision to be labeled "irrational."

Cultural Aspect

A critical component of decision modeling is the prediction of a single human's behavior, within the limitations of the uncertainty principle. And behavior cannot be predicted with any confidence without putting it in the actor's social and cultural context. An analyst needs to understand such elements of a culture as how it trains its youth for adult roles and how it defines what is important in life. In behavioral analysis, culture defines the ethical norms of the collective that a decision maker belongs to. It dictates values and constrains decisions.[13] In general, culture is a constraining social or environmental force. Different cultures have different habits of thought, different values, and different motivations. Straight modeling of a decision-making process without understanding these differences can lead the analyst into the "irrational behavior" trap, as happened to U.S. and Japanese planners in 1941.

Before Japan attacked Pearl Harbor, both the United States and Japan made exceptionally poor predictions about the other's decisions. Both sides indulged in "mirror imaging"—that is, they acted as though the opponent would use a "rational" decision-making process, as *they* defined "rational."

U.S. planners reasoned that the superior military, economic, and industrial strength of the United States would deter attack. Japan could not win a war against the United States; so a Japanese decision to attack would be irrational.[14]

The Japanese also knew that a long-term war with the United States was not winnable because of the countries' disparity in industrial capacity. But Japan's leadership believed that a knockout blow at Pearl Harbor would encourage the United States to seek a negotiated settlement in the Pacific and East Asia.[15] To validate this assumption, the Japanese drew on their past experience: A similar surprise attack on the Russian fleet at Port Arthur in 1904 had eventually resulted in the Japanese obtaining a favorable negotiated settlement. The Japanese did not mirror-image the United States with themselves but with the Russians of 1904 and 1905. Japan believed that the U.S. government would behave much as the tsarist government had.

Such errors in predicting an opponent's decision-making process are common when the analyst does not take cultural factors into account. Cultural differences cause competitors not to make the "obvious" decision. Intelligence analysts have to understand these different motivations, or they can be caught in the sort of surprise that U.S. television manufacturers encountered during the 1960s. At that time, all TV manufacturers foresaw a glut of TV sets on the market. U.S. manufacturers responded by cutting back production, assuming that other manufacturers would follow suit. Japanese manufacturers, working on different assumptions (giving priority to capturing market share instead of maintaining short-term profit), kept production up. As U.S. manufacturers' market share dropped, they found that their per-unit costs were rising, while the Japanese per-unit costs were dropping through economies of scale. The U.S. television industry never recovered.

Culture is often ignored or downplayed in both organizational and behavioral analysis. But history tells us that national declines are preceded by cultural declines.[16] Of immediate concern to intelligence analysis, *organizational* declines follow cultural declines. Culture has been described as representing the heartbeat and lifeblood of an organization.[17] Therefore, cultural analysis should always be a part of both organizational analysis and behavioral analysis.

For most countries and ethnic groups, a considerable volume of material is available to aid in cultural analysis, thanks to the work of many cultural anthropologists worldwide. Liam Fahey has described a methodology for cultural analysis that highlights four elements of an organizational culture: values, beliefs, norms, and behaviors. Fahey provides an example of the contrast in these four elements between a culture that is product or technology oriented and one that is customer or marketplace oriented.[18] But suppose that an analyst knows nothing about a country's culture and needs a quick lesson. How would she start?

An informal but effective way to grasp quickly some elements of a culture is to look at the culture's proverbs or "old wives' tales." The analyst should examine the similarities to and differences from those of her own culture. To illustrate, let's try a guessing game. The following are some proverbs from different cultures. Try to guess the culture or country of origin (the answers are in the notes at the end of the chapter):

Culture 1
Without bread and wine even love will pine.
Better a good dinner than a fine coat.
When the hostess is handsome the wine is good.[19]

Culture 2
Study others' advantages, and they will become your own.
We learn little from victory, much from defeat.
It is not wise to stay long when the husband is not at home.
Proclaim by your deeds who your ancestors are.
Women should associate with women.
A single arrow is easily broken, but not ten in a bundle.
Two birds of prey do not keep each other company.
It is the nail that sticks out that is struck.[20]

Culture 3
The weapon of a woman is her tears.
My brother and I against my cousin; my cousin and I against a stranger.
Be contrary and be known.
He who reproduces does not die.
We say, "It's a bull"; he says, "Milk it."[21]

Culture 4
In war there can never be too much deception.
Sit atop the mountain and watch the tigers fight.
Life and shame are never equal to death and glory.
Kill the chicken to frighten the monkey.
Fight only when you can win; move away when you cannot.[22]

Culture 5
If you are sitting on his cart you must sing his song.
If you see a Bulgarian on the street, beat him up. He will know why.
To live is either to beat or to be beaten.[23]

Organizations also have their own cultures, distinct from the national culture; but only long-established companies are likely to have standard sayings that are the equivalent of proverbs, and many of them no longer define the culture—if they ever did. Finding the information needed to assess an organizational culture can be difficult. Clues are sometimes available from unofficial (that is, not sponsored by the company) Web sites that feature comments from ex-employees. Those sites have to be used with caution, however; they rarely present the positive side of the organization's culture.

Part of assessing the culture of an organization is assessing the people in it—their attitudes or motivation, their educational background, and their commitment to the organization. It is in those features that countries and organizations vary markedly from their peers.

Some guidelines for assessing the motivations of the people in an organization were defined years ago by Professor A. H. Maslow and are widely known as the Maslow hierarchy of needs. Humans, according to this theory, have a basic set of prioritized needs, and as each need in turn is satisfied, the next need becomes predominant. The needs, in hierarchical order, are the following:

- *Physiological:* food, shelter, the essentials of survival
- *Safety:* freedom from physical danger
- *Belongingness:* friends and affection
- *Esteem:* self-respect and the esteem of others
- *Self-actualization:* to "be all that you can be"[24]

The effectiveness of organizations in developed countries depends on their ability to meet the higher order needs in the hierarchy. In less developed countries, food, shelter, and safety may be the upper limit of employee expectations. Innovation, in particular, depends on satisfying the need of the innovators for self-actualization.

Finally, all organizations have what is called a *psychological contract* with their members—an unwritten agreement on the rules each side is expected to follow.[25] People form bonds with organizations and develop expectations of how organizations should behave toward them. The strength of the employees' commitment and the strength of the organizational culture depend on how well the organization lives up to its half of the contract.

Assessing employees' educational backgrounds as a part of an organization's culture involves more than simply counting the number and levels of university degrees in the organization. Particularly in comparing organizations in different countries, one should be aware that there are important trade-offs between breadth of knowledge and depth of specialization. Each has its advantages. Universities in countries such as Japan and Russia tend to develop specialists who are highly trained in a field that is currently needed by industry. For example, each year Russia graduates large numbers of "engineers," but a breakdown of specialties shows that many of them are welding engineers or individuals who have some similarly narrow specialty. In fact, most Russian engineers have no particular interests outside their specialty and are remarkably inflexible, though they tend to be very good within their narrow specialty. U.S. universities, in contrast, have tended to develop generalists—people who have a broad area of expertise, who tend to be flexible and to draw on disciplines outside their primary field. The U.S. employment pattern tends to reinforce that flexibility; white-collar workers have high mobility and change companies and fields easily.

Japanese and Russian white-collar workers traditionally have tended to stay with one company for a long time, though the pattern may be changing in both countries.

Emotional Aspect

The final aspect of the decision process to consider when analyzing behavior is the emotional aspect. We do many things because they are exciting or challenging. Russell Ackoff tells the story of a hand-tool manufacturer whose executive team was eager to get into the business of manufacturing the (then) newly discovered transistor—not because they knew what a transistor was but because they were bored with their existing business and wanted a new challenge.[26] Pride and revenge are also motivators. Business leaders, generals, and even presidents of the United States make some decisions simply because they want to pay back an opponent for past wrongs. The emotional aspect of behavioral prediction cannot be ignored, and personality profiling is one way to grasp it.

Business intelligence analysts have developed a methodology for personality profiling of competitors that is based on the lesson that personal idiosyncrasies and predisposition will have a greater bearing on an executive's decisions than will a calculated assessment of resources and capabilities. The resulting profile is a model that can be used to assess likely decisions.[27]

In evaluating the likely decision of an executive, it may help to apply the Myers-Briggs model discussed in chapter 5. A decision by one Myers-Briggs type will predictably be different from a decision made by another Myers-Briggs type. An executive who was the linebacker of the college football team will likely have a completely different decision-making style than an executive who was president of the chess club.[28]

Collective Decision Making

Very often a decision will be made by a group instead of by one person. Such cases require a collective decision-prediction approach. It is somewhat easier to predict what a group will decide than to predict what an individual will decide—which is not to say that it is easy. In such decision modeling, one must identify the decision makers—often the most difficult step of the process—and then determine the likely decisions. The organization and management structures that make collective decisions vary from company to company and from country to country.

Some analytical tools and techniques can predict the likely outcome of group decision making. These tools and techniques are based on the theories of social choice expounded by the Marquis de Condorcet, an eighteenth-century mathematician. He suggested that the prevailing alternative should be the one that is preferred by a majority over each of the other choices in an exhaustive series of pairwise comparisons. Another technique is to start by drawing an influence diagram that shows the persons involved in the collective decision.

Collective decisions tend to have more of the rational elements and less of the emotional. But unless the decision participants come from different cultures, the end decision will be no less cultural in nature.

The collective decisions of an organization are usually formalized in its plans, especially its strategic plans. The best way to assess a strategic plan is to identify, and then attempt to duplicate, the target organization's strategic planning process. If the analyst comes from the same culture as the target, a duplication may be relatively easy to do. If that is not the case, it may be necessary to hire some executives from the target culture and have them attempt the duplication. The analyst also can order a collection operation to determine which strategic planning books the target's planners have read or which approach they favor.

Process

The functions of an organization are carried out by processes. Different types of organizations—civil government and law enforcement, military, and commercial organizations—will have markedly different processes. Even similar types of organizations will have different processes, especially in different cultures. The processes that a terrorist organization such as al Qaeda uses are quite different from those used by the Tamil Tigers of Sri Lanka. There are a correspondingly large number of analytical techniques for analyzing processes, many of which are industry specific. Analysts tend over time to develop process methodologies that are unique to their area of responsibility. Political, military, economic, and weapons systems analysts all use specialized process-analysis techniques. Here we address a few that are widely used: operations research, schedule, and cost. Chapter 14 discusses some process-analysis techniques that are specific to weapons systems analysis.

Operations Research

Operations research is a specific type of performance simulation that objectively compares alternative means of achieving a goal or solving a problem and selecting an optimum choice. It is widely used to help design complex systems. Operations research techniques grew out of the military sciences in World War II. One of the first applications was in antisubmarine warfare against German U-boats. Analysts looked at the effectiveness of searching from aircraft and surface ships, the disposition of escorts around a convoy, and methods of attacking submarines. They subsequently formulated a model of U-boat operations in the North Atlantic.[29] Operations research has been used since then to predict bombing effectiveness, to compare weapons mixes, and to assess military strategies.[30] In the communications arena, operations research techniques have helped planners and decision makers to select transmitter locations and satellite orbits, to provide competitive services that stay within goals for efficiency and costs, and to increase overall system reliability.

Two widely used operations research techniques are linear programming and network analysis. They are used in many fields, such as network planning, reliability analysis, capacity planning, expansion capability determination, and quality control.

Linear programs are simply systems of linear equations or inequalities that are solved in a manner that yields an optimum value—the best way to allocate limited resources, for example.[31] The optimum value is based on some single goal statement (provided to the program in the form of what is called a *linear objective function*). Linear programming is often used in intelligence for estimating production rates, although it is applicable in a wide range of disciplines.

Suppose that an analyst is trying to establish the maximum number of tanks per day that a tank assembly plant can produce. Intelligence indicates that the primary limits on tank production are the availability of skilled welders and the amount of electricity that can be supplied to the plant. These two limits are called *constraints* in linear programming. The plant produces two types of tanks:

- The T-76 requires 30 hours of welder time and 20 kilowatt-hours of electricity per tank.
- The T-81 requires 40 hours of welder time and 5 kilowatt-hours of electricity per tank.

The plant has 100 kilowatt-hours of electricity and 410 hours of welder time available per day. The goal statement, or objective function, is to determine the maximum possible number of tanks produced per day, where

Tanks per day = (# of T-76s) + (# of T-81s),

subject to two constraints, represented by inequalities. It takes four times as much power to produce a T-76 than a T-81, so one inequality is

20 (# of T-76s) + 5 (# of T-81s) ≤ 100 kilowatt-hours.

And a T-76 takes only three-quarters as many welder hours to produce as does a T-81, so the second inequality is

30 (# of T-76s) + 40 (# of T-81s) ≤ 410 welder hours.

The solution to the linear program is most easily observed in a graph like the one shown in Figure 13-4. The two constraints appear as solid lines. Both are inequalities that define a limit; an acceptable solution must lie below and to the left of both lines to satisfy both inequalities. According to the lines, the plant could produce ten T-81s and no T-76s, or five T-76s and no T-81s. The objective function or goal statement is shown as a dotted line representing the total number of tanks produced. Anywhere on this dotted line, the total number of tanks produced is a constant, which changes as the

Figure 13-4 Linear Programming Solution for Tank Production

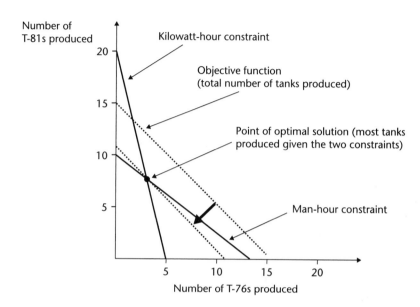

Note: The large arrow between the two dotted lines shows how the objective function was moved down and to the left to a point where it intersected the two constraints and created a point of optimal solution.

line is moved up and to the right, or down and to the left. We start the line at a total of fifteen tanks produced, and move it down and left, as indicated by the large arrow, until it touches a point that meets both constraints. This point—approximately eight T-81s and three T-76s, for a total of eleven tanks—represents the optimal solution to the problem.

Another operations research technique widely used in intelligence is network analysis. We previously introduced the concept of network analysis as applied to relationships among entities. Network analysis in an operations research sense is not the same. Rather, in this context networks are interconnected paths over which things move. The things can be automobiles (in which case we are dealing with a network of roads), oil (with a pipeline system), electricity (with wiring diagrams or circuits), information signals (with communication systems), or people (with elevators or hallways).

In intelligence against such networks, we frequently are concerned with such things as maximum throughput of the system, the shortest (or cheapest) route between two or more locations, or bottlenecks in the system. Network analysis is frequently used to identify the points in a complex system that are vulnerable to attack or subject to countermeasures.

Schedule

A new system—whether a banking system, a weapons system, or computer software—develops and evolves through a process commonly known as the program cycle or the system life cycle. Beginning with the system requirement and progressing to production, deployment, and operations, each phase bears unique indicators and opportunities for collection and synthesis/analysis. Customers of intelligence want to know where a major system is in this life cycle.

Each country, industry, or company has its own version of the program cycle. Figure 13-5 illustrates the major components of a generic program cycle. Different types of systems may evolve through different versions of the cycle, and product development differs somewhat from systems development. It is therefore important for the analyst first to determine the specific names and functions of the cycle phases for the target country, industry, or company and then to determine exactly where the target program is in that cycle. With that information, analytic techniques can be used to predict when the program might become operational or begin producing output.

It is important to know where a program is in the cycle to make accurate predictions. In assessing both Libya's and Iraq's WMD capabilities, analysts tended to take procurement actions as indicating that a weapons capability existed—though the two occur at quite different phases in the program cycle. The tendency was partially a result of receiving a large volume of procurement-related intelligence, possibly leading analysts to overestimate its importance.[32]

Figure 13-5   Generic Program Cycle

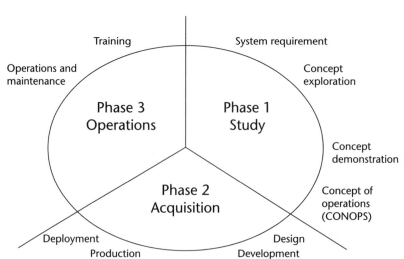

A general rule of thumb is that the more phases in the program cycle, the longer the process will take, all other things being equal. Countries and organizations with large, stable bureaucracies typically have many phases, and the process, whatever it may be, takes that much longer.

Project or Program Loading. The duration of any stage of the cycle shown in Figure 13-5 is determined by the type of work involved and the number and expertise of workers assigned. Fred Brooks, one of the premier figures in computer systems development, defined four types of projects in his well-known book *The Mythical Man-Month.*[33] Each type of project has a unique relationship between the number of workers needed (the project loading) and the time it takes to complete the effort.

The graph at the upper left of Figure 13-6 shows the time-labor profile for a perfectly partitionable task—that is, one that can be completed in half the time by doubling the number of workers. It is referred to as the "cotton-picking curve": Twice as many workers can pick a cotton field in half the time. Few projects fit this mold, but it is a common misperception of management that people and time are interchangeable on any given project, such that a project that could be done in ten months by one person could be completed in one month by ten. Brooks notes that this is the dangerous and deceptive myth that gave his book its title.

A second type of project involves the unpartitionable task, and its profile is shown at the upper right of Figure 13-6. The profile is referred to here as the "baby production curve" because no matter how many women are assigned to the task, it takes nine months to produce a baby.

Figure 13-6   **Brooks Curves for Projects**

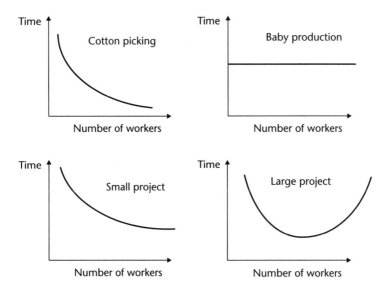

Most small projects fit the curve shown at the lower left of the figure, which is a combination of the first two curves. In this case a project can be partitioned into subtasks, but the time it takes for people working on different subtasks to communicate with one another will eventually balance out the time saved by adding workers, and the curve levels off.

Large projects tend to be dominated by communication. At some point—shown as the bottom point of the lower right-hand curve in Figure 13-6—adding more workers begins to slow the project because all workers have to spend more time in communication. The result is simply another form of the familiar bathtub curve. Failure to recognize this pattern or to understand where a project is on the curve has been the ruin of many large projects. As Brooks observed, adding workers to a late project makes it later.[34]

Risk Analysis. Analysts often assume that the programs and projects they are evaluating will be completed on time and that the target system will work perfectly. They would seldom be so foolish in evaluating their own projects or the performance of their own organizations. Risk analysis needs to be done in any assessment of a target program. It is typically difficult to do and, once done, difficult to get the customer to accept. But it is important to do it because intelligence customers, like many analysts, also tend to assume that an opponent's program will be executed perfectly.

One fairly simple but often overlooked approach to evaluating the probability of success is to examine the success rate of similar ventures. In planning the 1980 Iranian hostage rescue attempt, the Carter administration could have looked at the Vietnam prisoner of war rescue attempts, only 21 percent of which succeeded. The Carter team did not study those cases, however, deeming them irrelevant, even though the Iranian mission was more complex.[35] Similar miscalculations are made every day in the world of information technology. Most software projects fail. The failure rate is higher for large projects, although the failures typically are covered up.

Risk analysis, along with the project-loading review discussed earlier in this chapter, is a common tool for predicting the likely success of programs. Risk analysis is an iterative process in which an analyst identifies and prioritizes risks associated with a program, assesses the effects of the risks, and then identifies alternative actions to reduce the risks. Known risk areas can be readily identified from past experience and from discussions with technical experts who have been through similar projects. The risks fall into four major categories for a program—programmatic, technical, production, and engineering. Analyzing potential problems requires identifying specific potential risks from each category, such as the following:

- *Programmatic:* funding, schedule, contract relationships, political issues
- *Technical:* feasibility, survivability, system performance
- *Production:* manufacturability, lead times, packaging, equipment
- *Engineering:* reliability, maintainability, training, operations

Risk assessment assesses risks quantitatively and ranks them to establish those of most concern. A typical ranking is based on the *risk factor,* which is a mathematical combination of the probability of failure and the consequence of failure. Such an assessment requires a combination of expertise and software tools, in a structured and consistent approach to ensure that all risk categories are considered and ranked.

Risk management is the definition of alternative actions to minimize risk and set criteria on which to initiate or terminate the activities. It includes identifying alternatives, options, and approaches to mitigation. Examples are initiation of parallel developments (for example, funding two manufacturers to build a satellite when only one satellite is needed), extensive development testing, addition of simulations to check performance predictions, design reviews by consultants, or focusing management attention on specific elements of the program. A number of decision analysis tools are useful for risk management. The most widely used tool is the Program Evaluation and Review Technique (PERT) chart, which shows the interrelationships and dependencies among tasks in a program on a time line.

Risk management is of less concern to the intelligence analyst than risk assessment; but one factor in evaluating the likelihood of a program failure is how well the target organization can assess and manage its program risks.

Cost

Estimating the cost of a system is usually a matter of comparative modeling. You start with an estimate of what it would cost your organization or an industry in your country to build something. You multiply that number by a factor that accounts for the difference in the costs to the target organization (and they will always be different). The result is a fairly straightforward cost estimate that is only as good as your understanding of the differences in the ways the two firms build a system. There is much room for error in this understanding, especially when the two firms are located in different countries.

Another way is to start by applying the problem breakdown methodology of chapter 2 to the system, breaking it down into its component parts. The analyst then produces estimates for building each component of the system and for each phase of the system development process shown in Figure 13-5. In more sophisticated versions of this approach, the analyst can run multiple simulations of each component cost, in effect "building" the system on a computer repeated times to get a most likely cost. This simulation process is used by the U.S. intelligence community on most major hardware development programs.

When several system models are being considered, cost-utility analysis may be necessary. Cost-utility analysis is an important part of decision prediction. Many decision-making processes, especially ones that require resource allocation, make use of cost-utility analysis. For an analyst assessing a foreign military's decision whether to produce a new weapons system, it is a useful place to start. But the analyst must be sure to take "rationality" into account. As noted earlier, what is "rational" is different across cultures and from one individual to the next. It is important for the analyst to understand the logic of the decision maker—that is, how the opposing decision maker thinks about topics such as cost and utility. Chinese leaders' decision to implement a manned space program can be subjected to cost-utility analysis, but doing such an analysis illustrates the pitfalls. Hardware and launch costs can be estimated fairly well. Utility is measurable to some extent—by most standards, it is low. The benefits in prestige and advancements in Chinese space technology have to be quantified subjectively, but these factors probably were dominant in the decision-making process.

In performing cost-utility analysis, the analyst must match cost figures to the same time horizon over which utility is being assessed. This will be a difficult task if the horizon is more than a few years away. Life-cycle costs should be considered for new systems, and most new systems have life cycles in the tens of years.

Perhaps the most widely used approach to cost-utility analysis of competing alternatives is simply to create a graph in which cost and utility are the two axes. An example of such a graph is shown in Figure 13-7. The Xs in the graph represent the alternatives being considered. Each alternative has a utility and a cost, and these two factors determine various alternatives' places on the graph. The alternatives that lie high and to the left (low cost, high utility) generally form a curve known as the Pareto frontier. The optimal choices lie along this frontier, although as the curve levels out, utility increases only at higher and higher costs.

Figure 13-7   Cost/Utility Plot

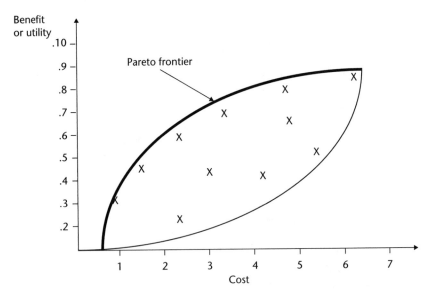

Note: X = Alternative.

The total set of options usually group into a roughly oval shape, as shown in Figure 13-7. This oval is often referred to as the "football" in cost-utility analyses. All of the options lying on the interior of the football are suboptimum choices, compared with those lying on the Pareto frontier.

Summary

To analyze an organization, one must examine its structure, function, and process. The result should be a series of models, usually in scenario form, which describe likely future states of the structure, the functions it will perform, and the processes it will use.

Within the organizational structure, relationship analysis usually is of most interest to the intelligence customer. Structural position confers power. A powerful individual has high centrality, meaning high degree (having many ties to other members), high closeness (being close to many other members), and high betweenness (being the only connection between members). Another important measure of individuals in an organization is their uniqueness—that is, whether or not they have equivalents.

Functional analysis tends to focus on behavior, specifically on the decision-making process. Decision making has three aspects—rational, emotional, and cultural, with the cultural probably being the dominant aspect.

Many process analysis techniques exist, and they vary by organization type and across cultures. Operations research techniques are useful for many types of process analysis. Linear programming is used to establish optimum values for a process. Network analysis is used to define flows and vulnerable points within a physical network, such as a communications or transportation network. Intelligence also is commonly interested in measuring programs' probabilities of success. Comparative analysis and risk analysis are frequently used to measure those probabilities. Cost-utility analysis is often used to support predictions about an opponent's program decisions. Most leaders go through some form of cost-utility analysis in making major decisions; the trick is to apply the proper cultural and individual biases to both cost and utility. What appears to be a high cost in the analyst's culture can appear to be very modest in the target's culture.

Organizational analysis is almost always a significant force to consider in predicting the development or use of a technology. We will return to it in the next chapter.

Notes

1. Liam Fahey, *Competitors* (New York: John Wiley and Sons, 1999), 403.
2. The curve is named after Professor Art Laffer, an adviser to President Ronald Reagan in the 1980s.
3. Antony Jay, *Management and Machiavelli* (London: Bantam, 1967), 67.
4. Fahey, *Competitors*, 237.
5. Ibid., 238.
6. See Defense Advanced Research Projects Agency, "DARPA Evidence Extraction and Link Discovery Pamphlet," November 22, 2002, www.darpa.mil/iso2/EELD/BAA01-27PIP.htm.

7. Jamshid Gharajedaghi, *Systems Thinking: Managing Chaos and Complexity* (Boston: Butterworth-Heinemann, 1999), 34.

8. Russell Ackoff, *The Art of Problem Solving* (New York: John Wiley and Sons, 1978), 62.

9. Oskar Morgenstern and John von Neumann, *Theory of Games and Economic Behavior* (Princeton: Princeton University Press, 1980).

10. M. R. Wehr and J. A. Richards, *Physics of the Atom* (Boston: Addison-Wesley, 1960), 199.

11. Ralph M. Barnes, *Motion and Time Study: Design and Measurement of Work* (New York: Wiley, 1968), 662–663.

12. David W. Miller and Marin K. Starr, *Executive Decisions and Operations Research* (Englewood Cliffs, N.J.: Prentice Hall, 1961), 45–47.

13. Gharajedaghi, *Systems Thinking*, 35.

14. Harold P. Ford, *Estimative Intelligence* (Lanham, Md.: University Press of America, 1993), 17.

15. Ibid., 29.

16. Gharajedaghi, *Systems Thinking*, 174.

17. Fahey, *Competitors*, 444.

18. Ibid., 419.

19. The proverbs are French. Wolfgang Mieder, *Illuminating Wit, Inspiring Wisdom* (Englewood Cliffs, N.J.: Prentice Hall, 1998).

20. The proverbs are Japanese. Guy A. Zona, *Even Withered Trees Give Prosperity to the Mountain* (New York: Touchstone, 1996).

21. The proverbs are Arabic. The last one, "We say, 'It's a bull'; he says, 'Milk it,'" is another way of saying, "Don't confuse me with the facts." Primrose Arnander and Ashkhain Skipwith, *The Son of a Duck Is a Floater* (London: Stacey International, 1985).

22. The proverbs are Chinese. The second one, "Sit atop the mountain and watch the tigers fight," means, "Watch two opponents contend and hope that they will eliminate each other." The fourth one, "Kill the chicken to frighten the monkey," means "Punish the less-important to warn the real culprit." Theodora Lau, *Best Loved Chinese Proverbs* (New York: HarperCollins, 1995).

23. The proverbs are Russian. The quote about Bulgarians is from an unpublished manuscript by John Hollister Hedley, "The School of Hard Knocks: Living with and Learning from Intelligence Failures," March 2004. The other two are from Mieder, *Illuminating Wit*, 32, 135.

24. A. H. Maslow, "A Theory of Human Motivation," in *Psychological Review* 50 (1943): 370–396.

25. Harry Levinson, *Psychological Man* (Cambridge: Levinson Institute, 1976), 90.

26. Ackoff, *The Art of Problem Solving*, 22.

27. Walter D. Barndt Jr., *User-Directed Competitive Intelligence* (Westport, Conn.: Quorum Books, 1984), 78, 93.

28. Comment by Michael Pitcher, vice president of i2Go.com, in *Competitive Intelligence Magazine*, 3 (July–September 2000): 9.

29. Brian McCue, *U-Boats in the Bay of Biscay* (Washington, D.C.: National Defense University Press, 1990).

30. Theodore J. Gordon and M. J. Raffensperger, "The Relevance Tree Method for Planning Basic Research," in *A Practical Guide to Technological Forecasting*, ed. James R. Bright and Milton E. F. Schoeman (Englewood Cliffs, N.J.: Prentice Hall, 1973), 129.

31. The two sides of an equation are connected by an "equals" or "=" sign. The two sides of an inequality are connected by an inequality sign, such as "is less than ($\leq$)" or "is equal to or less than ($\leq$)."

32. *Report of the Commission on the Intelligence Capabilities of the United States Regarding Weapons of Mass Destruction,* March 31, 2005, www.wmd.gov/report/wmd_report.pdf, 261.

33. Frederick P. Brooks Jr., *The Mythical Man-Month* (Reading, Mass.: Addison-Wesley, 1975), 16–19.

34. Ibid., 16–25.

35. Hossein Askari, "It's Time to Make Peace with Iran," *Harvard Business Review,* September–October 1993, 13.

14

Technology and Systems Analysis

A weapon has no loyalty but to the one who wields it.
Ancient Chinese proverb

The impact of technologies such as computers and telecommunications, nanoengineering, and bioengineering reaches across most fields of intelligence. Advanced technologies are particularly relevant to terrorism intelligence and intelligence about weapons of mass destruction (WMD), such as chemical, biological, and nuclear weapons. Technology assessment and systems analysis are important specialized fields of intelligence analysis that depend on creating models. Systems analysis in particular makes more use of target models, especially simulation models, than does any other intelligence subdiscipline. Both routinely use all of the sources discussed in chapter 6.

The technology intelligence discipline is often called *scientific and technical* (S&T) intelligence. But scientific developments generally are openly published. They are seldom of high intelligence interest. When you *do* something with science, however, the result is technology, and it can be of intelligence interest. Science is of intelligence interest only insofar as it has the potential to be implemented as a technology. Analysts often are strongly tempted to investigate an interesting scientific breakthrough that will not become a system or a product for decades.

Technology, in turn, is of interest only insofar as it has the potential to become part of a *system* that is of intelligence interest, for example, a weapons system or, in business intelligence, a competing product. This is a simple paradigm but a valid one that is often forgotten by S&T and weapons systems analysts.

Technology Assessment

Technology assessment makes extensive use of open source information. No other source contains the technical detail that open source material can provide. No matter how highly classified a foreign project may be, the technology involved in the project eventually appears somewhere in the open literature; scientists and technologists want to publish their results, usually for reasons of professional reputation. This rule holds true even with respect to targets that heavily censor their open publications; one merely has to know where to look. For example, a collector can trace even the most sensitive U.S. defense or intelligence system developments simply by following the right articles over an extended period of time in journals such as *Aviation Week and Space Technology*.

The key to using open source material in technical intelligence is identifying and analyzing the relationships among programs, persons, technologies, and organizations, and that depends on extensive use of relationship or network analysis (chapter 13).

Technology helps shape intelligence predictions and is the object of predictions. The three general types of technology predictions have to do with the following:

- The future performance of a technology
- A forecast of the likelihood of innovation or breakthroughs in a technology
- The use, transfer, or dissemination of the technology

Future Performance

Pattern analysis is used extensively in making technology estimates based on open literature. Articles published by a research group identify the people working on a particular technology. Patents are an especially fruitful source of information about technology trends. Tracking patent trends over time can reveal whether enthusiasm for a technology is growing or diminishing, what companies are entering or leaving a field, and whether a technology is dominated by a small number of companies.[1] Patent counting by field is a technique used in creating technology indicators; in technology policy assessments; and in corporate, industry, or national technological activity assessments. Corporate technology profiles, based on patents, are used for strategic targeting, competitor analysis, and investment decisions. They are used to create citation network diagrams (which show the patterns of citations to prior relevant research) for identifying markets and forecasting technology.

Another publications pattern analysis tool, citation analysis, involves counting the number of citations to a particular report. A high number of citations is a proven indicator of the impact, or quality, of the cited report.[2] Citation analysis indicates relationships and interdependencies of reports, organizations, and researchers. It can indicate whether a country's research is internally or externally centered and show relationships between basic and applied research. Productivity in research and development has been shown to be highly concentrated in a few key people.[3] Citations identify those people. Commercial publications now routinely track citation counts and publish citation analysis results.

A technology assessment methodology must correctly characterize the performance of the technology; that is, it must use the correct measures of performance. For example, one useful measure of high-power microwave tube technology is average power as a function of frequency. Second, the methodology must identify the critical supporting technologies (forces) that can make a difference in the target technology's performance. Third, it must allow comparison of like developments; it is misleading, for example, to compare the performance of a one-of-a-kind laboratory device with the performance of a production-line component or system. Finally, the methodology must take time into account—the time frame for development in the country or organization of interest, not another country's or organization's time frame—since the methodology requires a projection into the future.

A five-stage, generic target model has been used for describing the development of a technology or product. It is commonly used to predict future development of a technology. The five stages of technology growth are often represented on the S curve introduced in chapter 5. The technology has a slow start, followed by rapid growth and, ultimately, maturity, wherein additional performance improvements are slight.[4] The vertical axis of the curve can represent many things, including the performance of the technology according to some standard, or its popularity or the extent of its use.

Transitions between stages are difficult to establish because there is a natural overlap and blending between stages. The scheme provides for development milestones that can be measured on the basis of how much or how little has been published on the research involved in the technology.

In the S curve in Figure 14-1, which shows the progress of a technology through the five stages of its lifetime, the vertical axis represents the number of patents or publications about the technology. Another type of S curve measures the performance improvement of the technology at some stage of its development, generally at the fourth (production) stage, though it can be drawn for all stages simultaneously. The horizontal axis for both curves is time. A technology is available for industrial use when it reaches the steepest slope on the S curve, as Figure 14-1 illustrates. In this region, the technology is a "hot" item and is being widely publicized.

When the S curve for technology use flattens, the technology is mature, and only incremental performance improvements are possible. Generally, at this point, the technology has reached some fundamental limit defined by physical laws. Incremental improvements may flow from clever design techniques, increases in scale size, or improvements in materials, but the changes will bring only modest improvements in the technology's performance.

The S curve is the fundamental tool in a widely used formal methodology for technology assessment. This methodology, called TRIZ-based technology intelligence, assists technology managers in identifying competing industrial technologies in order to forecast their development and determine their potential. (TRIZ is a Russian acronym for Theory of Inventive Problem Solving.) The TRIZ methodology incorporates a number of techniques for locating the

Figure 14-1   S Curve for Technology Development

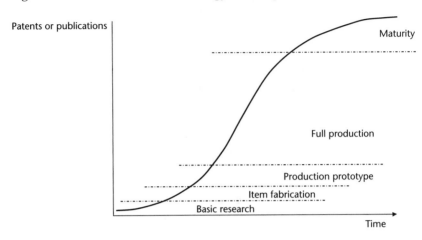

technology's position on the S curve, including the dates and quality of patent applications and measurements of performance improvements.[5] All of the techniques, though, at best can determine the current position of the technology on the S curve and its technological limits only qualitatively.

Innovation

The general nature of advances in any field of technology can be foreseen through the use of such criteria as current activity in the field, the need for a solution to a particular problem, and the absence of fundamental laws prohibiting such advances.[6] If those criteria have been met, one looks for an innovative development using the techniques described in this section.

Innovation is a divergent, not a convergent, phenomenon; no body of evidence builds up to an inevitable innovation in a technical field. Predicting innovation is an art rather than a science. As noted earlier, the U.S. intelligence community long ago gave up trying to predict a divergent act such as a coup, for good reasons.[7] When we attempt to predict innovation, we are trying to predict a breakthrough, which is of the same nature as a coup. A breakthrough is a discontinuity in the S curve of technology development. We cannot predict when an innovation will happen, but as with a coup we can determine when conditions are right for it, and we can recognize when it starts to develop.

Because technology development follows the S curve, we have some prospects for success. Guidelines based on past experiences with innovation can sometimes help predict who will produce an innovation. We say *sometimes* because innovation often comes from a completely unexpected source, as noted later in this chapter. Finally, standard evidence-gathering and synthesis/analysis techniques can help determine what the innovation will be, but only very late in the process.

Predicting the Timing of Innovation. Predicting when the timing is right for innovation in a technology is a matter of drawing the S curve of performance versus time for the technology. When the curve reaches the saturation level and flattens out, the timing is right. The replacement technology normally will start to take over sometime after that point and will eventually reach a higher level of performance. It will not necessarily start at a higher level. Over time in a given field, we obtain a series of S curves on one graph. In each case the replacement technology begins at a lower performance level but quickly surpasses its predecessor technology.

Predicting Sources. Innovation generally comes from an individual or a small organization that is driven by an incentive force and is not held back by restraining forces. Consider DuPont's innovation record between 1920 and 1950. During that time, only five of eighteen major DuPont innovations—neoprene, nylon, teflon, orlon, and polymeric color film—originated within the company. The rest came from small companies or individual inventors and were acquired by DuPont. Many came from a U.K. chemical company under a technology exchange agreement. For comparison, five of DuPont's seven major product and process improvements over the same period originated within DuPont. The DuPont case is one of many examples that suggest that innovation does not typically take place in a large organization, but product and process improvements do.

It is worth asking why DuPont chose to acquire those outside innovations. In the time frame of the study, DuPont maintained one of the best business intelligence operations in the world. Its business intelligence group, which remains largely unpublicized, achieved success by a combination of solid collection (open literature search, human intelligence, and materials acquisition and testing) with good technical analysis to identify promising targets and acquire needed technology effectively and cheaply.

The same generalization held true in the planned economy of the former Soviet Union: Most innovations came from outside the country, and those that came from within were developed by individual scientists or very small groups in Academy of Sciences laboratories. Soviet defense and industrial laboratories did very well on engineering improvements but almost never innovated. And like DuPont's, Soviet commercial espionage was reasonably effective at acquiring technology. The Soviets, however, were considerably less effective in analyzing, evaluating, and adopting technology than was DuPont.

These examples, along with others discussed later in this chapter, have a common theme: a revolutionary project has a much better chance of success if it is placed under a management structure completely separate from that used for evolutionary developments. In evaluating an organization that is pursuing a potential breakthrough technology, the analyst therefore should assess the organizational structure, as discussed in the preceding chapter, and note how the organization has handled new technologies in the past. Does the organization welcome and aggressively pursue new technologies, as DuPont, 3M, Biotech, and most Internet companies do? Or does it more closely resemble the former Soviet industrial ministries, which saw new technologies as a hindrance?

Evaluating the Innovation Climate. The following example sets the stage for a discussion of two forces—freedom and demand-driven incentive—that foster innovation and that need to be considered in any force analysis.

Back in 1891 an American named Almon B. Strowger developed one of the most significant innovations in telecommunications history—the step-by-step electromechanical switch. The Strowger switch made the dial telephone possible. Strowger's innovation is remarkable because he was not an engineer; he was an undertaker. But Strowger had two things going for him that are at the core of all innovation: freedom and incentive. He had freedom because no one required him to be an electrical engineer to develop communications equipment. He did not even have to work for Bell Telephone Company, which at that time had an entrenched monopoly. And he had a special kind of incentive. Strowger was one of two morticians in Kansas City. The other mortician's wife was one of the city's telephone switchboard operators. Strowger was convinced that she was directing all telephone calls for mortician services to his competitor. Strowger had a powerful economic incentive to replace her with an objective telephone call director.

The elements of freedom and incentive, which we see in Strowger's case, appear in most significant innovations throughout history. The incentive does not have to be economic; in fact, we can use the nature of the incentive to define the difference between scientists and engineers or technologists: Science is driven primarily by noneconomic incentives, and engineering or technology is driven primarily by economic incentives. The difference is important: It explains why the Soviet Union produced so many competent scientists and scientific discoveries yet failed so miserably in technological innovation. Soviet scientists, like their U.S. counterparts, had as incentives knowledge, recognition, and prestige. But the engineer, in contrast, tends to depend on economic incentives, and those are notably absent in planned economies such as the Soviet one. The Soviet patent system was almost confiscatory and provided no more financial return to an innovative engineer than the typical U.S. company's patent-rights agreement does. Patents aside, the Soviet engineer who developed something new would likely see his manager take credit for the innovation.

Freedom is a more subtle factor in the innovation equation, but it is just as important as incentive. In the 1920s the Soviet Union and the United States were world leaders in genetics. At that time, Russian geneticist Trofim D. Lysenko proposed the theory that environmentally acquired characteristics of an organism were inheritable. Lysenko rejected the chromosome theory of heredity and denied the existence of genes. Lysenko was dismissed as a charlatan by Russia's leading geneticists, including N. I. Vavilov. But he had one powerful argument in his favor: Josef Stalin liked his theories. They were compatible with Stalin's view of the world. If people could pass on to their descendants the behavior patterns they acquired in Soviet society, then the type of state that Stalin sought to establish could become a permanent one. So, with the backing of the Communist Party, the environmental theory became the only acceptable theory of genetics in the Soviet Union. In August 1940 Vavilov was arrested and subsequently died in prison. At least six of Russia's other top geneticists disappeared. In later years, the Soviets would admit that "Lysenko-ism" set back their effort in genetics by about twelve years.

Intelligence analysts sometimes looked on the Lysenko affair as an aberration. It was in fact a fairly accurate picture of the research environment of the Soviet Union. Although there were no more cases as dramatic as Lysenko's, the contamination of Lysenkoism spread to many other scientific fields in the Soviet Union during the 1930s and 1940s. Restrictions on freedom to innovate contributed substantially to the country's economic decline. Most of the restrictions stemmed from two phenomena—the risk aversion that is common to most large, established organizations and the constraints of central economic planning that are unique to state-run economies such as that of the Soviet Union.

The Soviet Union was organized for central economic planning, and meeting the plan had first priority. That gave Soviet industries a powerful incentive to continue their established lines. Inertial forces, discussed in chapter 12, dominated. If current production declined, a plant manager would strip his research and development organization to maintain production. Furthermore, central planning seems inevitably to imply short supplies. Supplies would become even shorter if a plant manager attempted to innovate, and new types of supplies needed for innovation wouldn't be available at all. The Soviet plant that needed something out of the ordinary—a special type of test instrument, for example—had to build the device itself at a high cost in resources.

Moreover, Soviet management subscribed, at least in principle, to Marx's labor theory of value, in which if one device takes twice as much labor to produce as another, it should command twice the price. Such theories provide a powerful deterrent to both innovation and automation.

In sum, the Soviet industrial structure provided severe penalties for risk taking if a project failed. It provided little reward if the project succeeded, and it provided no special penalty for doing nothing. This set of pressures often led the Soviet or East European plant manager to an interesting response when he was required to start a new project: Because there were no rewards for success, and severe penalties for failure, the manager would choose an expendable worker—usually someone who was due to retire shortly—and place him in charge of the project. When the project failed—and the cards were always stacked against it—the plant manager could blame his carefully prepared scapegoat and fire or retire him.

A poor innovation climate has on occasion adversely affected U.S. firms. General Electric (GE), in its race with Bell Laboratories to invent the transistor, paid dearly for the inertial constraint of dependence on familiar technology. As Lester Thurow described in his article "Brainpower and the Future of Capitalism," Bell Laboratories developed the transistor exactly one day ahead of GE.

The reason that Bell was able to trump GE, in spite of GE's large technological edge in the field, was that GE gave the job of testing the transistor to its vacuum tube engineers, who spent three years trying to prove that the transistor would not work. Bell Laboratories, on the other hand, spent its time trying to prove that the transistor would work. As Thurow so clearly puts it, "There were five companies in America that made vacuum tubes and not a single one of them ever successfully made transistors or semiconductor chips. They could not adjust to the new realities." If GE had spun off a new company based solely on the viability of the transistor, GE might now have all the patents and Nobel prizes and revenues from the transistor that Bell enjoyed. More important, GE would also have been in a better position to benefit from the revolution in miniaturization that came with the introduction of the transistor. Instead, GE ended up having to buy transistors and semiconductors from suppliers.[8]

The lesson of these examples for the analyst is this: In evaluating the ability of an organization or a country to develop a new technology, look at the culture. Is it a risk-accepting or a risk-averse culture? Does it place a high priority on protecting its current product line? What political, economic, organizational, or social constraints does the organization place on development of technology?

Technology Use, Transfer, and Diffusion

Use. In tracking a technology that may have military use, analysts use a generic target model called the *bathtub curve*—a time-versus-visibility curve shaped like a bathtub. The basic research on a technology is usually visible, because scientists and engineers need to communicate their findings. As this research is applied to a military system or moves toward production, the work becomes more secret and disappears from publication (the bottom of the "bathtub"). Finally, as a weapons system emerges from the research and development stage and enters testing, the program becomes visible again.

Keeping track of a technology on the bathtub curve requires skillful use of a combination of open literature and classified sources. The technique has enabled analysts to determine the capabilities of a technology and the time phases of technical developments and innovations even when the program was at the bottom of the "bathtub."

Patents are a valuable source for determining what use is being made of a technology. There are several guidelines for working with patents:

- Obtain the names of all coauthors and any institutional affiliations in a patent. In sifting through the great volume of patents, the first search an experienced open literature analyst usually makes is of names or institutions; this preliminary screening allows relevant work to be identified. The second screening is on the specific technology discussed in the patent.
- Abstracts are useful for screening and identifying patents of interest, but the full text is essential for technology evaluation. The full text also

may contain indicators that a patent is of interest to the military or to a particular company.

- Some patent literature describes patented devices that have been introduced in industry. These provide a filtered set of the most interesting patents—those that are sufficiently applications oriented to be used by an industry.

When an analyst is assessing the usage of a technology, it is easy to become entranced with its performance and promise. Technology does not exist in a vacuum; it is a resource like any other, and it can be well applied or poorly applied. What matters is not just the technology itself but what an organization does with it. Throughout the 1970s and 1980s Xerox Corporation funded a think tank called the Palo Alto Research Center (PARC). PARC's staff was perhaps the greatest gathering of computer science talent ever assembled. PARC developed the concept of the desktop computer long before IBM launched its PC. It created a prototype graphical user interface of icons and layered screens that evolved into Microsoft Windows. It developed much of the technology underlying the Internet. But despite PARC's many industry-altering breakthroughs, Xerox repeatedly failed to exploit the financial potential of the achievements (although the return on investment to Xerox from laser printers alone more than paid for PARC). PARC's culture was well suited to developing new technologies but not so well suited to exploiting them for financial gain.

The various constraints on innovation also may constrain use of a new technology. A technology may carry with it risks of liability or action by government regulatory agencies. Pollution control regulations increasingly shape technology decisions. Possible tort liability or patent infringement suits are risks that might cause a technology to be rejected.

The assessment of regulatory forces (discussed in chapter 12) has become a key decision point for innovations in recent years. Analysts need to ask: Can the product be produced within environmental restrictions on air and water pollution? Does it meet government safety standards? Does it face import barriers in other countries? Can the innovation be protected, either by patents or trade secrets, long enough to obtain a payoff of production costs?

Within the framework of questions such as these, large and small companies have strikingly different approaches to the acquisition of new technology. Within large companies, the rejection rate of new technology is high. Less than one idea in a hundred is taken up, and when commercialized, two of three new products fail. Institutional resistance to change is endemic, and new technologies face enormous hurdles—even though a large company's access to new technologies is typically much greater than that of small companies.

In large companies, a "champion" of a major new technology typically must emerge before the company will accept the new technology. Such champions, also described as "change agents," are innovators who are willing to risk their personal and professional future for a development of doubtful success.

The unpopularity of such champions in large companies is understandable because of two circumstances: the vulnerability of established product lines to the new technology and the high costs of converting the established production line. These factors are particularly important in a large and complex industry such as the automotive industry, where new technology is welcome only if it is incremental and evolutionary.

As a consequence, revolutionary technologies often are brought to the market by outsiders after being rejected by leaders in the relevant industry. Witness Kodak's rejection of Dr. Edwin H. Land's instant photography process and its subsequent development by Polaroid; or the refusal of several large corporations to accept the challenge of commercializing the photocopying process that led to the creation of Xerox.

Transfer or Diffusion. It is often important to assess the effectiveness of technology transfer or diffusion—an especially critical topic in the fields of WMD and weapons proliferation. In assessing the effectiveness of technology diffusion, an analyst has to consider several factors:

- Is the technology available, and if so, in what form? In transferring software, for example, a receiving organization can do far more with the source code than with the compiled code.

- Does the receiving organization reach out for new technologies or resist their introduction? Resistance to change is a severe constraint on technology diffusion. Everyone knows that, but intelligence analysts often ignore it, blithely assuming that instant diffusion exists and forgetting about inertial forces and the "not invented here" factor (see chapter 12).

- What mechanisms are used to transfer? Some transfer mechanisms are very effective, others less so. Table 14-1 summarizes the effectiveness of various transfer mechanisms.

Technology transfer and diffusion occur rapidly in countries that are open, relatively free from government interference, and technologically advanced. Technology diffusion works extremely well in the United States, with its high mobility of workers and information. The lower mobility of Japan's workers slows its diffusion mechanism somewhat, but Japan does well at acquiring and assimilating foreign technology because of other, unique aspects of its culture. Multinational corporations provide a powerful international technological diffusion mechanism because they use the most effective of the mechanisms enumerated in Table 14-1 to transfer technology among their subsidiaries.

In contrast, technology diffusion was extremely poor in the former Soviet Union because of a tight compartmentation system and Soviet leaders' insistence on secrecy—both of which were especially severe in defense industries but carried over into the civil industries as well. The situation was aggravated

Table 14-1 Effectiveness of Technology Transfer Mechanisms

Effectiveness	Transfer mechanism
High	Sale of firms or subsidiaries
	License with extensive teaching effort
	Joint ventures
	Technical exchanges with ongoing contact
	Training programs in high-technology areas
	Movement of skilled personnel between companies
Medium	Industrial espionage
	Engineering documents plus technical data
	Consulting
	Licenses plus know-how
	Documented proposals
	Sale of processing equipment without know-how
	Commercial visits
Low	Licenses without know-how
	Reverse engineering of the product
	Undocumented proposals
	Open trade literature, technical journals
	Trade exhibits and conferences

by the low mobility of Soviet workers; so technology did not spread through employees' relocations either. As a result, a technology that found application in naval weapons systems, for example, would be unknown in the rest of the military and in civil industries.

Transfer of technology depends also on the motivations of both the transferee and transferrer. Organizations that have the best technologies may not have the motivation to transfer. Industry's approach to technology transfer is evaluative and selective. Industrial transferrers of technology expect a return benefit that outweighs the cost of transfer, and they tend to evaluate the feedback of information on benefits, costs, and risks with reasonable objectivity. Among industrial transferrers, large firms tend to be more cautious in applying new technologies than do small firms.

When a technology has been developed within a company, the company has incentives to transfer the technology to others. The technology so developed is a time-perishable company asset. If its transfer would result in a return benefit to the company that would more than offset the loss occasioned by the transfer, then the transfer will likely occur.

In making a decision whether or not to transfer, a company must consider many factors that can weigh for or against. The existence of a competing technology; the speed of assimilation and obsolescence of the technology; the vulnerability of established company products; the capability of the company to exploit the technology in-house; the competitiveness of the industry; the capability to protect the technology as a trade secret or under patent laws—all can weigh either way in the decision.

Some factors clearly weigh against a decision to transfer. Most important is the irreversibility of the release of technology. If the company's analysis of the situation proves wrong, the technology cannot be "recalled." Second is the advantage of lead time, an advantage that varies greatly according to the nature of the industry.

Other factors weigh for a decision to transfer. In some technologies, a potential return flow of benefits exists because others can build on the disclosed technology; the existence of cross-licensing or technical exchange agreements increases the value of these benefits. In other technologies, transfer is favored for the opposite reason: It makes the transferee dependent on the transferrer's R&D and inhibits the transferee from developing an independent R&D capability. The threat of loss of the technology through industrial espionage or personnel raids is another major factor. Also, it is usually easier to license the technology (for both sides) than it is to contest infringement. Easy transfer is also encouraged by the desire of companies for recognition as leaders in their fields. Furthermore, early release of a technology may result in an industry's adopting the releasing company's standards, with consequent competitive advantage to the releasing company.

Systems Analysis

Any entity having the attributes of structure, function, and process can be described and analyzed as a system, as noted in previous chapters. Air defense systems, transportation networks, welfare systems—all of these and many others have been the objects of systems analysis. Many of the formal applications of systems analysis were pioneered in the U.S. Department of Defense during the 1960s.

Much systems analysis is parametric, sensitivity, or "what if" analysis; that is, the analyst must try a relationship between two variables (parameters), run a computer analysis and examine the results, change the input constants, and run the analysis again. Systems analysis must be interactive; the analyst has to see what the results look like and make changes as new ideas surface.

Analysis of any complex system is, of necessity, multidisciplinary. Systems analysts have had difficulty dealing with the multidisciplinary aspects; they are more comfortable sticking to the technical aspects, primarily performance analysis. In its National Intelligence Estimate on Iraqi weapons of mass destruction, the WMD Commission observed, "The October 2002 NIE contained an extensive technical analysis . . . but little serious analysis of the socio-political

situation in Iraq, or the motives and intentions of the Iraqi leadership. . . .
[T]hose turn out to be the questions that could have led the Intelligence Community closer to the truth."[9] In fact, too much technical analysis is done in a vacuum, with no consideration of political and economic constraints. The following sections address examples of the need to consider those constraints.

Future Systems

The first step in analyzing future systems, and particularly future weapons systems, is to identify the system(s) under development. Two approaches traditionally have been applied in weapons systems analysis, both based on systems of reasoning drawn from the writings of philosophers: deductive and inductive.

- The deductive approach to prediction is to postulate objectives that are desirable in the eyes of the opponent; identify the system requirements; and then search the incoming intelligence for evidence of work on the weapons systems, subsystems, components, devices, and basic R&D required to reach those objectives.

- The opposite method, an inductive or synthesis approach, is to begin by looking at the evidence of development work and then synthesize the likely advances in systems, subsystems, and devices that are likely to follow.[10]

A number of writers in the intelligence field have argued that intelligence uses a different system of reasoning: *abduction,* which seeks to develop the best hypothesis or inference from a given body of evidence. Abduction is much like induction, but its stress is on integrating the analyst's own thoughts and intuitions into the reasoning process. Abduction has been described as "an instinct for guessing right."[11] Like induction, it is problematic in that, as Roger George and James Bruce note, "different analysts might arrive at different conclusions from the same set of facts." So both induction and abduction are inherently probabilistic.[12]

The deductive (or abductive) approach can be described as starting from a hypothesis and using evidence to test the hypothesis. The inductive approach is described as evidence-based reasoning to develop a conclusion.[13] Evidence-based reasoning is applied in a number of professions. In medicine, it is known as evidence-based practice—applying a combination of theory and empirical evidence to make medical decisions.

Both (or all three) approaches have advantages and drawbacks. In practice, though, deduction has some advantages over induction or abduction in identifying future systems development. If only one weapons system is being built, it is not too difficult to identify the corresponding R&D pattern and the indicators in the available information, and from that to synthesize the resulting systems development. The problem arises when two or more systems are under development at the same time. Each system will have its R&D process, and it is very difficult to separate the processes out of the mass of incoming raw intelligence. This is the "multiple pathologies" problem that is well known in the medical profession: When two or more pathologies are present in a patient, the symptoms are mixed together, and diagnosing the separate illnesses becomes very difficult. Generally, the deductive technique works better for handling simultaneous developments in future systems assessments.

Experience with predictive techniques in weapons systems development has shown that extrapolation works for minor improvements in a weapons system over periods of five years or fewer. It works poorly after that. Projection works in the five- to fifteen-year time frame.[14] But whatever predictive technique is used, you should consider the force of inertia (discussed in chapter 12). Institutional momentum has resulted in more weapons systems development than new requirements have.[15]

Once a system has been identified as in development, analysis proceeds to the second step: answering customers' questions about the system. At the highest level of national policy, details on how a future weapon system may operate are not as important as are its general characteristics and capabilities and a fairly precise time scale.[16] As the system comes closer to completion, a wider group of customers will want to know what specific targets the system is designed against, in what circumstances it will be used, and what its effectiveness will be. These matters typically require analysis of the following:

- The cost of the system
- The schedule for development of the system and associated risks
- The system's performance, including its suitability in operating in its environment or in accomplishing the mission it was designed for

Cost and schedule were discussed in chapter 13. The following section focuses on performance.

Performance Analyses

Systems performance analyses are done on two different types of systems—simple and complex. Determining the performance of a narrowly defined system, such as a surface-to-air missile system, is straightforward. More challenging is assessing the performance of a complex system, such as an air defense system or a narcotics distribution system. Because of the complexity of the systems performance problem, most such analysis is now done by using simulation, a topic to which we will return.

Much systems analysis for both policymakers and the military is focused on weapons systems performance. Weapons systems analysts operate in a different environment from political, military, and economic analysts—their conclusions are less often challenged and more frequently accepted without question. Policymakers and military leaders seldom have the technical expertise to engage weapons systems analysts at the detailed level.

Traps in Performance Analysis. A major problem of weapons systems analysis is that analysts tend to get lost in the details and lose sight of the main objective. It is a matter of professional pride to get to the last pound of thrust of a rocket or to go to fractions of a decibel on radar performance analysis. The customers usually don't care. Sometimes, though, the difference can be critical. In the case of the Backfire bomber, it was.

Throughout the 1960s U.S. Air Force intelligence had consistently predicted that the Soviets would develop a new heavy bomber capable of striking U.S. targets. In 1969 photos of a plant at Kazan revealed the existence of a new bomber, subsequently codenamed Backfire. Two alternative missions for Backfire became the center of controversy: Air Force analysts took the position that Backfire could be used for intercontinental attack. CIA analysts argued that the aircraft's mission was peripheral attack—that is, attack of ground or naval targets near the Soviet mainland.

Over the next several years, National Intelligence Estimates shifted back and forth on the issue. The critical evaluation criterion was the aircraft's range. A range of 5,500 miles or more would allow Backfire to strike U.S. targets from Soviet bases on one-way missions. A range of less than 5,000 miles would not allow such strikes, unless the Backfire received in-flight refueling. The answer was important for the U.S. Department of Defense, and particularly the air force, because a Backfire threat to the United States would justify defense budgets to counter the threat. CIA analysts, who had no stake in defense funding, strongly opposed what they saw as an attempt to shape intelligence estimates to serve parochial air force interests.

The air force and the Defense Intelligence Agency (DIA) produced estimates from McDonnell Douglas engineers that the Backfire had a range of between 4,500 and 6,000 miles. The CIA produced estimates from a different set of McDonnell Douglas engineers that showed a range of between 3,500 and 5,000 miles. Each side accused the other of slanting the evidence.

The range of the Backfire bomber became even more important because the issue became enmeshed in Strategic Arms Limitation Talks (SALT). A Soviet intercontinental bomber would have to be counted in the Soviet array of strategic weaponry. The Russians eventually agreed, as part of the SALT II process, to produce no more than thirty Backfires a year and not to equip them for in-flight refueling; the United States agreed not to count the Backfires as intercontinental bombers. In later years, evidence made clear that Backfire was in fact a somewhat overdesigned peripheral attack bomber, never intended for intercontinental attack missions.

The Backfire bomber case illustrates some of the analytical traps that were discussed in the introduction: premature closure, in that analysts were trapped by previous predictions that the Soviets would develop a new intercontinental bomber, and parochial interests that led analysts to make judgments in conformity with their organization's interests. It also illustrates the difficulty of applying multidisciplinary analysis in systems analysis. A serious consideration of Soviet systems designs and requirements, and of what the Soviets foresaw as threats at the time, would likely have led analysts to zero in more quickly on the Backfire's mission of peripheral attack.

The case also illustrates the common systems analysis problem of presenting the worst-case estimate: National security plans often are made on the basis of a systems estimate; so it is better to base the estimate on the worst case that is reasonably possible. Analysts tend to present the worst case in fear that the policymaker will otherwise become complacent. Hunger for recognition also tends to drive analysts to the more disturbing conclusion. For example, the WMD Commission noted that "the Intelligence Community made too much of an inferential leap, based on very little hard evidence, in judging that Iraq's unmanned aerial vehicles were being designed for use as biological warfare delivery vehicles and that they might be used against the United States"[17]—a case of moving to the most disturbing conclusion.

The Backfire bomber example illustrates the importance of having alternative target models. It also illustrates the two main techniques of performance analysis: comparative performance analysis and simulation.

Comparative Performance Analysis. Comparative performance analysis is similar to benchmarking, discussed previously, but it has a different focus. It includes analysis of one group's system or product performance versus an opponent's. The method has a number of pitfalls; for example, the opponent's system or product (such as an airplane, missile, tank, or supercomputer) may be designed to do different things or to serve a different market from the one with which it is being compared. U.S. Air Force analysts in the Backfire bomber case tended to compare the Backfire to the slightly larger U.S. B-1A, which was an intercontinental bomber under development at the time. The risk in comparative performance analysis is therefore one of mirror-imaging, much the same as can occur in decision making. U.S. analysts of Soviet military developments made a number of bad calls during the cold war years as a result of mirror-imaging. It is useful to review some of the major differences we observed in the Soviet case.

Technological asymmetry. Technology is not used in the same way everywhere. An analyst in a technologically advanced country, such as the United States, tends to take for granted that certain equipment—test equipment, for example—will be readily available and will be of a certain quality. This is a bad assumption with respect to the typical state-run economy.

It took some time to recognize how low the productivity of Soviet engineers could be, and the reasons had nothing to do with their competence. Soviet engineers often had to build their own oscilloscopes and voltmeters—items available in the United States at a nearby Radio Shack. Sometimes plant engineers would be idle for weeks while they waited for a resistor so that they could finish the oscilloscope they needed to test the microwave tube for the radar they were supposed to build.

As a result, Soviet weapons systems might be designed quite differently from those in the United States to take advantage of the country's technology strengths and compensate for weaknesses. For example, the United States and the Soviet Union took strikingly different paths in ballistic missile development. U.S. missiles had simple rocket engines operating at fixed thrust, with very sophisticated guidance systems using onboard computers. The Soviets could build good rocket engines but had difficulty building guidance systems for their missiles. So they used more sophisticated, variable-thrust engines, with simple guidance systems having almost no onboard computation capability. The Soviet approach had the advantages of simplicity and quick achievement of satisfactory reliability.[18]

Unexpected simplicity. In effect, the Soviets applied a version of Occam's razor (choose the simplest explanation that fits the facts at hand) in their industrial practice. Because they were cautious in adopting new technology, they tended to keep everything as simple as possible. They liked straightforward, proven designs. When they copied a design, they simplified it in obvious ways and got rid of the frills that the United States tends to put on its weapons systems. The Soviets made maintenance as simple as possible because the hardware was going to be maintained by people who did not have extensive training.

In a comparison of Soviet and U.S. small jet engine technology, the U.S. model engine was found to have 2.5 times the materials cost per pound of weight. It was smaller and lighter than the Soviet engine, of course, but it required twelve times as many maintenance hours per flight hour as the Soviet model, and overall the Soviet engine's life cycle cost was half that of the U.S. engine.[19] The ability to keep things simple was the Soviets' primary advantage over the United States in technology, especially military technology. This was a major pitfall in the attempt to compare the Backfire bomber with U.S. bombers; a U.S. bomber of Backfire's size and configuration could easily have had intercontinental range.

A narrowly defined mission. The Soviets built their systems to perform specific, relatively narrow (by U.S. standards) functions. The MIG-25 is an example of an aircraft built this way—overweight and inefficient by U.S. standards but simple and effective for its intended mission. The Backfire also was designed for a very specific mission—countering U.S. naval forces in the North Atlantic. The United States tends to optimize its weapons systems for a broad range of missions.

The advantage of being number two. A country or organization that is not a leader in technology development has the advantage of learning from the leader's mistakes, an advantage that helps it keep research and development costs low and avoid wrong paths. A basic rule of engineering is that you are halfway to a problem solution when you know that there is a solution, and you are three-quarters there when you know how a competitor solved the problem. It took much less time for the Soviets to develop atomic and hydrogen bombs than U.S.

intelligence had predicted. The Soviets had no principles of impotence or doubts to slow them down. They knew that the bombs would work.

Quantity may replace quality. U.S. analysts often underestimated the number of units that the Soviets would produce. The United States needed fewer units of a given system to perform a mission, since each unit had more flexibility, quality, and performance ability than its Soviet counterpart. The United States forgot a lesson that it had learned in World War II: U.S. Sherman tanks were inferior to the German Tiger tanks in combat, but the United States deployed a lot of Shermans and overwhelmed the Tigers with numbers.

Patterns of Comparative Modeling. Comparative modeling—comparing your country's or organization's developments with those of an opponent—can involve four distinct fact patterns. Each pattern poses challenges of vested interest or bias. The first possible pattern is that Country A has developed a certain capability (for example, a weapon, a technology, or a factory process), and so has opponent Country B. In this case the analyst from Country A has the job of comparing Country B's capability with that of Country A. The other three possible patterns are that Country A has developed a particular capability, but Country B has not; that Country A has not developed a particular capability, but Country B has; or that neither country has developed the capability. In short, the possibilities can be described as follows:

- We did it—they did it.
- We did it—they didn't do it.
- We didn't do it—they did it.
- We didn't do it—they didn't do it.

There are many examples of the "We did it—they did it" sort of intelligence problem, especially in industries where competitors typically develop similar products. The United States developed intercontinental ballistic missiles (ICBMs); the Russians developed ICBMs. Both sides developed antiballistic missile systems and missile-firing submarines. Many countries build aircraft, cruise missiles, tanks, electric power distribution systems, computers, and so on. In these cases the intelligence officer's analysis problem is not so difficult because she can turn to her own country's or organization's experts on that particular system or product for help.

For example, in World War II both the British and the Germans developed and used radar. So when, in 1942, a British reconnaissance aircraft photographed a bowl-shaped antenna near the French coast, British intelligence could determine, with help from their experts, that it was a radar. Because the radar, which was later nicknamed the Würzburg, posed a threat to British aircraft attacks on Germany, the British undertook some rather direct materiel collection means to gather additional information about it. The result was the Bruneval raid, described in chapter 6.

Analysis of the Würzburg also provides a good example of some pitfalls that can exist when a country uses its own experts. The Würzburgs were normally deployed in pairs, one radar in a pair having one to three searchlights collocated with it. British radar experts believed that the second radar was a spare, to be used when the first radar was inoperative, since that was the normal British practice. British intelligence officer R. V. Jones, however, argued that the Würzburg with searchlights was intended to track bombers, whereas the second radar had the job of tracking the fighters that would be guided to the bomber. British experts disagreed, since this would require an accuracy in coordinate transformation that was beyond their technical skill at the time. They failed to appreciate the accuracy with which German radars operated as a matter of course. As it turned out, Jones, armed with a better understanding of the German way of building defense systems, was correct.

In the second case, "We did it—they didn't do it," the intelligence officer runs into a real problem: It is almost impossible to prove a negative in intelligence. The fact that no intelligence information exists about an opponent's development cannot be used to show that no such development exists.

After the British created the magnetron (a microwave transmitter tube widely used in radar) and discovered what wonders it could do for a radar system, their constant worry was that the Germans would make a similar discovery and that the British would then have to face radars with capability equal to their own. In fact, the Germans learned about the magnetron only when they captured one from a downed British aircraft late in the war, but the threat kept British intelligence on edge.

The third pattern, "We didn't do it—they did it," is the most dangerous type that we encounter. Here the intelligence officer has to overcome opposition from skeptics in his country. Jones faced a case like this when he pieced together the operating principles of a new German aircraft navigation system called Knickebein.

Knickebein was a radio beam system that the Germans used to guide their bombers to their bomb drop point (usually London) at night. At one point, when Jones was attempting to convince top government officials to send radio-equipped aircraft aloft to search for the Knickebein signal, he was opposed by Britain's leading authority on radio wave propagation—Thomas Eckersley, of the Marconi Company. Eckersley argued that radio waves would not propagate sufficiently far at 30 megahertz to be observed over London. Fortunately for Jones, the ELINT search aircraft collected the signal before its flights could be halted.

The central premise of the movie *The Hunt for Red October* is another example of this type. In the movie, the Soviets had developed a low-noise caterpillar drive for their submarine the *Red October,* making it almost undetectable when under way. The United States had no equivalent development; so understanding the submarine's quiet performance was difficult.

"We didn't do it—they didn't do it": This seems to be a ridiculous case. After all, if we haven't developed a weapon and they haven't developed a weapon, who cares? The answer is that people do care, and intelligence analysts spend a great deal of their time on just this sort of problem.

Back in World War II, British intelligence received reports about classified testing going on at a secret installation inside Germany. According to the reports, automobiles driving near this installation would suddenly stall and could not be started again. After a while a German sentry would step out of the nearby woods, tell the automobile drivers they could proceed, and the automobiles would start again and run normally.

As one might imagine, the thought of a weapon that could stall internal combustion engines caused British intelligence some concern, since British tanks, trucks, and airplanes relied on such engines. Although the threat was a continuing concern to British intelligence, they found out after the war that the order of events had become transposed in the reports. What actually happened was that the Germans were testing very sensitive radio equipment that was vulnerable to automobile ignition noise. When testing was under way, German sentries throughout the area around the plant would force all automobiles to stop and shut down their ignitions until testing was over.

This sort of transposition of cause and effect is not uncommon in human source reporting. Part of the skill required of an intelligence analyst is to avoid the trap of taking sources too literally. Occasionally, intelligence analysts must spend more time than they should on problems that are even more fantastic or improbable than that of the German engine killer. In chapter 7 we discussed the particle beam weapon scare of the 1970s. The particle beam weapon appears to have been a classic case of "We didn't do it—they didn't do it." The United States didn't build one and neither did the Soviets; in fact, no one could.

Systems Simulation

A conceptual model that is to be used in a simulation (usually referred to as a "simulation model" to distinguish it from other model types) was introduced in chapter 5. Systems models are often created and run as simulations. Simulation models have several applications in intelligence.

Simulations Used in Intelligence Analysis

Intelligence analysts use simulation models extensively to assess the performance of foreign weapons systems, military forces, and economies. These simulations comprise computer programs that solve individual equations or systems of equations and graphically portray the results. They should be interactive; the analyst has to see what the result looks like and change it as new intelligence information is received.

Weapons Systems Simulations. These are well-defined problems ranging in complexity from simulating the performance of a single entity, such as an aircraft, to simulating that of an elaborate, interconnected system, such as an air defense system. Even simulating the performance of a single weapon can be a complex undertaking. For example, the design of a nuclear weapon requires complex modeling and simulation of the weapon detonation process. High-speed computers and sophisticated simulation codes are necessary. The models used to support one's own nuclear weapons development can be used to assess the performance of another country's nuclear weaponry.

Many simulation models of weapons systems already exist. The U.S. Department of Defense and its contractors possess a large suite of performance models of missiles, ships, submarines, and air and missile defense systems that they use to evaluate their own systems. These models can be modified to simulate the performance of foreign systems. The Backfire bomber case involved two competing simulation models, both derived from existing models of U.S. aircraft. Commercial simulation models also are available to simulate the performance of radars and communications systems and the orbits of satellites. Both the U.S. and foreign intelligence services, for example, use commercial software to create satellite orbit simulations to identify the occurrences of hostile satellite surveillance in order to conduct denial and deception.

Military Simulations. These are closely related to weapons systems simulations and often incorporate them. They are used by defense organizations in planning systems acquisition and determining force mixes and for training. Some examples are logistics models; vulnerability and weapons effects models; system reliability models; and force-on-force and campaign models that simulate combat between opposing forces. As with weapons systems simulations, the Defense Department and its contractors possess and regularly use military simulations, which can be adapted for use in assessing foreign military systems as well. When models are set up to simulate combat, the intelligence and military operations communities have to work together: The military operations analysts understand your side, the intelligence analysts understand your opponent, and inputs from both sides are necessary to make the simulation run effectively.

Economic Simulations. Econometric models were introduced in chapter 5. They can be used to simulate the performance of an entire economy or any segment of it, such as a particular industry. Intelligence analysts often run econometric models to support trade negotiations. For example, an analyst can create a simulation of another country's economy to show that his own government's trade proposals will benefit the other country's economy. A particularly effective technique is to obtain and run the other country's econometric model, since it should be more credible with the opposing negotiation team.

Political and Social Simulations. Simulations of political and social systems have been developed to analyze such diverse topics as the interactions of political parties, the clash of cultures, and population migration patterns. One interactive simulation, *SimCity*, has even been produced as an educational computer game. The CIA has used a simulation model of political processes, *Policon*, to assess topics such as these:

- What policy is Egypt likely to adopt toward Israel?
- What will the Philippines likely do about U.S. bases?
- What stand will Pakistan take on the Soviet occupation of Afghanistan?
- To what extent is Mozambique likely to accommodate with the West?
- What policy will Beijing adopt toward Taiwan's role in the Asian Development Bank?
- How much support is South Yemen likely to give to the insurgency in North Yemen?
- What is the South Korean government likely to do about large-scale demonstrations?
- What will Japan's foreign trade policy look like?
- What stand will the Mexican government take on official corruption?[20]

However, political and social simulations have not gained the wide acceptance within the intelligence community that military and weapons systems simulations enjoy. In part, that is a result of attitudes of the customers of political analysis, which we will take up in chapter 15.

Creating and Running a Simulation

The process of developing and running a simulation is similar to the analysis process described in chapters 2 and 3.

Formulate the Problem. Start with problem definition (discussed in chapter 2). Then identify the parts of the overall problem that can be answered by simulation. As part of this effort, it is almost always necessary to define the desired outputs of the simulation. The outputs are measurements of such things as benefit, impact, effectiveness, or affordability of the system. These analytic measures are often called *measures of effectiveness.* They are also known as *figures of merit* and are used to quantify how well a system meets its objectives. In commercial ventures, return on investment is such a measure. In aircraft performance, top speed is a measure of effectiveness. In an air defense system, probability of kill (P_k) is a measure. Measures of effectiveness are used extensively in systems performance analysis.

Identify the Needed Input Information. Simulation models usually don't work if input data are missing. You have to begin by identifying information that is already available; then identify information that it may be possible to collect; and finally identify information that probably will not be available under any circumstances. The answers will help define the model used for the simulation.

Select the Simulation Software. Depending on the topic, a simulation model may already be available either commercially or within the government.

It usually will require some modification to simulate the target system adequately. If no usable model exists, one has to be built. Fortunately, there are a number of commercial modeling packages that can be used to build even very sophisticated models. Many of these require an experienced modeler, but increasingly analysts find packages that they can use without extensive simulation training.

Develop a Valid and Credible Model. Once developed, a simulation model has to be validated. That is, you must confirm that the model accurately simulates what it is supposed to simulate. It is far preferable to use a proven, validated model, such as one that has had its simulations checked repeatedly against real-world results. If this is not possible, a number of standard methods exist for validating a model. But sophisticated models can be very complex, and independent checks are difficult to run on them. Examining the results to see if they "feel" right may be the best possible check.

As an example of the validation problem, it is well known that combat models tend to overrate an opponent's defense. One of the better-known examples of the problem is modeling that was done of the offense and defense prior to the B-52 strikes on Hanoi during the Vietnam War. The prestrike model predictions were that enemy fire would inflict significant losses on U.S. forces. In the initial raids, however, no losses were suffered. A similar disparity existed in models of allied force losses in the Desert Storm operation in Iraq.

These are examples of the observation that models tend to be overbalanced in favor of the defense in the initial stage of any conflict. The reason is that most such models assume a steady state; that is, they assume that both offense and defense have some awareness of what is going to happen. But in the initial stages of an engagement, the offense has a big advantage: It can dictate the rules of engagement, knows what it has to do, and has the advantage of surprise. The defense must prepare for the estimated threat and react. Furthermore, the defense must make every link in the chain strong; the offense needs only to find the weak link in a system and then attack it. Al Qaeda operatives demonstrated the very large advantage that a determined offense has in their September 11, 2001, attacks on the World Trade Center and the Pentagon. Islamic militants again demonstrated the attacker's advantage in Great Britain on July 7, 2005, when they killed with no warning fifty-two London bus and Underground passengers in coordinated suicide bombing attacks. It is very difficult for a model to take this initial offensive advantage, and defensive disadvantage, into account.

Run the Simulation and Interpret the Results. Once a model has been developed and validated, the analyst runs the simulation and examines the results. Analyzing the results of any modeling effort requires that one do a "sanity check" on the model results. In intelligence simulations, where considerable uncertainty often exists about the input data, it usually will be necessary to make many runs with different possible inputs to do sensitivity analysis and to compare alternative conclusions. Another type of validation becomes important here. A valid model can give invalid results if the inputs are improper. Econometric models, for example, can produce almost any desired simulation results, depending on the different inputs chosen. A smart customer of intelligence knows this and will want to know not only what model was used but what the inputs were.

Summary

Technology analysis is used in business intelligence, where it can provide companies with a competitive advantage, and in military intelligence, where it is of value in assessing the performance of current and future weapons systems. It can be used to assess the future performance of a technology, the use or transfer of the technology, or in forecasts of technology breakthroughs. The most difficult task is to assess how a technology will be used. It is the use to which a technology will be put, not the technology itself, that matters.

The natural starting point for technology performance analysis is to project how the technology will evolve assuming no major breakthroughs. It is necessary to identify the supporting or ancillary technologies that drive such evolution. All technologies evolve through an S curve of performance improvement, eventually reaching the top of the S and becoming mature. When a technology is mature, the analyst should be alert for the advent of a replacement technology.

The next step is identifying innovative developments that represent a break in the S curve. This step is an art, not a science. The technique is to identify new forces or technologies, or synergies among existing technologies, and look outside the established companies or organizations in an industry. Technology evolutions and improvements come from within establishment organizations; innovation seldom does. The shaping forces discussed in chapter 12—inertia, contamination, synergy, and feedback—all promote or constrain innovation. Organizational forces, especially culture and the decision-making process, are often critical in determining whether a technology will be developed or used when it has been developed.

Most technology predictions rely on open literature, and publications pattern analysis is used to tell where a technology is on the S curve and to identify emerging innovations in the technology.

Future systems analysis can take an inductive, a deductive, or an abductive approach, but the deductive approach works better in practice. For analysts predicting systems developments as much as five years into the future, extrapolations work reasonably well; for those looking five to fifteen years into the future, projections usually fare better. The predictions typically require analysis of a system's performance, cost, and schedule. Comparative performance analysis is widely used in such predictions. Simulations are used to prepare more sophisticated predictions of a system's performance.

Simulations have long been a tool to assess the capabilities of an opponent's military hardware, such as aircraft, tanks, and naval vessels. They are increasingly being used to assess the performance of larger systems—air defense systems or entire economies, for example. Such complex targets are best analyzed by using simulation models.

Most simulation models are systems of equations that must be solved for different input assumptions. The critical issues in dealing with simulation models are to define the problem to be solved, validate the model (ensure that it approximates reality), and select appropriate measures of effectiveness for the output.

Notes

1. Francis Narin, Mark P. Carpenter, and Patricia Woolf, "Technological Performance Assessments Based on Patents and Patent Citations," *IEEE Transactions on Engineering Management* 4 (November 1984): 172.
2. Ibid.
3. Ibid.
4. Joseph P. Martino, "Trend Extrapolation," in *A Practical Guide to Technological Forecasting*, ed. James R. Bright and Milton E. F. Schoeman (Englewood Cliffs, N.J.: Prentice Hall, 1973), 106.
5. Günther Schuh and Markus Grawatsch, "TRIZ-Based Technology Intelligence," presentation at the European TRIZ association meeting, TRIZFutures 2003, May 15–16, 2003, www.triz-journal.com/archives/2004/04/05.pdf.
6. Herbert C. Rothenberg, "Identifying the Future Threat," *Studies in Intelligence* 12, no. 4 (1968): 13–21.
7. John Prados, *The Soviet Estimate* (Princeton: Princeton University Press, 1987), 324.
8. Lester Thurow, "Brainpower and the Future of Capitalism," in *The Knowledge Advantage: Fourteen Visionaries Define Marketplace Success in the New Economy*, ed. Rudy Ruggles and Dan Holtshouse (New York: John Wiley/Capstone, 1999).
9. *Report of the Commission on the Intelligence Capabilities of the United States Regarding Weapons of Mass Destruction*, March 31, 2005, www.wmd.gov/report/wmd_report.pdf, 13.
10. Rothenberg, "Identifying the Future Threat."
11. Stéphane J. Lefebvre, "A Look at Intelligence Analysis," Poster presentation TC99, International Studies Association Conference, Portland, Oregon, February 27, 2003, 25.
12. Roger Z. George and James B. Bruce, *Analyzing Intelligence* (Washington, D.C.: Georgetown University Press, 2008), 175–176.
13. Jeffrey R. Cooper, "Curing Analytical Pathologies" (Washington, D.C.: Center for the Study of Intelligence, Central Intelligence Agency, December 2005), www.fas.org/irp/cia/product/curing.pdf.
14. Ibid.
15. David S. Brandwein, "Maxims for Analysts," *Studies in Intelligence* 22, no. 4 (Winter 1978): 31–35.
16. Rothenberg, "Identifying the Future Threat."
17. *Report of the Commission*, 143.
18. David S. Brandwein, "Interaction in Weapons R&D," *Studies in Intelligence* 12, no. 1 (Spring 1968): 13–20.
19. Arthur J. Alexander, "The Process of Soviet Weapons Design," Technology Trends Colloquium, U.S. Naval Academy, Annapolis, Md., March 29–April 1, 1978.
20. Bruce Bueno de Mesquita, "The Methodical Study of Politics," New York University and Hoover Institution, October 30, 2002, www.yale.edu/probmeth/Bueno_De_Mesquita.doc.

15

The Analyst and the Customer

Intelligence is best done by a minimum number of men and women of the greatest possible ability.
R. V. Jones, Assistant Director of Britain's Royal Air Force
Intelligence Section During World War II

Intelligence can be thought of as having three phases—information acquisition (building the model), analysis, and customer acceptance. An exceptional analyst needs to call on different personal qualities to shepherd each phase along. He or she also needs a good understanding of the characteristics of intelligence customers and should know how best to present intelligence results to win their acceptance.

The Analyst

During the information acquisition and analysis stages, staying objective and keeping a broad perspective are crucial to success. Just as important, however, is the ability to lead a team. It is the premise of this book that collaboration is the only practical future for a relevant and successful intelligence community, and the analyst functions as the project manager for the team.

Objectivity

It may seem obvious that to remain objective is a credible analyst's first commandment. She knows that a search for evidence to support preconceived notions has no place in intelligence. She knows that she cannot discard observations because they are contrary to what she expected. In fact, she knows that her goal is to function like the physical scientist: In the physical sciences, an astronomer is not emotionally affected by finding that stars follow a certain development pattern. An astronomer does not think that this is good or bad; it simply is.

Unfortunately, intelligence analysts are typically in a position more like that of a social scientist. Their thinking may be complicated by an inability to isolate their own emotional needs from the problem being studied. Put simply, they *care* about the outcome. But if an analyst wishes to assess foreign events, for example, he must put aside personal opinions about war, poverty, racism, police brutality, and governmental corruption, to name a few tough ones. For instance, "political corruption" is a normal way of life in many areas of the world. Neither good nor bad in an absolute sense, it is merely the accepted standard of conduct. An analyst who receives the task of assessing the international narcotics trade cannot begin with the view that the traffickers are opportunistic scum. Instead, she must practice empathy, or the concept of putting herself in the shoes of the target. Empathy is a tool of objectivity in that it allows the analyst to check her biases. The analyst must try to see things from the traffickers' perspective—they are a group of small businesspeople working to uphold the free enterprise system in the face of excessive government regulation. (As an aside, a well-rounded analyst who has read Machiavelli sometime in the past might find it helpful to reread him, this time from the analyst's vantage point. One of Machiavelli's great strengths was his ability to assess conduct rather than values.)

If the intelligence customer is in the business world, the challenge for the analyst of keeping an objective attitude reaches new heights. In business the intelligence analyst often must make a recommendation, though without specifically telling the decision maker what to do.[1] Intelligence professionals in government and in the military service would undoubtedly be amused at the suggestion that they should offer advice such as, "General, you should move your tank battalions to the positions I have indicated," or "Madam Secretary, it would be prudent if your ambassador in Botswana initiated a dialogue with the rebel alliance." Recommendations such as these are career enders for government intelligence officers, who typically have neither the policymaking nor the operations experience—nor the current knowledge of operational factors—needed to give such advice. Conversely, in many companies the business intelligence analyst has both the operations expertise and the credibility to make operational recommendations. It remains a valid question whether the government intelligence officer should be more like the business intelligence analyst—qualified to make judgments on policy or operational issues. In a collaborative environment that includes the customer, making judgments is likely to happen. But when analysts make recommendations, they find objectivity tough to maintain.

Broad Perspective

Successful analysts have an inherent inquisitiveness and a lifelong interest in learning about subjects and ideas that may seem to have little or no relevance to their current subject area. Relevant and wide-ranging reading on other cultures, their economies, military traditions, religious and political doctrines, philosophy, and the like, gives analysts a breadth of substantive competence that will serve them well throughout their careers.

A long-term, historical perspective is essential in making predictions about a culture, a government, an industry, a system, or a technology. Each of these concerns, even technology, has a long history. With few exceptions, the policymakers or executives who control industries, military forces, and governmental organizations today earned their credentials ten to twenty years ago. Their organizations thus are bureaucracies shaped by the worldview of key controlling individuals who likely retain biases based on the lessons they learned through earlier experience. An analyst cannot comprehend the present shape of an organization—public or private—or predict its likely evolution and organizational behavior without an understanding of what has happened within it during its history. One cannot understand the 1989 crackdown by the People's Republic of China on student demonstrators in Tiananmen Square, and the average Chinese person's view of the crackdown, without understanding the Cultural Revolution and its impact on the Chinese people.[2] And it is important to learn a nation's history as its people teach the subject—which may be quite different from what you were taught.[3]

A historical perspective requires more than just knowledge of the past few decades. The study of organizations, management, and decision making has gone on for centuries, and some of the most pertinent observations on these subjects trace back to the thinking of Machiavelli, Sun Tzu, and Plato.

Analyst as Team Player

The target-centric approach requires teamwork, and analysts should expect that customers will be part of the team. Because many people have something at stake in how an intelligence question is answered, the process of getting to the answers, especially the answers to complex intelligence problems, is fundamentally a *social* one. Most complex problems involve many stakeholders: Some of them, such as the analyst's managers, are involved in defining the intelligence problem; others, such as the customers, may add constraints to the solution. Teams working on related projects have a particularly large stake because one team's answer is the next team's problem. For instance, an economic analyst's assessment that the economy of Egypt is headed for serious trouble would present a number of challenges to an analytical team assessing the political future of Egypt. Any member of the team—a collector, an analyst, a customer—is no longer confined to using his or her expertise in just one area or at just one time during the process. Instead, synergistic discoveries and opportunities occur, as pooled expertise and talents are brought to bear on one relevant focus: the target model that was introduced in chapter 3.

No team leader is brilliant or experienced enough to go off and solve complex problems alone. It is not even possible to assemble a team of brilliant people to go off and solve the problem, because the moment they go off they leave behind the stakeholders whose input is essential. Again, a target-centric approach helps solve this problem by emphasizing the benefit of sharing information and expertise among stakeholders. In this way the approach breaks down the long-held compartmental barriers that collectors, analysts, and customers have traditionally experienced in solving intelligence problems. All stakeholders contribute to the target model, which is an initial representation of the intelligence problem. The model remains accessible to all the participants and available for their input as it evolves. Thus interpersonal skills (including the ability to express and present ideas clearly) cannot be overemphasized. Admittedly, analysts who live by logic and the scientific method are not often described as "naturals" when it comes to soft skills. But practicing empathy, conflict resolution techniques, facilitation skills, and the art of knowing when and how to advocate, versus when to follow and reflect, are crucial to analysis and the resulting product. These project management skills, along with some mastery over one's ego, can be learned (albeit sometimes through painful trial and error). Even the most logical and objective creature in popular television history, *Star Trek's* Mr. Spock, was a consummate listener, dialoguer, and when appropriate, advocate.

There are likely several thousands of books nowadays dedicated to the art of teamwork. If there is a single key to successful team outcomes, it is efficient collaboration built on mutual trust—something that is very difficult to build and very easy to destroy in a large intelligence organization. Effective teams require cohesion, formal and informal communication, cooperation, shared mental models, and similar knowledge structures. Without such a common process, an interdisciplinary team will quickly fall apart.[4]

Precisely because a coordinated team approach will have been implemented, an analyst will consistently produce credible analysis reports of excellent quality by following these imperatives:

- As part of the analyst's interpersonal skill set, he or she must be a strong team leader, who can execute a team intelligence effort, but who also understands and is committed to the *inclusive* nature of complex problem solving. This person must be capable of fostering active participation by the customer community, which will improve the quality of the synthesis and analysis of intelligence problems, as well as improve support for the results. When customers are integrated into the study process, not only is their assistance invaluable but they will have confidence in, and use, the product. A competent team leader also recognizes how difficult it is for one team member to confront or criticize another, the disincentive being strongest when a junior analyst must oppose a veteran.[5]

- In managing this process, the analyst should encourage every possible form of communication—welcoming disagreement as a sign that the stakeholders are putting their cards on the table and using meetings as occasions for learning and building shared mental models. Finally, the analyst should use technologies that support communication among the stakeholders and promote the value of capturing and sharing soft information, such as ideas, questions, problems, objections, opinions, assumptions, and constraints.

- The analyst should remember that he or she is managing an *opportunity-driven* process and look for opportunities for breakthroughs, synergies, connections, and allies. The skillful team manager drives for making decisions quickly, even before the team is ready, knowing that decisions and partial solutions will flush out new contributions. This is equivalent to the concept of rapid prototyping in software development.

- Perhaps most important, the team leader must manage the scope of the problem—determining which stakeholders to include in the process and how to include them; choosing which constraints to be ruled by, which to bend, and which to ignore. In this way, the analyst can make conscious and responsible choices about the scope of the problem.

U.S. and British intelligence have two distinctly different approaches to this process in producing their top-level estimates. In the United States, National Intelligence Estimates are prepared in a meeting exclusively of intelligence officers. In Britain, the process is more like the one outlined above: Equivalent estimates are prepared by a group that comprises both intelligence officers and policymakers."[6] Even in the NIE meetings, though the policymakers themselves are absent, their preferences are usually known and presented. Jack Davis refers to this phenomenon as the "elephant in the room."[7] The drawback is that, unlike in the British model, the policymaker–analyst dialogue does not take place. The analysts are like the blind men of Hindustan, each perceiving the elephant differently.

Once the fact-finding and analysis have been completed, it is time for the analyst to set objectivity aside and assume the opposite role—that of persuader. The analyst now must turn his attention toward getting the team's results read or heard and understood. This means presenting them to the customer in the most compelling way possible. Before the presentation, however, the analyst must first seek to know the customer.

The Customer

The numbers of customers of intelligence have expanded steadily over the past century from the traditional two groups—military and national leadership—to include a diverse customer set. In the United States since 9/11, for example, law enforcement and emergency response teams have become regular customers of intelligence. In many countries, such as China and France, commercial firms are major customers of government-provided commercial intelligence because of the competitive advantage that such intelligence gives them.

Policymakers

Policymakers in the political, economic, and S&T arenas are strikingly different in how they interact with analysts. Policymakers in the political arena are probably the most difficult customers. They frequently understand politics better than the analysts do and have their own sources of information independent of the intelligence community. They got where they are because of great interpersonal skills, and they believe that they read people well, independent of cultural background. Customers of S&T and weapons intelligence are more likely not to be able to match the technical competence of the analyst and accordingly will give the analyst's opinions more respect. Customers of economic intelligence tend to fall in between those extremes.

The Policymaker's Environment. A typical senior government executive works under severe time pressures in a disruptive environment. Former secretary of defense Robert McNamara was typical of executives and policymakers. On his Vietnam mistakes, he observed, "One reason [we] failed to take an orderly, rational approach . . . was the staggering variety and complexity of the other issues we faced. Simply put, we faced a blizzard of problems, there were only twenty-four hours in a day, and we often did not have time to think straight. This predicament is not unique to the administration in which I served or to the United States. It has existed at all times and in most countries."[8] The implications are clear: Government executives need good analytical insights to deal with complex problems in a short time frame. But as a result:

- Policymakers have little time to make their needs known or to dialogue with the analyst.

- The intelligence message has to be clear, unequivocal, and usually brief—on one page or even in the title of the article.

- Policymakers have short memories; they need to be reminded of past material—you cannot assume past knowledge—and they usually don't retain copies of prior intelligence.

- They have a "today's news" orientation; they tend to prefer current intelligence, and in-depth analysis often is not valued. Long-term research has to answer a question that the policymaker considers important.

The Policymaker's Mindset. Policymakers frequently adopt a mindset, and after they have done so the evidence must be overwhelming to change it. Their receptivity to intelligence changes over time. At the start of a new administration, intelligence analysts have their greatest impact. As policy views begin to harden, it takes more and more evidence to change anyone's mind.[9] Policymakers demand more proof if intelligence negatively affects their agenda, and they accept a much lower standard of proof when intelligence complements their agenda.

Many policymakers want to see the raw intelligence, often to select items to support their mindsets. National security adviser Zbigniew Brzezinski insisted on seeing raw intelligence, claiming that the intelligence community could not provide the broad, sweeping, and bold insights into the future that he needed.[10] The policymaker or leader mindset has existed since there were leaders:

- Perhaps the earliest example recorded (in the Bible) occurred when the Israelites spied out the land of Canaan. Their leader's objective (and mindset) was to conquer Canaan. His spies brought back unwelcome news, reporting, "They are stronger than we. . . . There we saw the giants" (Numbers 13: 31–33). (This also was the earliest example of intelligence's propensity to overstate a threat.) The Israelites wound up spending forty more years in the wilderness (there is no indication what happened to the spies). Not surprisingly, there were no giants in the reports from the next set of spies, forty years later.

- In the sixteenth century Philip II ruled the Spanish empire. Philip was the ultimate "hands on" executive and typical of leaders before and since. His policy was to accept incoming information from his far-flung intelligence network that supported his preconceived ideas and to avoid or ignore anything that contradicted them.[11] Like many executives since, Philip II was prone to wishful thinking.

- A CIA analyst in 1951 was studying the movements of the Chinese and had reached the conclusion that the Chinese had surreptitiously introduced their forces into North Korea. He briefed the assistant secretary of state for Far Eastern affairs, Dean Rusk, who later was the secretary of state under Presidents John F. Kennedy and Lyndon B. Johnson. Rusk listened politely to the briefing, and at the end of it he said, "Young man, they wouldn't dare."[12] Weeks later, the Chinese forces attacked UN forces in Korea.

- Even directors of central intelligence have been trapped in mindsets. Former DCI Stansfield Turner believed that Ayatollah Ruhollah Khomeini was just another Iranian politician. Despite the arguments of his analysts, Turner briefed the National Security Council that after the overthrow of the shah of Iran things would go on pretty much as they had before.[13]

Business Leaders

Business consumers of intelligence are very similar to political policymakers for many of the same reasons. They like to feel that they are in control and that they understand the competitive environment better than their business intelligence staff. They have mindsets. They face constant time pressures and are action oriented. But because they pay for their intelligence, they are more inclined to give specific guidance, more willing to listen, and more apt to take the analyst to task for poor outcomes.

Military Leadership

Military customers are usually clear about what they want from intelligence. Intelligence is an integral part of their world; they are used to seeing it and understand its value. Military leaders, like policymakers, vary greatly in articulating needs. All of them, to some degree, want to act as their own analysts—though policymakers are probably most inclined to do that.

Most executives, including policymakers and military leaders, are guided in decision making by a principle known as *prospect theory.* Prospect theory says that people will pay a higher price, or risk more, to prevent losses than they will to seek gains. Executives, especially in large bureaucracies, tend to be conservative and cautious. So they tend to want intelligence that warns of losses and to pay less attention to intelligence that suggests opportunities for gain.

One opportunity for gain that will always catch the policymaker's or military leader's attention, however, is the chance to deliver an asymmetric response. While *asymmetric response* is currently a phrase with cachet, it is an old technique in conflict. The Dutch conducted asymmetric warfare against the Spanish in the Netherlands around 1600. They could move by water in the rivers more quickly than the Spaniards could, in some cases reaching in two days places that the Spaniards could only reach in fifteen.[14] The Dutch built their successful conflict strategy around this advantage. The Farewell case, discussed in chapter 9, was a superbly crafted asymmetric response to Soviet intelligence, and the U.S. intelligence officers supporting it received commendations. Intelligence that identifies opportunities for asymmetric response will always be welcome. So it is worthwhile to highlight the opponent's weaknesses and identify his vulnerabilities in constructing the target model.

Military Operations

At the military operational and tactical levels, intelligence has a well-established role that is spelled out in military doctrine. Unit commanders are familiar with what intelligence can and cannot do. The relation of intelligence to operations has been well settled by tradition. However, intelligence has become much more valuable to war fighters as it has gotten better. As noted earlier, precision strikes require precise intelligence. The role of intelligence in war fighting is expanding, and intelligence is a central part of what has been called a "revolution in military affairs."[15]

Law Enforcement

Law enforcement officials fall somewhere between policymakers and military operations customers. Some, such as counternarcotics teams, have experience in dealing with intelligence. Local police traditionally have had very little experience with, or understanding of, intelligence. Increasingly, however, law enforcement groups have crime fusion centers that correlate and analyze intelligence and deliver it to police officers. Cyber and computer crime centers have been created in many states to bring together intelligence from national and local sources. Acceptance of the value of intelligence analysis is increasing in the U.S. law enforcement community.

The classification of intelligence is an ongoing problem for law enforcement. Raw reporting from HUMINT, IMINT, or COMINT sources is typically classified at the secret level or higher, and local law enforcement officials normally have no security clearance. Conventionally this problem is handled by sharing information without source details—"I can't tell you why, but. . . ." Law enforcement officers are comfortable with that; they are used to taking unverified tips. Intelligence officers also frequently use fictional sources, often creating very elaborate reports to conceal the true source and get the material released at a lower classification. You have to deal with the trade-off between protecting sources and misleading analysts (who will evaluate a report depending on its source). Ideally, you use a fictional source that has the same general level of credibility.

Analyst-Customer Interaction

All of the types of customers described in the preceding section have mindsets. In the close interaction that is necessary to make the target-centric approach work, the pressures to conform analysis to policy are subtle. Intelligence that supports policy will readily be accepted and the analyst suitably rewarded; intelligence that contradicts policy will be ignored. This section discusses some ways of dealing with those pressures.

Going back to the discussion of the intelligence cycle in chapter 1, the "dissemination" block in the cycle tends to leave analysts believing that their job is done when the report goes out the door. What consumers do with the report is up to them. But the most brilliant piece of intelligence analysis may as well have gone into the trash if it is not read by the right people in time for them to act on it. Make sure that the person who initiated the request sees your report or receives a briefing—ideally, both. Get copies to other people who may have an interest in the results. Get feedback from as many of them as possible.

As an analyst, you have to enter the interaction at the customer's level—which can be quite different when dealing with a president's national security adviser, a combat commander, or a police captain. The effectiveness of this interaction depends critically on the level of mutual trust and confidence between the customer and the analyst. And for policymakers the road to trust can be a long, hard one. A military commander and his intelligence officer can usually establish a high degree of mutual trust; they are working together for a common goal against a common enemy. Neither is much concerned that the other will share his confidences with the enemy. The policymaker and the analyst often have neither the common goal nor the common enemy. In Washington, D.C., the policymaker's enemy is often located just down Constitution Avenue, and she has to be aware that the intelligence officer might defect to that enemy at any time. For his part, the analyst constantly has to be concerned that his assessments will be twisted or misconstrued to fit a policy preference.

Assuming that some level of trust can be established, the analyst next has to do two things: get the customer to understand the message and get buy-in—that is, get the customer to accept the message and act on it.

Analyst as Communicator: Getting the Customer to Understand the Message

A major problem of intelligence in sixteenth-century Europe was that spies could readily acquire information, but governments could not readily grasp its significance and act accordingly.[16] Issues are much more complex today, and the challenge for analysts is still to help customers grasp the significance of intelligence.

If one is to be an effective analyst, one must learn the skills of effective communication, both in writing and in speaking. There are procedures for writing a report or presenting a briefing, some generally recognized across professions and some that are institution specific. It is the responsibility of the analyst to learn the technical quality and style requirements of his or her particular intelligence organization and then pay strict attention to them. Analysts who develop communications skills must follow the conventional standards for publications in their area and use terminology that their customers understand. In general, they should address problems and issues that interest the customer and present results that

- are forward looking, with detailed predictions of future developments or of major trends in the subject area and descriptions of the factors driving those trends;
- contain clearly stated conclusions supported by thorough research and technical reasoning; and
- include clear tutorials or explanations of complex technical subjects, aimed at the expected customer.

A major cause of intelligence failure is what has been referred to as the "pathology of communication"; that is to say, it is often hard to get the customer to believe intelligence judgments where policy issues are concerned.[17] Furthermore, analysts must convey areas of uncertainty and gaps in their knowledge. The Iraqi WMD Commission noted, "Analysts also have a responsibility to tell customers about important disagreements within the Intelligence Community. . . . In addition to conveying disagreements, analysts must also find ways to explain to policymakers degrees of uncertainty in their work."[18] To do these things without causing the customer to totally disregard the intelligence is a challenge.

The answer to both of these problems lies in the target-centric process introduced in chapter 2. You have to make the customer a part of the intelligence process—difficult in the case of the busy policymaker. But once the customer is engaged in the process, communicating the results becomes much less difficult, and the customer is much more likely to understand and use the intelligence. The British model, discussed earlier in this chapter, has demonstrated that this approach can work.

Finally, in preparing intelligence on technical subjects, there is always an easier way, always a clearer way, always a more accurate way to say something. Unfortunately, they are not the same way. It is almost axiomatic that if a report is readable and understandable, it is technically inaccurate. Only a masterly analyst can achieve technical accuracy and readability in one document. The answer? Don't place consuming emphasis on technical accuracy. It is far more important to have the message understood.

This demand for precision of expression causes problems in S&T intelligence, but that is true across all fields of intelligence, and for a good reason. Intelligence analysts often find that their words are interpreted (or misinterpreted) by policy customers to fit with the customers' preferred course of action. The response by analysts, especially in preparing National Intelligence Estimates, is to make precise expression an art form that is studied and practiced. As Michael Herman has noted, precision of expression is rated very highly by analysts and their managers in intelligence communities in both Britain and the United States.[19]

Analyst as Advocate: Getting Buy-In

If analysis is conducted as has been discussed in this book, the customer will usually accept and make use of the analysis results. But if the customer does not give a positive response, the analyst must shift his or her interpersonal skills in the direction of advocacy and act as a spokesperson supporting the conclusions.

In chapter 2 we said that determining requirements and needs is marketing—finding out what the customer wants. This section is about sales—getting the intelligence customer to want (and use) what you have. Recognize, however, that this is a controversial recommendation. The Iraqi WMD Commission report criticized this tendency, saying, "In ways both subtle and not so subtle, the daily reports seemed to be 'selling' intelligence—in order to keep its customers, or at least the First Customer, interested."[20]

Analysts often have no choice but to sell the product. Ideally, intelligence would be a commodity like food: Consumers would buy it because they need it. In operations, especially in military operations, that may be the case. Unfortunately, at least in policy support, intelligence is more like insurance: It has to be sold, and buyers have to be convinced that they are getting a good product. Former secretary of state Henry Kissinger, on being reminded by an analyst that he had been warned about the impending outbreak of a war, reportedly said, "You warned me, but you didn't convince me."[21] The invitation could not be clearer. If policymakers expect intelligence analysts to convince them, analysts have to sell.

One problem of looking at intelligence as sales, especially in policy matters, is that it increases the danger of telling customers what they want to hear.[22] Another challenge is that the analyst needs a good sense of timing (as every salesman knows).[23]

Although the proper analytic attitude is one of objectivity, once analysis is finished, political realities set in. The analyst must sell the product because here again she quickly encounters one of the fundamental principles of physics that is also a fundamental principle in intelligence (Analysis Principle 12-2, previously discussed): Every action produces an equal and opposite reaction. If the analyst's results are at all worthwhile, they likely will meet with skepticism or outright opposition.

Furthermore, if the customer is a U.S. government policymaker, the analyst typically must interact with lawyers, a relationship that is much different from what analysts are used to and one in which advocacy skills are useful. Lawyers prefer to use intelligence experts as they would use scientific experts in a courtroom—receiving testimony on the facts and opinions, cross-examining, determining the key issues, and deciding. The existence of controversy and of differing opinions is essential, in the lawyer's view, to establishing the truth. Lawyers are uncomfortable with a single expert opinion and with the intelligence compartmentation system. To them, the intelligence community's traditional compartmentation system for protecting sources and methods is suspect because it tends to conceal evidence and is therefore inconsistent with the goal of the discovery process in civil litigation.

Most intelligence analysts have difficulty being advocates because it goes against their objective nature. The advocacy process is an adversarial one, and the guidelines for conduct come from the legal profession, in which advocacy has been raised to a fine art and the pitfalls of improper advocacy are well understood. R. V. Jones once observed, "When an analyst participates in an adversary process he is, and should conduct himself as, and should expect to be treated as, an advocate. The rules for an adversary process are different from those of research. The former permit biased or slanted testimony and the latter are directed toward objective evaluation."[24] Jones did, however, reserve judgment as to whether the giving of "biased or slanted testimony" was compatible with honor in a scientist.[25]

One answer to this dilemma is the same one that Machiavelli gave to his Prince: The conduct that I am describing may not be proper or honorable, but it seems to work where proper and honorable conduct does not.[26] Jones himself went on to cite some examples of how he had slanted or strained the evidence when, in his judgment, it was the right thing to do. Most analysts would give a different answer: Slanting the intelligence reporting is unethical and is always a bad idea, even if the customer consequently makes a bad decision.

Furthermore, obtaining acceptance from any customer depends on the analyst's reputation. A reputation for credibility and veracity among customers is an analyst's most valuable asset. It takes a long time to build and can be lost in a day. Or, as David Landes has observed, "In the public domain, a reputation for veracity is worth more than valor and intelligence, and this especially in a world of ubiquitous guile and duplicity."[27] You need to make the customer pay attention, but you cannot sacrifice credibility or truth to do it. If you do, you might as well get out of the business. A few examples:

- The KGB was discredited in the eyes of Soviet leadership when the Farewell deception became public, and all of its materiel acquisition results were called into question.

- During the Vietnam War, the CIA discounted and underestimated the magnitude and significance of the North Vietnamese support reaching the Viet Cong through Cambodia's port of Sihanoukville. Subsequent information from a newly recruited source in the Cambodian port showed that the agency's estimates were wrong and the military's were more accurate. Afterward, whenever the CIA disagreed with the Pentagon, the White House would ask DCI Richard Helms: "What about Sihanoukville?"[28]

- The Iraqi WMD miscall damaged the credibility of several intelligence community analysis groups, especially the CIA's. It will take years to overcome that damage.

The Defense Analysis Challenge

The intelligence analyst in a defense organization must deal with two distinctive challenges: the premium placed on warning and the pressure to produce threat assessments that align with policy.

The Premium Placed on Warning. Defense analysts have a special obligation to give their leaders warning of hostile military actions. The failure to warn has more severe consequences than does excessive warning. As Herman said, "Underestimation is less readily forgiven than overestimation" and "it is more satisfying, safer professionally, and easier to live with oneself and one's colleagues as a military hawk than as a wimp."[29]

This tendency of defense analysts to overestimate a threat is well documented, and policymakers compensate for it—which leads to the desensitization problem discussed in chapter 4.[30] The result, though, is that the credibility of the defense analyst suffers.

Threat Assessments that Support Funding and Policy Decisions. Herman also observed that "Threat assessments have always been one of the military cards in bargaining with treasuries."[31] The Backfire bomber case cited in chapter 14 and the particle beam weapon case of chapter 7 are examples of such threat assessments as bargaining tools. The tendency is to overstate the threat to justify funding or to support defense policy positions. The resulting problem, as Herman notes, is that U.S. defense intelligence organizations "have always had fairly low esteem."[32]

Defense analysts have to break away from the trap of aligning assessment with funding or policy decisions by providing objective analysis even when it runs contrary to the official position of their service or of the defense establishment. Those who have the courage to stand up for their beliefs don't always fare well, however. Gordon Negus, former executive director of the Defense Intelligence Agency (DIA), tells of how Maj. Gen. Lincoln Faurer, while director of the DIA, dealt with pressure to conform intelligence analysis to policy. When Jimmy Carter was president, the White House was considering options for dealing with the Soviet Union's improved air defense system. Two of the options were to build the B-1 bomber or to arm the existing B-52 fleet with cruise missiles. The U.S. Air Force wanted the B-1. But the DIA's intelligence indicated that the Soviets felt much more threatened by the cruise missile option, which would nullify the Soviet Union's massive air defense investment. The air force chief of staff told Faurer, in unequivocal terms, to revise the DIA estimate to support the air force position. Faurer refused and was gone from the DIA within a month.[33]

Although the pressure to conform estimates to policy is especially severe in the military, it is not unique to defense. Any analytic group that is closely connected to a policy group has to deal with this problem. As I noted in the introduction to this book, the British Foreign and Commonwealth Office forced the intelligence process to its desired conclusion that Argentina would not attack the Falklands in 1982. In the United States, departmental intelligence units such as the State Department's Bureau of Intelligence and Research (INR), for example, face pressure to make intelligence fit policy. The State Department has long recognized this potential problem and attempts to keep its analysts separate and organizationally shielded from the pressures of the policymaker.

Appropriators of funding also recognize this tendency, and they usually follow the rule for using an organization's test results that was discussed in chapter 7. That is, if the reporting organization has a stake in what an intelligence report says, and if the report supports the organization's position or interests, the appropriator will typically view the conclusions with suspicion.

Presenting Analysis Results

Even if you have followed the guidance in chapter 2 in detail, you still, in the end, need a vehicle to communicate the results. In intelligence, that almost always means either a written report or a verbal report (typically, a briefing). The remainder of this chapter concentrates on delivering the presentation and getting feedback.

An intelligence presentation may require a written report or the development of a briefing, either of which can be a time-consuming activity. Each has its advantages. The report gets wider circulation and typically has a longer life. Most analysis projects conclude with some type of written report. The briefing allows direct and immediate feedback to the analyst. Briefings are probably the primary communication method for executives. They usually value the two-way exchange, and you in turn should value the feedback.

The important thing is to fit your presentation to the style of the key customer. Although most executives prefer briefings, some like written reports; an increasing number want e-mails. You may have to conduct an intelligence effort on the key customer (which his or her staff will usually cooperate in). Find out the customer's favorite way to get information. Some prefer more text; some want graphics; a few may want lots of facts and figures. Following are some guidelines for presenting analysis results:

Support Every Analytic Conclusion

All conclusions must be clearly traceable to the results of your effort and explained in the body of the report. Provide, explain, and emphasize key intelligence insights. The reader should be able to follow your reasoning at every turn. Highlight key words, phrases, or sentences to stress their importance.

Often an analyst is so close to a study that results and conclusions are clear to him or her but not so clear to someone not involved in the study. Furthermore, results and conclusions should be carefully scrubbed for both apparent and actual contradictions. Consider having several nonparticipants review your results and conclusions prior to the presentation. Take advantage of every opportunity you get for a peer review of your final product. Your peers can provide excellent feedback on the flow, logic, and clarity of your message.

Most reports include two levels of detail: a brief but complete summary for decision makers and another, more detailed description for fellow analysts. Your detailed description can contain as much detail as you deem necessary in order to allow another analyst to duplicate the results.

The final written study report should include a concise executive summary right up front to allow the busy reader to get "the bottom line" without poring through page after page of details. Limit your executive summary to one page.

Write or Brief with a Purpose

Because most intelligence products provide information, your customers expect to hear clear, concisely stated conclusions and projections up front. This means that you write with a purpose—which, if you began by defining the problem as you should have, will be straightforward.

Separate Facts from Analysis

Make it abundantly clear when you move from fact to analysis. Never cover up evidence with slick writing. As noted in chapter 7, you inevitably have to work with incomplete and conflicting information. For this reason your finished presentation has to clearly articulate what is known (the facts), how it is known (the sources), what drives the judgments (linchpin assumptions), the impact if these drivers change (alternative outcomes), and what remains unknown. Customers expect logical and objective arguments. Detailed facts may or may not be appropriate, depending on the scope of the topic and the technical sophistication, interest, and need of the audience. But the reader or listener should never be in doubt about whether they are getting facts or analysis.

State the Facts. As noted earlier, a typical segment of intelligence includes a summary or brief description of relevant facts, written by answering these questions:

- Who?
- What?
- When?
- Where?
- How?

Occasionally, you have to present results that conflict with what the customer wants to hear—the results undercut existing policy, for example. Facts become critical in such a case. Your only chance to change a policy decision (and a slim chance, at that) is to present concrete, persuasive evidence, and solid, factual evidence is the best kind.

Analyze the Facts. The *Who-what-when-where-how?* questions elicit the facts of the situation. The second part of the segment answers, typically, two other questions:

- Why?
- So what?

The *Why?* and *So what?* questions require analysis that extends beyond the facts. *So what?* answers the customer's question, Why should I be concerned about this issue? Then comes the second question, What should I do about it?—assuming that your customer wants you to answer that question.

The *Why?* and *So what?* questions require that you offer your opinion. At this point, you are no longer reciting facts or simply reporting; you are doing *analysis*. Answering these questions may also require that you evaluate source reliability, using the guidelines established in the Data Sources section in chapter 6.

Get to the Point

Plunge right in. Don't build up to your main point. Put it in the beginning of each section. Give recommendations before justifications, answers before explanations, conclusions before details. You are not in the business of writing mystery novels. Shorter is better. Ten pages is far too long; two or three pages is the limit for a busy policymaker (and they all are busy). Ideally, keep everything that the policymaker needs to know on one page.

We have all encountered the securities or insurance sales rep who telephones out of the blue—you've never heard of him before, but his first words are, "How are you?" He doesn't care how you are; what he really means is, "Do you have some money you'd like to spend on . . . ?"

Beating around the bush irritates people. Don't do it.

Write or Brief to Inform, Not to Impress

The formal communication skills most of us learned in school usually involved presenting material to a teacher. Your main purpose then was impressing upon someone who knew more than you did how well you, too, had mastered the subject area. The audience in a work environment is drastically different. Consequently the style and technical content of your products should change too.

In intelligence work, the expert is the presenter, not the customer. Hence, you must write to inform rather than to impress. This means that you must make certain that your intended message is as clear as possible to your audience. You cannot assume that the reader will be familiar with technical jargon or with the consequences or implications of observations or calculations. To communicate effectively, you must use vocabulary familiar to both the intelligence community and the reader. You can introduce new terms, but you must start from some common ground, some common understanding. It is this commonalty of understanding that permits analysts to introduce something new. The new term or concept then becomes common and can be used in turn to introduce something else that is new. You must work from old to new, and you must do so in a logical, easy-to-follow manner.

Make It Easy and Enjoyable to Read or Listen To

To be effective, each product must have, in addition to a clear purpose, a technical content and organization tailored to its audience. That means you should use a vocabulary and thought process familiar to your audience. Orient and motivate the reader in each section and subsection. Don't let her wonder, Why am I reading or listening to this?

Good writing is hard work. But hard work on your part is necessary to make it easy for readers to digest the message that is intended. If you care whether your customers get your message, it is a dangerous gamble to make them work unnecessarily. They always have the choice of not reading your analysis or not finishing it. It is essential therefore that you make a reader's work as easy and as fruitful as possible. If a paper is a struggle to read, chances are it won't be read.

Statistics show that most intelligence customers look at the summary of a paper, and a slight majority will read the preliminaries, but few will read the technical discussion or the appendixes. Furthermore, it is well known that audiences will pay attention for about the first five minutes of a briefing; their attention drops off markedly thereafter. Since, as a writer or briefer, you spend a great deal of effort on the body of the presentation, why not raise the odds of getting this portion of a paper read or that part of the briefing absorbed?

The best ways to do that, given that you have no authority over a reader or listener, are to make your prose fun to read, your briefings entertaining, and your messages obvious.

Standardize the products you create and the source information. Customers need to see a standard product line and know where to look to find information. For example, don't have both one- and two-column products. Avoid continuous text; it is difficult to read, and the all-caps message format is the worst. It frustrates the reader. If longer text is necessary, use bold text, bullets, and text boxes.

Write as You Would Talk

Write as you would talk to someone. Use declarative sentences. Avoid the passive voice. Writing should not be quite as informal as conversation, however. There are two extremes to avoid: stilted writing and its opposite— informality that detracts from your message or reduces its credibility.

Avoid Acronyms

Don't use acronyms without defining them. Even standard acronyms in common use throughout an organization may cause problems for consumers from the outside. It is acceptable to use a standard list of acronyms that is defined in an appendix or a glossary.

Use Graphics

Graphics and tables are the primary tools for organizing and presenting data in understandable form. Use figures, tables, bullets, multimedia, and other devices freely to make the report look interesting. Refer to every figure and table in the text.

It is important to show probabilities and statistics to be convincing, but never do it with numbers alone. A general rule is that the more graphics you use, the better. They help to explain the text, support it, and summarize data; the old rule that a single picture is worth a thousand words still holds. Maps and time lines are very useful. Liberally annotate maps and pictures; make them self-explanatory. Graphics that provide a tour of the conclusions are remembered, whereas text is not. Annotated pictures that include all the main points of the article are always well received.

One of the most memorable intelligence graphics ever produced was prepared in 1971 by an engineer from outside the intelligence community— James Headrick of the Naval Research Laboratory. Intelligence analysts were assessing a new Russian radar, which at the time had the most massive antenna in the world. Headrick used a picture of the National Mall in Washington, D.C., and put in it a white block scaled to the size of the radar antenna. The white block filled the Mall and was taller than the Washington Monument. This graphic was greatly admired, and copies of it were widely circulated because it carried a clear and easily understood message: The Russians know how to build really big and powerful radars.

Summary

A few attributes are essential in a top-rate analyst. Having the proper investigative attitude is the starting point. That is, analysts must be prepared to take an objective approach, relying on the scientific method. Ideally, they should not care what the answer is to an intelligence problem when they begin an analytic effort. They should be prepared to observe and investigate the anomaly, the unexpected, and the things that simply don't fit into the existing target model. But when the analysis is done, they often must drop the objective attitude and act as an advocate. A good analyst at times has to become a salesperson and sell the analytic product to customers. To do this well, the analyst needs a well-developed ability to express ideas orally and in writing.

Because the synthesis/analysis process is increasingly a collaborative process, analysts should be adept at teamwork. They should be familiar with the culture, processes, and problems of team partners. Specifically, they should understand the information collectors and work closely with them to obtain intelligence and evaluate the collection process. They should also understand the intelligence customers' sensitivities and boundaries.

Intelligence customers vary greatly in their willingness to express their needs and to make use of intelligence. Policymakers are probably the most difficult customers because of their pressure-cooker work environment and their tendency to adopt a mindset. Customers of political intelligence are the least receptive of the group; S&T and weapons systems intelligence customers are the most receptive.

Military leaders and military operations customers understand and value intelligence. Intelligence has a well-established role, and it is becoming more important, especially at the tactical unit level. Law enforcement officials also increasingly understand the value of intelligence and how to use it; their problem is that they don't usually have the clearances needed to deal with classified material.

In dealing with these customers, analysts have two challenges: getting customers to understand the message and getting them to accept and make use of the analytical results. Making intelligence understandable requires communication skills and empathy—the ability to put oneself in the place of the customer. Getting the customer to accept and make use of intelligence may require that the analyst become an advocate—a controversial and risky step. Acceptance also depends on the customer's view of the analyst's reputation.

Preparing and presenting analysis results are most effectively achieved by a rapid prototyping approach that starts with the problem breakdown (from chapter 2) and expands an outline into a final report or briefing. The type and the format of the presentation are shaped by the preferences of the customer or customer class; generally, a short, to-the-point, graphically oriented presentation works best.

Notes

1. John H. Hovis, "CI at Avnet: A Bottom-Line Impact," *Competitive Intelligence Review* 11 (third quarter 2000): 11.
2. Rob Johnson, *Analytic Culture in the U.S. Intelligence Community* (Washington, D.C.: Center for the Study of Intelligence, Central Intelligence Agency, 2005), 76–79.
3. Martin Petersen, "The Challenge for the Political Analyst," *Studies in Intelligence* 47, no. 1 (Winter 2003), www.csi.cia/studies/vol47no1/article05/html.
4. Johnson, *Analytic Culture,* 70.
5. Ibid., xiv–xv.
6. Michael Herman, *Intelligence Power in Peace and War* (Cambridge: Cambridge University Press, 1996), 275.
7. Quoted in Roger Z. George and James B. Bruce, *Analyzing Intelligence* (Washington, D.C.: Georgetown University Press, 2008), 167.
8. Robert S. McNamara, with Brian VanDeMark, *In Retrospect: The Tragedy and Lessons of Vietnam* (New York: Random House, 1995), xxi.
9. Center for the Study of Intelligence, Central Intelligence Agency, "Watching the Bear: Essays on CIA's Analysis of the Soviet Union," conference, Princeton University, March 2001, www.cia.gov/cis/books/watching thebear/article08.html, 18.
10. Ibid., 19.
11. Geoffrey Parker, *The Grand Strategy of Philip II* (New Haven: Yale University Press, 1998), 74.
12. CIA Center, "Watching the Bear," 14.
13. Ibid., 18.
14. Parker, *The Grand Strategy of Philip II,* 284.
15. Anthony D. McIvor, ed., *Rethinking the Principles of War* (Annapolis, Md.: Naval Institute Press, 2005), part 5.
16. Parker, *The Grand Strategy of Philip II,* 213.
17. Douglas H. Dearth and R. Thomas Goodden, *Strategic Intelligence: Theory and Application,* 2nd ed. (Carlisle Barracks, Pa.: U.S. Army War College, and Washington, D.C.: Defense Intelligence Agency, 1995), 197.
18. *Report of the Commission on the Intelligence Capabilities of the United States Regarding Weapons of Mass Destruction,* March 31, 2005, www.wmd.gov/report/wmd_report.pdf, 419.
19. Herman, *Intelligence Power in Peace and War,* 105.
20. *Report of the Commission,* 14.
21. Quoted in George and Bruce, *Analyzing Intelligence,* 80, 113.
22. Dearth and Goodden, *Strategic Intelligence,* 153.
23. Ibid., 156.
24. "The Obligations of Scientists as Counsellors: Guidelines for the Practice of Operations Research," *Minerva* 10 (January 1972): 115.
25. R. V. Jones, "Temptations and Risks of the Scientific Adviser," *Minerva* 10 (July 1972): 441.
26. Niccolò Machiavelli, *The Prince* (New York: Bantam Classics, 1984).
27. David S. Landes, *The Wealth and Poverty of Nations* (New York: W. W. Norton and Company, 1998), 167.
28. David S. Robarge, "Richard Helms: The Intelligence Professional Personified," *Studies in Intelligence* 46, no.4 (2002), www.cia.gov/csi/studies/vol46no4/article06.html.
29. Herman, *Intelligence Power in Peace and War,* 247.
30. George and Bruce, *Analyzing Intelligence,* 80, 113.
31. Herman, *Intelligence Power in Peace and War,* 248.
32. Ibid., 240.
33. Gordon Negus, unpublished briefing notes on the Intelligence Reform and Terrorism Prevention Act of 2004, Washington, D.C., 2007.

Appendix

A Tale of Two NIEs

In 1990 the National Intelligence Council (NIC) produced a National Intelligence Estimate—the most authoritative intelligence assessment that the intelligence community produces—on Yugoslavia. Twelve years later, the NIC similarly produced a National Intelligence Estimate (NIE) on Iraq's weapons of mass destruction (WMD) program. The Yugoslavia NIE

- used a sound prediction methodology,
- got it right,
- presented conclusions that were anathema to U.S. policymakers, and
- had zero effect on U.S. policy.

The Iraqi weapons NIE, in contrast,

- used a flawed prediction methodology,
- got it wrong,
- was exactly what U.S. policymakers wanted to hear, and
- had a significant effect on U.S. policy.

This appendix contains a discussion of the differences in analytic approach used in the two National Intelligence Estimates.

The Yugoslavia NIE

The opening statements of the 1990 Yugoslavia National Intelligence Estimate contained four remarkably prescient conclusions:[1]

1. Yugoslavia will cease to function as a federal state within one year and will probably dissolve within two. Economic reform will not stave off the breakup.
2. Serbia will block Slovene and Croat attempts to form an all-Yugoslav confederation.

3. There will be a protracted armed uprising by Albanians in Kosovo. A full-scale, interrepublic war is unlikely, but serious intercommunal conflict will accompany the breakup and will continue afterward. The violence will be intractable and bitter.
4. There is little the United States and its European allies can do to preserve Yugoslav unity. Yugoslavs will see such efforts as contradictory to advocacy of democracy and self-determination.

I focus on the Yugoslavia NIE because it illustrates prediction that uses force field analysis and the creation of alternative target models in the form of scenarios. It also is an example of clear and unequivocal communication to that most difficult of intelligence consumers, the policymaker. Finally, it was about a country torn apart by religious and ethnic divisions, but which U.S. policy was determined to try to keep together; and Yugoslavia was a place where U.S. troops might wind up in harm's way. It is a scenario that continues to have relevance. The same scenario appeared in the 1980s U.S. involvement in Lebanon and more recently in Iraq.

The Setting

Yugoslavia, a federation of six republics, had a long history of instability. It was created in the aftermath of World War I, and for political reasons it united three distinct nations—Serbs, Croats, and Slovenes. Yugoslavia's internal boundaries roughly reflected ethnic and historical divisions, but the population was so thoroughly mixed that it proved impossible to separate the various ethnic groups clearly. This was especially true of the dominant ethnic group, the Serbs, who were widely dispersed in the republics. Nationalist tensions had long plagued the region. Religious divisions added to the problems: the Croats and Slovenes were primarily Roman Catholic, the Serbs were Eastern Orthodox, and Bosnia-Herzegovina and Kosovo had large Muslim populations. However, strongman Josip Broz Tito ruled Yugoslavia from 1945 until his death in 1980, and he proved very effective at suppressing tensions and keeping the country united.

In 1990, though, Tito was gone. The federal central government that was Tito's legacy was not working well. Foreign debt, inflation, and unemployment had created a troublesome situation. The economy was faltering, and nationalist pressures were causing increasing instability. In March and April 1990 Slovenia and Croatia held their first multiparty elections in almost fifty years. The Communist reformers lost to parties favoring national sovereignty within Yugoslavia.

The national intelligence officer (NIO) for Europe in 1990 was Marten van Heuven. In May of that year he visited Yugoslavia to assess the situation. He concluded that pressures were building for a collapse of the federation. The ethnic problems alone, he thought, were fast becoming irresolvable. After returning from Belgrade, van Heuven directed the preparation of an NIE on Yugoslavia. The NIE was prepared in two successive drafts. Both involved force field analysis, but they differed in the conclusions drawn from the analysis because they created starkly different target models.

First Draft (the "Muddle Through" NIE)

Van Heuven initially assigned the task of drafting the NIE to a State Department analyst who had extensive background on Yugoslavian and Eastern European affairs. In the first draft, which was completed during the summer of 1990, the author reviewed the evidence for and against the probability of Yugoslavia's disintegration and concluded that there was more reason for the republics to stay together than to split apart. That first draft is sometimes referred to as the "muddle through" NIE because, as van Heuven noted, it predicted that Yugoslavia would somehow muddle through. It identified a number of forces that were working to hold Yugoslavia together. Those forces are summarized in the influence net shown in Figure A-1 (see chapter 11 for a discussion of influence nets). The primary forces for cohesion that it identified were the following:

- The threat of Soviet intervention had held Yugoslavia together during Tito's life and for ten years after his death.

- The numerically dominant Serbs strongly preferred a united Yugoslavia. The officer corps of the Yugoslav Army (the JNA) was overwhelmingly Serbian and was thought to be in a position to prevent the nation's collapse.

- Economic incentives for remaining integrated were strong, since the republics' economies by themselves were too small to be viable.

- Fear of the future, specifically fear of ethnic and religious conflict, was considered a force that would restrain potential breakaway republics.

Some of the failures of objectivity discussed in the introduction to this book may have influenced the first NIE. The U.S. State Department had a vested interest in preserving Yugoslavia as a state, or at least seeing a peaceful

Figure A-1   Influence Net Model: Yugoslavia NIE First Draft

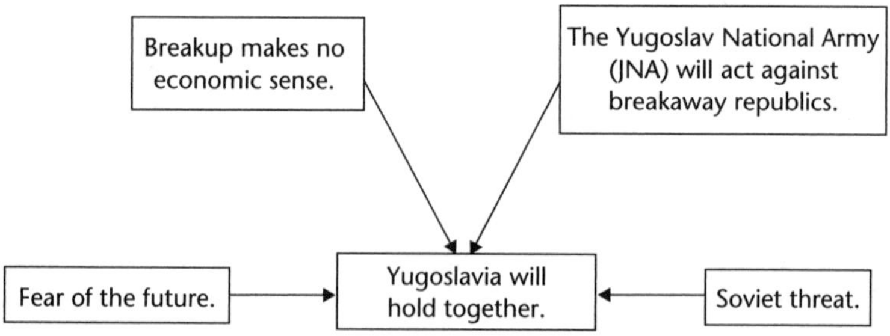

Note: The arrows come from boxes that support the conclusion that Yugoslavia will hold together.

breakup if Yugoslavia could not hold together, an organizational bias that may have shaped the analysis. Wishful thinking may also have played its part. One of the forces keeping Yugoslavia together was "fear of the future." But it appears that the fear was on the U.S. side. When a National Security Council staff member told the Slovenes and Croats that a declaration of independence would start a war, they replied, "So what?" Finally, in Yugoslavia the United States encountered a different way of thinking, and ethnocentric biases may have been at work. Both the U.S. culture and its legal system stress religious and ethnic tolerance. The republics of Yugoslavia have a long history of religious and ethnic strife and intolerance. The first NIE draft simply didn't take this critical force into account.

Van Heuven was skeptical of the conclusions; they didn't fit with the situation he had observed in his visit to the region. He wanted to see an alternative model, and he got it in the form of a second draft NIE.

Second Draft: Force Field Analysis

Van Heuven assigned the task of producing a second NIE draft to other experienced observers of events in Yugoslavia, including CIA analyst Harry Yeide, who had served in the region and was intimately familiar with the issues involved. The second NIE draft presented an alternative model or scenario of the future. It concluded that the forces that had held Yugoslavia together in the past were weak or nonexistent and that current forces were acting to tear Yugoslavia apart. Those forces are summarized in the influence net diagram in Figure A-2:

- The Yugoslav National Army was less inclined than before to intervene unless Serbian interests were seriously threatened. It would not intervene in Croatia in any event, since Croatia had no Serbs.
- No strong central leadership had replaced that of Tito.
- The Soviet threat was gone.
- The breakup made no economic sense for Yugoslavia taken as a whole, as the first draft indicated. But Croatia and Slovenia would be better off economically as independent states.
- The first draft downplayed what were probably the dominant forces in action: the ethnic and nationalistic differences among the peoples of Yugoslavia, the history of hostility and suspicion, and the religious divisions.
- Fear of the future was not a factor. As noted earlier, the United States may have feared the future, but the breakaway states of Croatia and Slovenia did not.

The resulting NIE was remarkable in several respects. All of the major contributors to it agreed on the facts. Most NIEs have footnotes indicating that a

Figure A-2 Influence Net Model: Yugoslavia NIE Second Draft

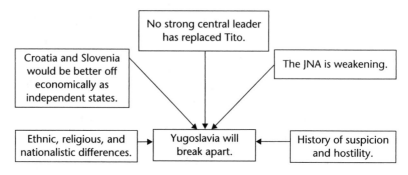

Note: The arrows come from boxes that support the conclusion that Yugoslavia will break apart.

segment of the intelligence community disagrees with some of the conclusions, but this one did not. The predictions that I quoted at the beginning of this appendix were exceptionally accurate. And the NIE had almost no effect on U.S. policy.

The Customer View

From a policymaker's point of view, the Yugoslavia NIE was unwelcome. It predicted what would happen, but it gave the policymakers nothing to do. U.S. policy preferences were, first, to keep Yugoslavia together. Failing that, the policymakers wanted a peaceful breakup, and, if all else failed, a managed disaster. They got none of those. The disintegration began in 1991, and it was brutal and bloody. The fighting and "ethnic cleansing" that resulted claimed about 200,000 lives.

If the NIE had a flaw, it was that it did not constructively engage the policymakers. The key judgments flatly predicted a breakup accompanied by long and bitter conflict but offered no suggestions for what might ease the impact of the breakup. Furthermore, U.S. government attention at the time was rapidly becoming focused on events in the Middle East, where Iraq was about to invade Kuwait. So, as one analyst said, the United States simply stopped caring until the atrocities mounted.

Finally, the NIE apparently was leaked to the *New York Times*. Its publication in the *Times* may have hastened the dissolution of Yugoslavia by indicating to all of the parties involved that the United States recognized the inevitable. The argument could be made that, as a result of its open publication, the NIE was a net disservice to the U.S. government.

The Iraqi Weapons of Mass Destruction NIE

In October 2002, at the request of members of Congress, the National Intelligence Council produced an NIE on the Iraqi weapons of mass destruction (WMD) program. That document concluded that Iraq

- was reconstituting its nuclear weapons program and was actively pursuing a nuclear device;
- possessed a biological weapons capability that was larger and more advanced than what it had before the Gulf War and that included mobile biological weapons production facilities;
- had renewed production of chemical weapons, including mustard, sarin, GF (cyclosarin), and VX, and that it had accumulated chemical stockpiles of between 100 and 500 metric tons; and
- possessed unmanned aerial vehicles (UAVs) that were probably intended for the delivery of biological weapons.[2]

All of these conclusions were wrong. Concerning this NIE, the Commission on the Intelligence Capabilities of the United States Regarding Weapons of Mass Destruction (the WMD Commission) said:

> We conclude that the Intelligence Community was dead wrong in almost all of its pre-war judgments about Iraq's weapons of mass destruction. This was a major intelligence failure. Its principal causes were the Intelligence Community's inability to collect good information about Iraq's WMD programs, serious errors in analyzing what information it could gather, and a failure to make clear just how much of its analysis was based on assumptions, rather than good evidence. (Quoted from the WMD Commission report cover letter)

There were failures in both collection and analysis, and the WMD Commission report covers them exhaustively. I focus here on the analytic failures, beginning with one that the WMD Commission report touched on but did not emphasize.

Poor Problem Definition

Poor problem definition was perhaps the root cause of the NIE's analytic failures. The effort failed at its beginning because the NIE began by failing to ask the right question, and it consequently ran afoul of the framing effect that was discussed in chapter 2. The NIE drafters, constrained by the unreasonably short deadline imposed on them by Congress, accepted the problem as it was presented. A problem breakdown that is too narrowly constrained, as this one was, overly restricts both the target model and the conclusions. Most of the other failures derived from failing to properly define the problem.

The problem definition focused solely on the question of whether Iraq had WMD programs, and, if so, what they were. By focusing on weapons of mass destruction, analysts had a tendency to fit all evidence into a WMD model. Analysts assumed that Iraq had WMD programs, and analysis proceeded from that point. A broader look at Iraq's overall military capability would have found more logical explanations for some of the evidence. For example,

- In March 2001 intelligence reporting indicated that Iraq was acquiring high-strength aluminum alloy tubes.[3] CIA and Defense Intelligence Agency analysts concluded that Iraq's purchase of aluminum tubes was intended to support a gas centrifuge uranium enrichment program. Focusing only on whether the tubes could be used for centrifuges, analysts ignored evidence that the tubes were better suited for use in rockets. The tubes in fact had precisely the same dimensions and were made of the same material as tubes used in Iraq's conventional rockets. In a classic example of premature closure, the CIA cited the existing judgment as a reason for rejecting the suggestion of one of its officers that they obtain the precise specifications of the rocket to evaluate the possibility that the tubes were in fact intended for rockets (57, 68).

- The NIE concluded that Iraq was developing small UAVs that were probably intended to deliver biological weaponry agents. In reaching this conclusion, the intelligence community (except for the air force) failed to consider other possible uses for the UAVs and dismissed countervailing evidence. As one CIA analyst explained, the purpose of the NIE was to discuss Iraq's WMD programs; so the analysis did not explore other possible uses (145). A broader problem definition would probably have concluded, correctly, that the preponderance of evidence indicated that the UAVs were intended for battlefield reconnaissance.

A better problem definition—one that required inputs from political, economic, and military analysts, as well as weapons systems analysts—would probably have avoided some of the most serious analytic lapses in the NIE. As the WMD Commission noted, multidisciplinary issues were in fact key. The Yugoslavia NIE considered military, political, economic, and social forces. But there was little serious analysis of the sociopolitical situation in Iraq or the motives and intentions of the Iraqi leadership. Weapons systems analysts are not likely to ask questions such as, Is Saddam Hussein bluffing? Or, Could he have decided to suspend his weapons programs until sanctions are lifted? An analyst of Iraq's politics and culture likely would ask such questions (13).

Poor Evaluation of Sources and Evidence

The WMD Commission faulted analysts for making judgments based on insufficient evidence. Analysts were too willing to find confirmation of their judgments in evidence that should have been recognized at the time to be of dubious reliability. They readily accepted any evidence that supported their theory that Iraq had stockpiles and was developing weapons programs, and they explained away or simply disregarded evidence that pointed in other directions. Two of the most egregious examples were the evaluation of a key human source on Iraq's biological weapons program and of both human and imagery sources on Iraq's chemical weapons program.

The conclusions about Iraqi biological weapons (BW) relied heavily on a single source, an Iraqi chemical engineer nicknamed "Curveball." This source claimed that Iraq had several mobile units for producing BW agents. The evidence Curveball presented fell short of being credible by the criteria advanced in chapter 7:

- *Competence.* Curveball was variously described as a drinker, unstable, difficult to manage, "out of control," and exhibiting behavior that is typical of fabricators (91, 97).

- *Access.* There was no evidence of access to BW laboratories. Corroborating evidence only established that Curveball had been to a particular location, not that he had any knowledge of BW activities being conducted there (113).

- *Vested interest or bias.* Curveball had a motivation to provide interesting intelligence to obtain resettlement assistance and permanent asylum (96).

- *Communications channel.* The reporting came through liaison with the German intelligence service, and U.S. intelligence officials were not provided direct access to Curveball. The communications channel between Curveball and U.S. WMD analysts therefore had many intermediate nodes, with consequent possibilities for the analysts to receive a distorted message.

Analysts evaluating Curveball's information were aware of some of these problems but nonetheless took his reporting as reliable and continued to make it the basis for judgments in the NIE and for subsequent judgments about Iraq's biological weapons program. They dismissed imagery evidence of flaws in Curveball's reporting as being due to denial and deception by the Iraqis (92). That Curveball was a fabricator was subsequently confirmed.

The NIE also erroneously concluded that Iraq had restarted chemical weapons production and increased its chemical weapons stockpiles; the conclusions were based on poor evaluation of both imagery and human sources:

- Analysts relied heavily on imagery showing the presence of "Samarra type" tanker trucks at suspected chemical weapons (CW) facilities. The distinctive trucks had been associated with CW shipments in the 1980s and during the Gulf War. Analysts also believed that they were seeing increased Samarra truck activity at the sites. They apparently did not consider an alternative hypothesis—that the trucks might be used for other purposes, as turned out to be the case. And they failed to recognize that the more frequent observed activity of the trucks was an artifact of increased imagery collection (122, 125). The trucks were simply observed more often because of more imagery reporting.

- One of the human sources, an Iraqi chemist, provided extensive reporting, about half of which was absurd. Despite evidence that he might not be a credible source, analysts used his report that Iraq had successfully stabilized the nerve agent VX in the NIE because it fit their existing mindset (127). Another source reported that Iraq was producing mustard and binary chemical agents but also reported on Iraq's missile, nuclear, and biological programs. Given Iraq's known use of compartmentation to protect sensitive weapons programs, analysts should have recognized that the source was unlikely to have had access to all these programs (128).

Failure to Consider Alternative Target Models

The Iraqi WMD NIE contained numerous examples of analysts' selecting a single hypothesis (or target model) and attempting to fit all evidence into that model. The failures to seriously consider alternative missions for Iraq's UAV program and alternative uses for the aluminum tubes have already been noted. In addition:

- Analysts failed to consider flaws in the target model they were using. If Iraqis had used all the aluminum tubes they were acquiring for centrifuges, they would have wound up with 100,000–150,000 machines, far more than any nuclear weapons proliferators would build (85). All target models should undergo a sanity check: Does the model intuitively make sense?

- They also failed to consider the Occam's razor alternative (see chapter 7)—that the reason they could find no mobile BW laboratories after an intensive search was that the labs didn't exist (93). It is virtually impossible to prove a negative in the intelligence business, but the negative at least deserves to be considered.

Poor Analytic Methodology

The raw intelligence that was available to analysts was mostly historical, largely as a result of Iraq's denial and deception programs. Intelligence about developments since the late 1990s depended heavily on IMINT and some questionable HUMINT. MASINT, COMINT, and open sources contributed very little (165). As a result, analysts had, in effect, to "predict" the present state of the WMD programs.

They did so by extrapolation based on past history. The intelligence community, prior to the 1991 Gulf War, had underestimated Iraq's nuclear program and had failed to identify all of its chemical weapons storage sites. That history shaped the community's selection of the forces acting to shape Iraq's WMD effort. Specifically, Iraq had the same leadership, presumably with the same objectives concerning WMD; a history of WMD development; and a history of concealment. Those forces provided the starting point for what was a straight-line extrapolation, much like the extrapolation that resulted in the muddle-through Yugoslavia NIE draft. Analysts assumed that the forces that were present in 1991 were still present, making no allowance for changes since 1991. The constant international scrutiny and the consequent high risk that any continuing WMD program would be discovered and bring on additional sanctions or military action were not taken into account. And a continuing, very important force was not considered: Saddam's ambition to be a major player in Mideast power politics, a motivation that would cause him to conceal his lack of weapons of mass destruction. The result of a combination of poor force field analysis and lack of intelligence was an estimate based on extrapolations (168–169).

The UAV estimate, for example, was based heavily on a straight-line extrapolation. Before the Gulf War, Iraq had been in the early stages of a project to convert MiG-21 jet aircraft into UAVs for biological weapons delivery. Iraq had also experimented in 1990 with a BW spray system, designed to be used with the MiG-21 UAV. In the mid-1990s Iraq began testing another modified jet aircraft, the L-29, as a UAV. Analysts concluded that the L-29 was a follow-up to the MiG-21 program. When the new and smaller UAVs made their appearance, analysts wrongly extrapolated that these UAVs were simply a continuation of the BW delivery program (141–145).

The most compelling analytic methodology failure, however, was the one that Martin van Heuven avoided. As the national intelligence officer in charge of the Yugoslavia NIE, van Heuven forced the consideration of a second target model, which ultimately was used in the NIE. The Iraqi weapons NIE drafters gravitated to a single model and apparently failed to consider a logical, top-level alternative hypothesis or model: that Iraq had abandoned its WMD programs.

Poor Interaction with Collectors and Customers

A major theme of this book has been the importance of a shared target model—shared with both collectors of intelligence and customers of intelligence. The project of creating an NIE on Iraqi weapons of mass destruction failed on both counts. Analysts did not share with collectors the extent to which they were relying on intelligence from sources that the collectors knew to be unreliable—Curveball and the Iraqi chemist who reported on Iraq's purported chemical weapons program being two examples. And in dealing with the customers, analysts left the impression that their sources were much more credible than was actually the case. As the WMD Commission report said, the NIE did not communicate how weak the underlying intelligence was. Analysts did not adequately communicate to the policymakers their uncertainties. Many of the analytic products obscured how heavily their conclusions rested on inferences and assumptions (12). The NIE started out on the wrong foot with a poor problem definition. It ended badly, as the WMD Commission noted (3), in a failure to communicate.

Notes

1. The facts in this appendix are taken from a case study prepared by Thomas W. Shreeve for the National Defense University in May 2003, titled "A National Intelligence Estimate on Yugoslavia." See Thomas W. Shreeve, "The Intelligence Community Case Method Program: A National Intelligence Estimate on Yugoslavia," in *Intelligence and the National Security Strategist: Enduring Issues and Challenges,* ed. Roger Z. George and Robert D. Kline (Washington, D.C.: National Defense University Press, 2004).

2. *Report of the Commission on the Intelligence Capabilities of the United States Regarding Weapons of Mass Destruction,* March 31, 2005, www.wmd.gov/report/wmd_report.pdf, 8–9.

3. Ibid., 55. Subsequent references to the report are by page number in the appendix text.

Index

Abacha family money laundering case, 70–71, 156–157, 243
Absence of evidence problem, 135
Abstracts, 27, 272
Abubakar, Yaya, 162
Accelerometers, 102
Access of sources, 126, 317
Accuracy of evidence, 131
Ackoff, Russell, 248, 254
Acoustic intelligence, 117
Acronyms, use of, 307
Active deception, 170
Active sensors, 110
Activity patterns, 66
Adaptive prediction techniques, 209
Advanced strategy development, 163–164
Advocates, analysts as, 300–302
Afghanistan
  al Qaeda and, 193–195
  human terrain models in, 81–82
  intelligence collaboration in, 15
  UAV use in, 17
Air Force Strategic Air Command (SAC, U.S.), 232
Air sampling, 110
Akademik Tupolev (ship), 83–84
"Alert fatigue," 58
Allen, Charles, 57
Almanac Trial (1858), 126
Al Qaeda
  convergent phenomena and, 186
  organization analysis of, 255
  predictive assessment of, 193–195
  prevention and deterrence methods against, 50
  simulation modeling for, 287
Alternative target models, 145–147
Analysis approach, 36–48. *See also*
  Analysts
  capabilities, 55
  collateral models for, 45–47
  combination methods, 43–47
  conflict spectrum, 49–52
  to counterintelligence, 42–43
  current intelligence, 53–54
  indications and warning (I & W), 55–58
  intentions, 55

model concept, 37–40
operational intelligence, 51
plans, 55
presentation of results, 303–307
research, long-term, 53–54
strategic intelligence, 50–51
submodels for, 44–45
tactical intelligence, 51–52, 100
target models for, 40–42
temporal spectrum, 52–55
Analysts, 290–294
  as advocates, 300–302
  broad perspective of, 291–292
  case-based reasoning and, 201–202
  as communicators, 299–300
  customer interaction with, 298–303
  defense analysis challenge and, 302–303
  intelligence failures, 2–5
  objectivity of, 5, 290–291
  presentation of results by, 303–307
  teamwork and, 292–294
  tradecraft of, 181–182
  veteran vs. novice, 156–157
Analytic spectrum, 49–59
  capabilities, plans, and intentions, 55
  conflict spectrum in, 49–52
  indications and warning, 55–58
  temporal analysis and, 52–55
Argumentation, structured, 25, 34, 141–144
Arms traffickers, 74, 170
Armstrong, Duff, 126
Arquilla, John, 8, 21, 53
The Art of Problem Solving (Ackoff), 248
Art of War (Sun Tzu), 80
Asimov, Isaac, 229
Assad, Hafez, 27
Assassinations, 187
Assimilation of technology, 276
Asymmetric response, 297
AT&T, 238
Audio transmitters, 101
Audit trail, 214
Australia, liaison relationships of, 103
Authenticity of evidence, 131
Autobahn securities trading system, 22
Autocorrelation, 209

About the Author

Robert M. Clark has been an intelligence analyst for thirty-nine years. He currently serves as an independent consultant assessing threats to U.S. space systems. He helped develop the DNI's Intelligence Community Officers' course and currently teaches the DNI's Introduction to the Intelligence Community course. Clark is the former president and CEO of the Scientific and Technical Analysis Corporation. He served in the U.S. Air Force as an electronics warfare officer and intelligence officer, reaching the rank of lieutenant colonel, and in the CIA as an analyst and as the chief of the Directorate of Intelligence's Analytic Support Group. He is the author of *The Technical Collection of Intelligence* (2010). Clark holds an SB from MIT, a PhD in electrical engineering from the University of Illinois, and a JD from George Washington University. He is a presidential interchange executive, a member of the Virginia state bar, and a patent attorney.